MATHS
IN ACTION

Mathematics in Action Group

Members of the Mathematics in Action Group associated with this book:
D. Brown, R. D. Howat, E. C. K. Mullan, K. Nisbet, A. G. Robertson

STUDENTS'
BOOK

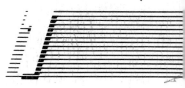

Nelson
Nelson House   Mayfield Road
Walton-on-Thames   Surrey
KT12 5PL   UK

Cover photograph by David Usill

© Mathematics in Action Group 1993

First published by Blackie and Son Ltd 1986
New edition published by Thomas Nelson and Sons Ltd 1993

ISBN 0-17-431416-7
NPN 9

Printed in China

CONTENTS

INTRODUCTION

Maths in Action—New Edition provides a course in mathematics that covers the Mathematics 5-14 National Guidelines in Scotland, the Northern Ireland Curriculum and the National Curriculum in England and Wales.

The new edition builds on experience gained in the classroom with the original series, and particular attention has been paid to providing a differentiated course with exercises graded at three distinct levels—A, B and C. Every chapter starts with a Looking Back exercise, which can be used for revision and to assess readiness for the topic, and ends with a Check-up exercise giving a further element of revision and assessment. Investigative work features prominently in each chapter in the many puzzles, projects, challenges, brainstormers and investigations. Answers to every question (except puzzles, challenges, brainstormers and investigations) are to be found at the back of this book.

Each *Students' Book* is supported by a *Teacher's Resource Book* and, in the first two years, by revised books of *Extra Questions* and *Further Questions*.

The *Teacher's Resource Book* contains 5-14, Northern Ireland Curriculum and National Curriculum references for every exercise, photocopiable worksheets, notes and suggestions for further activities, and the answers to the puzzles, challenges, brainstormers and investigations in the *Students' Book*. In addition, there are grids which may be photocopied and used to record and assess students' progress.

Extra Questions 1 and *Further Questions 1* consist of exercises which are directly related to those in the *Students' Book*. *Extra Questions* contains easier questions than those found in the *Students' Book*, and *Further Questions* consists of harder questions to extend the more able.

LOOKING BACK

1 Harry is playing golf. He scores 5, 6, 4, 5, 2, 3, 6, 5 and 1 at the first nine holes. What is his total score?

2 A car's mileometer reads 980 km. What will it read after another 100 km?

0	0	9	8	0

3 Sue won a prize of $1000. How many $10 notes will she receive? How many $100 notes?

4 Write down the numbers the arrows are pointing to:

a

b

5 Round these distances to the nearest 10 miles:
a Bristol to Exeter, 81 miles
b Edinburgh to York, 191 miles
c Glasgow to Southampton, 436 miles.

6 Round the distances in question **5** to the nearest 100 miles.

7 Calculate these in your head:
a 57×0 **b** 18×1 **c** 48×10 **d** 11×100
e $30 \div 6$ **f** $900 \div 10$ **g** $2000 \div 100$

8 This is the story of 5.

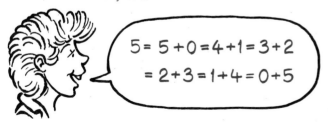

$$5 = 5+0 = 4+1 = 3+2$$
$$= 2+3 = 1+4 = 0+5$$

Write down the story of:
a 4   **b** 7   **c** 10

9 Write down two more numbers in each sequence.
a 4, 10, 16, ...   **b** 32, 29, 26, ...
c 1, 3, 9, ...   **d** 16, 8, 4, ...

10 Find the IN and OUT numbers:

a

b

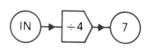

c

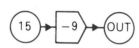

d

11 a In Tech City School, how many pupils are:
(i) boys   (ii) girls?
b How many more pupils are in the lower school than in the upper school?

Tech City School	Boys	Girls
Upper school	171	163
Lower school	235	217

12 Ali's new bicycle will cost him £3 a week for 35 weeks. How much is this altogether?

13 A piece of wood is 60 cm long. How many whole pieces could you cut from it of length:
a 2 cm   **b** 3 cm   **c** 4 cm   **d** 5 cm   **e** 6 cm
f 8 cm   **g** 9 cm   **h** 15 cm?

14 Pens cost 18p each, or 6 for 90p. What is the least you could pay for 20 pens?

USING WHOLE NUMBERS

EXERCISE 1A

1 This is the Isle of Arran in the Firth of Clyde. Distances between the villages are shown in miles.

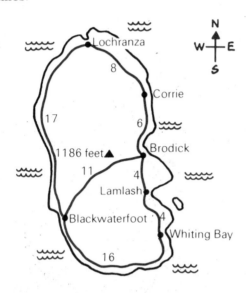

a How many routes are shown from Brodick to Blackwaterfoot?
b Find the distance along each route.

2 How far is it from Lochranza to Whiting Bay:
a down the west coast
b down the east coast
c How many miles are saved by taking the shorter route?

3 A bus trip goes right round the coast road of the island. How many miles is this?

4 Look at the dart board. Why are two of the rings called double and treble?

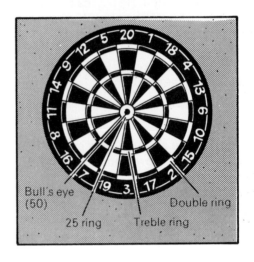

5 a Find the score if your dart lands in:
    (i) Double 4   (ii) Double 7   (iii) Treble 7
    (iv) Treble 3   (v) Treble 8   (vi) Double 15
    (vii) Treble 12 (viii) Double 18 (ix) Treble 14
    (x) Double 19 (xi) Treble 17 (xii) Treble 19
b What is the highest score possible with one dart?

6 Robert and Liz are playing darts. Robert needs 7 to win and Liz needs 9. Each has two darts left and the game must finish with a double. List all the possible scores they can make with their darts to win the game.

EXERCISE 1B/C

1

Capital city				
28	North-port			
38	66	South-port		
29	51	42	East-port	
31	35	43	60	West-port

This mileage chart shows the distances between five towns. For example, by reading down and across, you can see that the distance from Northport to Eastport is 51 miles. Copy the map, and mark in the distances between the towns.

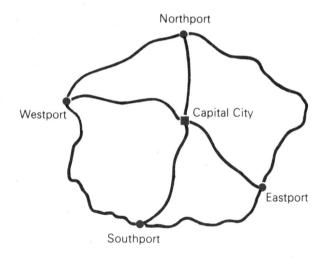

Northport

Westport

Capital City

Eastport

Southport

2 Karen, Bobby and Wendy played a round of golf. Their scorecards showed that:
Karen had 2 threes, 6 fours, 8 fives and 2 sixes.
Bobby had 3 fours, 6 fives, 3 sixes, 4 sevens and 2 nines.
Wendy had 2 fours, 7 fives, 4 sixes, 4 eights and 1 nine.
Calculate their scores for the round.

3 In need of practice, the three friends tried the putting green. Calculate their scores from this table.

	Twos	Threes	Fours	Fives	Sixes
Karen	7	8	3		
Bobby	2	8	7		1
Wendy	4	10	3	1	

4 Bobby and Wendy enjoyed their golf so much that they decided to buy second-hand sets of golf clubs.
Bobby bought four woods at £17 each and seven irons at £12 each.
Wendy bought three woods at £19 each and six irons at £11 each.
How much did they pay for their sets of clubs?

5 Mr Williams is travelling from Reading to Swindon. Between junctions 11 and 12 on the M4 motorway he hears on his car radio that an overturned lorry is blocking the motorway between junctions 12 and 13. He must leave the motorway.

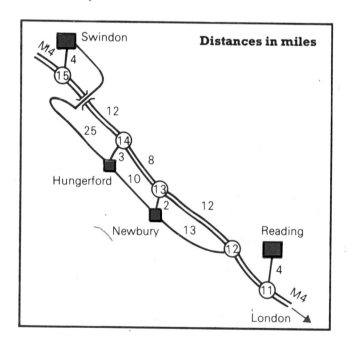

a What then is the shortest route to Swindon?
b How far is it from junction 12 to Swindon by this route?
c Why might he decide to take a longer route?

A DIVERSION—MAGIC SQUARES AND TRIANGLES

EXERCISE 2

1 a Add up the numbers in each row of the magic square above.

  b Add up the numbers in each column.

  c Add up the numbers in each diagonal. What do you notice about all of these?

Rows → Diagonal   Columns

2 Copy and complete these boxes to make them magic squares.

a

2		
	5	
4		8

b

8	1	6
	5	

c

		4
	5	
6		2

d

2		
7		
6	1	

3 Make up a '3 by 3' magic square of your own. Use each number from 1 to 9 once only, and put 5 in the middle. Make sure that the numbers in each row, column and diagonal add up to 15.

4 This magic triangle contains three smaller triangles whose numbers add up to 20. Find the three triangles.

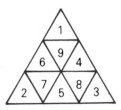

5 Copy these magic triangles, and use the numbers from 1 to 9 to fill them in.

a

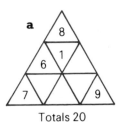

Totals 20

b

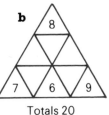

Totals 20

c

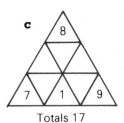

Totals 17

CHALLENGE

This supermagic square has many secrets.

4	22	6	9
5	10	3	23
11	8	20	2
21	1	12	7

Explore the square to find sets of four numbers which add up to 41. The numbers may be in straight lines, or in '2 by 2' squares, or grouped in other ways.
How many can you find?

WORKING WITH NUMBERS

EXERCISE 3A

1 The calculator and the abacus both show the number 1264. What is *each* bead worth on:
a Wire A   **b** Wire B   **c** Wire C   **d** Wire D?

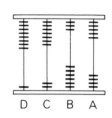

D   C   B   A

2 What numbers are shown on each abacus here?
a   **b**   **c**

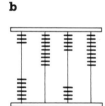
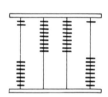

3 5678 can be changed to 5078 by subtracting 600.
How can you change 5678 to:
a 5608   **b** 678
c 5680   **d** 5700?

4 In a computer game, Olivia scores 8005, Sarah 3905, Salim 6480, Matthew 995, Darren 1050, Naima 7895.
a List the scores in order, with the highest one first.
b Write the highest and lowest scores in words.

5 Write down the numbers marked by the arrows on these scales:

a
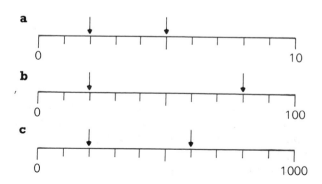

6 These bags are full of 10p coins.

How many coins are in each bag?

7 These bags are full of £1 coins.

How many coins are in each bag?

8 In a local election, Joginder Singh got 1873 votes, Amy Anderson 2005 votes and Harry Goodall 972 votes.
a Who won, and by what majority over the person who came second?
b How many votes were cast altogether?

9 Find the IN and OUT numbers.

a
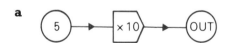

b
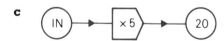

c
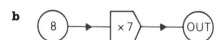

10 Find the numbers behind the stars.

	a	b	c
	4*	76	6*
	+12	+**	+*4
	*9	99	90

	d	e	f
	*8	8*	73
	−2*	−*3	−1*
	56	26	*4

EXERCISE 3B

1 The diagram shows a radio tuning scale.

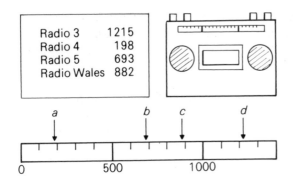

Radio 3   1215
Radio 4   198
Radio 5   693
Radio Wales   882

a Which station does each letter point to?
b Write the wavelength 1215 in words.

2

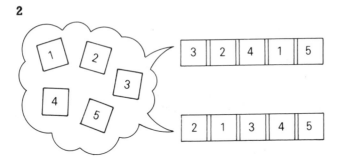

The five cards can be arranged side by side to make five-figure numbers, like the two that are shown. Find the largest and smallest possible numbers, and calculate the difference between them.

3 Each number in the second and third rows is the sum of the two numbers just above it. Copy and complete:

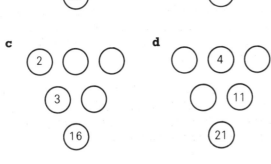

a

b

c

d

4

Sat	14 Feb	41 223
Sat	21 Feb	28 622
Sat	28 Feb	27 971
Sat	7 Mar	28 239
Sat	14 Mar	28 134
Sat	21 Mar	55 039

Arrange these football attendances in a table, with the largest attendance first, like this:

1	21 Mar	55 039
2		
3		

5 Find the OUT numbers:

a

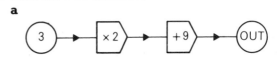

b

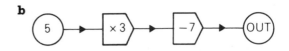

c

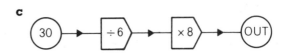

6 A carton of crisps contains 40 bags. 290 bags were sold. How many cartons had to be opened?

7 A sheet of 26p stamps consists of 15 rows with 12 stamps in each row. What is its total value?

8 Find the numbers behind the stars.

a   65
    + **
    *04

b   5*
    + *3
    *28

c   *3
    + 7*
    *00

d   75
    − **
    27

e   5*
    − 28
    *8

f   23*
    − *23
    8

EXERCISE 3C

1 Chris has to write a 3000 word essay. She estimates that she can fit 55 lines of type on each page, and about 14 words in each line. How many sides of paper will she use?

2 a List these cities in order, largest first.

City	Athens	Berlin	Madrid	Paris
Population	3 027 000	3 001 000	3 188 000	2 189 000

b Write the largest population in words.

3 This number machine converts kilometres to miles, approximately.

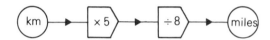

a Convert, to the nearest mile: 64 km, 88 km, 50 km.
b How many kilometres convert to: 20 miles, 35 miles, 10 miles?

4 This number machine converts Fahrenheit temperatures to Celsius temperatures.

a Convert to Celsius: 59°F, 212°F.
b How many degrees Fahrenheit convert to: 10°C, 75°C?

5 Each number in a circle is the sum of the numbers in the neighbouring squares. Copy and complete:

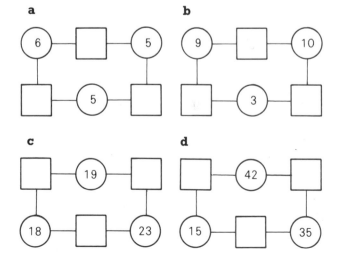

A CALCULATOR CROSSWORD

Copy the grid onto squared paper. Use your calculator for the calculations, and after each one turn it upside down to read the word needed to fit into the grid.

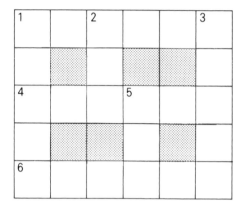

Across
1 125×3691
4 $107 \times 13 \times 9 \times 5 \times 4 \times 2 + 1$
6 $567\,890 + 9876 - 321 - 100$

Down
1 $47 \times 45 \times 9 \times 3$
2 $8796 \div 12$
3 $(4 \times 4 \times 4 \times 4 - 47) \times 4 \times 4 \times 4 \times 4$
5 $678 + 54 - 32 + 10$

A FEW PUZZLES

1 *A frog is climbing a well 31 feet deep. It climbs 4 feet in one hour, but then slides back 1 foot as it rests for an hour. How long will it take to climb out of the well?*

2 *Think of a number. Add 3 and multiply your answer by 10. Add 15 and divide your answer by 5. Subtract 9 and divide by 2. What do you notice about the result? Try it again, starting with a different number.*

3 *Think of a number. Double it and add 4. Multiply by 6 and subtract 18. Divide by 3, subtract 2 and divide by 4. How does your answer compare with the number you first thought of?*

SEQUENCES OF NUMBERS

A list of numbers such as 2, 4, 6, 8, . . . is called a *sequence of numbers*.
For many sequences there is a rule which helps you to find the next number in the sequence.
A possible rule for the sequence 2, 4, 6, 8, . . . is *Add 2*.

EXERCISE 4A

1 Think of the house numbers in the picture above:
2, 4, 6, . . .
What will the numbers of the houses across the road be?
Write down a rule for finding the next number in this sequence.

2 Write down a rule for each of the following sequences.
Use your rule to write down the next number in each sequence.
a 2, 5, 8, 11, . . .   **b** 1, 6, 11, 16, . . .   **c** 10, 9, 8, 7, . . .
d 20, 40, 60, . . .   **e** 100, 95, 90, . . .   **f** 101, 102, 103, . . .
g 7, 16, 25, . . .   **h** 46, 39, 32, . . .

3 List the number of dots in each pattern.
Then write down the next two numbers in the sequence.

a

b

c

d

4 What is the missing number in each of these sequences?
Describe the rule you have used for each one.
a 15, 20, __, 30   **b** 12, __, 8, 6   **c** 3, 6, __, 12
d 7, __, 21, 28   **e** 60, 48, 36, __
f 1, 10, 19, __, 37   **g** __, 100, 110, 120
h 49, 44, __, 34

5

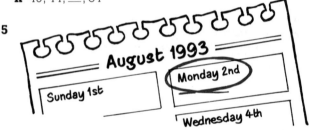

August 2nd 1993 was a Monday. Write down the dates of:
a the other Mondays in August   **b** all the Fridays in August.

6 Make up some sequences of your own, and list the first four numbers in each one.
Ask your neighbour to find the rule you used for each one.

EXERCISE 4B

1 Write down two more numbers in each of these sequences:
  a 0, 2, 4, 6, ...   **b** 5, 10, 15, ...   **c** 1, 11, 21, ...
  d 33, 30, 27, ...

2 What rule can you find for each of these sequences?
  a 9, 27, 81, 243   **b** 1, 2, 4, 8, 16   **c** 1000, 100, 10, 1
  d 64, 16, 4, 1

3 A number is missing in each sequence. Can you work out the one missing?
  a 13, 17, 21, __, 29   **b** 300, 200, 100, __
  c 77, 88, 99, __, 121   **d** 99, 87, 75, __

4 Find four different rules for sequences beginning 1, 2, ...
  Write down the next three numbers in each sequence.

5 Copy this pattern of numbers, which is called Pascal's triangle. Make the triangle larger by writing down the next three rows. Describe the rule that you have used.

```
        1
      1   1
    1   2   1
  1   3   3   1
1   4   6   4   1
```

6 a Copy and complete this table of stopping distances for cars.

Speed (mph)	20	30	40	50	60	70
Thinking distance (feet)	20	30	40			
Braking distance (feet)	20	45	80			
Stopping distance (feet)	40					315

  b If you double the speed of the car do you double the stopping distance?

EXERCISE 4C

1 Find a rule for each of these sequences:
  a 1, 3, 5, 7, ...   **b** 10, 9, 8, 7, ...
  c 1, 3, 9, 27, ...   **d** 60, 30, 15, ...
  e 1, 2, 4, 7, ...   **f** 1, 4, 9, 16, ...
  g 1, 2, 1, 3, 1, 4, ...   **h** 1, 0, 5, 2, 0, 4, 3, 0, 3, ...

2 In question **1e** it would be possible to show the differences between the terms like this:
```
1   2   4   7   ...
  1   2   3     ...   first differences
    1   1       ...   second differences
```
What are the first and second differences for **1f**?

3 Find the first, second and third differences for the sequence 1, 2, 4, 8, 15, 26, ...

4 Find the terms named in the list on the right of these spreadsheet sequences:

	A	**B**	**C**	**D**	**E**	**F**	**G**	**H**	**I**	
1	1	10	100	1000	...					G1
2	100	90	81	73	...					F2
3	1	3	7		31	63				D3
4	6		20	30	42					B4
5	1	2	3	1	2		1	2	5	F5

5 The chess piece can move only in the directions shown. Copy the board.

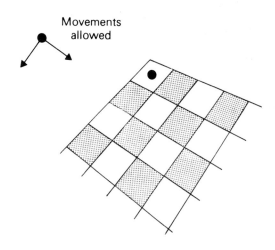

Movements allowed

  a In each square enter the number of different routes the piece can take in moving from the top square to that square.
  b Examine the pattern of numbers you get, and work out how to continue it.
  c Find the sum of the numbers along each 'level'. Can you extend the sequence of sums?

6 Find the rules, and a few more terms for these sequences:
  a The Fibonacci sequence 1, 1, 2, 3, 5, 8, ...
  b 1 × 3, 3 × 4, 5 × 5, 7 × 6, ...

1 A ball bounces downstairs, either one step or two steps at a time. Investigate the number of ways in which the ball can bounce down 1, 2, 3, 4, 5 steps. Can you find a rule?

2 Each cube is built from a number of small cubes, and all the outside faces are painted red. Find sequences of the number of small cubes with:
  a exactly three red faces
  b exactly two red faces
  c only one red face
  d no red faces.

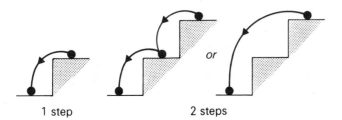

1 step   2 steps

or

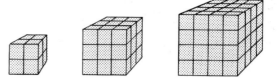

MULTIPLICATION AND DIVISION BY 10, 100 AND 1000

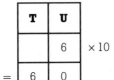 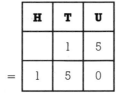

T	U	
	6	× 10

= | 6 | 0 |

H	T	U	
	1	5	× 10

= | 1 | 5 | 0 |

Th	H	T	U	
	2	4	7	× 10

= | 2 | 4 | 7 | 0 |

When a whole number is multiplied by 10, each figure moves 1 place to the left.
Units become tens, tens become hundreds and hundreds become thousands.

Th	H	T	U	
		3	5	× 100

= | 3 | 5 | 0 | 0 |

2 places to left

Th	H	T	U	
			7	× 1000

= | 7 | 0 | 0 | 0 |

3 places to left

Multiply by 10, 100, 1000.

Answer is a larger number.

Be careful when multiplying by zero!
Examples: $2 \times 0 = 0$, $673 \times 0 = 0$, $0 \times 1 = 0$.

EXERCISE 5A

Calculator out of action! Answer these questions mentally, or using pencil and paper.

1 Multiply by zero:
  a 9 **b** 14 **c** 87 **d** 129 **e** 1000

2 Multiply by 10:
  a 1 **b** 17 **c** 66 **d** 101 **e** 5321

3 Multiply by 100:
  a 8 **b** 80 **c** 234 **d** 1 **e** 0

4 Multiply by 1000:
  a 23 **b** 1 **c** 0 **d** 100 **e** 1000

5 Calculate:
  a 94×10 **b** 38×100 **c** 64×0
  d 85×1000 **e** 10×100 **f** 50×100
  g 10×204 **h** 91×1000 **i** 100×100
  j $24\,680 \times 0$

6 Calculate:
  a 6×5 **b** 6×7 **c** 8×8 **d** 5×9
  e 7×7 **f** 7×9 **g** 5×8 **h** 8×4
  i 9×3 **j** 9×9 **k** 54×3 **l** 54×30
  m 54×300 **n** 54×3000 **o** 54×0

EXERCISE 5B/C

Calculator out of action here again!

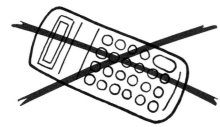

1 Calculate:
  a 100×100 **b** 1000×0 **c** 240×10 **d** 100×204
  e 0×2468

2 Calculate:
  a 45×2 **b** 27×3 **c** 33×4 **d** 84×5
  e 64×6 **f** 71×7 **g** 35×8 **h** 32×9
  i 99×0 **j** 123×5 **k** 4×47 **l** 40×47
  m 400×47 **n** 4000×47 **o** 0×47

3 Find these products:
  a 17×2 **b** 17×20 **c** 17×200 **d** 17×0
  e 0×17 **f** 5×62 **g** 4×74 **h** 6×76
  i 62×8 **j** 599×1 **k** 82×20 **l** 76×50
  m 54×60 **n** 33×70 **o** 132×80

4 Calculate:
  a $2 \times 7 \times 5$ **b** $4 \times 6 \times 10$ **c** $5 \times 19 \times 2$
  d $2 \times 17 \times 10$ **e** $4 \times 25 \times 100$ **f** $25 \times 16 \times 4$
  g $19 \times 3 \times 10$ **h** $5 \times 17 \times 20$ **i** $2 \times 33 \times 50$
  j $5 \times 20 \times 0$ **k** $50 \times 41 \times 2$ **l** $0 \times 111 \times 0$

5 Divide by 10:
  a 80 **b** 560 **c** 100 **d** 700 **e** 1040

6 Divide by 100:
  a 600 **b** 900 **c** 12 000 **d** 3800 **e** 14 500

7 Divide by 1000:
  a 3000 **b** 75 000 **c** 80 000 **d** 1000
  e 1 000 000

8 Calculate:
  a $90 \div 10$ **b** $100 \div 100$ **c** $120 \div 10$
  d $1000 \div 10$ **e** $2300 \div 100$ **f** $58 \div 2$
  g $93 \div 3$ **h** $72 \div 4$ **i** $435 \div 5$
  j $366 \div 6$ **k** $999 \div 9$ **l** $552 \div 8$
  m $511 \div 7$ **n** $312 \div 4$ **o** $234\,000 \div 1000$
  p $204 \div 2$ **q** $558 \div 9$ **r** $808 \div 8$
  s $396 \div 6$ **t** $1002 \div 3$

WHOLE NUMBERS IN ACTION

Here is a good rule for calculations:

$$\boxed{\text{Estimate}} \rightarrow \boxed{\text{Calculate}} \rightarrow \boxed{\text{check}}$$

Example 1
Park High School has 1283 pupils, of whom 609 are boys. How many are girls?

Estimate: 1300 − 600 = 700
Calculate: 1283 − 609 = 674
Check: 609 + 674 = 1283
Answer: 674 girls

Example 2
Quicksell employ 28 assistants, who are each paid £94 per week. What is the total weekly wage bill?

Estimate: 30 × £90 = £2700
Calculate: 28 × £94 = £2632
Check: £2632 ÷ 28 = £94
Answer: £2632

EXERCISE 6A

1 Riverside School has 492 boys and 429 girls. Estimate, calculate and check the number of pupils at the school.

2 The number of miles this car had travelled at the beginning and end of one year are shown on the windscreens. Estimate, calculate and check the number of miles covered during the year.

3 Kevin has 12 video tapes. Each can record for 180 minutes. Estimate, calculate and check the total number of minutes he can record. How many hours is this?

4 A Parents' Association gives the school £200 to buy calculators. If each one costs £7, how many can the school buy?

5 A batsman played in 29 cricket matches. He scored an average of 47 runs per game. Calculate the total number of runs he made.

6 168 pupils are starting a new school. They will be divided into six classes. How many pupils will be in each class?

7 How many:
a months in 18 years   **b** weeks in 105 days?

8 Each cat eats one tin of Whiskers cat food every day. A tin costs 38p. What is the September food bill for these two cats?

9

Sovereign	Year crowned
Victoria	1837
Edward VII	1901
George V	1910
Edward VIII	1936
George VI	1936
Elizabeth II	1952

a For how long did each king or queen reign?
b For how many years between 1837 and 1952 was there a king on the throne?
c Who reigned longer—the two Edwards or the two Georges?

10 182 pupils and 9 teachers are going on a theatre visit. They hire 42-seater buses.
a How many buses will they need?
b Will there be extra seats if any more pupils decide to go?

EXERCISE 6B

1 The diagram shows the heights in metres above sea level of camps in an Everest expedition.

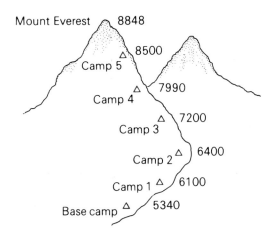

Mount Everest 8848
8500
Camp 5
7990
Camp 4
7200
Camp 3
6400
Camp 2
6100
Camp 1
Base camp 5340

a Give the heights, to the nearest 100 m, of each camp above the base camp.
b What height, to the nearest 10 m, is the summit above the base camp?

2 Estimate, calculate and check the difference in price between these used cars:
a the Escort and the Sierra
b the Fiesta and the Sierra.

£6 599 FIESTA   £7 849 ESCORT   £8 275 SIERRA

3 a (i) Write down the distances from Bristol to Aberdeen, and from Aberdeen to Glasgow.
(ii) Estimate, then calculate, the total distance from Bristol to Glasgow.
b Repeat **a** for journeys from Glasgow to Cardiff, and then to Birmingham.

Aberdeen				
430	Birming- ham			
511	85	Bristol		
532	107	45	Cardiff	
149	291	372	393	Glasgow

4 The leader of a youth club has £1000 to spend on tables and chairs. He buys eight tables at £80 each. He then spends the money he has left on chairs which cost £15 each. How many chairs can he buy?

5 Sita is collecting for charity. Her can contains these coins. How much money has she collected?

Coin	1p	2p	5p	10p	20p	50p	£1
Number	18	27	34	26	16	8	3

6 Lampposts are being put up along one side of a straight road 380 metres long. They have to be placed 20 metres apart, with one at each end. How many are needed?

7 a Does anything strike you as odd about these figures? Round each to the nearest thousand.

City	Population
Aberdeen	190 565
Dundee	174 345
Edinburgh	420 169
Glasgow	765 830

b Use the rounded figures to calculate:
(i) the total population of Glasgow and Edinburgh.
(ii) the difference between the largest and smallest populations.

8 Gareth Davies is paid expenses for using his car on business. Each month he receives: 28p per mile for the first 500 miles, 21p per mile for the next 1000 miles, then 14p per mile for the rest.
a One month he travelled 1940 miles. How much was he paid?
b Next month he received £444.92. How many miles had he travelled?

EXERCISE 6C

1 a Round the weight of each ship to the nearest 1000 tonnes.

238 700 tonnes

79 600 tonnes

386 200 tonnes

94 100 tonnes

b Estimate, then calculate, the total weight, using the rounded weights.

c What is the difference between the *actual* weights of the heaviest and lightest ships?

2 A firm has 30 000 leaflets to hand out. They employ 40 young people, and pay them £1.25 for every 50 leaflets they issue. Each person is given the same number of leaflets. How much does each one earn, and what is the total cost to the firm?

3 Is the janitor correct? If so, how many empty seats will there be?

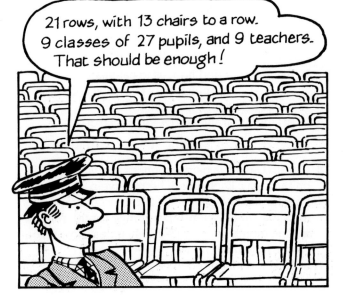

21 rows, with 13 chairs to a row.
9 classes of 27 pupils, and 9 teachers.
That should be enough!

4 Rashid weighs 58 kg, Simon 55 kg and Sarah 43 kg. Estimate, then calculate, their average weight by dividing their total weight by three.

5 Mr Baxter, who is a lorry driver, logs these distances one week.

Day	Mon	Tue	Wed	Thur	Fri
Distance (km)	182	248	213	195	222

Estimate, then calculate, the average distance he drives each day.

6 The sales staff at Grand Garages earned £2000, £1300, £1300, £1000, £800 and £800 in a month. Estimate, then calculate, their average salary for the month.

GRAND GARAGES

CHECK-UP ON WHOLE NUMBERS IN ACTION

1 Which prize fund paid out:
  a most money
  b least money?
  c Write out both amounts in words.

2 The bags are full of £10 notes. How many notes are in each bag?

3 Find the IN and OUT numbers.

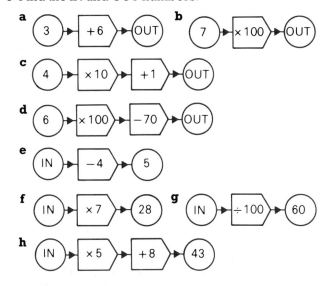

4 How many days are there in a hundred weeks?

5 To pay for a skiing trip, Robert saves £30 a week for twelve weeks. What is the cost of the trip?

6 Copy and complete these magic squares.

a

9	5	1
		8

b

6		2
	5	
		4

c

	70	
	50	
40	30	

7 Continue these sequences of dots for two more patterns, and write down the number of dots in each pattern.

  a

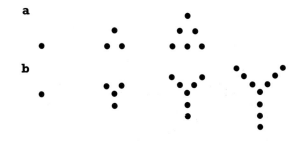

  b

8 Find two more terms for each sequence, and write down the rule you used.
  a 0, 2, 4, 6, ...   **b** 1, 7, 13, 19, ...   **c** 91, 83, 75, ...
  d 9, 27, 81, ...

9 Without using a calculator:
  a Multiply 84 by 10, by 100 and by 1000.
  b Divide 37 000 by 10, by 100 and by 1000; and divide a million by a thousand.

10 In 1991 the number of pupils at Riverside Comprehensive was 1035. At the end of the session 243 pupils left school, and next session 196 new pupils arrived. How many pupils were at the school then?

11 The attendances at three football matches were 25 067, 32 741 and 19 558.
  a What was the total attendance?
  b How many short of 100 000 is this?

12 Find the numbers behind the stars:

$$\begin{array}{r} \textbf{a}\quad 28 \\ +1* \\ \hline *5 \end{array} \qquad \begin{array}{r} \textbf{b}\quad *9 \\ +6* \\ \hline 94 \end{array} \qquad \begin{array}{r} \textbf{c}\quad 235 \\ +*** \\ \hline 1000 \end{array}$$

$$\begin{array}{r} \textbf{d}\quad 1*7 \\ +4* \\ \hline *83 \end{array} \qquad \begin{array}{r} \textbf{e}\quad 72 \\ -** \\ \hline 45 \end{array} \qquad \begin{array}{r} \textbf{f}\quad 9* \\ -68 \\ \hline *0 \end{array}$$

13 A box of six tennis balls costs £15. How much does each ball cost?

14 Pete pays £1.20 for eight shots to win a prize at the fair. How much did each shot cost?

2 ANGLES AROUND US

LOOKING BACK

1 What kind of angle is marked in this picture?

2 a Which angles below are smaller than a right angle?

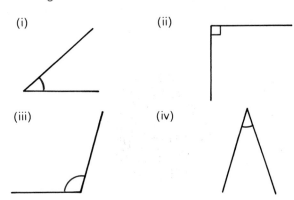

(i)

(ii)

(iii)

(iv)

b What do you call an angle which is smaller than a right angle?

3 How many degrees are in:
a a right angle **b** a straight angle?

4 What do you call an angle which is larger than a right angle and smaller than a straight angle?

5 Draw an acute angle and an obtuse angle.

6 Are the angles below acute, right, obtuse or straight?
a 72° **b** 126° **c** 90° **d** 15° **e** 180°

7 a Which two angles below can be put together to make a right angle?

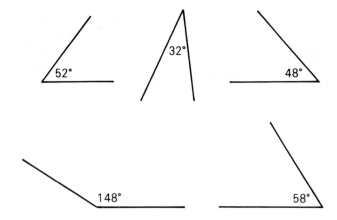

b Which two can make a straight angle?

8 Calculate the sizes of the angles marked with arcs.

a

b

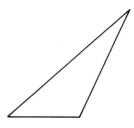

Straight angle

Right angle

9 a How many angles are there in the triangle?
b What kinds are they?

10 Can two acute angles be put together to make a straight angle? Give a reason for your answer.

CLASS DISCUSSION

1

Where are there right angles?

Which angles can change size?

Which angles are fixed?

2 Discuss the questions in **1** above for angles you can find in the classroom.

3 Can you name streets near your home or school which meet at:
   a right angles   **b** an acute angle
   c an obtuse angle?

TYPES OF ANGLE

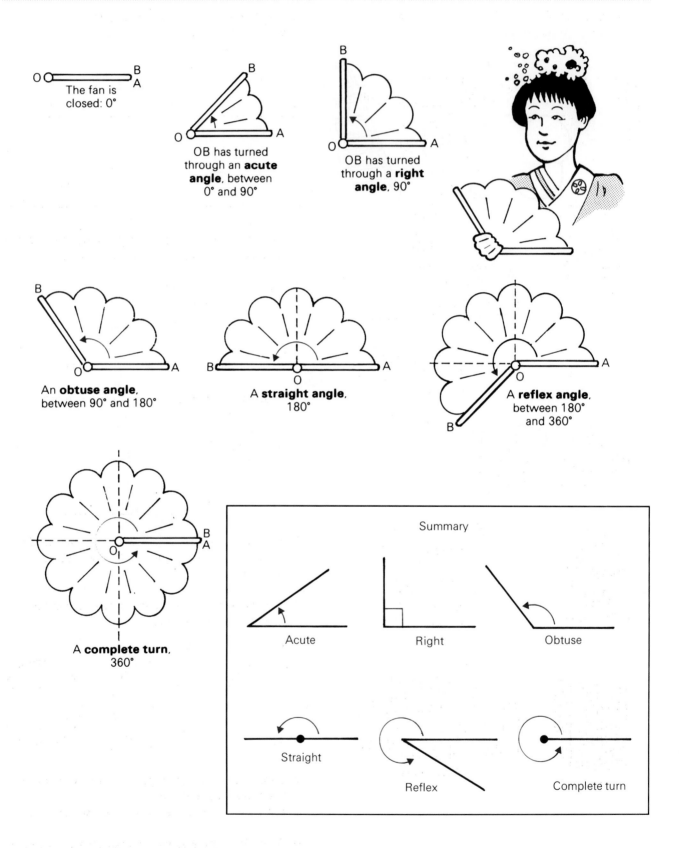

The fan is closed: 0°

OB has turned through an **acute angle**, between 0° and 90°

OB has turned through a **right angle**, 90°

An **obtuse angle**, between 90° and 180°

A **straight angle**, 180°

A **reflex angle**, between 180° and 360°

A **complete turn**, 360°

Summary

Acute

Right

Obtuse

Straight

Reflex

Complete turn

EXERCISE 1A

1 Say whether each angle marked below is acute, obtuse, right or straight.

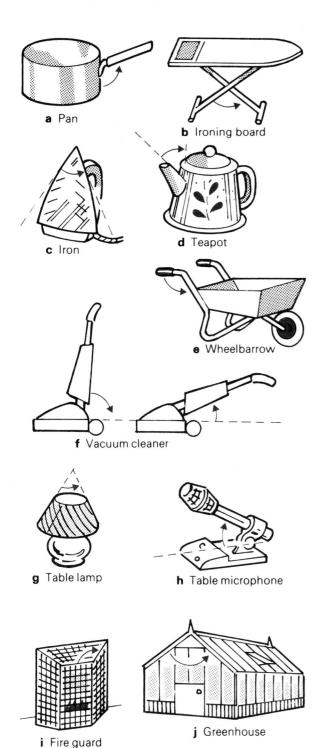

a Pan

b Ironing board

c Iron

d Teapot

e Wheelbarrow

f Vacuum cleaner

g Table lamp

h Table microphone

i Fire guard

j Greenhouse

2 Draw a right angle, and mark its size in degrees.

3 List these angles in order, smallest first:

a   **b**   **c**

d   **e**

4 Estimate the size of each angle in question **3** in degrees. Remember that a right angle is 90°.

5 If you are facing north, through how many degrees must you turn to face:
a east **b** south
c north again?

6 Ignoring the flag, how many angles in the picture are:
a right
b obtuse
c acute?

7 Find two times of the day when the hands of a clock are at right angles and show them in diagrams.

8 Calculate the angle between neighbouring spokes on each wheel.

a   **b**   **c**

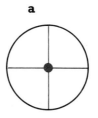
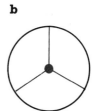
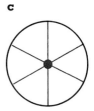

9 Through how many degrees does the *minute* hand of a watch turn in:
a 1 hour **b** 2 hours **c** ½ hour **d** 1 minute?

10 Describe right angles, acute angles and obtuse angles you can see in the classroom.

EXERCISE 1B

1 Correct the labels below which are wrong.

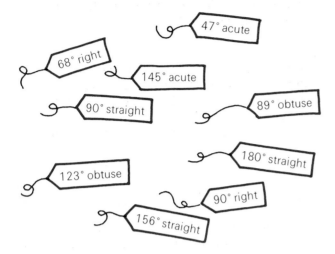

2 How many degrees are there in:
  a a right angle **b** a straight angle
  c a complete turn?

3 How many degrees are there in each of the angles below?

a The doorstop makes sure this door can only make ¼ turn.

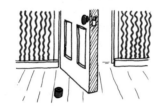

b 10 complete turns are needed to screw the nail right in.

c Geraldine goes round the helter-skelter three times on her way down.

4 Say whether each angle is acute, obtuse, right or straight: 8°, 180°, 80° 123°, 90°, 99°.

5 Sketch angles of 80°, 100° and 170°.

6 Calculate each angle at the centre of these objects:

a

Floor tiles

b

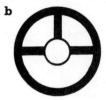

Steering wheel

c

Needlework box

d

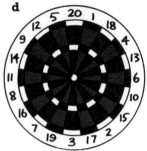

Slice of dart board

e

Clock hands

f

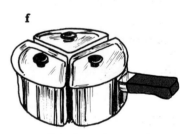

Set of pans

7 The cooker control turns clockwise. How many degrees does it turn through from:
  a OFF to 1
  b OFF to OFF
  c 3 to OFF
  d 1 to 4?

8 Can you fit:
  a two acute angles into a right angle
  b two acute angles into an obtuse angle
  c two obtuse angles into a straight angle?
  If you can, draw a diagram to show how. If you cannot, explain why not.

EXERCISE 1C

1 Sketch angles of 45°, 135°, 225° and 315°.

2 Draw a large capital letter A. On it, mark three acute angles, two obtuse angles, two straight angles and a reflex angle.

3 What fractions of a complete turn are: 180°, 90°, 60°, 45°, 1°?

4 The radio has four controls:
Volume—1 turn   Tuning—4 turns
Wavelength—$\frac{3}{4}$ turn   Tone—$\frac{1}{2}$ turn.

Through how many degrees can each control be turned?

5 The Speedy wheel company are testing wheels with different numbers of spokes. Copy and complete this table:

Number of spokes	6	8			12	18
Angle between spokes	60°		40°	36°		

6 The floor of this roundabout is made up of eight equal slices, or sectors, of a circle, with one car on each sector.

a Calculate the size of a sector angle.
b How many cars would there be if each sector had an angle of 40°?

7 A clock maker spaces the numbers equally around the face.
a What angles does he mark at the centre?
b Sub-divisions for minutes are made between the numbers. What angle has to be made at the centre for each of these?

c Through what angle does the minute hand move in 5 seconds?

8 An LP makes $33\frac{1}{3}$ revolutions, or complete turns, every minute. How many degrees does it turn through each minute?

9 Can you fit:
a two obtuse angles into an obtuse angle
b three acute angles into a reflex angle
c an obtuse angle and a reflex angle into a complete turn?
If you can, draw a diagram to show it. If you cannot, explain why not.

BRAINSTORMERS

1 a *Draw round the edge of your setsquare as in OAB. Keep the point at O fixed, and turn the setsquare to OCD, and draw round it again. Keep doing this until you return to OA.*

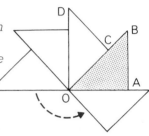

b *How many equal angles have you made at O? How many degrees are there in the complete turn at O?*
So what size is the angle of your setsquare at O?
c *Repeat **a** and **b** for other angles of your setsquare, and for any other setsquares you have.*

2 a *List all the whole numbers which divide exactly into 360.*
b *Why do you think 360 was chosen as the number of degrees in a complete turn?*

3 a *Count the total number of angles on all the faces of each pyramid in the diagram.*

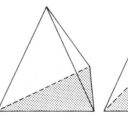
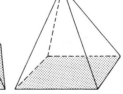
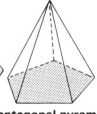

Tetrahedron   **Square pyramid** **Pentagonal pyramid**
(3-sided base)   (4-sided base)   (5-sided base)

b *Deduce the total number of angles on pyramids with 6-sided, 7-sided, . . . , 10-sided, . . . , n-sided bases.*

NAMING ANGLES

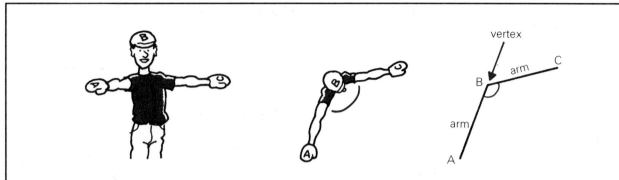

Angle ABC can be written ∠ ABC, or ∠ CBA. B is the *vertex* of the angle, and AB and BC are its *arms*.

EXERCISE 2A

1 In each picture name an angle, its vertex and its arms.

a

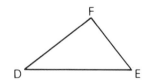

b

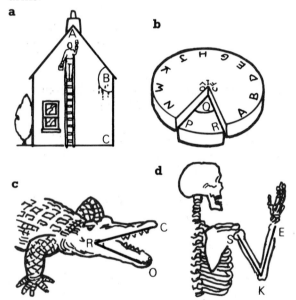

c

d

2 Draw and name a right angle ABC.

3 Name the three angles in the triangle, and the four angles in the rectangle.

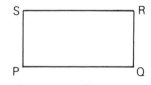

4 ∠ ABC is a right angle. Calculate ∠ ABD.

5 ∠ EFG is a straight angle. Calculate ∠ HFG.

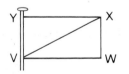

6 The three angles make a complete turn. Calculate ∠ KMP.

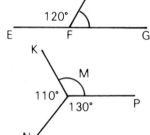

7 In this diagram of a road crossing, name:
a two acute angles
b two obtuse angles.

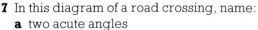

8 Name three angles on this flag which have vertex V.

9 Name each angle which is marked with an arc, and calculate its size.

a

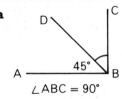

∠ABC = 90°

b

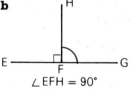

∠EFH = 90°

c

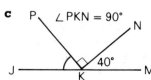

∠ PKN = 90°

d

140° 140°

∠Q S R

EXERCISE 2B/C

1 Two pages of the book are raised.
Name:
 a all the acute angles at O
 b the obtuse angles at O.

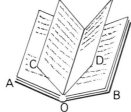

2

 a Name three angles which
 have XY as an arm.
 b Name all the angles which
 have YW as an arm.

3 Sketch ∠ABC = 120°. What size is reflex angle ABC?

4 Calculate the angles marked with arcs:

 a

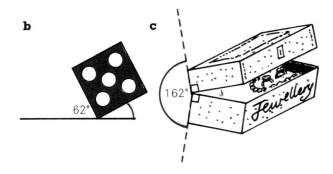

 b **c**

5 Ossie, the team captain, is taking a penalty.

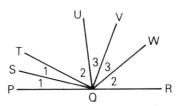

 a Name the angle within which he must kick the ball if he is to score.
 b The goalkeeper can save any ball which crosses the line between B and C. Which angles must Ossie now use to score?

6 ∠KON = ∠POM.
Calculate ∠KON.

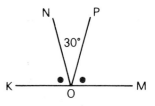

7 ∠ABE = ∠CBD.
Calculate ∠ABE.

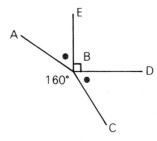

8 Copy the diagram, and fill in the sizes of all the angles.

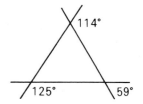

9 Which four of these angles fit exactly round a point? 23°, 65°, 77°, 92°, 124°, 168°.

10 Two straight lines MN and KP cross at O. By calculating the angles, show that if ∠KON = 2 ∠KOM then ∠MOP = 2 ∠PON.

11 ∠RSU = 90°. Calculate ∠RST and ∠TSU when:
 a ∠TSU is 30° less than ∠RST
 b ∠RST is 20° more than ∠TSU
 c ∠TSU is 36° less than ∠RST.

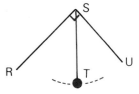

12 PQR is a straight line, and the angles are equal in pairs, as marked.

 a Calculate ∠SQV.
 b Explain how you got your answer.

MEASURING ANGLES

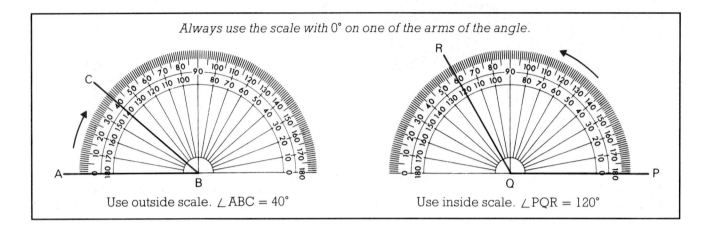

Always use the scale with 0° on one of the arms of the angle.

Use outside scale. ∠ABC = 40°   Use inside scale. ∠PQR = 120°

EXERCISE 3A

1 Write down the size of each angle in degrees. For example, ∠PQR = 120°.

2 First *estimate* the size of each angle, then measure it with your protractor.

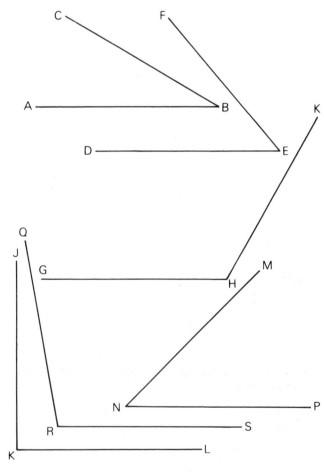

3 Look again at the angles in question **2** and name:
  a the smallest and largest angles
  b the acute angles
  c the obtuse angles.

4 Cheese wedges are packed in circular boxes.
  a Measure ∠ABC.

  b How many wedges will fit in a full box?
  c Suggest two other possible wedge angles. How many of these wedges would fill a box?

5 Measure the acute angle between each arrow and the target.

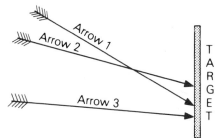

6 On squared paper draw a rectangle 8 cm long and 6 cm broad. Call it ABCD, and draw diagonal AC. Measure all the angles, and write down their sizes.

EXERCISE 3B/C

1 Estimate, then measure, the sizes of the angles marked with arcs. Make a table:

Angle	Estimate	Measure

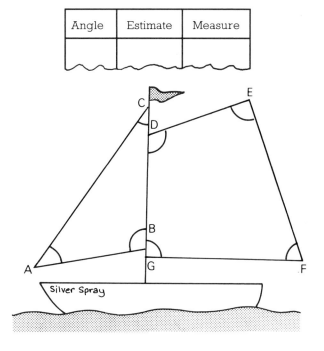

2 a Measure angles RSU, USV and VST and write in their sizes.

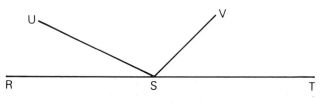

  b ∠RST is a straight angle. What should your total be in part **a**? How far out were you?

3 a Sketch an angle of about 45°, then measure it exactly. How many degrees out were you?
  b Repeat part **a** for angles of 120° and 200°.

4 Estimate, then measure, the reflex angles marked in the diagrams below.
  a

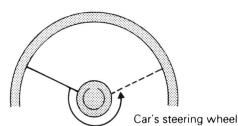

Box lid

  b

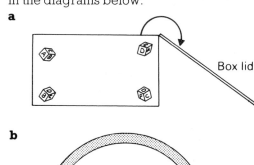

Car's steering wheel

CHOOSE A CHALLENGE

1 a *Draw a large triangle. Measure its angles, and calculate their sum.*
  b *Repeat **a** for several triangles. What do you deduce about the sum of the angles of a triangle?*
  c *Repeat **a** and **b** for a quadrilateral (four-sided).*

2 *Investigate the angles in a bicycle—in the frame, pedals, spokes, saddle, handlebars and so on. Devise ways of measuring the angles. Prepare a report, including diagrams and descriptions.*

DRAWING ANGLES

EXERCISE 4

1 Draw ∠ABC = 40°, like this:
  a Draw arm AB 6 cm long, and place your protractor on it as shown.
  b Count round the edge from 0° to 40°, and mark C.
  c Remove the protractor, and join BC.

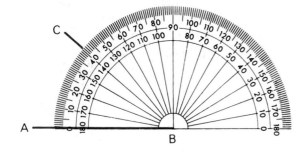

2 Follow the method used in question **1** to draw angles of:
  a 30° **b** 90° **c** 120° **d** 175°

3 Draw an 8-point compass by following these steps:
  a Use compasses to draw a circle with centre O and radius 5 cm.
  b Draw the line WOE across the middle.
  c Measure ∠WON = 90°, and draw NOS.
  d Measure angles of 45° on OE and OW, and draw the NE-SW and NW-SE lines.
  Note. North and South are the main directions, hence **N**E, **N**W, **S**E, **S**W.

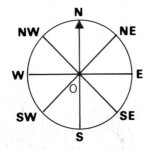

4 In the compass diagram:
  a Which direction is:
     (i) opposite NW (ii) midway between N and E?
  b If you are facing W and turn to face E, through how many degrees do you turn?
  c Name two directions which are at right angles to: (i) W (ii) NW.
  d What is the size of the smallest angle between:
     (i) N and E (ii) N and NE (iii) N and SE?

5 a A ship sailing north changes course by 45° clockwise. In which direction is it sailing now?
  b A ship sailing south-west changes its course 90° anti-clockwise. In which direction is it sailing now?

6 The wind in the morning is blowing from the west. By midday it is from the south. Through what angle has it turned?

7 a Use a ruler and protractor to make accurate drawings of these angles.

  (i)
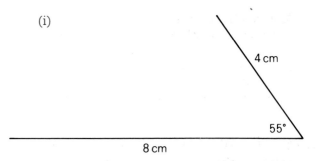

  (ii)
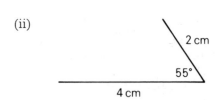

  (iii)
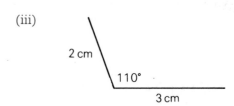

  b Is angle (i) larger than angle (ii)?
  c Is angle (ii) larger than angle (iii)?

8 Make an accurate drawing of this trowel. Start by drawing BD 12 cm long.

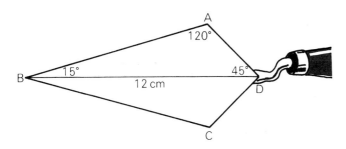

9 A patchwork quilt design consists of pentagons, hexagons and octagons.

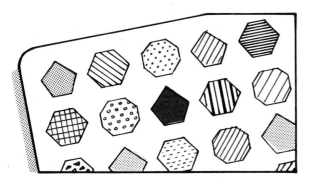

Construct, accurately:

a a pentagon with sides 5 cm long, and angles of 108°

b a hexagon with sides 4.5 cm long, and angles of 120°

c an octagon with sides 4 cm long, and angles of 135°.

10 Make an accurate drawing of this arrowhead. Mark the sizes of all the sides and angles.

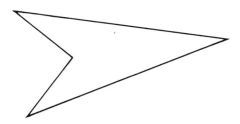

/ **INVESTIGATION**

1 Place your hand on a blank sheet of paper. Spread your fingers as wide as you can. Trace round the outline of your hand.

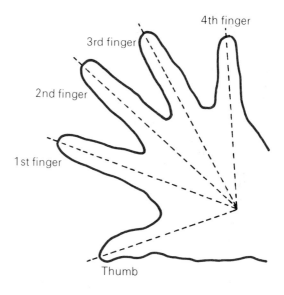

You will find that the directions of your fingers can be extended back to meet at a point.

2 Copy this table, and use your protractor to help you complete it.

My finger chart

angle between → ↓	4th finger	3rd finger	2nd finger	1st finger
Thumb				
1st finger				
2nd finger			
3rd finger			

*3 **a** Which of the measurements in the table should be used to judge the 'spread' of the hand?*

*   **b** Who has the largest hand-spread in the class?*

*   **c** Do small hands give small angles, and large hands large angles?*

*   **d** What sort of measurements would pianists like for their hands? Why?*

HORIZONTAL AND VERTICAL

CLASS DISCUSSION

1 Here is a marble on a board. The board is **horizontal**.

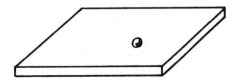

Will the marble roll?

2 The balanced pencil is **vertical**.
How many horizontal pencils are there?

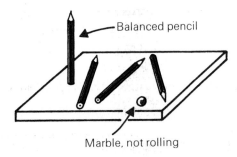

Balanced pencil

Marble, not rolling

Why is the marble not rolling?
If the marble starts to roll, what has happened to the board? Will the balanced pencil still be vertical?

3 How many pencils are vertical and how many are horizontal?

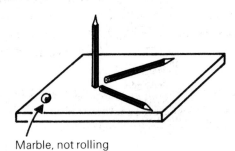

Marble, not rolling

If the horizontal pencils are at right angles to each other, how many right angles do the three pencils form?

4 a Describe any horizontal lines or surfaces you can see in the classroom or outside the school.
b Repeat part **a** for vertical lines and surfaces.

5 Lines like these which keep the same distance apart are called **parallel**.

Can you see any parallel lines in the classroom?

6 Do you think that the dark lines shown here are parallel?

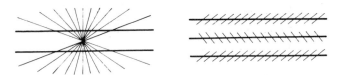

Hold the page level with your eyes and look along the lines. Do they look parallel now?

7 Lines which are at right angles are **perpendicular** to each other.

Can you see any perpendicular lines in the classroom?

8 Draw a rectangle, and mark its parallel and perpendicular sides as shown:

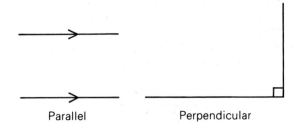

Parallel   Perpendicular

EXERCISE 5

1 Sketch these pictures. Then go over horizontal lines in one colour, and vertical lines in another colour.

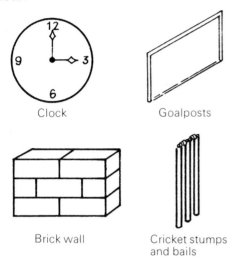

Clock   Goalposts

Brick wall   Cricket stumps and bails

2 Describe horizontal and vertical lines and surfaces in these pictures.

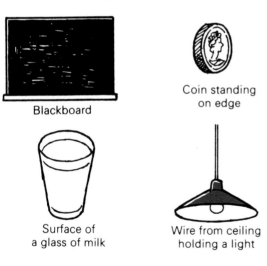

Blackboard

Coin standing on edge

Surface of a glass of milk

Wire from ceiling holding a light

3 The book stands on a table. On the front cover:
a Which edges are horizontal, and which are vertical?
b Name two pairs of parallel edges, and four pairs of perpendicular edges.

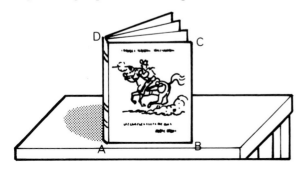

4 The wire cube and pyramid sit on a horizontal table. Count the number of horizontal edges and faces, and vertical edges and faces on each.

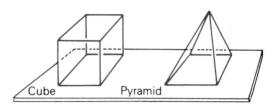

Cube   Pyramid

5 Name all the pairs of:
a perpendicular lines in the rectangle
b parallel lines in the octagon.

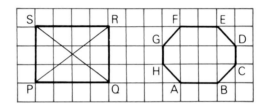

6 Which of these statements are true, and which are false?

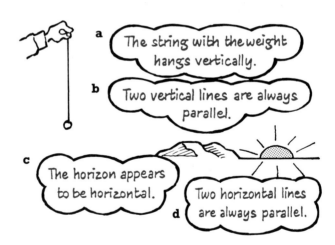

a The string with the weight hangs vertically.

b Two vertical lines are always parallel.

c The horizon appears to be horizontal.

d Two horizontal lines are always parallel.

7 List in a table the number of horizontal edges and surfaces, and vertical edges and surfaces, on these solids. The table is horizontal.

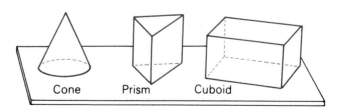

Cone   Prism   Cuboid

CHECK-UP ON ANGLES AROUND US

1 Say whether each angle is acute, obtuse, right, or straight.

a   **b**   **c**   **d**

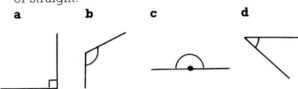

2 List the acute, obtuse, right and straight angles in:
10°, 90°, 170°, 110°, 180°, 89°, 98°

3 Estimate the size in degrees of each angle below, and say which type it is.

a   **b**   **c**

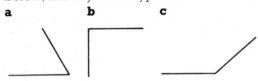

4 How many degrees are there between the hands of a clock at 6 am?

5 a In the rectangular gate, ABCD, name three angles with vertex B, and one with vertex C.
b What types of angles are they?

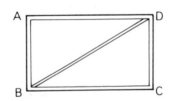

6 Name the largest and smallest angles in the window PQRS.

7 Name and calculate the sizes of the angles marked with arcs.

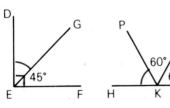 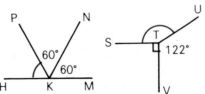

8 Estimate, then measure, the sizes of these angles:

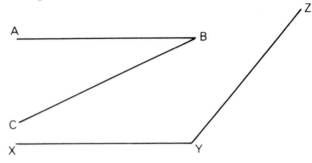

9 a Write down the sizes of angles AOB, AOC and AOD below.
b Calculate ∠COD and ∠BOD.
c Name all the obtuse angles.

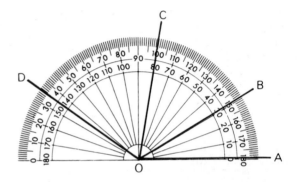

10 A tap needs three turns to open it fully. Through how many degrees must it be turned?

11 The angle of the slice of cake is 40°.

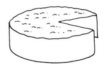

a What size is the reflex angle at the centre?
b How many slices of the same size can be cut?

12 Through how many degrees does the pointer on the dial turn clockwise from:
a OFF to 1 **b** OFF to 3 **c** 1 to 5?

13 Construct triangle PQR, with PQ = 6 cm, ∠PQR = 50° and ∠QPR = 50°. Measure ∠PRQ.

3 LETTERS AND NUMBERS

(volcano illustration with expressions: 3m, x=1, x+y, 6, x, 5, 2a, 2-t, y+1, y=3)

LOOKING BACK

1 Which numbers should be put in the boxes?
  a $\square + 3 = 8$ **b** $7 + \square = 12$ **c** $8 - \square = 6$
  d $14 - \square = 10$ **e** $2 \times \square = 10$ **f** $\square \times 7 = 28$
  g $\square \div 10 = 10$ **h** $9 \div \square = 1$

2 Write down three more numbers for each sequence.
  a $1, 3, 5, \ldots$ **b** $5, 10, 15, \ldots$ **c** $10, 9, 8, \ldots$
  d $40, 35, 30, \ldots$

3 Which numbers do the letters stand for in these sequences?
  a $5, 6, 7, x, \ldots$ **b** $40, 30, 20, y, \ldots$
  c $1, 2, 4, 8, m, \ldots$ **d** $3, 9, 27, n, \ldots$

4 In the sequences of numbers inside this table, describe the rules for moving:
  a along the rows from left to right
  b down the columns.

	A	B	C	D	E
1	3	4	5	6	7
2	5	6	7	8	9
3	7	8	9	10	11

5 The same rules as in question **4** are used to fill in these new tables. Copy and complete them.
  a

	A	B	C
1	5		
2			
3			

  b

	A	B	C
1			
2			
3			14

6 Find the IN and OUT numbers.
  a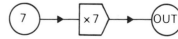
  b
  c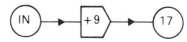

EXERCISE 1A

This weighing machine
is in a bank.
It shows the number
of £1 coins on it.

In this example:
$x + 1 = 7$
So $x = 6$
There are 6 coins in the bag.

Find the number each letter stands for in questions **1** and **2**. Give your answers like this: $x = 6$.

1 a   **b**

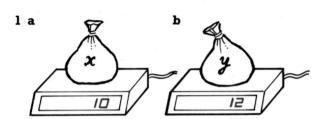

c   **d**

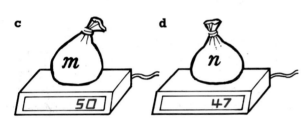

2 a   **b**

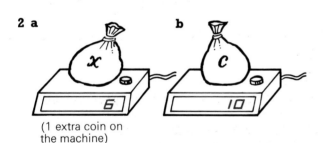

(1 extra coin on the machine)

c   **d**

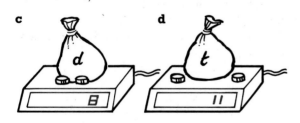

Each letter in the sequences in questions **3–5** stands for a number. Find the numbers. Give your answers like this: $u = 5$.

3 a $2, 4, 6, x, \ldots$ **b** $10, 20, 30, y, \ldots$
  c $5, 4, 3, t, \ldots$ **d** $12, 10, 8, v, \ldots$

4 a $4, 6, k, 10, \ldots$ **b** $3, p, 9, 12, \ldots$
  c $20, q, 18, 17, \ldots$ **d** $20, 15, w, 5, \ldots$

5 a $x, 3, 5, 7, \ldots$ **b** $y, 2, 4, 6, \ldots$
  c $m, 99, 98, 97, \ldots$ **d** $n, 6, 3, 0, \ldots$

6 In this spreadsheet, one number in each sequence has been replaced by a letter. Which number? Give your answers like this: $n = 30$.

	A	B	C	D	E
1	7	8	9	a	11
2	9	10	b	12	13
3	11	c	13	14	15
4	13	14	15	16	d
5	e	16	17	18	19
6	17	18	19	20	f
7	19	g	21	22	23
8	h	22	23	24	25

7 In these four magic squares, the numbers in each row, column and diagonal add up to 15. Which number does each letter stand for?

a

4	c	8
d	5	b
2	a	6

b

8	1	e
g	5	h
f	9	i

c

2	m	t
7	k	n
6	1	j

d

r	s	4
t	5	q
6	p	2

EXERCISE 1B

In questions **1**–**3** find the number that each letter stands for. Give your answers like this: $x = 6$.

1 a
b

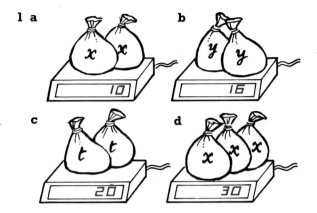

c
d

2 a
b

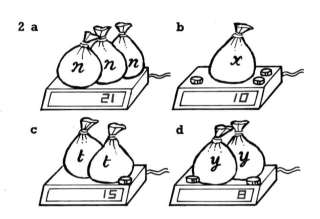

c
d

3 a
b

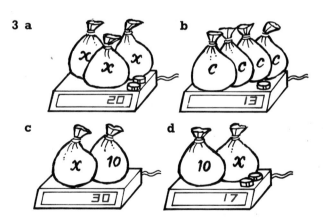

c
d

4 Karen drives at s mph, always 10 mph below the speed limit. Find s for each of these limits:

a   **b**   **c**

5 a Find the numbers which the letters represent in these sequences.
   b Calculate the numbers needed for spaces D1 and A6 (where the question marks are).

	A	B	C	D
1	15	12	x	?
2	30	t	18	
3	y	48	r	
4	120	96	d	
5	240	w	144	
6	?			

6 The lift can hold n persons. Five people enter the empty lift on the ground floor, and two more get in on the first floor. If the lift is now full, what is the value of n?

7 Ahmed has £x to spend on tapes. He has just enough to buy four tapes at £6.50 each. Find x.

8 In a sale, bags cost £y each. Eight bags cost £56. Find y.

9 In this spreadsheet:
   a Which number will appear in spaces A6, B6 and C6?
   b Calculate A1 + B1 + C1, A2 + B2 + C2, A3 + B3 + C3 and A6 + B6 + C6.
   c Can you write down the value of A12 + B12 + C12 without calculating each part separately?

	A	B	C
1	3	27	5
2	6	25	9
3	9	23	13
4	12	21	17
5	15	19	21
6			

EXERCISE 1C

(3 coins missing)

There were x coins in the bag, but three have been taken out.
The weighing machine shows eight coins in the bag now, so when
it was full it must have held 11 coins. $x = 11$

Find the numbers which the letters stand for in
questions **1** and **2**. All the bags were labelled before
any coins went missing.

1 a

(2 coins are missing
from the bag)

b

(5 coins are missing
from one of these bags)

c

(1 coin is missing
from each of the bags)

2 a

(3 coins are missing
from one of the bags)

b

(Each bag has 2 coins
missing from it)

c

(2 coins are missing
from one bag, but
there are 5 coins too
many in the other bag)

3 In each balance, the number of coins on the left is
equal to the number of coins on the right. Find the
number that each letter stands for.

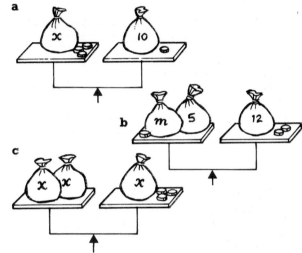

a

b

c

4 In this spreadsheet,
$B1 = A1 + 1$, $C1 = B1 + 1, \ldots$ and $A2 = 2 \times A1$
$B2 = A2 + 2$, $C2 = B2 + 2, \ldots$ $A3 = 3 \times A2$
$B3 = A3 + 3$, $C3 = B3 + 3, \ldots$ $A4 = 4 \times A3$

	A	**B**	**C**
1			
2			
3			
4			
5			

a Copy the table, and put 3 in space A1. Then fill
in all the spaces.
b If 5052 appears in space C6, what number had
been put in space A1?

5 In these sequences, each term is found by adding
the same number to the one before it. Which
numbers do the letters stand for?
a $5, x, y, 14$ **b** $3, p, q, r, 27$ **c** $a, 12, b, 22, c$

EXERCISE 2A

x coins have been put into a bag marked x. Now there are:

  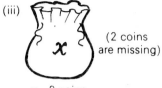

(i)   (ii)   (iii) (2 coins are missing)

x + 3 coins   x + 10 coins   x − 2 coins

How many coins are in each picture in questions **1–4**?

1 a   **b**   **c**   **d**

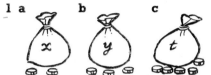

2 a   **b**

c   d

3 a   **b**

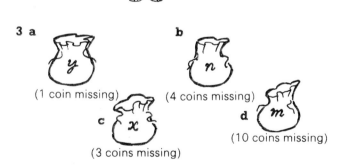

(1 coin missing)   (4 coins missing)

c   d

(3 coins missing)   (10 coins missing)

4 a   **b**

(2 coins missing)

c (5 coins missing)   d

5 Find the letters and numbers that go into the IN and OUT circles.

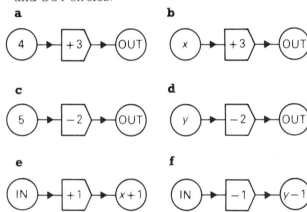

a   **b**

$4 \rightarrow +3 \rightarrow$ OUT $x \rightarrow +3 \rightarrow$ OUT

c   **d**

$5 \rightarrow -2 \rightarrow$ OUT $y \rightarrow -2 \rightarrow$ OUT

e   **f**

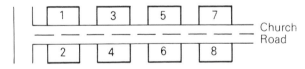

IN $\rightarrow +1 \rightarrow x+1$ IN $\rightarrow -1 \rightarrow y-1$

6 Here are the first eight houses in Church Road, Nos 1–8.

	1		3		5		7	

Church Road

	2		4		6		8	

Copy these houses in Church Road, and fill in their missing numbers.

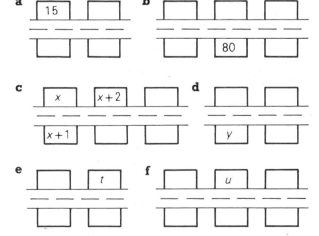

a   15

b   80

c   x   x+2

x+1

d   y

e   t

f   u

EXERCISE 2B/C

1 Find the letters and numbers that go into the IN and OUT circles.

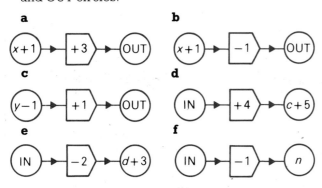

a $(x+1) \rightarrow [+3] \rightarrow (\text{OUT})$

b $(x+1) \rightarrow [-1] \rightarrow (\text{OUT})$

c $(y-1) \rightarrow [+1] \rightarrow (\text{OUT})$

d $(\text{IN}) \rightarrow [+4] \rightarrow (c+5)$

e $(\text{IN}) \rightarrow [-2] \rightarrow (d+3)$

f $(\text{IN}) \rightarrow [-1] \rightarrow (n)$

2 This is the ground floor plan for a new block of flats. The floors above have similar plans, with flat numbers continuing in sequence.

4	5	6	
Corridor			
3	2	1	

Entrance

a Draw and number the flats on the first floor.
b On one of the higher floors the flat directly above No. 1 is No. x. Sketch this floor, and fill in all the flat numbers in terms of x.

3 These school lockers have to be renumbered.

There are three possible schemes:

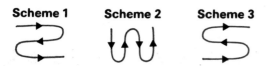

Scheme 1 **Scheme 2** **Scheme 3**

a If the lockers are numbered 1, 2, 3, ... find the number of the bottom right-hand locker under each scheme.
b The top left-hand locker is marked x. List the numbers of all the other lockers as they would appear in each scheme.
c Investigate which lockers would have the same numbers under different schemes.

BRAINSTORMERS

1 The face to which the arrow is pointing must show 6, since the two numbers on opposite faces always add up to 7.

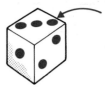

In terms of x, what should be marked on the faces opposite those marked x, $x+1$ and $x+3$?

 x $x+1$ $x+3$

Test your answers by putting $x = 1, 2, 3, \ldots$

2 Train A has 150 trucks, train B has 100 and train C has 90. x trucks are removed from train A and added to train B. Then 20 trucks are taken from train B and added to train C. $x+10$ trucks are now removed from train C and added to train A. If train B and train C are now coupled together, will the resulting train have more trucks than the new train A now? Show your reasoning clearly.

Train A

Train B

Train C

EXERCISE 3A

How many marbles are on each skateboard?

$$5+5$$
$$=2\times5$$
$$=10$$
(Two bags of 5 marbles)

$$n+n$$
$$=2\times n$$
$$=2n$$
(Two bags of n marbles)

$$y+y+y+2$$
$$=3\times y+2$$
$$=3y+2$$
(Three bags of y marbles, and one bag of 2 marbles)

How many marbles are on each skateboard?

1 a   **b**

4 a    **b**

c

c

2 a    **b**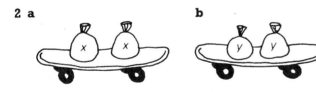

5 a 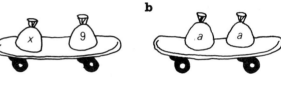   **b**

c

c

3 a 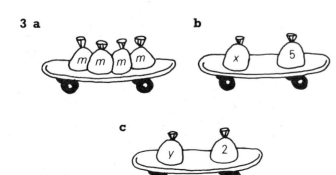   **b**

6 a    **b**

c

Target practice

Match each arrow with the correct target.

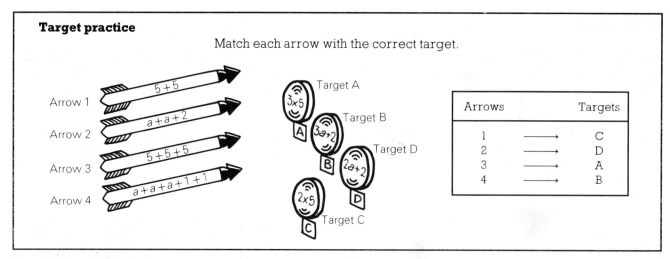

Arrows		Targets
1	$\longrightarrow$	C
2	$\longrightarrow$	D
3	$\longrightarrow$	A
4	$\longrightarrow$	B

Match the arrows with the targets. Show how they match up in a table, as above.

7

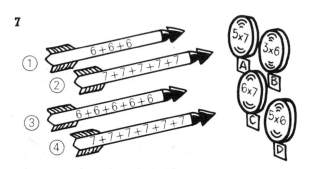

8

9

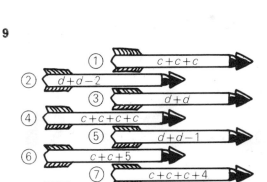

Making sure

  (i) $4+4+4+4+4 = 5 \times 4 = 20$
 (ii) $a+a+a = 3 \times a = 3a$
(iii) $x+x+4-1 = 2x+3$
 (iv) $y+2+y-1 = y+y+2-1 = 2y+1$

Write each of these in a shorter form.

10 a $7+7$ **b** $6+6+6$
    c $1+1+1+1+1$ **d** $9+9+9+9$
    e $x+x$ **f** $y+y$
    g $a+a+a$ **h** $b+b+b+b$

11 a $c+c+c$ **b** $d+d$
    c $t+t+t+t$ **d** $k+k+k+k+k$
    e $x+x+5$ **f** $y+y-1$
    g $m+m+m+4$ **h** $n+n-2$

12 a $t+t+t+3$ **b** $v+v-4$
    c $a+a+a+a+1$ **d** $b+b+b-3$
    e $x+2+3+x$ **f** $y+4-1+y$
    g $3x+2-2-3x$ **h** $5a-2a+4+5a$

EXERCISE 3B

1 Match the arrows with the targets. Notice that some arrows have missed their targets, and more than one arrow may hit the same target.

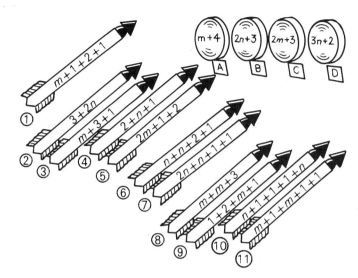

2 Julie and Jamie open bank accounts on a Monday. Each puts in £*x*. List the amount of money in their accounts each day from Monday to Saturday.

Julie

Day	Action	Amount (£)
Monday	Puts in £*x*	*x*
Tuesday	Puts in £5	
Wednesday	Takes out £3	
Thursday	Puts in £*x*	
Friday	Takes out £2	
Saturday	Puts in £10	

Jamie

Day	Action	Amount (£)
Monday	Puts in £*x*	*x*
Tuesday	Puts in £*x*	
Wednesday	Puts in £8	
Thursday	Puts in £2*x*	
Friday	Takes out £6	
Saturday	Takes out £4*x*	

3 Each car in the queue is *x* metres long, and each bus is 2*x* metres long. There is a one metre space between vehicles. Find the total length of each queue in terms of *x* and numbers.

a

b

c

4 One evening Channel 6 showed six short television programmes, each *m* minutes in length, and three longer programmes, each 3*m* minutes in length. There were also six commercial breaks, each two minutes long.
Find the total length of:
  a the short programmes
  b the longer programmes
  c the commercial breaks
  d the whole evening's viewing.

Write all of these in shorter form:

5 a $x+x+3+1$ **b** $y+y+2-1$
  c $p+2+p+1$ **d** $r+1+r-1+r$
  e $3+x-2+x$ **f** $4+a-4+a$
  g $2a+2a$ **h** $x+8+4x$

6 a $3+2x+4+x$ **b** $a+7+b+2+a+b$
  c $4y-2y$ **d** $5x-3x+2$
  e $8+2x-x$ **f** $7+3r-r+2$
  g $5w-w+t+4t$ **h** $8a+4x-2a-x$
  i $5-x+3x$ **j** $x-7+8-x$
  k $2w-t+4t-w$ **l** $18+7y+2x-7+y$

EXERCISE 3C

Study each diagram until you see how it works.

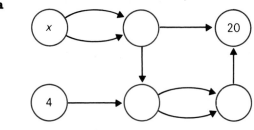

1 Find the numbers which go in the empty circles:

a

b

c

d

e
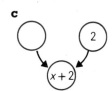

f
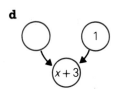

g
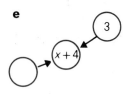

h
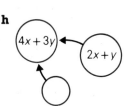

i
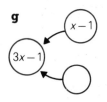

j
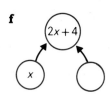

k
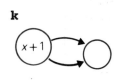

l
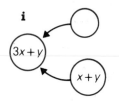

2 Copy these arrow diagrams, and fill in the spaces. Then find the values of x and y.

a
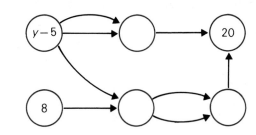

b
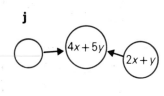
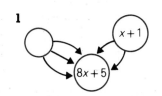

Simplify.

3 a $x+x+y+y$ **b** $2a-a+3b-b$
  c $c+d+c-d$ **d** $2e+2f+3e+4f$
  e $8g-8h-g+9h$ **f** $m+2+n+1$
  g $2p-3+q+3$ **h** $6+r+8+9r$

4 a $s-1-t+4$ **b** $3u-3v+5-u$
  c $6w+3-w+v$ **d** $8x+5-3y-3$
  e $5a+2b+6a+b-a$ **f** $c+7d+2e-c-7d$
  g $1-f-1+f-g+g$ **h** $11+m+3n+9+m-n$

5 If n is a whole number, explain why:
  a $2+2n+4+3n+6+5n-12$ will always be an even number
  b $1+n+3+2n+5+3n-8$ will always be an odd number.

BRAINSTORMER

All the water in each left-hand container is poured into each right-hand one as shown.

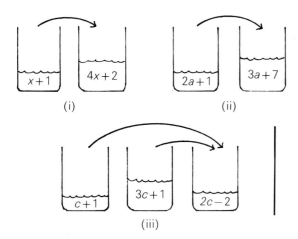

Each right-hand container now has 18 litres of water. Find the values of *x*, *a* and *c*.

CHALLENGE

a *In each game below the player starts with 6 points, and moves one square at a time. Follow each board from Start to Finish to find the total score.*

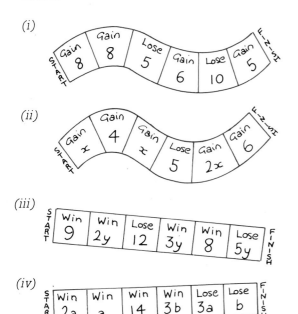

b *Now make up your own Win-Lose board game where letters or numbers are given with each move. Ask a partner to work out the score.*

INVESTIGATION

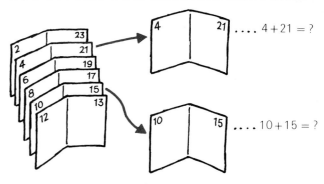

Look at a newspaper to see if its pages are numbered like those above.

a *What do you notice when you add the numbers on facing pages of the same sheet as shown above?*

b *Write down the numbers which these letters stand for.*

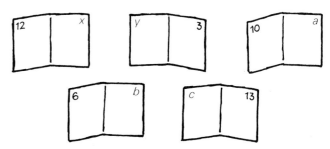

c *What is the page number on the back of page 2?*

d *Find the value of x in each of these:*

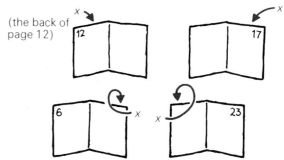

e *Find numbers to replace the letters in these:*

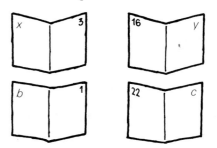

f *Investigate answers to questions like those above for a newspaper of your own.*

CHECK-UP ON LETTERS AND NUMBERS

1 Find the value of x for each diagram:

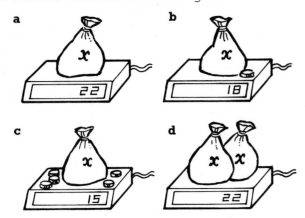

a   b

c   d

2 How many coins are in each picture?

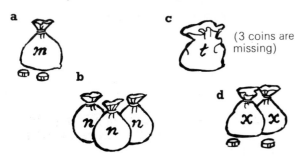

a

c

(3 coins are missing)

b

d

3 Find the numbers and letters that fit the OUT circles.

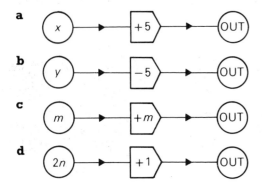

a

b

c

d

Write questions **4** and **5** in shorter form:

4 a $m+m+2$ **b** $4+x+3+x$
   c $2x+4+x$ **d** $t+1+3t-1$
   e $4x-2x+1$ **f** $6+8y+2-3y$
   g $a+1+2a-1$ **h** $5+3x-2-2x$

5 a $5a-1-2a$ **b** $1-6b+6b$
   c $3z-z+6z-2z$ **d** $k-k+k-k$
   e $9c-7c-2c+1$ **f** $5-5x-5+5x$
   g $y+y+z+z$ **h** $m+n-m+n$

6 a In this spreadsheet, what numbers must go in spaces F1, A6 and F6 to continue the sequences?

	A	**B**	**C**	**D**	**E**
1	1	2	3	4	5
2	3	4	5	6	7
3	5	6	7	8	9
4	7	8	9	10	11
5	9	10	11	12	13

b (i) and (ii) below are parts of the main spreadsheet. Copy and complete them.

(i)

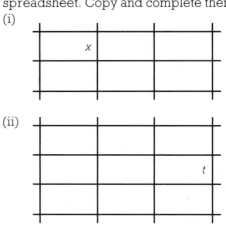

(ii)

7

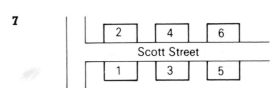

2   4   6

Scott Street

1   3   5

a Copy and complete (i) and (ii) for house numbers in Scott Street.

(i)

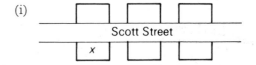

Scott Street

x

(ii)

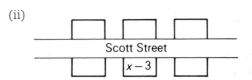

Scott Street

$x-3$

b June lives in Scott Street, in an odd-numbered house $y+6$. Her friend Rachel lives on the opposite side, three houses nearer the road junction. What number house does she live in?

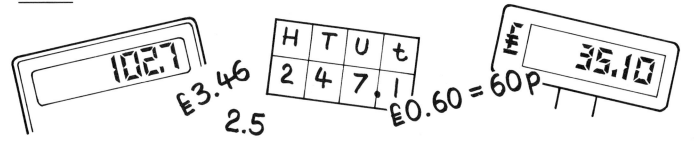

1 Write down these numbers, and underline the tens figure in each:
  a Thirty-four b Seven hundred and fifteen
  c Six thousand and twenty

2 In the number 7903, how many hundreds and how many units are there?

3 Write down the amount of money each girl has in her purse, using the £ sign, like this: £2.50.

  a Sabina

  b Tessa

  c Kim   d Ann

4 The amounts shown on these calculators are in £s. Write each in words.

  b
  a
  c

5 Write out these sums of money with £ signs, for example £0.65.
  a Two pounds forty pence
  b Twenty pounds nine pence
  c Sixty pence
  d Eight pence
  e One hundred and ten pence.

6 Multiply each number by 10:
  a 7 b 17 c 55 d 105 e 986

7 Round to the nearest £:
  a £7.99 b £3.27 c £45.60 d £52.09

8 Who has most money, and who has least?

Matt	David	Mike
£8.20	£8.22	£8.02

9 Meena buys two magazines, one for 40p, the other for 45p. Calculate the total cost, and her change from £1.

10 Boxes of chocolates cost £1.20 each.
  a What is the cost of five boxes?
  b How many boxes can you buy with a £5 note?

11

Jim   Asher

  a How much money does each boy have?

  b Who can buy two of the magazines? Which ones?
  c Together, can they buy all three?

COUNTING IN TENS; DECIMAL FRACTIONS

CLASS DISCUSSION/EXERCISE 1

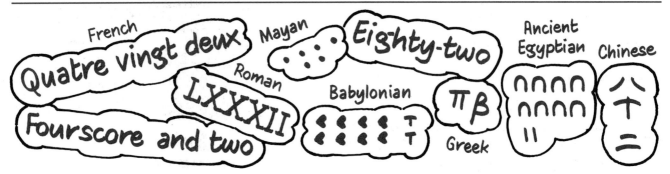

1 Lots of different systems of counting have been used at other times and in other parts of the world. How many of the systems shown above can you understand and explain?

2 Our **decimal** system is based on the ten numerals 0, 1, 2, 3, 4, 5, 6, 7, 8, 9, and on counting in 10s. When a number is multiplied by 10, each figure moves one place to the left, making the number 10 times larger, as shown in the table.

	Th	H	T	U	
				1	× 10
=			1	0	× 10
=		1	0	0	× 10
=	1	0	0	0	

Multiply each number below by 10, 100 and 1000.
a 5 **b** 20 **c** 100

3 Building up a number with a decimal fraction
Look at the length of the javelin throw. The number is built up like this:

H	T	U		t	h
1	0	0		0	0
	0	0		0	0
		6		0	0
				8	0
					2
1	0	6	.	8	2

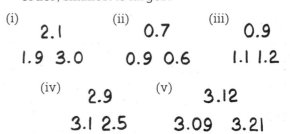

t = tenth
h = hundredth

The javelin travelled 106 metres, 8 tenths and 2 hundredths of a metre. .82 is a **decimal fraction**. If there were no whole number in front of it, it would be 0.82.

The decimal point separates the whole number from the fraction.

What is the whole number, and what is the decimal fraction, in each measure given below?
a 1 inch = 2.54 centimetres
b 1 yard = 0.914 metre
c 1 gallon = 4.546 litres
d 1 ounce = 28.35 grams
e 1 pound = 453.6 grams
f 1 litre = 1.76 pints

4 Whole numbers and decimal fractions in order
a The ruler shows the whole numbers from 0 to 5, and their tenths, in order:

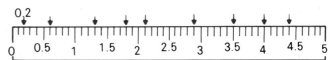

The first arrow points to 0.2. Which numbers are the other arrows pointing to, in order?
b Numbers with decimal fractions can be arranged in order, smallest to largest, like this:

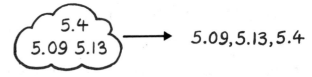

Arrange the numbers in each set below in order, smallest to largest.

(i)	(ii)	(iii)
2.1	0.7	0.9
1.9 3.0	0.9 0.6	1.1 1.2

(iv)	(v)
2.9	3.12
3.1 2.5	3.09 3.21

5 Money

Example

In a money calculation the calculator display shows:

This means £2.21, or two pounds, twenty-one pence.

a These calculators show sums of money in £s. Give each one in the two ways shown in the example.

b When you fill in a cheque you have to write the sum of money in words and in figures.

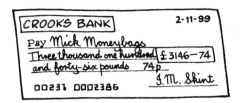

Write out these sums of money in full.
(i) £349   (ii) £2071   (iii) £5.43
(iv) £17.05   (v) £1234.56

EXERCISE 2A

1 Write down the numbers that **a–c** represent. Remember to include the decimal point in your answers.

a U t	b T U t	c H T U t
2 0	7 0 0	3 0 0 0
4	3 0	1 0 0
	2	2 0
		7

2 Write these numbers in figures:
a Five point six
b Thirty-one point two
c Nought point three
d Twenty point five
e One hundred point four
f Nought point nought one

3 The first arrow points to 0.1. Which numbers do the other arrows point to?

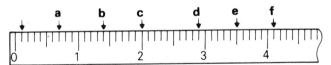

4 Draw, or trace, a ruler like the one above. Mark arrows at:
a 0.1 **b** 0.9 **c** 1.7 **d** 2.5 **e** 3.8 **f** 4.2

5 Copy and complete this table.

Numbers	8.35	1.7	0.04	0.2	5.08	15.63
Tenths	3					
Hundredths	5	0				

6 Which is greater in each pair?
a £5.56 or £5.65   **b** 1.9 m or 2.1 m
c 0.71 or 0.17   **d** 1.22 or 2.11
e £10.01 or £9.99   **f** 76.04 or 76.40
g 3.09 or 3.10   **h** 0.1 or 0.02

7 a List the numbers which the arrows point to, in order, smallest to largest.
b Which number is:
  (i) halfway between 0 and 1
  (ii) two small divisions clockwise from 2?

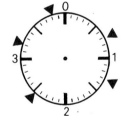

8 Bernie keeps a record of the growth of his prize sunflower, but all the labels have blown off. Which label goes in which space?

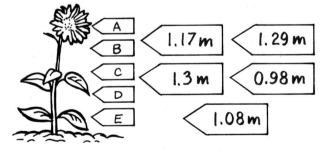

9 Write out these payments in words, as you would on a cheque:
a £12.52   **b** £22.90   **c** £160.05

10 Arrange these numbers in order, smallest to largest:
14.78   14.5   15.01   14.99
14.28   14.93   14.75   15.1

EXERCISE 2B/C

1 The magnifying glass shows the part of the ruler between 8.2 and 8.7. The first arrow points to 8.34. Which numbers do the other arrows point to?

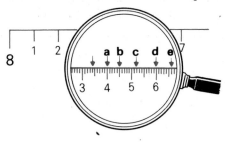

2 Arrange in order, smallest to largest: 10.04, 9.95, 10.104, 10.004, 9.876, 10

3 Write the number 1 234 567.890 in words.

4 Write down the readings on the scales of these instruments.

  a Thermometer

  b Tyre gauge

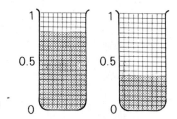

  c Pressure gauge (2 arrows)

  d Barometer (2 arrows)

5 Each jar can hold one litre of liquid.

  a Write down the volume of liquid in each jar as a decimal fraction of a litre.

  b What fraction of each jar is empty?

6 Copy and complete this table of populations.

Country	Population in millions	Population in full
Great Britain	57.2	
Germany		78 630 000
United States	248.84	
China		1 113 900 000

7 These are some old measures of length—list their names in order, shortest first.

Name	Length in metres
Rod, pole or perch	5.0292
Fathom	1.8288
Iron	0.000 53
Telegraph nautical mile	1855.32
Link	0.201 168
Chain	30.48
Mil	0.000 025 4

CHALLENGE

  a *(i) What is the least number of these coins needed to make each of these amounts? 10p, 20p, 30p, 40p, 50p, 60p, 70p, 80p, 90p, £1*

  (ii) Continuing to £1.10, £1.20, . . . how far can you go before you have to use four coins?

  b

  Show that if you had this set of coins you could make up 10p, 20p, 30p, . . . , £1.90 with no more than three coins.

INVESTIGATION

The Roman number system is based on these numerals:

Roman	Decimal
I	1
V	5
X	10
L	50
C	100
D	500
M	1000

Investigate how a number is built up using Roman numerals, and how calculations were carried out. Find out other facts in reference books or encyclopaedias.

ADDITION AND SUBTRACTION

14.75	8.3
+9.30	−1.6
24.05	6.7

When adding and subtracting numbers with decimal fractions, the decimal points must be kept in line, one below the other. Why is this?

EXERCISE 3 (MENTAL, OR PENCIL AND PAPER)

Calculator out of action! Try this exercise without it.

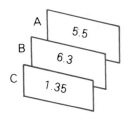
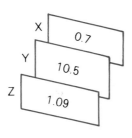

A 5.5
B 6.3
C 1.35

X 0.7
Y 10.5
Z 1.09

1 Choose two cards, one from each pile (for example AX), and add the numbers on the two cards. Repeat this for as many pairs as you can.

2 Repeat question **1**, but this time subtract the smaller number from the larger in each pair.

3 Copy and complete these triangle patterns where each number is the sum of the two above it. For example, in part **a** 1.7 = 0.9 + 0.8.

a
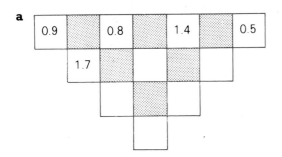

0.9		0.8		1.4		0.5
	1.7					

b
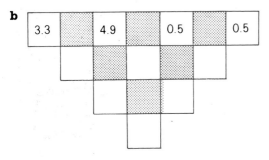

3.3		4.9		0.5		0.5

c
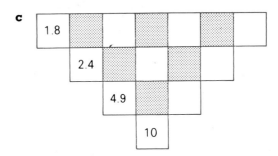

1.8				
	2.4			
		4.9		
			10	

4 17-year-olds at a job interview were asked to do calculations like these mentally. Can you do them?
a 1.5 + 2.6 − 3   **b** 5.4 − 3.2 + 1.6
c 6.5 + 9 − 5.5   **d** 2.8 − 1.2 − 0.7

5 Copy and complete this cross-number puzzle.

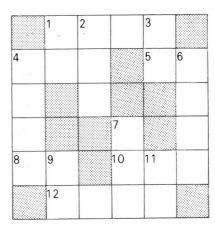

Enter 7.2 as 7 .2

or 7
.2

Across	**Down**
1 13.2 + 14.37	**1** 0.05 + 2.05
4 20.18 − 12	**2** 80 − 1.9
5 1.2 − 0.86	**3** 9.6 − 2.3
8 6.13 + 3.07	**4** 90 − 0.01
10 74.3 − 56.1	**6** 237 + 200.2
12 597.7 − 57	**7** 0.02 + 0.19
	9 16.55 − 16.30
	11 2.36 + 6.34

6 Make up some 'triangle' calculations of your own, like those in question **3**.

EXERCISE 4A

1 Neil buys a magazine for 75p and a book for £2.15.

  a How much will he have to pay?
  b What change will he get from £5?

2 Andrew is 1.72 m tall, and Rebecca is 1.57 m.
  a How much taller is Andrew?
  b Calculate the sum of their heights.

3 Salman has a job as a part-time waiter. The tips he receives total £6.20 on Friday, £8.05 on Saturday and £4.80 on Sunday.
  a Calculate the total amount that he receives in tips.
  b How much more does he make in tips on Saturday than on Sunday?

4

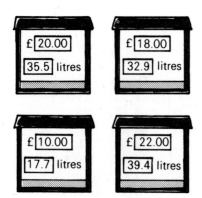

Here are the readings on four petrol pumps.

£ 20.00   35.5 litres
£ 18.00   32.9 litres
£ 10.00   17.7 litres
£ 22.00   39.4 litres

  a How much did the four motorists spend on petrol altogether?
  b What was the total amount of petrol put in their tanks?

5 David Murray was given £10 for his birthday. He bought a paperback book for £1.95, a knife for £3.16 and a box of chocolates for £1.54. He paid for them with his £10 note and was given the wrong change of £3.25. What was the correct change?

6 Calculate the perimeter of each shape (the distance round the edge):

  a
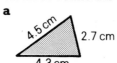
4.5 cm   2.7 cm   4.3 cm

  b
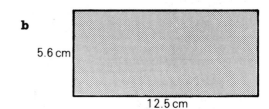
5.6 cm   12.5 cm

  c
2.2 cm   4.2 cm   7.1 cm   5.8 cm   2.9 cm   8 cm

7 In May 1954, Roger Bannister became the first person to run a mile in less than four minutes. He ran the four laps of the race in 57.5, 60.7, 62.3 and 58.9 seconds.
  a What was his total time?
  b By how much did he break the four minute barrier?

8 In a diving competition, Chris scored 43.56, 37.27 and 53.26 points. Gary scored 51.26, 33.76 and 49.37. Who won? By how many points?

EXERCISE 4B/C

1

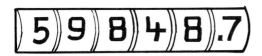

This is the mileometer reading on a motor car before a journey. The car travels 258.5 miles. Write down the new reading.

2

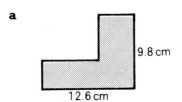

a How much dearer is the video recorder than the television set?

b What is the total cost of both?

3 The dimensions of these cars are shown in metres.

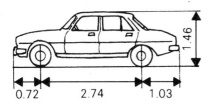

a Calculate the difference between:
(i) their lengths (ii) their heights.

b The wheelbase is the distance between the front and back wheels. What is the difference between the wheelbases of the two cars?

4 Jacqui Green buys a cassette recorder for £37.50, a pack of cassettes for £8.35 and a small transistor radio for £15.09. What change will she be given from £70?

5 Calculate the perimeters of these shapes based on rectangles.

a

9.8 cm

12.6 cm

b

8.65 cm

5.15 cm

11.75 cm

8.25 cm

36.55 cm

6 An electrician has 100 metres of wire on a drum. He uses 13.6 metres and 28.7 metres of wire in one house, and the same lengths again in another house. What length of wire will be left?

7 In an indoor athletics stadium four laps of the track are run in an 800 metre race. An athlete ran the first lap in 24.9 seconds, the first two laps in 51.4 seconds and the first three laps in 78.9 seconds. Her time for 800 metres was 1 minute 46.5 seconds.

a What were her times for the second, third and fourth laps?

b Which was her fastest lap?

8 Six radar masts are linked by underground cables whose lengths are shown in kilometres.

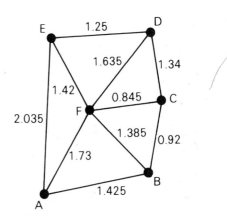

a Calculate the total length of cable.

b In a new plan, each mast is only linked directly to F. How much cable is saved?

MULTIPLICATION AND DIVISION BY 10, 100, ...

(i) On page 10 we saw that when a number is multiplied by 10, each figure moves one place to the left, making the number 10 times larger.
$8.5 \times 10 = 85$
Multiplying by 10 again, $8.5 \times 100 = 850$

	T	U	t	
		8 . 5		$\times 10$
=	8	5 . 0		

(ii) When a number is divided by 10, each figure moves one place to the right, making the number 10 times smaller.
$120 \div 10 = 12$
Dividing by 10 again, $120 \div 100 = 1.2$

	H	T	U	
	1	2	0	$\div 10$
=		1	2	

Examples
1 3.14×10
$= 31.4$

2 47.1×100
$= 4710$

3 0.3×1000
$= 300$

4 $26 \div 10$
$= 2.6$

5 $5.3 \div 100$
$= 0.053$

EXERCISE 5 (MENTAL, OR PENCIL AND PAPER)

Again, do not use a calculator in this exercise.

1

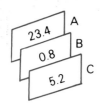
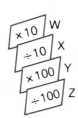

23.4 A
0.8 B
5.2 C

×10 W
÷10 X
×100 Y
÷100 Z

a Choose two cards, one from each pile, then carry out the calculation.
b Repeat **a** for as many pairs as you can.

2 Write down the cost of ten of each item.

a Lolly £0.20
b Chew £0.08
c Toffee £0.12
d Sweets £2.35
e Chocs £5.30

3 Calculate:
a £3.25 × 10   **b** £27.03 × 100   **c** £85 ÷ 10
d £6.20 ÷ 10   **e** 12 750 ÷ 100

4 Calculate the weight of 100 identical quantities of each of these:

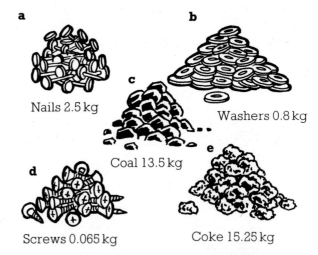

a Nails 2.5 kg
b Washers 0.8 kg
c Coal 13.5 kg
d Screws 0.065 kg
e Coke 15.25 kg

5 Divide each of these by 10 and by 100:
a £360   **b** 185 metres   **c** 23.5 seconds
d 1047 kilograms.

6 £1 buys:
a France   **b** Austria   **c** Portugal   **d** Italy
   9.44 Fr   19.71 Sch   240.80 Esc   2105 L
How much of each currency should you receive for £10, £100 and £1000?

7 a Multiply each number by 20:
(i) 5   (ii) 12   (iii) 3.4   (iv) 25.1
b Now multiply each number by 200.

MULTIPLICATION AND DIVISION BY ANY NUMBER

You must always make sure that the decimal point is in the correct place in the answer.
It is useful to make a rough estimate first.
Examples
1 8.8×6 **2** 3.14×8 **3** $12.6 \div 7$
Estimation: $9 \times 6 = 54$ *Estimation*: $3 \times 8 = 24$ *Estimation*: $13 \div 7 =$ between 1 and 2
Calculation: $8.8 \times 6 = 52.8$ *Calculation*: $3.14 \times 8 = 25.12$ *Calculation*: $12.6 \div 7 = 1.8$
A further check   In multiplication, the number of figures after the decimal point in the answer is the same as the number before multiplication.
(1 in Example **1**, 2 in Example **2**)

EXERCISE 6 (MENTAL, OR PENCIL AND PAPER)

Calculator still out of action!

1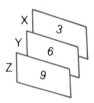

A 7.2
B 0.54
C 21.6

X 3
Y 6
Z 9

Choose two cards, one from each pile. Multiply the numbers on the cards, but estimate each answer first.
Repeat this for as many pairs as you can.

2 Repeat question **1**, but this time divide the A, B or C number by the X, Y or Z number.

3 Copy and complete these triangle patterns in which each number is the product of the two above it.

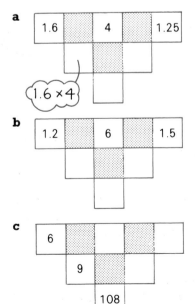

a

| 1.6 | | 4 | | 1.25 |

(1.6 × 4)

b

| 1.2 | | 6 | | 1.5 |

c

6				
	9			
		108		

4 Copy and complete this cross-number puzzle.

1	2		3	4	
	5	6		7	8
9		10	11		
12	13		14	15	
	16	17		18	19
		20			

Enter 7.2 as $\boxed{7}\boxed{.2}$

or $\boxed{7}$
$\boxed{.2}$

Across
1 $5.7 - 2.8$
3 0.9×5
5 $51.1 + 9.9$
7 0.25×100
10 0.9×0.9
12 $103.6 - 25.6$
14 $1.68 \div 2$
16 $1.4 \div 4$
18 3×1.9
20 $38.4 \div 6$

Down
2 4×0.24
4 0.26×2
6 0.9×2
8 $10 \times 10 \times 0.5$
9 3.7×10
11 $0.6 + 0.6 + 0.6$
13 $141.1 - 132.8$
15 100×0.45
17 5×11.2
19 0.19×4

5 a Match the numbers
1, 2, 3, ..., 10 with the letters A, B, C, ..., J.

1 =   3 =   7 =   4 =
5 =   8 =   9 =   6 =
2 =   10 =

A. $5 - 5 + 0.5 + 0.5$ B. $0.5 + 0.5 + 0.5 + 0.5$
C. $5 + 5 - (5 \div 5)$ D. $5 - (5 \div 5)$
E. $5 - (5 \times 0.5) + 0.5$ F. $(5 \times 5 - 5) \times 0.5$
G. $5 + (5 \times 0.5) - 0.5$ H. $(55 \div 5) - 5$
I. $5 \times 0.5 + (5 \times 0.5)$ J. $5.5 + (5 \times 0.5)$

b Try to use four 5s to complete:
(i) $11 = \ldots$ (ii) $12 = \ldots$ (iii) $13 = \ldots$

6 Make up some 'triangle' calculations of your own, like those in question **3**.

ROUNDING TO THE NEAREST PENNY

> **a** £10 is shared equally among 12 pupils. Each receives £10 ÷ 12 = £0.833..., or 83.3...p.
> Rounded to the nearest penny, this is 83p.
> **b** If the £10 is shared equally among 7 pupils, each receives £10 ÷ 7 = £1.428....
> Rounded to the nearest penny, this is £1.43 (although this would cost £10.01).
>
> | **Rule**: If the next figure is 5 or over, round up the penny. |
> | --- |
>
> | *Examples* | Amount | 12.4p | 12.5p | £1.283 | £8.316 | £1.205 | £1.298 |
> | --- | --- | --- | --- | --- | --- | --- | --- |
> | | Round to | 12p | 13p | £1.28 | £8.32 | £1.21 | £1.30 |

EXERCISE 7A

1 Round these to the nearest penny.
   a 23.8p **b** 16.2p **c** 7.4p **d** 49.5p
   e 10.9p **f** 95.6p **g** £1.237 **h** £2.463
   i £4.185 **j** £8.394 **k** £1.395 **l** £35.506

2 These calculators show money in £s. Round each amount to the nearest penny.

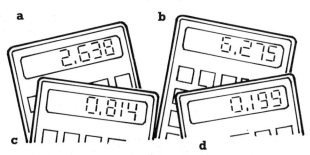

3 Douglas is buying a personal stereo. He pays £1.45 a week for 18 weeks. How much does it cost?

4 Eight friends buy ice-cream. The bill is £3.60. How much should each pay?

5 Dress material costs £8.50 a metre. Calculate the cost of:
   a 0.2 m **b** 0.8 m **c** 2.5 m
   d 12.75 m, to the nearest penny.

6 Six prizewinners share £123. How much does each receive?

7 Value Added Tax (VAT) is added to most things you buy. In the early 1990s the amount of VAT on an item could be found by multiplying the cost by 0.175.

Use this method to calculate the VAT on the items below to the nearest penny.

8 Mr Smart fills the tank in his car with 44.3 litres of diesel. If one litre costs 47.5 pence, how much does he have to pay?

9 The organisers of a Youth Club calculate that the cost of running a Disco will be £210. How many tickets at £1.75 each must they sell to cover the cost?

10 A tradesman completes a job in 14 hours. He charges £9.75 an hour.
   a How much does the job cost?
   b If his labour charge is £195 for another job, how many hours did he spend on it?

11 Calculate the cost per day of each holiday, to the nearest penny.

SKIING HOLIDAYS
7 days £276
14 days £395

EXERCISE 7B/C

1 £1 = $1.85, so £7.30 = $7.30 × 1.85 = $13.505. Rounded to the nearest cent, or two decimal places, this is $13.51. Convert these sums of money to dollars and the nearest cent.
  a £8.24   **b** £12.50   **c** £125.75   **d** £5733

2 Laura saves £4.75 every month and Susan saves £1.25 every week, for holiday spending money. How much will they have altogether after a year?

3 3.5 metres of dress material cost £24.15. Calculate the cost per metre.

4 Which is the cheaper method of buying the TV set? By how much?

£168·95 cash OR
£45 cash and
26 weekly
payments of £4·99

5 Linda buys seven balls of wool for £6.58. She uses six of them, and the shop refunds her money on the seventh ball. How much did she get back?

6 Gladys fills her petrol tank.
  a Calculate the cost, to the nearest:
    (i) penny   (ii) 10p   (iii) £.
  b How many litres could she buy for £20, to the nearest:
    (i) litre   (ii) 0.1 litre?

PRICE PER LITRE
47.4p
NO. OF LITRES
37.20

7 Calculate Mr Patel's telephone bill. Start by finding the number of units he used between the readings on 18 March and 16 June.

The Talky Telephone Co.	BILL
RENTAL FOR 3 MONTHS £ 17·75	

DATE	READING
18 MARCH	5708
16 JUNE	6066

.........UNITS at 5·25p = £ _____

TOTAL £ _____

8 Here are the prices of some items on sale at a supermarket.

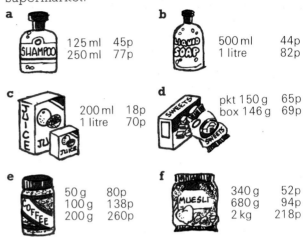

a 125 ml   45p   250 ml   77p

b 500 ml   44p   1 litre   82p

c 200 ml   18p   1 litre   70p

d pkt 150 g   65p   box 146 g   69p

e 50 g   80p   100 g   138p   200 g   260p

f 340 g   52p   680 g   94p   2 kg   218p

Look at the quantities and prices. Do you think the larger pack always gives better value? Find out by calculating the amount of each (rounded to one decimal place) that you get for one penny.

CHALLENGE

A	B	C	D	E	F	G	H	I	J	K	L	M
↑	↑	↑	↑	↑	↑	↑	↑	↑	↑	↑	↑	↑
0	0.1	0.2	0.3	0.4	0.5	0.6	0.7	0.8	0.9	1	1.1	1.2

N	O	P	Q	R	S	T	U	V	W	X	Y	Z
↑	↑	↑	↑	↑	↑	↑	↑	↑	↑	↑	↑	↑
1.3	1.4	1.5	1.6	1.7	1.8	1.9	2	2.1	2.2	2.3	2.4	2.5

Use the code to read this message:
$\| 2 \times 0.9 | 0.1 + 0.1 | 4.2 \div 6 | 0.2 \times 7 | 12.6 \div 9 | 1.21 \div 1.1 \|$
$0.23 + 0.47 | 23.8 \div 17 | 9.9 - 8.8 | 2.32 \div 2.9 | 0.001 \times 300 |$
$| 0 \div 9.99 | 1.2 \times 10 \times 0.2 | 14.3 - 12.5 \| 11.34 \div 6.3 | 0.7 |$
$0.007 \times 200 | 0.24 \div 0.12 | 6.69 - 5.59 | 0.11 + 0.19 \|$
$77 \div 770 | 0.16 \div 0.4 \| 0.83 + 0.27 | 2 \times 0.7 | 7.15 \div 5.5 |$
$| 2.9 - 2.3 | 400 \div 1000 | 8.5 \div 5 \|$

BRAINSTORMER

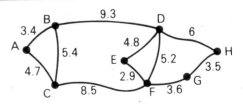

A salesman has to visit all the shops marked by dots. The distances between them are shown to the nearest tenth of a kilometre. Find the shortest route he could take to visit every shop, starting C → A.

CHECK-UP ON DECIMALS IN ACTION

1 Write these numbers in figures:
   a Sixteen point two
   b One hundred and five point eight
   c Nought point one four

2 What numbers are these arrows pointing to?

a

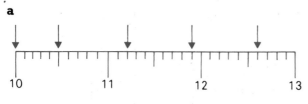

b

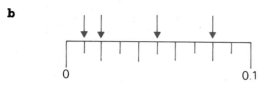

3 Arrange these numbers in order, smallest first:
   a 15.6, 16.5, 17.0, 16.1, 16
   b 9.96, 10.81, 9.68, 11.12

4 Calculate:
   a 3.5 + 2.5, and 3.5 − 2.5
   b 5.67 + 2.34, and 5.67 − 2.34

5 Calculate:
   a 2.25 + 1.76 − 0.56
   b 0.68 + 0.79 − 0.54
   c 123.4 − 90.2 + 77.6

6 In a Diving Competition the gold medallist scored 49.68, 47.52 and 60.03 points, and the silver medallist scored 46.86, 51.84 and 55.38 points in the final. Find the total score of each. By how many points was the gold medallist the winner?

7 Steven drives 236.5 km, 168.7 km, 97.6 km, and 302.8 km. How much farther does he have to travel to complete a total distance of 1000 km?

8 Calculate the perimeter of this L-shape.

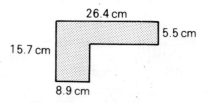

Would you have been able to do this if the 5.5 cm and 8.9 cm lengths had not been given?

9 Multiply each number by 10 and by 100.
   a 3.4   **b** 12.5   **c** 1.09   **d** 234.5   **e** 0.1

10 Estimate, then calculate:
   a 7.8 × 5   **b** 3.2 × 9   **c** 12.4 × 4
   d 25.3 × 6   **e** 1.89 × 3

11 Divide each number in question **9** by 10 and by 100.

12 Estimate, then calculate:
   a 14.7 ÷ 3   **b** 26.5 ÷ 5   **c** 49.5 ÷ 9
   d 10.4 ÷ 4   **e** 6.4 ÷ 8

13 Round to the nearest penny:
   a £5.632   **b** £1.246   **c** £0.092
   d £7.125   **e** £3.199

14 Colour films cost £2.95, or £9.74 for four. How much do you save by buying four?

15 Calculate the cost of this telephone bill.

METER READING		CHARGES	AMOUNT
PRESENT	PREVIOUS		
15499	14994	RENTAL	£19.00
		...... units at 5·65p each ⟶	£
		TOTAL	£

16 The distance by rail between two towns is 31 km. A day return ticket costs £5.60. Calculate the cost in pence per km.

5 FACTS, FIGURES AND GRAPHS

LOOKING BACK

1 Here is a picture of Cara's class.

She made this table of the number of girls and boys in the class.

	Tally	Number
Girls	⍁⍁⍁⍁⍁ ⍁⍁⍁⍁⍁	
Boys	⍁⍁⍁⍁⍁ IIII	

a What is the number of girls, and the number of boys in Cara's class?

b How many pupils are in her class altogether?

2 Cara also made a table of the number of pupils with different colours of hair. Copy the table, and fill it in, using the picture of her class above.

	Tally	Number
Dark hair		
Fair hair		
Red hair		

3 This pictogram also shows the number of girls and boys in Cara's class.

⍟ = 1 pupil

Girls	⍟⍟⍟⍟⍟⍟⍟⍟⍟⍟
Boys	⍟⍟⍟⍟⍟⍟⍟⍟⍟

Use your table from question **2** to draw a pictogram of the number of pupils in her class with dark, fair and red hair.

4 The bar graph shows one month's sales of lollipops in the school shop.

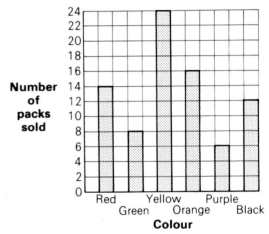

a What colour was most popular?

b What colour was least popular?

c How many packs of yellow lollipops were sold?

d Calculate the total number of packs of lollipops sold.

5 The table shows sales of soft drinks during the month.

Flavour	Cola	Soda	Lime	Orange	Lemon
Number of crates	6	7	5	9	3

a Using squared paper, copy and complete the bar graph.

b Which drink sold best?

c List the flavours in order, from most popular to least popular.

6 The number of packets of chocolate biscuits sold in the same month was:
Snap—4, *Yummy*—1, *Fab*—7, *Chewy*—10, *Crunch*—8, *Fudge*—3, *Nutty*—5.
Show these sales in a bar graph.

COLLECTING AND ORGANISING INFORMATION

EXERCISE 1A

1

To settle the argument, Nick and Simon's teacher suggested that they should collect some information. Here are the results they collected from their class:

Pet	Tally	Number
Dog	⟋⟍⟋⟍⟋ II	
Cat	⟋⟍⟋⟍⟋ IIII	
Budgie	IIII	
Snake	I	
Tortoise	III	
Fish	⟋⟍⟋⟍⟋	
None	I	

List the totals. Who said 'I told you so'?
Their teacher said 'Don't be too sure. Try another class'.

2 Here are the statistics for the other class. List the totals. Who said 'I told you so' now?

Pet	Dog	Cat	Budgie	Hamster	Guinea Pig	None
Tally	⟋⟍⟋⟍⟋ ⟋⟍⟋⟍⟋	⟋⟍⟋⟍⟋ III	⟋⟍⟋⟍⟋	I	I	IIII
Number						

3 Draw up a table like the one in question **2** for your own class. Fill in the tallies as pupils say which pets, if any, they have at home.

4 Make a tally table for the colour of pupils' eyes in Zoe's class.
Blue, blue, brown, grey, blue, green, grey, blue, brown, hazel, grey, grey, blue, grey, blue, brown, grey, green, hazel, grey, blue, blue, blue, blue, grey, brown, blue.

5 Here is a pictogram of the number of pupils in Riverside High School:

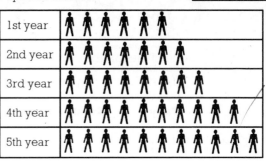

Pupils in school

a How many pupils are there in:
   (i) each year   (ii) the whole school?
b Write a sentence about the trend in the number, year by year.

<hr>

PRACTICAL PROJECT

Working on your own, or with a partner, or in a group, investigate some of the following for the pupils in your class.
Collect the statistics in a table, and then illustrate them with pictograms.
1 *The ways in which they travel to school.*
2 *Their favourite sports.*
3 *Their favourite pop groups.*
4 *The months in which they were born.*
5 *The number of children in their families.*
6 *Their shoe sizes.*

EXERCISE 1B

1 Salim made a survey of the number of pupils who were members of school clubs. Here is his pictogram:

Choir	☺	☺	☺	☺	☺	☺
Chess	☺	☺	☺	☺		
Sports	☺	☺	☺	☺	☺	
Drama	☺	☺	☺	☺		

$$☺ = 5 \text{ pupils}$$

a Why do you think he made each figure stand for 5 pupils?

b How are 4 pupils shown in the table?

c How many pupils are there in each club?

2 Miss James, in the school office, made this table of how all 12-year-old pupils took lunch.

School lunch	Packed lunch	Café	Home
40	27	24	31

Show the results in a pictogram, in which

$$☺ = 5 \text{ pupils}$$

3 Mr Davis taught two classes of 12 year olds. He thought that Class A1 was better at French than A2. On Friday he gave both classes a test, marked out of 10.

Here are the results.

A1 1, 5, 0, 4, 3, 5, 1, 6, 5, 4, 4, 4, 4, 5, 4, 2, 4, 5, 3, 4, 9, 2, 2, 3, 4, 0, 7, 3, 1, 4, 10, 4

A2 10, 9, 8, 7, 0, 1, 3, 4, 5, 4, 8, 9, 10, 1, 2, 5, 4, 5, 5, 5, 7, 3, 2, 1, 8, 8, 9, 6, 4, 4, 6, 7

a Make a tally table for each class.

b Do you think that A1 is better than A2? Give a reason for your answer.

4 Jean was captain of the Junior Hockey Team. Eighteen games were played during the season. Jean kept a note of the scores. She always wrote the goals scored by her team first:
2–1, 1–1, 2–1, 4–2, 0–0, 0–2, 3–4, 2–2, 5–3, 1–0, 4–0, 2–4, 1–1, 1–2, 0–3, 3–1, 2–1, 0–2

a Copy and complete Jean's table.

	Tally	Number
Won		
Drawn		
Lost		

b How many points did her team gain if there were 2 points for a win and 1 for a draw?

c Do you think her team had a good season? Explain your answer.

PRACTICAL PROJECT

Try the one at the end of Exercise 1A, if you did not do it then.

EXERCISE 1C

1 Mr Mills, the mathematics teacher, set an examination, marked out of 100. Here are the marks of 50 pupils:

```
71  63  13  31  51  65  48  75  59  75  22
 1  87  32  37  95  65  45  91  45  31  73
25  36  93  53  96  94  57  74  42  35  32
19  28  65  76  51  74  41  38  29  63  58
64  54  76  69  54  98
```

He prepared a table using class intervals of 10: 1–10, 11–20, 21–30, . .

Copy and complete this table.

Class interval	Tally	Frequency
1–10	I	1
11–20	II	2
21–30	IIII	4
31–40	ЖЖ III	8

2 Later, Mr Mills decided that a table with class intervals of 20, starting 1–20, 21–40, . . . , would be more useful. Draw up this table.

3 Next term, Mr Mills set another examination for the same 50 pupils. Here are the results:

```
 4  32  75  93  63  47  44  25  53  43  14
95  66  24  35  94  57  51  26  79  72  34
44  18  27  25  86  55  86  42  75  97  67
44  31  37  52  84  27  77  67  91  36  87
46  85  83  27  48  80
```

  a Use class intervals 1–20, 21–40, . . . to organise this new set of marks in a table.

  b Is this set of marks better than the last set, or not?

  c Choose a different set of class intervals, and make a new table.

4 The best throw of each of the 36 entrants in the javelin contest at Action Academy is given below, to the nearest metre:

```
28  26  31  37  33  41  28  37  48  52  42
47  35  31  25  29  38  40  49  35  34  37
42  44  27  48  32  34  45  43  38  37  42
42  40  36
```

List the throws in a table with class intervals of 5, starting 25–29, 30–34, . . .

PRACTICAL PROJECT

Make a class survey of:
a the times taken by pupils to travel to school, or
b the distances they live from school.
  Arrange the data in a table, with suitable class intervals of times or distances.

DISPLAYING AND INTERPRETING INFORMATION

After information has been collected and organised, it can be displayed in many different ways. Here are some examples; notice all the titles, scales, etc.

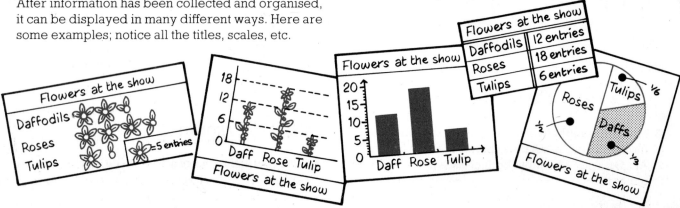

EXERCISE 2A

> **Bar graphs** are easy to draw and to interpret.

1 This bar graph shows the number of boxes of crisps sold in the school shop.
  a Which flavour is:
    (i) most popular
    (ii) least popular?
  b (i) How many boxes of each flavour were sold?
    (ii) How many boxes were sold altogether?

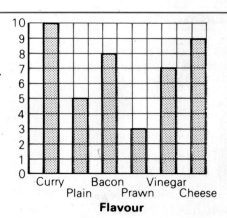

2 a On squared paper draw a bar graph for these crisps sales. Remember to put in the titles and the scale at the left-hand side as in question **1**.

Flavour	Plain	Curry	Tomato	Cheese	Beef	Onion
Number of boxes sold	8	6	3	7	5	1

b List the flavours in order, from most popular to least popular.

3 Accidents often happen in playgrounds. One local council registered 40 accidents during the summer holidays.

Swings	Slides	Roundabout	Rocking horse	Climbing frame
20	4	4	2	10

a Draw a bar graph on squared paper, with axes as shown.

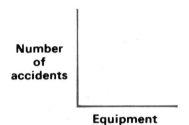

b What fraction of the accidents involved swings?
Why do you think there were so many?

Pie charts display information 'at a glance'.

---

4 The circles are divided into equal parts. What fraction of each circle is shaded?

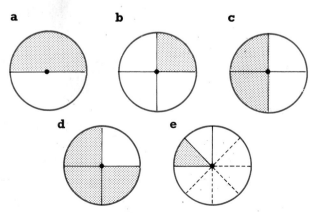

5 What fraction of the employees at the Top TV factory:

a are women   **b** eat in the canteen

c walk to work   **d** work part-time?

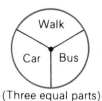

(Three equal parts)

6 Each of these pie charts shows different information about Hilltop High School. What fraction of the pupils:

a are girls   **b** take school lunches

c walk to school   **d** like mathematics?

(Five equal parts marked)

7 The pie chart shows the sales in the school's drinks vending machine during the winter term. What fractions of the sales were for:

a coffee
b hot chocolate
c tea
d Fizzo?

> **Line graphs** are useful for showing trends in the data.

8 Luke, was born on 30th June. His weight was measured every month. His sister Katie drew this line graph.

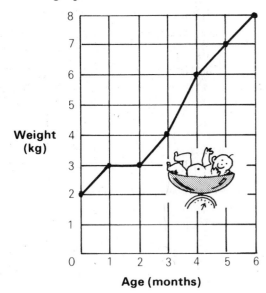

Age (months)

a What weight was Luke when he was born?
b What weight was he at:
   (i) 3 months   (ii) 6 months?
c When did he weigh 6 kg?
d His parents were worried between months 1 and 2. Why?

9 Growmore Garage's sales graph has its ups and downs.

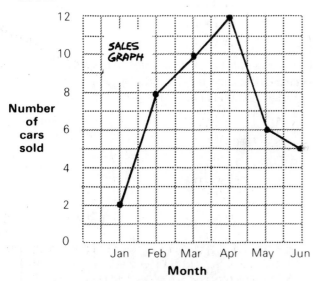

Month

a Which month saw the most sales?
b In which month were only six cars sold?
c How many cars were sold altogether in these six months?

d Copy and complete this table:

Month	Jan	Feb	
Cars sold	2		

10

Tony kept a note of his ice cream sales each day, to the nearest £5.

Day	Mon	Tue	Wed	Thu	Fri	Sat	Sun
Sales (£)	40	55	60	45	60	75	65

a On squared paper draw these axes and scales. Plot the points, and draw a line graph of his daily sales.

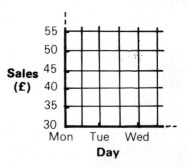

Day

b On which day was most ice cream sold? Why do you think this was?
c Write a sentence about the trend of the sales— up or down during the week.

/**PRACTICAL PROJECT**/

Choose another of the topics listed in the project on page 56. Collect the data and present your results in a bar graph and a line graph—also a pie chart, if you feel able to. Write a sentence about the results.

EXERCISE 2B

1 In an environmental experiment, the height of a seedling is measured daily.

Day	1	2	3	4	5	6	7	8
Height (mm)	2	3	5	8	12	18	20	21

a Copy and complete the bar graph and the line graph to illustrate the seedling's growth.

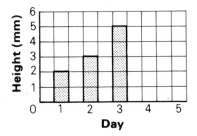

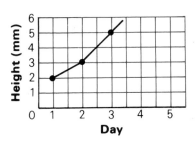

b Which graph illustrates plant growth better? Why?

2 The bar graph shows the number of telephones per 100 of the population in six countries.

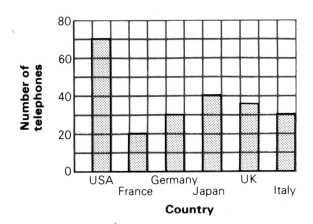

a Which country has:
   (i) most telephones   (ii) fewest telephones?
b How many telephones per 100 of the population does each country have?

3 Sue had flu. The graph shows her temperature, day by day. By Sunday it was back to normal.

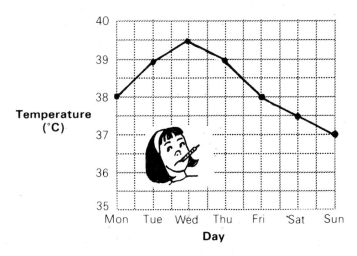

a On which day was her temperature highest? What was this temperature?
b On how many days was her temperature 38°C or higher?
c What is her normal temperature?

4 Sue's baby sister, Fiona, was born on 1st January. Sue drew this line graph of her weight at the start of each month.

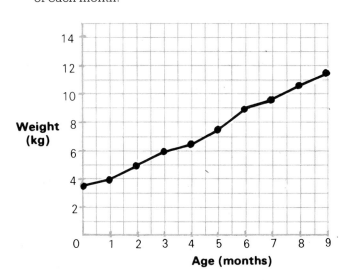

a How many kilograms does each box on the left-hand scale stand for?
b What weight was baby Fiona at:
   (i) birth   (ii) 3 months   (iii) 6 months?
c During which month did she gain most weight (where the graph is steepest)?
d By which month had her birth weight doubled?

5

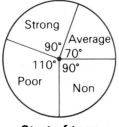

THERE ARE FAR MORE BRITISH CARS ON THE ROAD THAN ANY OTHER KIND

TRY TAKING A SAMPLE IN THE TOWN CAR PARK, JANE

This is what Jane found:

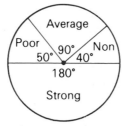

a Was Jane right? Explain why or why not.
b What do you think she means by 'others'?
c List her results in order, from most common to least common.
d Estimate the fraction of cars that were:
  (i) British   (ii) Japanese.

6 Mr Armstrong gave his class swimming tests at the beginning and end of term. The pie charts show the grades of swimmers he found. Why was he pleased with the results? Give several reasons.

Start of term   **End of term**

7 The tables show the average monthly temperatures in Glasgow.

Month	Jan	Feb	Mar	Apr	May	June
Temperature (°C)	4	4	6	8	11	13

Month	July	Aug	Sep	Oct	Nov	Dec
Temperature (°C)	15	15	13	10	7	5

a Draw the axes, and mark the scales, on squared paper. Plot the temperatures, and draw a line graph.
b Write a sentence or two describing how the temperature changes throughout the year.

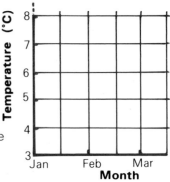

8 Which types of diagram would you use to illustrate the results of surveys on these topics? Explain why you would choose them.
a Pupils' pocket money.
b Time spent by pupils watching television.
c A patient's temperature over 24 hours.
d Types of pets in pupils' homes.
e Pupils' shoe sizes.
f The length of a supermarket queue from 8am–8pm.

/**PRACTICAL PROJECT**

Try the one at the end of Exercise 2A, if you did not do it then.

EXERCISE 2C

1 This graph shows sales of the hit record 'It counts'.
a In which week were most records sold? How many?
b For how many weeks were more than 50 000 records sold?
c Between which weeks did the sales remain the same?
d Describe the trend of sales over the 12 weeks.

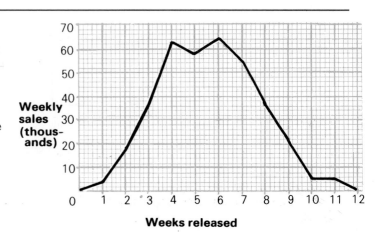

2 The speeds in mph of 50 vehicles on a motorway were checked as follows:

62	54	56	73	78	63	68	70	66	54	58
65	55	57	69	67	61	64	53	56	68	76
57	48	57	68	82	78	72	75	65	67	64
54	58	62	67	80	87	69	74	78	70	76
46	60	63	68	74	67					

a What was the range of speeds?

b Starting at 45 mph, with class intervals 45–49, 50–54, ... mph, make a tally table of speeds.

c Draw a bar graph.

d How many vehicles were exceeding 70 mph?

3 A large crowd turned out for the City v. United football match. It was estimated that half of them were City supporters, one third United supporters, and the rest were neither.

The angle at the centre of a circle is a complete turn of 360°. How many degrees are there in the slices of a pie chart for City supporters, United supporters and others? Draw the pie chart.

4 The 30 pupils in class 2B were asked which country in the United Kingdom they would like to have a holiday in. The results were:
England—10; Scotland—10; Wales—5; Ireland—5.

They calculated the angles for the slices of a pie chart like this:

England's slice $= \frac{10}{30} \times 360° = 120°$
Scotland's slice $= \frac{10}{30} \times 360° = 120°$
Wales' slice $= \frac{5}{30} \times 360°$
$= 60°$
Ireland's slice $= \frac{5}{30} \times 360°$
$= 60°$

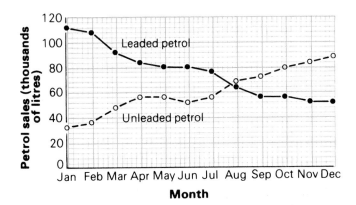

Use your protractor to help you draw the pie chart.

5 Claire calculated the number of hours of 'repeats' on television in one week.

Channel	1	2	3	4	
Hours of repeats	7	6	8	3	Total hours = 24

She calculated the angle of the first slice in a pie chart like this:
Channel 1: $\frac{7}{24} \times 360° = 105°$
Calculate the other angles, and draw the pie chart.

6 Suzanne asked her class to vote on the television programmes they like best. Their votes were:
Sport—6 Cartoons—3 Films—9 Quizzes—3
Plays—1 Other—8

a How many votes were there altogether?

b How many degrees on the pie chart should she give for each type of programme?

c Draw the pie chart. Mark in the programmes, and write the vote opposite each one.

7 This graph shows the monthly sales of petrol at the Green Star Filling Station.

a What were the total sales of petrol in March?

b Calculate the total sales of leaded petrol in 1990.

c What fraction of January's sales was unleaded?

d Write a few sentences about the two line graphs, giving reasons for the way they look.

8 A traffic census was started at 8 am. Every hour, a note was taken of the total number of vehicles which had passed so far.

Time	09 00	10 00	11 00	12 00	13 00
Total number of vehicles	250	400	500	550	700

Time	14 00	15 00	16 00	17 00	18 00
Total number of vehicles	850	950	1000	1250	1550

a Draw a line graph on 2 mm squared paper. Take 1 cm to represent 100 vehicles on the vertical axis.

b By what time had 1500 vehicles passed the census point?

c Did more vehicles per hour arrive before noon or after noon?

d Describe any trends you see in the number of vehicles passing the census point.

SAMPLING

CLASS DISCUSSION

1 Manufacturers' claims are often based on **samples**.

(i) Average contents 47 matches
(ii) Average life 100 hours

(iii) '9 out of 10 people can't tell the difference between butter and margarine'

Why do the manufacturers not:
a count the matches in every box
b test every lightbulb
c ask everyone's opinion about butter and margarine?

2 The first ever Top Ten singles chart was published on 22nd January 1955. It was based on the sales in a sample of record shops. Can you think of advantages and disadvantages of sampling like this?

3 You have to find which sports are preferred by all the pupils in the school.
a How many pupils would you ask?
b Which pupils would you ask?
c How would you choose the pupils?
d What questions would you ask?
e How would you record, analyse and present the results?

4 Describe the samples you would collect in order to estimate:

a The amount of water wasted in one day from a dripping tap

b The time taken to count to 1000 000

c The number of words in a dictionary

d The number of hairs on your head

e The popularity of different makes of motorcar

> The aim is to choose a sample that will represent the whole population.

PRACTICAL PROJECTS

1 You have to order supplies for the class outing, and want to find out which is the flavour of crisps pupils prefer.
a Give each pupil a table, and ask them to put a mark opposite their favourite.

Cheese	Tomato	Onion	Bacon	. . .

b First draw a pie chart using all the data.
c Then choose 12 tables at random, and draw a pie chart for this sample. Repeat this a few times.
d How do the samples compare with the whole class pie chart?

2 In the game of Scrabble, each player is given a set of tiles which have letters and scores on them, like this:

A	B	C	D	E	F	G	H	I	J	K	L	M	N	O
1	3	3	2	1	4	2	4	1	8	5	1	3	1	1

P	Q	R	S	T	U	V	W	X	Y	Z	Blank
3	10	1	1	1	1	4	4	8	4	10	0

The aim of the game is to make words. Letters like Q and Z are worth more points as they are harder to use.
a Choose a passage from a book, and make a tally table of the number of times different letters are used in this sample passage.
b Compare the frequency of the letters with the scoring system in Scrabble.
c Repeat **a** and **b** for different passages from the book, or from other books.

3 Opinion Polls ask samples of people about all sorts of things. Choose one of the following, or a subject of your own choice, and carry out a poll. Decide on the topic, the questions to ask and the way to record, analyse and present the results.

4 Sample some different newspapers in order to compare their:
a word length **b** sentence length
c picture area **d** sports coverage
e popularity.

CHECK-UP ON FACTS, FIGURES AND GRAPHS

1 This pictogram shows the number of pupils absent from school each day in one week.

Mon	⚇	⚇	⚇	⚇	⚇	⚇	⚉		
Tue	⚇	⚇	⚇	⚇	⚉				
Wed	⚇	⚇	⚇	⚉					
Thu	⚇	⚇	⚇	ₒ					
Fri	⚇	⚇	⚇	⚇	⚇	⚇	⚇	⚇	⚇

⚇ = 5 absent pupils

a On which day were there fewest absences? How many were there?

b On which day were there most absences? How many were there?

c How many absences were there altogether that week?

2 The label on a box of SPARKY matches says there are 45–47 matches in each box.
The number of matches in each of 50 boxes was counted. Here are the results.

Number of matches	42	43	44	45	46	47	48
Number of boxes	4	7	5	10	12	9	3

a Draw a bar graph of the results.

b How many boxes did not contain 45–47 matches?

3 The numbers of goals scored in West League football on Saturday 14th April were:
0, 1, 2, 3, 1, 3, 4, 0, 0, 1, 3, 3, 2, 1, 2, 3, 4, 2, 4, 5, 3, 2, 0, 1, 0, 1, 2, 1, 3, 1, 2, 0, 0, 1, 2, 0, 1, 1

a Draw and complete a table with the headings Goals, Tally and Number.

b How many teams scored:
(i) less than 2 goals   (ii) more than 2 goals?

4 Twenty-five pupils sat a test which was marked out of 50. Their marks were:

21   46   25   17   32   33   11   22   2   26   23
35   8   24   7   15   12   21   47   28   29   26
28   16   24

a Arrange the marks in class intervals 1–10, 11–20, and so on.

b Draw a bar graph. Into which class interval do most marks fall?

5 Angie works in a hairdressing salon. The pie chart shows how she spends her wages each week.

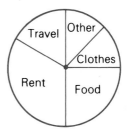

a List the items in order, from largest to smallest.

b Estimate the fraction of her money that she spends on:
(i) food   (ii) rent   (iii) travel.

c Her take home pay is £120 a week. Estimate the amount she spends each week on each item.

6 Alison's height was measured each year at the school medical inspection.

Age	8	9	10	11	12	13	14	15	16
Height (cm)	135	137	140	145	148	155	158	160	161

a Draw a line graph.

b Did Alison grow by the same amount each year?

c Estimate her height at:
(i) age 8½   (ii) age 17.
How does your graph allow you to do this?

6 MEASURING TIME AND TEMPERATURE

LOOKING BACK

1 Name the next three months: January, February, March, . . . , . . . , ...

2 Arrange these years in order, starting with 1795: 1905, 1855, 1795, 1950, 2001.

3 What are the next three days in this sequence: Monday, Wednesday, Friday, . . . , . . . , . . . ?

4 In the picture above, Big Ben shows 5 o'clock. What is the time on each of these clocks?

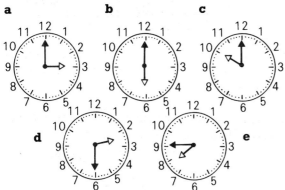

5 Quarter past ten can be written as 10.15. Write 'half past ten' and 'quarter to eleven' in the same way.

6 If *Neighbours* is on at 5.35 pm and the News starts at 6.00 pm, how long does *Neighbours* last?

7 Eurosport starts at 11.30 pm, and lasts for 45 minutes. When does it finish?

8 Lyn bought the cheesecake on 18th June. How many days could she safely keep it?

9 Write the following as am or pm times:
 a twenty past nine in the morning
 b five to ten in the evening.

10 Here is part of the calendar for June.

M	T	W	T	F	S	S
–	–	1	2	3	4	5
6	7	8				

 a Write down the dates of all the Wednesdays.
 b What day is 30th June?

11 A shop sale lasts 7 days a week, for all of November and December. How many days is this?

12 a *Signed J. Jones* 17. 8. 99
 Write this date in words.
 b Now write 'Fourth of October 1996' in figures, as in part **a**.

13 What would John's watch show at these times?
 a Five past nine in the morning.
 b Quarter to eleven in the morning.

14 What are the temperatures on these thermometers?

15 The temperature in the classroom at 9 am was 16°C.
 a By midday it had risen 5°. What was the temperature then?
 b By 3.30 pm it had fallen to 15°C. How many degrees did it fall?

MEASURING TIME—THE CALENDAR

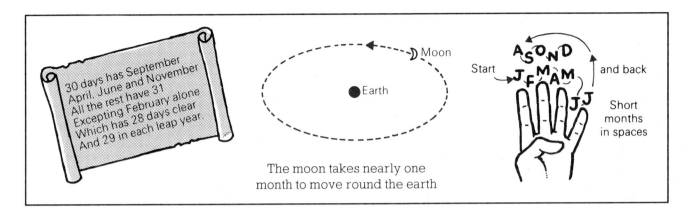

30 days has September
April, June and November
All the rest have 31
Excepting February alone
Which has 28 days clear
And 29 in each leap year

The moon takes nearly one
month to move round the earth

Start   and back

Short
months
in spaces

EXERCISE 1A

1 How many days are there in:
a January **b** June **c** December?

2 How many months have 31 days?

3 a Copy and complete this page from a calendar.

June						
Sun	Mon	Tue	Wed	Thu	Fri	Sat
–	–	–	–	1	2	3
4	5					

b What day of the week was 17th June?
c What was the date of the third Tuesday in June?

4

The sale notice goes up on Monday. On what day does the sale end if the shop is open every day?

5 The first of April is a Saturday. What day is the thirtieth?

6 Write down the next three days in these sequences:
a Sunday, Tuesday, Thursday, . . .
b Monday, Thursday, Sunday, . . .

7

⌐07. 10. 98⌐

This is the date stamped on a library book. Write the date in words.

8 List these years in order, with the earliest one first.

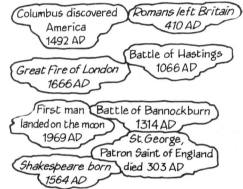

Columbus discovered America 1492 AD

Romans left Britain 410 AD

Great Fire of London 1666 AD

Battle of Hastings 1066 AD

First man landed on the moon 1969 AD

Battle of Bannockburn 1314 AD

St. George, Patron Saint of England died 303 AD

Shakespeare born 1564 AD

9 Olympic Games are held every four years. They were held in 1992. When will the next three Games be held?

10 The Earth moves round the sun in about $365\frac{1}{4}$ days. What happens to the $\frac{1}{4}$ day?

11 a Copy and complete this month:

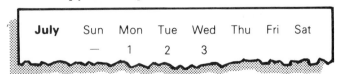

July	Sun	Mon	Tue	Wed	Thu	Fri	Sat
	—	1	2	3			

b Ian's birthday is on 22nd July. Which day is this?
c Anita goes on holiday on the last Saturday in July. What date is this?

EXERCISE 1B/C

1 How many days are there in the autumn months, September, October and November?

2 January 1st 1993 was on a Friday. Make a calendar for January.

3 a Helen's holiday starts on a Monday and lasts for 9 days. On what day does it finish?
 b From the first day of term to the last is 80 days including Saturdays and Sundays. Term begins on a Monday. On what day does it end?

4 Write down the numbers that go in these spaces:
 . . . seconds in a minute
 . . . minutes in an hour
 . . . hours in a day
 . . . days in a week
 . . . days in a fortnight
 . . . or . . . or . . . or . . . days in a month
  . . . or . . . days in a year
  . . . weeks in a year
  . . . months in a year
  . . . years in a decade
  . . . years in a century

5 Including both given dates, for how many days is this rail ticket valid?

> FAST RAIL FARE
> Valid 20. 4. 98 to 20.5.98

6 Spring starts on March 20th, and ends on June 20th. To calculate the length of Spring, copy and complete:
 March: 20 to 31 = 12 days
 April :
 May   :
 June :   20
         Total ____ days

7 Calculate the number of days (including both dates, as in question **6**) from:
 a January 1st to February 24th.
 b June 28th to August 18th.

8 How many days are there (including both dates) from:
 a 3.5.94 to 3.6.94
 b 20.8.93 to 10.10.93
 c 1.4.95 to 22.9.95?

9 Apart from century years, like 1900, a year which is divisible by 4 is a leap year. Which of these are leap years?
 a 1990 **b** 1992 **c** 1994 **d** 1996 **e** 2002
 f 2004

10 List the years given in question **8** of Exercise **1A**, and opposite each say which century it is in.

> ### Table of centuries
> | 0 – 100AD | : | 1st Century AD |
> |---|---|---|
> | 101 – 200 AD | : | 2nd Century AD |
> | _ _ _ _ | | _ _ _ _ |
> | 1901 – 2000 AD | : | 20th Century AD |
> | 2001 – 2100 AD | : | 21st Century AD |

11 Christmas Day in 1992 was a Friday.
 a Explain why it was a Saturday in 1993.
 b Copy and complete the table up to 1999.

Year	Christmas day
1992	Friday
1993	Saturday

BRAINSTORMER

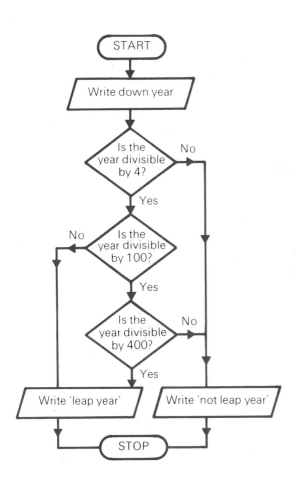

1 Use the flowchart to find out which of these years
are leap years:
 a 1900 **b** 1980 **c** 2000
 d 2020 **e** 2050 **f** 2100

2 a Is the present year a leap year?
 b If not, when was the last leap year?

3 With the help of the flowchart write one or two
sentences to explain how to find out whether or
not a year is a leap year.

INVESTIGATION

How to find the day of any date from 1900 to 1999.

Write down these numbers:	Example
	5th December 1991
A = the last two digits in the year	A = 91
B = A ÷ 4. Ignore remainders; if remainder = 0, it is a leap year	B = 22 (remainder 3)
C = month value; see table	C = 6 (from table)
D = date in month	D = 5
E = A+B+C+D	E = 124
E ÷ 7. The remainder gives the day of the week:	E ÷ 7 = 17, remainder 5
	Date is a Thursday

1 = Sunday
2 = Monday
3 = Tuesday
4 = Wednesday
5 = Thursday
6 = Friday
0 = Saturday.

Month value		
Jan 1 (0 in leap year)	Jul	0
Feb 4 (3 in leap year)	Aug	3
Mar 4	Sep	6
Apr 0	Oct	1
May 2	Nov	4
Jun 5	Dec	6

1 Check that the calculation works for today's date.
2 Find the day of the week on which you were
born.
3 On which weekdays were the letters with these
postmarks posted?

MEASURING TIME—CLOCKS

'It's 4 o'clock.'
But is it 4 am ('ante meridiem' means before noon),
or 4 pm ('post meridiem' means after noon)?
It's impossible to tell from the 12 hour clock.

EXERCISE 2A

1 What are the two possible times shown by each of these clocks (am and pm)?

a

b

c

d

2 Draw clock faces showing these times:
  a 4 pm **b** 6.15 am **c** 10.30 pm **d** 1.55 am

3 Write these afternoon times in figures:
  a half past one   **b** twenty past two
  c quarter to three **d** twenty-five to five

4 Write these times in words:
  a 5.30 am **b** 11.45 pm **c** 3.05 pm

5 How long is it from:
  a 10 am until noon   **b** noon until 5 pm
  c 9 am until 3 pm   **d** 2 am until 11 am
  e 5 am until 3 pm   **f** 7 am until midnight
  g 10 pm until 8 am   **h** 3.30 pm until 11.30 pm?

6 Bill waited for a bus from quarter to five until ten past five. How long was this?

7 Grace has to be at the airport at least an hour and a half before her plane is due to take off at 10.15 pm. When should she be there?

8 Alex hands in his shoes at 1.20 pm. When will they be ready?

SHOE REPAIRS
ONLY TAKE ¾ HOUR

9 A football match begins at 2.30 pm. Each half lasts 45 minutes, and there is an interval of 15 minutes at half time. When does:
  a the first half finish
  b the second half begin
  c the game end?

10 Sunrise is at 7.30 am, and sunset is at 9.15 pm. How long is it from:
  a 7.30 am until 7.30 pm
  b 7.30 pm until 9.15 pm
  c sunrise until sunset?

EXERCISE 2B/C

1

How long does each of these programmes last?
a Operation Petticoat
b Animation Now
c The Money Programme

2 Find the starting and finishing times of:
a The Natural World, which lasts 50 minutes
b Snooker, which is on for 1 hour 35 minutes
c Not Mozart, lasting 45 minutes.

3 Lois is going to roast a chicken. She has to allow 20 minutes for each 500 g, plus 15 minutes over.
a How long will it take to roast a chicken weighing 2 kg?
b If the chicken is put in the oven at 3 pm, when will it be ready?
c If the chicken has to be ready at 6 pm, when should Lois put it in the oven?

4 a On August 1st the sun rose at 5.22 am and set at 9.24 pm. How long was it above the horizon?
b On the same day the moon rose at 10.21 pm and set at 5.16 am. For how long could the moon be seen?

5 a A bus service between two towns runs every 40 minutes. The first bus leaves the bus station at 7.30 am. When will the next two buses leave?
b The journey takes 1 hour 25 minutes. Write down the arrival times of these three buses.
c The third bus reaches its destination 25 minutes late. What time does it arrive?

6 If time were to be decimalised, with 100 seconds in a minute, 100 minutes in an hour and 10 hours in a day, which would be longer—the old second or the new second? Explain your method.

7 A puzzle. Given a 3-minute and a 5-minute eggtimer, how could you time exactly:
a 1 minute **b** 4 minutes **c** 7 minutes?

/ CHALLENGE /

Make a list of TV programmes. On your own, with a partner, or as part of a group, schedule a complete day's viewing. Your Channel opens at 7.25 am, and adult features must be screened after 9 pm. Your aim is to attract as many viewers as possible. Prepare your schedule, and then compare it with others.

/ PRACTICAL PROJECTS /

1 a *Estimate, then measure, the time taken by classmates to add ten 2-digit numbers (correctly). Compare results. What is the record time?*
b *Repeat part **a**, using calculators. Any conclusions?*

2 *Choose a length of time between 1 and 30 seconds. Then take it in turns to try to stop a stopwatch at that time, without looking at the dial. The number of seconds you are out is counted as a penalty. The person with the lowest total number of penalty points after five attempts is the winner. Vary the length of time and the penalty system. Try counting 'thousand 1, thousand 2, thousand 3, . . .' mentally to time the seconds.*

3 *Use a stopwatch with hundredths of a second to time yourself and your friends in a 100 m run, or over a shorter distance in the sports hall. Calculate the difference in times between different runs.*

4 *Compare the counter readings on a video cassette recorder or on a cassette player with the length of time left to play. Write a report, possibly including graphs to illustrate your findings.*

MEASURING TIME—THE 24 HOUR CLOCK

Many bus, train and plane timetables use the 24 hour clock, in order to avoid confusion; for example, 8.30 can mean 8.30 am or 8.30 pm.

Midnight to midday is am, or 00 00 to 12 00 hours

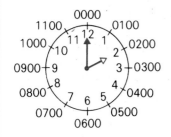

Examples
    2 am = 02 00 hours
    6.30 am = 06 30 hours

    09 00 hours = 9 am
    11 30 hours = 11.30 am

Midday to midnight is pm, or 12 00 to 24 00 hours

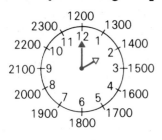

Examples
    2 pm = 14 00 hours
    5.15 pm = 17 15 hours
You have to add or subtract 12 hours for pm ↔ 24 hour times, since pm starts at midday (12, or 12 00 hours)

    20 00 hours = 8 pm
    23 30 hours = 11.30 pm

EXERCISE 3A/B

1 Write down the times on these clocks, using 24 hour time.

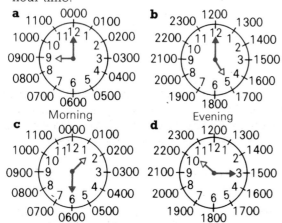

a Morning
b Evening
c
d

2 Write down the time on each clock in question **1**, using am/pm time.

3 Copy and complete this table. Remember to add or subtract 12 hours for pm ↔ 24 hour times.

12 hour clock	4 am	10 am	2 pm	5 pm			
24 hour clock					03 00 hours	16 00 hours	21 00 hours

4 What times, am or pm, are these watches showing?

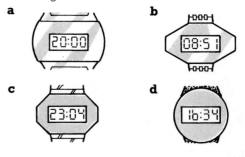

a
b
c
d

5 Draw digital watch faces which show these times:
    a 3 pm **b** midday **c** 11.30 am **d** 11.30 pm

6 Saturday Sport is on TV from 9.15 pm until 10.30 pm. Sandra wants to tape it on her video recorder, which uses a 24 hour clock. What starting and finishing times should she key in?

7 a The Allen family's plane to Majorca is due to take off at 19 45 hours. They have to be at the airport one hour earlier. What time is this in am/pm time?
    b They are due to land back at Gatwick at 3.20 am. What time is this on the 24 hour clock?

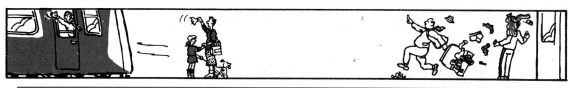

Edinburgh....	09 15	10 30	12 30	14 30	16 20	16 30	17 15	17 55	18 45	19 45	20 45	22 15	23 25
Haymarket....	09 18	....	....	....	16 23	....	17 18	17 58	18 48	19 48	20 48	22 18	23 28
Linlithgow....	....	....	....	....	....	....	17 36	....	19 06	20 06	21 06	22 36	....
Polmont.......	....	....	....	....	....	....	17 43	....	19 13	20 13	21 13	22 43	....
Falkirk........	09 41	11 03	13 03	15 03	....	17 03	17 49	18 20	19 19	20 19	21 19	22 49	23 53
Larbert.......	09 58	11 08	13 08	15 08	....	17 08	17 55	....	19 25	20 25	21 25	22 55	00 01
Stirling.......	10.08	11 19	13 19	15 19	....	17 19	18 05	18 33	19 35	20 35	21 35	23 05	00 11
Bridge of Allan	....	11 24	13 24	15 24	....	17 24	18 10	....	19 40	20 40	21 40	23 10	....
Dunblane.....	....	11 31	13 31	15 31	....	17 31	18 18	18 41	19 48	20 48	21 48	23 18	00 21
Gleneagles...	....	....	....	....	....	....	....	18 53	....	....	....	....	....
Perth.........	10 48	....	....	17 50	....	....	19 09	....	....	....	....	00 54

8 Caroline picked up this train timetable in her local station. It shows the times of trains from Edinburgh to Stirling and Perth on Sundays.
  a Which stations does the 09 15 train stop at?
  b How long does it take to travel to Perth from Edinburgh on this train?

9 When does the first train for Polmont leave Edinburgh?

10 When does the last train for Bridge of Allan leave Falkirk?

11 If you had to be in Stirling by 8 pm, what is the latest train that you could take from Edinburgh?

12 How many trains travel on Sundays from:
  a Edinburgh to Perth **b** Stirling to Dunblane?

13 How many trains leave Edinburgh for Stirling:
  a in the morning **b** between noon and 6 pm
  c after 6 pm?

14 a At which station on the line does only one train from Edinburgh call on a Sunday?
  b At which towns do most trains stop on a Sunday?

15 How long does it take from Edinburgh to Perth by:
  a the fastest train **b** the slowest train?

EXERCISE 3C

1 A bus leaves the bus station at 18 25 hours, and reaches its destination at 20 10 hours. How long did the journey take? Copy and complete this calculation:
  18 25 hours to 19 00 hours =   35 minutes
  19 00 hours to 20 10 hours = ... hour ... minutes
                     Total time = _____

2 A train leaves at 14 35 hours and arrives at 16 20 hours. How long does the journey take?

3 Tom is on holiday at the seaside. High tide today is at 15 30 hours. The next high tide will be in 12 hours and 24 minutes. What time will that be?

4 How long is it between these times?
  a 15 40 hours and 17 00 hours
  b 08 15 hours and 10 50 hours
  c 21 46 hours and 23 35 hours
  d 22 05 hours and 03 20 hours next day

5 Mark wants to set the timer on his video recorder to record a programme starting at 7.35 pm and lasting for 2 hours 45 minutes. If the recorder uses a 24 hour clock what times should he set?

6 The table gives the times of daily flights to Oslo.

London Airport	Depart	Arrive	Aircraft	Flight Number
Heathrow	08 25	10 20	Boeing 757	BA 642
Gatwick	10 35	13 45	Douglas DC9	SK 516
Heathrow	10 45	12 45	Douglas DC9	SK 514
Heathrow	14 05	16 00	Boeing 757	BA 644
Heathrow	17 50	19 50	Douglas DC9	SK 512

  a How long does the quickest flight take?
  b How long does the slowest flight take?
  c If you have to be in Oslo by 5 pm, which is the latest flight you can take from London?

MEASURING TEMPERATURE

Feeling the heat

Temperature is measured in degrees Celsius
(°C), using a thermometer.

How many degrees are there between the
temperatures at which water freezes and boils?

What is the temperature in your classroom?

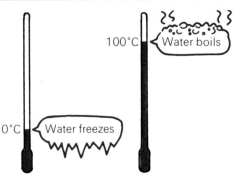

100°C   Water boils

0°C   Water freezes

Here are temperatures from around the world one day
in July, in degrees Celsius.

Alicante	31°C	London	20°C	Oslo	18°C
Athens	36°C	Los Angeles	30°C	Palma	30°C
Blackpool	19°C	Miami	30°C	Paris	24°C
Corfu	33°C	Moscow	25°C	Rome	33°C
Edinburgh	19°C	Naples	32°C	Sydney	17°C
Hong Kong	31°C	New Delhi	34°C	Toronto	24°C
Las Palmas	25°C	New York	32°C	Venice	26°C

EXERCISE 4A

1 a In the table above, which place was warmest?
 b Which place was coolest?
 c Calculate the difference in temperature
   between these two places.

2 Which places had temperatures of 33°C or more?

3 What was the difference in temperature between:
 a Blackpool and Hong Kong
 b New York and Moscow
 c Miami and Palma?

4

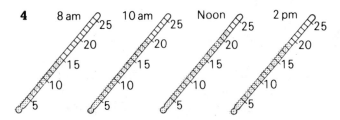

8 am   10 am   Noon   2 pm

 a List the room temperatures at 8 am, 10 am, noon
   and 2 pm.
 b Which of these times had the highest
   temperature?
 c What is the difference in temperature between
   10 am and noon?
 d Between which of the times did the
   temperature rise 5°C?

5 a When Adam leaves for school the temperature
   is 6°C. By midday it is 13°C. How many degrees
   has the temperature risen?
 b By the time Adam gets home the temperature
   has fallen from 13°C by 4 degrees. What is the
   temperature now?

6 Peter was not feeling well. His mother took his
   temperature with this thermometer.

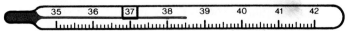

 a What was his temperature?
 b Why is there a box round the 37 on the scale?
 c Why does the scale only go from 35°C to 42°C?

7 Can you read the temperatures on these
   thermometers?

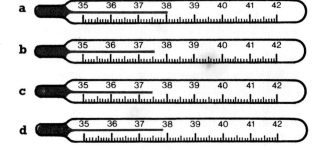

a

b

c

d

EXERCISE 4B/C

Becky, Kerry and Catherine were reading scales. Can you help them by writing down the numbers which the arrows are pointing to?

1 Becky

2 Kerry

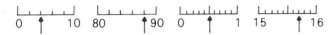

3 Catherine

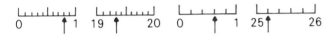

4 Different scales are used on different kinds of thermometer.
Look at these very carefully. Then write down the temperatures marked **a, b, c, d, e, f**.

Marked every degree	Marked every 2 degrees	Marked every 0·1 degree

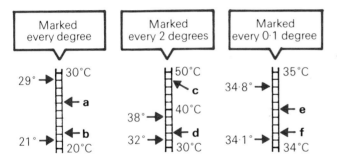

5 What are the temperatures on these thermometers (all in °C)?

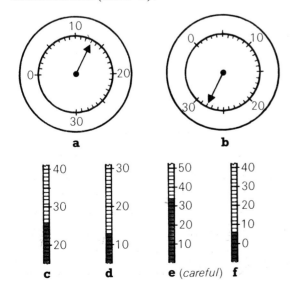

6 Copy and complete this table.

First temperature	Second temperature	Rise in temperature	Fall in temperature
64 °C	75 °C		—
52 °C	43 °C	—	
32 °C		9 °	—
	25 °C	6 °	—
28 °C		—	7 °
	13 °C	—	8 °
12.5 °C	15.8 °C		
21.4 °C	16.7 °C		

7 The oven tap on a gas cooker is marked 'OFF, $\frac{1}{4}$, $\frac{1}{2}$, 1, 2, 3, ..., 9'. These settings and their temperatures are shown in the table.

Setting	Temperature °C
$\frac{1}{4}$	110
$\frac{1}{2}$	130
1	140
2	150
3	170
4	180
5	190
6	200
7	220
8	230
9	240

a A recipe for a cake says that the oven temperature should be 190°C. What setting is this?

b Meringues are baked at a setting of $\frac{1}{2}$. What temperature is this?

c Estimate the temperatures of these three settings.

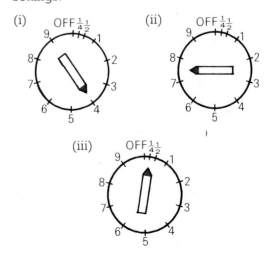

BELOW ZERO

The temperature on this thermometer is 5 degrees above zero (0°C). It is +5°C, which means +5° Celsius.
+5 is a positive number, and is read 'positive 5'. Often the '+' is left out, and 5 is taken to mean +5.

This temperature is 5 degrees below zero. It is −5°C.
−5° is a negative number, and is read 'negative 5', or sometimes 'minus 5'.

EXERCISE 5A

1 Copy this number line, and mark all the numbers from −5 to 5.

2 Copy this thermometer, and mark arrows at −10°, −2°, 0°, 14° and 28°.

3 Here is part of a thermometer scale from −5°C to 5°C.
Write down the temperatures at the points marked **a** to **f**.

4 Using negative numbers, write down these temperatures. Watch out for the different scales!

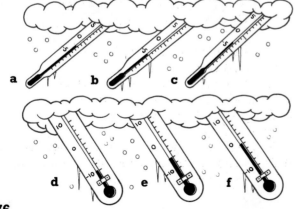

5 a Which temperature is colder: −7°C or −8°C?
b Which temperature is warmer: −12°C or −11°C?
c Which temperature is higher: 3°C or −3°C?
d Which temperature is lower: 0°C or −1°C?

6 Write down the highest and lowest temperatures in each of these:
a 0°C, −10°C, 5°C   **b** −3°C, −5°C, −4°C

7 In each of the following write down:
 (i) the temperatures in the glass and in the cup
(ii) the lower of the two temperatures.

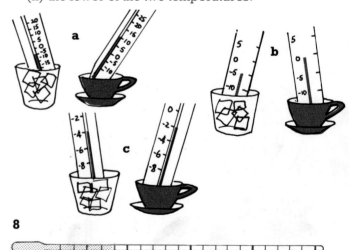

8

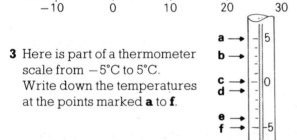

a The temperature rises by 5°C. What is the new temperature?
b The temperature then falls by 7°C. What is the new temperature now?

EXERCISE 5B/C

1 Using a number line thermometer if you wish, write down temperatures that are:
  a 4° lower than:
    (i) 6°C   (ii) 4°C   (iii) 0°C   (iv) −3°C
  b 5° higher than:
    (i) 0°C   (ii) −2°C   (iii) −5°C   (iv) −8°C.

2 Write these temperatures in order, from coldest to warmest:
  a 5°C, −3°C, 0°C, −1°C
  b −10°C, −20°C, 0°C, 10°C, 9°C
  c 100°C, −1°C, −19°C, 50°C, 0°C, −100°C.

3 The freezing point of water is 0°C. Use + or − to describe temperatures:
  a 18° above freezing point
  b 12° below freezing point.

4 These greenhouse thermometers show the maximum and minimum temperatures.

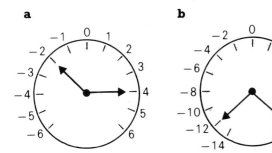

a   **b**

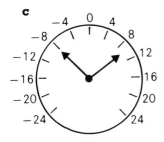

c

For each one find:
  (i) the maximum and minimum temperatures
  (ii) the number of degrees between these temperatures.

5 When a freezer is defrosted its temperature rises to 15°C. When set to 'freeze', the temperature drops by 25°. What is its temperature now?

6 Antifreeze is used in a car radiator so that it will not freeze unless the temperature drops down to −18°C. The temperature one evening is −5°C. How many degrees can it fall before the radiator will freeze?

7 The dotted lines on this map are called isotherms. These are lines joining points where the temperature is the same. All places on a dotted line have the same temperature.

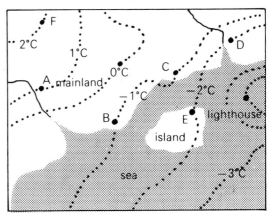

a What is the temperature at town A?
b Which town has the same temperature as town E?
c Name two towns on the coast that have the same temperature.
d Which two towns are colder than town C?
e What is the difference in temperature between town A and town E?
f Name a town which is 4° warmer than town D.
g By how much must the temperature of town B rise to be the same as town A?
h What would you expect the temperature to be at the lighthouse?

8 On 22nd January 1943 the temperature rose an astonishing 27.2° in two minutes at Spearfish, South Dakota, in America. It rose to 7.3°C at 7.32 am. What was the temperature at 7.30 that morning?

9 The temperatures every two hours at an airport on 5 January were:

00 00	02 00	04 00	06 00	08 00	10 00
0°C	−3°C	−4°C	−5°C	−4°C	−1°C

12 00	14 00	16 00	18 00	20 00	22 00
4°C	6°C	5°C	3°C	1°C	0°C

a When were the highest and lowest temperatures?
b How many degrees were there between the highest and lowest temperatures?
c In which two-hour period was there the greatest:
  (i) rise in temperature   (ii) fall in temperature?
d Draw a line graph of the temperature for the 24-hour period.

INVESTIGATION

Temperatures are sometimes still measured in degrees Fahrenheit.
The weatherman gives the temperature in both scales.

It will reach 16° Celsius, 61° Fahrenheit, today.

Here is his flowchart to change °C to °F.

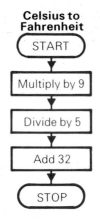

Celsius to Fahrenheit

START

Multiply by 9

Divide by 5

Add 32

STOP

1 Use his flowchart to change these temperatures to °F:
   a 20°C   **b** 40°C   **c** 0°C   **d** 100°C

2 Investigate the temperatures on both Celsius and Fahrenheit scales for:
   a a warm summer day   **b** a cold winter day
   c the lounge in your home   **d** a hot bath
   e your body   **f** the classroom

3 Draw a flowchart which changes °F to °C. Then test your flowchart by changing several temperatures.

PRACTICAL PROJECT

Many newspapers print the daily temperatures in various places in Britain and throughout the world. Each day for a week record the temperatures in the warmest and coldest places, and compare them with those in Britain. Draw some graphs, and write about your findings.

BRAINSTORMER

These tables list the melting points and boiling points of some elements in °C.

Element	Melting point	Boiling point
Potassium	64	760
Sodium	98	883
Lithium	187	1326
Copper	1083	2595
Silver	961	2200
Gold	1063	2950

Element	Melting point	Boiling point
Calcium	850	1440
Zinc	420	906
Carbon	3700	4830
Tantulum	3000	5427
Tungsten	3380	5930
Iron	1539	3070

a Say whether each element is solid, liquid or gas at 1000°C.
b For what range of temperatures is:
   (i) gold solid, silver liquid and zinc gas
   (ii) carbon solid, and tantulum and tungsten liquid?

CHECK-UP ON MEASURING TIME AND TEMPERATURE

1 How many days are there in:
a a week **b** the month of December
c a year (not a leap year)?

2 The 4th of May is a Monday. What day is the 12th of May?

3 How many days does the sale last?

SALE
1 July – 16 August

4 Judy watched a TV programme from quarter past one until half past two. How long was this?

5 Write down the time on each clock, using am or pm:

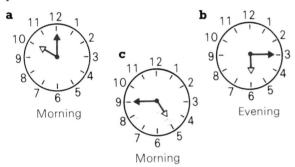

a Morning

c Morning

b Evening

6 How many hours are there from:
a 2 pm until 11 pm **b** 1.30 am until 11.30 am
c 9 am until 5 pm?

7 Including both dates, how many days are there from 11.5.95 to 12.6.95?

8 If the journey takes 43 minutes, when should the trains arrive at Edinburgh?

Trains to Edinburgh
depart at
8.30 am and 10 am

9 Elaine hands in her film at 11.30 am on Tuesday. When will it be ready to collect?

Films
ready in 24 hours

10 Copy and complete the table:

12 hour clock	5 pm	3 pm		
24 hour clock			08 00 hours	23 00 hours

11 Write down the times on the clocks in question **5** using 24 hour times.

12 How long does each journey take?

Depart	07 00	09 30	13 30	21 30
Arrive	08 30	11 45	15 30	23 00

13 *American Top 10*: 8.15 pm–8.45 pm
Frankenstein: 10 pm–11.50 pm
Alan wants to record these programmes on a 3-hour tape.
a What 24-hour times should he use?
b How much tape will be left?

14 The times, in seconds, for three runners in a 100 m race are shown on these watches.

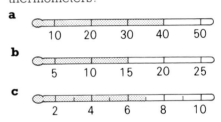

a Which is the best time?
b How much better is it than the next time?

15 What are the temperatures on these thermometers?

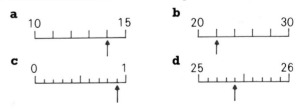

a

b

c

16 Arrange these temperatures in order, from coolest to warmest:
55°C, 100°C, 0°C, 19°C, 31°C

17 What is the rise in temperature from 12.7°C to 18.3°C?

18 What numbers do the arrows point to?

a 10 ⌐ 15

b 20 ⌐ 30

c 0 ⌐ 1

d 25 ⌐ 26

19 Write these temperatures in order, coldest first:
−1°C, 0°C, −3°C, 3°C, −4°C, 2°C

20 a Draw a thermometer scale, and mark on it each degree from −6 to 6.
b Put arrows at −4°C and 2°.
c How many degrees does the temperature rise from −4° to 2°?

LOOKING BACK

1 Meena sits at desk C2.
Who sits at these desks?
a A1 **b** B2
c C1 **d** C3

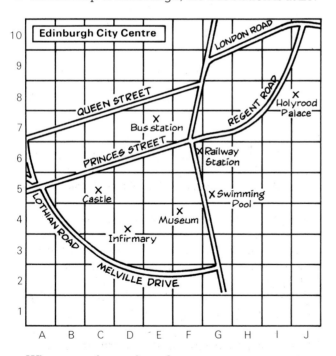

Where do these pupils sit?
e Tony **f** Ian **g** Balvinder **h** Jo
Sketch the desks or tables in your class or group,
and describe where you sit.

2 On this map of Edinburgh, the bus station is at E7.

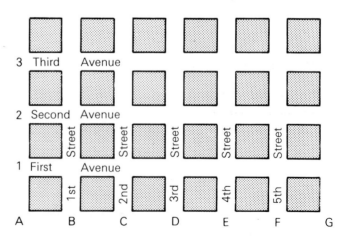

Where are these places?
  a The Castle   **b** Holyrood Palace
  c The railway station   **d** The museum
  Which roads meet at: **e** J10 **f** A5?

Where would you start and finish if you walked
the whole length of:
  g Queen Street   **h** Regent Road?

3 Use letters in this grid to send messages. For
example,
'G2, A2, F1, B1, D1' means 'TODAY'.

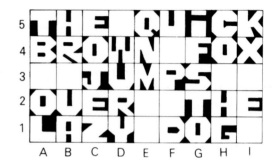

Which letters are in these squares?
a E3, B1, G2, H2, G3
What are these messages?
b H2, C2, A1, A1, H4
c A5, H2, G5, G3 : G5, G3 : C2, B1, G3, D1
d B1, A1, A1 : G2, H2, C2 : B1, A1, F3, H2, B1, A4,
   C2, A5 : G5, E4 : H1, B4, G5, F1

4 These are the streets in an American city. Check
that Third Avenue and 5th Street cross at F3.

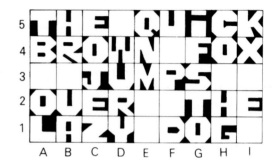

Where do these streets cross?
a Second Avenue and 4th Street
b Third Avenue and 1st Street
c First Avenue and 1st Street
d Third Avenue and 5th Street?

THE COORDINATE GRID

A system which describes positions with pinpoint accuracy was invented by a Frenchman called René Descartes in the 17th century. He would have said that P is the point (4, 2). Four units to the right of O and two units up from OX.

O (0, 0) is the origin, OX is the *x*-axis and OY is the *y*-axis.

The *x*-coordinate 4 comes first, then the *y*-coordinate 2; *along, then up.*

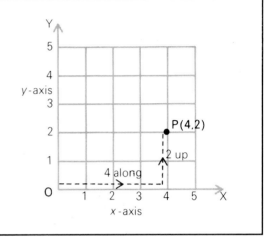

EXERCISE 1A

1 A treasure hunt at a fête is laid out using string and pegs. You have to guess the crossing where the treasure is hidden. A coordinate grid (see foot of page) is used to show all the places.

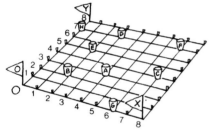

Amy guesses A (4, 3), *x*-coordinate first. Write down the other guesses in the same way.
Ben's guess B (. . . , 2)
Catriona's guess C (7, . . .)
Dave's guess D (. . . , . . .)
Elinor's guess E (. . . , . . .)
Fatima's guess F (. . . , . . .)
The *x*-coordinate of Gordon's guess is . . .
The *y*-coordinate of Harry's guess is . . .

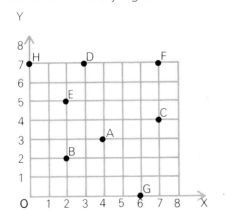

2 In a new game, eight more people try to guess where the treasure is. Copy and complete this list of guesses.
E (8, . . .),
F (1, . . .),
G (5, . . .),
H (. . . , 6),
J (0, . . .),
K (. . . , . . .),
L (. . . , . . .),
M (. . . , . . .).

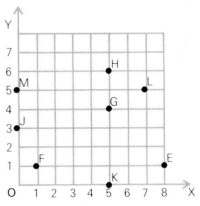

3 Prizes are buried at S (3, 3), T (4, 0), U (0, 6), V (5, 1) and W (1, 4). On squared paper draw axes OX and OY at right angles, and number them from 0 to 6. Plot the positions of the prizes.

4 A logo was designed for the front of the programme for 'The Old-Time Variety Show'. To draw the logo, plot these points on squared paper and join them up in the order given.
(4, 1), (12, 1), (8, 5), (8, 8), (6, 10), (6, 13), (8, 14), (7, 16), (6, 16), (4, 15), (5, 13), (1, 13), (0, 8), (2, 10), (1, 13), (3, 11), (3, 10), (4, 9), (4, 1).

5 Plot these points and join them up in the order in which they are listed. If you add an eye and a mouth you'll have a . . . . . . ? (0, 3), (7, 3), (8, 4), (9, 4), (9, 3), (10, 3), (9, 2), (8, 2), (8, 1), (7, 1), (7, 0), (6, 1), (3, 1), (2, 0), (2, 2), (0, 3).

EXERCISE 1B

1 In a 'Spot the Ball' competition you have to guess where the football might be in the picture.

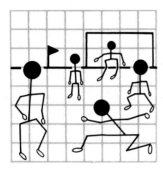

Brian made eight guesses.

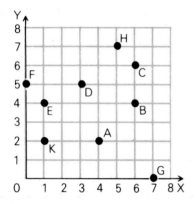

Copy and complete the following. For example, K (1, 2).

a A (4, . . .), B (. . . , 4), G (. . . , . . .)

b Two guesses with x-coordinate 6 are B (6, . . .) and . . .

c Two guesses with y-coordinate 5 are F (. . . , 5) and . . .

d One guess where the x and y-coordinates are the same . . .

e The point with x-coordinate zero is F (0, . . .)

f The point with y-coordinate zero is . . .

2 The sign writer uses coordinates to design his letters.

Plot each set of letters, joining the points as shown by the arrows.

a $(1, 1) \rightarrow (3, 1) \rightarrow (3, 2) \rightarrow (1, 2) \rightarrow (1, 3) \rightarrow (3, 3)$

b $(4, 3) \rightarrow (6, 3)$, then $(5, 3) \rightarrow (5, 1)$

c $(7, 1) \rightarrow (7, 3) \rightarrow (9, 3) \rightarrow (9, 1)$, then $(7, 2) \rightarrow (9, 2)$

d $(10, 1) \rightarrow (10, 3) \rightarrow (11, 2) \rightarrow (12, 3) \rightarrow (12, 1)$

e $(13, 1) \rightarrow (13, 3) \rightarrow (15, 3) \rightarrow (15, 2) \rightarrow (13, 2)$

f $(16, 1) \rightarrow (18, 1) \rightarrow (18, 2) \rightarrow (16, 2) \rightarrow (16, 3) \rightarrow (18, 3)$

g What does the shop sell?

3 On squared paper draw the word EXIT. Write down the coordinates of the points you would give the sign writer for this word. Then ask a friend to draw your word.

4 Robbers based at R rob a bank at B. The lines of the grid show a network of roads. Copy this on squared paper.

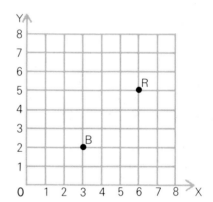

The police set up roadblocks at (1, 2), (2, 3), (3, 0), (3, 4), (4, 1), (4, 3) and (5, 2).

a Mark the roadblocks

b Can the robbers escape?

c If you think the robbers can escape, draw their shortest route from B to R.

d At what other point should the police have set up a roadblock?

EXERCISE 1C

Archaeologists explore stone circles on Machrie Moor in Arran. They use a coordinate grid to describe the positions of stones in an 'outer circle': $(2, 0)$, $(4, 0)$, $(6, 1)$, $(7, 3)$, $(6, 5)$, $(1, 6)$, $(0, 4)$, $(0, 2)$, $(4, 7)$.

1 a Plot the points on squared paper, and make a rough sketch of the 'circle'.
  b On the same diagram, plot these points in an 'inner circle': $(2, 1)$, $(4, 1)$, $(5, 2)$, $(5, 4)$, $(2, 5)$, $(1, 4)$. Now sketch this 'circle'.
  c Stones are found at $(1, 2)$, $(3, 7)$ and $(4, 5)$. Which circle is each stone part of?
  d A burial ground is found near the centre of the circles. What are its coordinates?

The archaeologists placed the origin O at a local farm. They made the x-axis run east, and the y-axis north. The stone at A is two units east and one unit north of O.

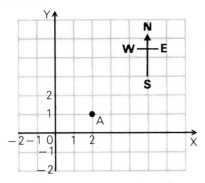

They soon found more stones west and south of the farm.

2 a Draw axes, and extend them to show points west and south of the farm, using negative numbers on the axes.
  b Mark points for these stones: B, 2 units west and 1 north of the farm; C, 3 units west and 2 south of the farm; D, 3 units east and 1 south of the farm. Write down the coordinates of B, C and D.

3 Find the coordinates of stones which are:
  a 3 units east and 2 south of A
  b 2 units west and 1 south of B.

4 How many units east or west, north or south, is:
  a B from A   **b** C from B   **c** D from C
  d D from A?

5 A special stone is found nine units west of A. Write down its coordinates.

/ **COORDINATE GAMES** /

1 Throw a dice twice. Use the numbers you throw for, first, the x, then the y-coordinate of a point to plot. Take turns with a partner. The winner is the one who gets most new points in a given time.

2 Keep your coordinate grid hidden, and mark a point on it. Your opponent then has to guess the coordinates of the point, and you have to give, in reply, the shortest distance along grid lines between the guessed point and your point. In this diagram, for example, for point (2, 4) and guess (4, 1) the distance is 5 units.

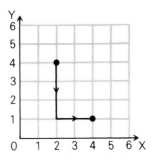

Count the number of guesses your opponent needs to reach your point. Then change places. The player with the smaller number of guesses is the winner.

BEYOND ZERO

Do you remember how we had to extend the number scale on the thermometer for temperatures below zero?

In the same way, we can extend the number scales on the x and y-axes to include negative numbers. We can now plot any point in the plane.

Look at these points, for example:
P (4, 2), Q (−5, 3), R (−4, −3), S (1, −3).
Always remember to mark the x-coordinate to the right or left, then the y-coordinate up or down.

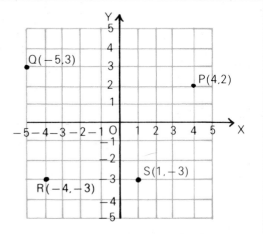

EXERCISE 2A

1 Another treasure hunt. Copy and complete the guesses, for example Paul's guess (−4, −2).

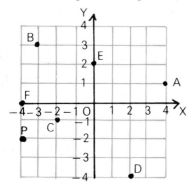

Alastair's guess A (4, . . .)
Barry's guess B (−3, . . .)
Carmen's guess C (. . ., −1)
David's guess D (. . ., . . .)
Emma's guess E (. . ., . . .)
Farah's guess F (. . ., . . .)

2 a For the rectangle ABCD below, copy and complete: A (3, −1), B (3, . . .), C (−1, . . .), D (. . ., . . .)

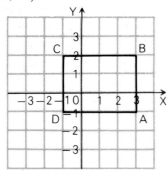

b List the vertices and coordinates of:

(i) the kite EFGH

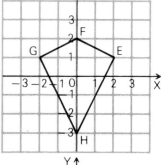

(ii) parallelogram JKLM

(iii) square OPQR.

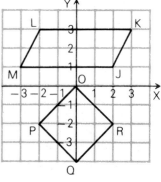

3 Draw axes on squared paper like those in question **2**. Plot these sets of points, joining them up as you go:
a (4, 1) → (2, 1) → (2, 4)
b (−1, 4) → (−2, 1) → (−3, 4)
c (−1, −1) → (−1, −4) → (−3, −1) → (−3, −4)
d (1, −4) → (1, −1) → (2, −3) → (3, −1) → (3, −4)

4 a Plot these points, and join them up:
(3, 0), (1, 1), (0, 3), (−1, 1), (−3, 0), (−1, −1), (0, −3), ($\frac{1}{2}$1, −1), (3, 0).
b Describe the shape you have drawn.
c What are the coordinates of its centre?

5 On squared paper, draw an *x*-axis from −20 to 20, and a *y*-axis from −20 to 10. Plot these points, joining them up in order in the five sets.
(−14, 6), (−11, 7), (−9, 9), (−6, 10), (−3, 9), (0, 7), (5, 5), (8, 3), (15, 5), (20, 5), (15, 3), (10, 1), (9, −2), (4, −7), (0, −7), (−5, −5), (−10, 0), (−12, 5), (−14, 6), (−11, 7), (−10, 6), (−12, 5). Stop.
Continue with the points on the right.

(0, 5), (5, 3), (10, 0), (12, −2), (9, −2), (3, −1), (−1, 0). Stop.
(0, −7), (−5, −11), (−8, −11), (−5, −11), (−8, −13), (−5, −11), (−6, −14), (−5, −11), (−1, −10). Stop.
(4, −7), (0, −12), (−3, −12), (0, −12), (−3, −14), (0, −12), (−1, −15), (0, −12), (4, −11). Stop.
(−9, 6), (−8, 7), (−7, 6), (−8, 5), (−9, 6). Stop.

EXERCISE 2B

1 More interesting finds have been made on Machrie Moor; a stone circle at B (3, 2), a single stone at P (−2, 3), a hut circle at M (6, −2) and a cairn at R (−4, −1).

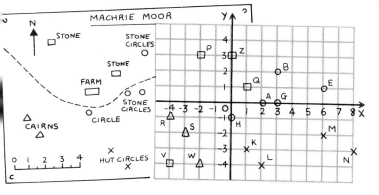

Write down the coordinates of:
a stone circles A, G, E, H
b single stones Q, V, Z
c hut circles K, L, N
d cairns S, W.

2 A rectangular area is roped off for study. Three of its vertices are at (−2, 2), (6, −2) and (4, −6). Plot these points, and complete the rectangle. Write down the coordinates of:
a the fourth vertex
b the centre of the rectangle
c the midpoints of its sides.

3 In many factories, machines for cutting shapes are controlled by computer. The coordinates of the corners have to be given to the computer in order.

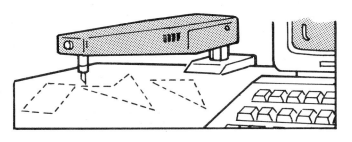

Write down the coordinates of the vertices of these shapes.

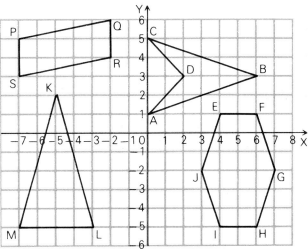

4 On squared paper, draw the *x*-axis from −12 to 12, and the *y*-axis from −16 to 16. Plot these points, joining them up in order.
(−2, −16), (−3, −15), (−4, −16), (−4, −14), (−5, −14), (−3, −12), (−2, −13), (−1, −10), (−2, −7), (−3, −7), (−5, −9), (−7, −10), (−8, −10), (−8, −9), (−9, −9), (−8, −8), (−9, −7), (−6, −7), (−5, −5), (−2, −4), (−3, −1), (−10, −3), (−11, −3), (−11, −2), (−12, −2), (−11, −1), (−12, 0), (−10, 0), (−9, −1), (−6, 1), (−9, 2), (−11, 5), (−12, 5), (−11, 6), (−12, 8), (−11, 8), (−11, 9), (−9, 8), (−9, 6), (−8, 4), (−4, 3), (−3, 6), (−5, 6), (−5, 7), (−3, 7), (−5, 8), (−5, 10), (−3, 10), (−2, 12), (2, 12), (4, 14), (4, 11), (6, 8), (4, 8), (5, 6), (3, 6), (4, 4), (3, 4), (4, 2), (3, 2), (3, −4), (4, −4), (7, −1), (7, 1), (8, 0), (9, 3), (8, 5), (9, 5), (9, 7), (10, 6), (11, 6), (9, 1), (10, 1), (8, −2), (9, −2), (7, −3), (5, −5), (3, −6), (2, −8), (3, −10), (3, −11), (−2, −16).

EXERCISE 2C

1 Mary has designed this cover for a nature magazine. Plot the points, and join them up to see the two foxes. You will need negative numbers on the axes.

Fox 1: $(0, 4)$, $(1, 5)$, $(1, 3)$, $(0, 2)$, $(2, 0)$, $(-3, 0)$,
$(-2, -1)$, $(-6, -1)$, $(-6\frac{1}{2}, -1\frac{1}{2})$,
$(-8\frac{1}{2}, -1\frac{1}{2})$, $(-7\frac{1}{2}, -\frac{1}{2})$, $(-5\frac{1}{2}, -\frac{1}{2})$, $(-4, 1)$,
$(-2, 1)$, $(-\frac{1}{2}, 2\frac{1}{2})$, $(-1, 3)$, $(-1, 5)$, $(0, 4)$
Fox 2: $(4, 1)$, $(5, 2)$, $(4, 3)$, $(4, 5)$, $(5, 4)$, $(6, 5)$, $(6, 3)$,
$(5\frac{1}{2}, 2\frac{1}{2})$, $(5\frac{1}{2}, \frac{1}{2})$, $(8, -2)$, $(8, -5)$, $(5, -5)$,
$(5\frac{1}{2}, -4\frac{1}{2})$, $(5\frac{1}{2}, -2)$, $(4, -\frac{1}{2})$, $(4, 1)$.

2 Plot the points A $(1, 2)$, B $(-2, 4)$, C $(2, -4)$, D $(-3, -3)$, E $(0, -5)$, F $(-6, 0)$ and G $(1, -2)$.
Which are:
a on the x-axis   **b** above the x-axis
c below the x-axis   **d** on the y-axis
e to the right of the y-axis
f to the left of the y-axis?

3 The axes divide the plane into four quadrants.

2nd quadrant	1st quadrant
3rd quadrant	4th quadrant

a In which quadrant does each point in question **2** lie, assuming that it is not on an axis?
b For a point (p, q), what can you say about p and q if the point is in:
(i) the first quadrant
(ii) the second quadrant
(iii) the third quadrant
(iv) the fourth quadrant?

CHOOSE A CHALLENGE

1 *Maps and atlases have grids marked on them. Some maps are fairly simple, like the one of Edinburgh on page 80, but others such as Ordnance Survey maps are more detailed. Choose a map or atlas, or a motorway handbook, and plan a route for a day out on foot, or by bicycle or car. Give details of grid references and as much other information as you can.*

2 *Have you ever been lost in a maze? Coordinates can help you out.*
a *Copy and complete this route through the first maze:* $(0, 0) \rightarrow (0, 2) \rightarrow (1, 2) \rightarrow (1, 1) \rightarrow (2, 1) \rightarrow \ldots$

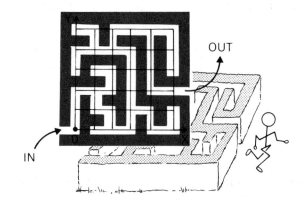

b *Place a tracing of the grid below over the second maze, and describe the route out by giving the coordinates of its turning points.*

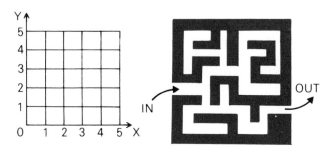

c *Invent a maze of your own, and a solution route using coordinates. Ask a friend to find, and describe, the solution route.*

POINTS AND LINES

EXERCISE 3A

1 a Plot the points A, B, C, D, E, F on squared
paper. What is the value of each *x*-coordinate?

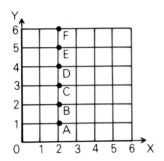

b Draw a straight line through the points. Which
axis is it parallel to?

2 a On the same diagram, plot the points $(0, 2)$,
$(1, 2)$, $(2, 2)$, $(3, 2)$, $(4, 2)$ and $(5, 2)$. What is the
value of each *y*-coordinate?
b Draw the line through the points. Which axis is
it parallel to?
c Write down the coordinates of the point where
the lines cross.

3 a Copy and complete this table for the fish tiling
pattern.

Fish	1	2	3	4	5	6
Eye	(0,2)	(2,2)	(4,2)			

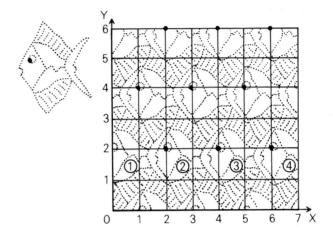

b To which axis is the line of eyes parallel?

4 a Copy and complete this sequence of eyes:
$(2, 2)$, $(2, 6)$, $(2, 10)$, $(2, \ldots)$, $(\ldots, \ldots)$, $(\ldots, 22)$.
b What direction would you expect this line of
eyes to have?

5 a Plot the points $(0, 0)$, $(2, 2)$, $(4, 4)$, $(6, 6)$, $(8, 8)$,
and draw a line through them. How would you
describe its direction?
b On the same diagram draw a line through O at
right angles to the line drawn in part **a**. List the
coordinates of five points on it.

EXERCISE 3B/C

1

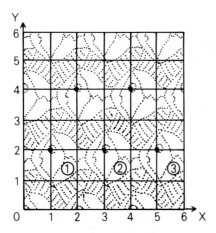

a Copy and complete this table.

Fish	1	2	3	4	5	6	10
Eye	(1,2)	(3,2)	(5,2)				

b Give the y-coordinate of every point on the line through the eyes.
The equation of the line is $y = 2$.

2 a Copy and complete this sequence of eyes.
$(1, 2), (2, 4), (3, 6), (4, \ldots), (\ldots, \ldots), (\ldots, 12)$
b Now complete this sentence: the y-coordinate of each point is ... times the x-coordinate.
The equation of this line is $y = 2x$.

3 Find the connection between x and y in these sets of points, in the form $y = \ldots x$, or $y = x + \ldots$.
a $(1, 3), (2, 6), (3, 9)$ **b** $(1, 4), (2, 8), (3, 12)$
c $(2, 1), (4, 2), (6, 3)$ **d** $(2, 3), (3, 4), (4, 5)$
e $(3, 5), (4, 6), (5, 7)$ **f** $(1, -1), (2, -2), (3, -3)$

4 $(1, -3), (2, -6), (3, -9)$ all lie on the line with equation $y = -3x$. Each of the following equations represents a line of points:
a $y = x$ **b** $y = -x$ **c** $y = 2x$ **d** $y = -2x$
e $y = x + 1$ **f** $y = x - 1$
 (i) Find three points on each line.
 (ii) Plot the points.
 (iii) Draw the line.

5 a How many points do you have to plot to draw a given line?
b Use the methods used in question **4** to draw the lines with these equations:
  (i) $y = \frac{1}{2}x$ (ii) $y = 5x$ (iii) $y = x + 2$
  (iv) $y = 2 - x$ (v) $y = -x - 1$

6 a Give the next two points to the right and left of the points in the sequence $(-2, 3), (0, 2), (2, 1), (4, 0)$.
b Find the equation of the line through the points.

INVESTIGATIONS

1 Copy this pattern from a radar screen, and mark several points on it to represent the positions of aircraft. Investigate different ways of defining the positions of the points on the screen.

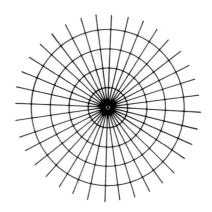

2 While designing wallpaper an artist draws a repeated pattern of 'stick' dancers.
Copy this picture of the dancers.

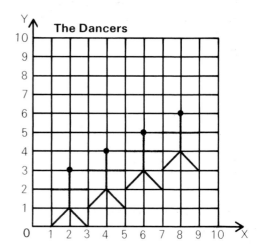

Look carefully at how one dancer follows another. Draw four more dancers in the pattern and write down the coordinates of the eight heads.
Look for a pattern in the coordinates. Write down the coordinates of the head of the twentieth dancer.
If a dancer's head is at (a, b), how are a and b connected? Investigate the sequence of positions of each dancer's feet.

CHECK-UP ON COORDINATES: X MARKS THE SPOT

1 Look at the jigsaw puzzle of Pirate Pete.

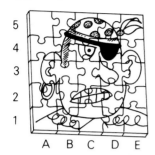

a What can you see in piece A2?
b Which piece contains:
  (i) the eyepatch (ii) the eye?
c Which three pieces lie between his ears?
d (i) What is special about pieces A1 and E1?
  (ii) Name two other pieces like this.

2 a Plot the points P (2, 1), Q (8, 1), R (8, 5) and S (2, 5) on squared paper.
  b (i) What shape is PQRS? Join PR and QS, crossing at T.
  (ii) What are the coordinates of T?

3

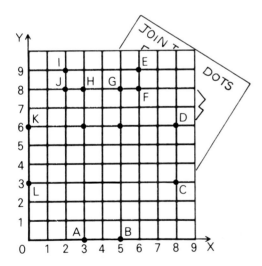

What goes in each space below?
a O is called the . . .
b OX is called the . . .
c OY is called the . . .
d The points with largest x-coordinates are . . . and . . .
e The points with largest y-coordinates are . . . and . . .
f A and B are on the x-axis, so their . . . coordinates are zero.
g Use tracing paper to draw the shape ABCD . . . KLA. What animal do you find?

4 Plot these points, joining each set as you go to find the letters:
  a $(1, 4) \rightarrow (1, 1) \rightarrow (3, 1)$
  b $(4, 4) \rightarrow (5, 1) \rightarrow (6, 4)$
  c $(7, 1) \rightarrow (7, 4) \rightarrow (9, 1) \rightarrow (9, 4)$
  d $(-4, -2) \rightarrow (-2, -2), \rightarrow (-4, -5) \rightarrow (-2, -5)$
  e $(-3, 1) \rightarrow (-3, 4) \rightarrow (-2, 2) \rightarrow (-1, 4) \rightarrow (-1, 1)$

5 Use the official map below to describe the solution route of the maze, giving the coordinates of turning points.

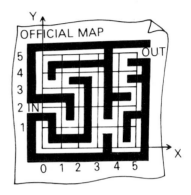

6 A laser draws the net of a cube. It never goes over the same route twice.

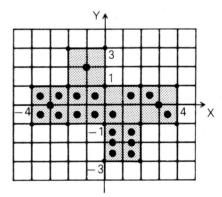

a One of its routes is shown below. Describe the route, using coordinates.

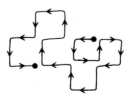

b Sketch some other routes. What is common to all successful routes?

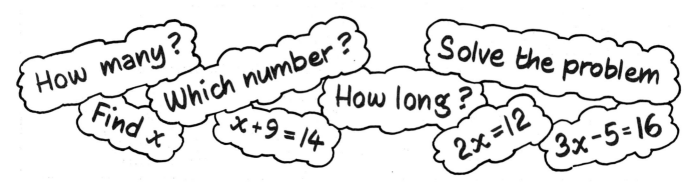

How many? Which number? Find x $x+9=14$ How long? Solve the problem $2x=12$ $3x-5=16$

LOOKING BACK

1 Which numbers go into the boxes?
  a $\Box + 7 = 11$ **b** $\Box - 7 = 11$
  c $\Box \times 6 = 54$ **d** $\Box \div 4 = 7$

2 Which numbers do the letters stand for in these sequences?

	A	**B**	**C**	**D**	**E**
1	7	8	9	10	a
2	9	b	11	12	13
3	11	12	c	14	15
4	13	14	15	16	d
5	e	16	17	18	19
6	17	18	19	20	f

3 Find the IN and OUT numbers or letters.
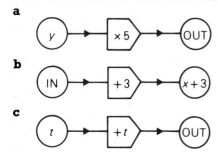

4 Simplify:
  a $n+n+n$ **b** $3m+2m$ **c** $2t+t$
  d $2t-t$ **e** $s+s-s$ **f** $3u+2u+u$
  g $5v-3v$ **h** $x+x+1$ **i** $2y+y-1$
  j $3z-2z+5$

5 Which numbers do the letters stand for in these sequences?
  a $10, 11, x, 13$ **b** $y, 16, 14, 12$
  c $1, k, 16, 64$ **d** $13, 21, 29, n$

6 The scales all balance. Which numbers do the letters stand for?
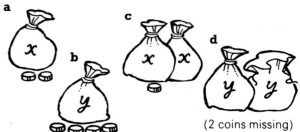

7 How many coins are in each picture? Bags were labelled before any went missing.
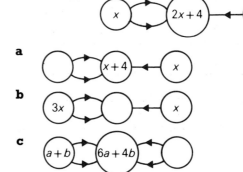

(2 coins missing)

8 Copy the diagrams and fill in the blanks. Remember:
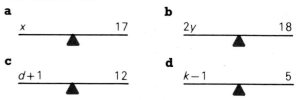

90

SOLVING EQUATIONS

A cover up

There are x weights in the bag, so $x+2 = 16$.
This is called an **equation**, since it involves **equals**.
To find x, cover it up:  $+2 = 16$.

What number is covered?
It must be 14, so $x = 14$. This is called the **solution** of the equation.

Example
Make an equation for the second picture, and
solve it to find the value of x.

$$x-4 = 8$$
$$x = 12$$

(4 weights missing)

EXERCISE 1A

Use the 'cover up' method to solve these equations.
Give the solutions like this: $x = 12$.

1 a $x+5 = 8$ **b** $x+1 = 9$
    c $x+3 = 10$ **d** $x+2 = 2$

2 a $y-1 = 4$ **b** $y-3 = 1$
    c $y-5 = 2$ **d** $y-4 = 4$

3 a $n+2 = 6$ **b** $n-2 = 1$
    c $n+5 = 9$ **d** $n-1 = 0$

4 a $k-1 = 1$ **b** $k-3 = 4$
    c $k+7 = 14$ **d** $k+10 = 19$

5 a $t+6 = 14$ **b** $t+9 = 15$
    c $t-8 = 0$ **d** $t-7 = 7$

6 a $u-6 = 6$ **b** $u+8 = 17$
    c $u-7 = 10$ **d** $u-8 = 9$

	A	**B**	**C**	**D**
1	3	4	a	6
2	$b-3$	5	6	7
3	5	6	7	$c+1$
4	6	7	8	9

From the sequences in the rows, we can make
and solve these equations:
(i) $a = 5$ (ii) $b-3 = 4$ (iii) $c+1 = 8$
                 $b = 7$ $c = 7$

Use this method to make and solve as many
equations as you can in these sequences:

7 a

	A	**B**	**C**	**D**
1	1	1	1	m
2	3	$n-6$	3	3
3	5	5	5	5
4	7	7	7	$p+6$

b

	A	**B**	**C**	**D**
1	1	1	1	1
2	2	2	$a-7$	2
3	$b+3$	3	3	3
4	4	4	4	$c+1$

8 a

	A	**B**	**C**	**D**
1	2	s	4	5
2	2	3	4	5
3	$t-1$	3	4	5
4	2	3	$u-10$	5

b

	A	B	C	D
1	d	2	3	4
2	2	$e - 10$	4	5
3	3	4	5	6
4	4	5	6	$f + 4$

Make equations for these pictures, and solve them.

9 a

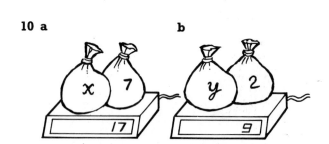

(a + 1 = 10)

b

c

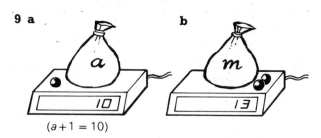

d

10 a

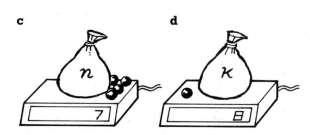

b

c

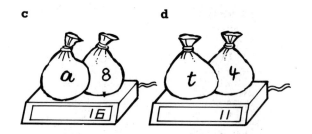

d

11 a

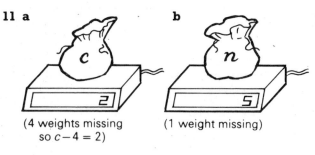

(4 weights missing
so $c - 4 = 2$)

b

(1 weight missing)

c

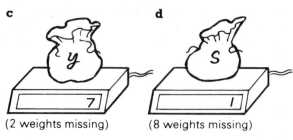

(2 weights missing)

d

(8 weights missing)

12 a

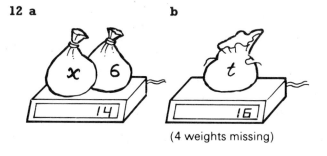

b

(4 weights missing)

c

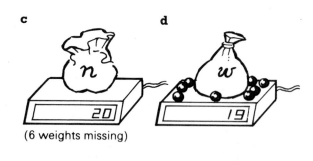

(6 weights missing)

d

The equation for this picture is:

$2y = 6$

$2 \square = 6$

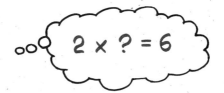

$2 \boxed{3} = 6$

$y = 3$

EXERCISE 1B

Use the 'cover up' method to solve these equations.

1 a $2x = 8$ **b** $3y = 9$ **c** $4z = 20$
 d $5k = 35$ **e** $6m = 54$

2 a $7p = 42$ **b** $8t = 64$ **c** $9u = 81$
 d $10w = 100$ **e** $12z = 60$

3 a $2x + 1 = 3$ **b** $3y - 1 = 5$ **c** $5a + 2 = 22$
 d $6b - 3 = 15$

4 a $8c + 5 = 13$ **b** $9d + 7 = 7$ **c** $7g - 2 = 33$
 d $4h - 9 = 15$

Make equations for these pictures, and solve them.

5 a 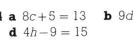   **b**

c   **d**

6 a 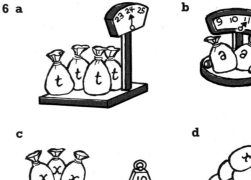   **b**

c    **d**

7 a 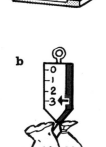   **b**

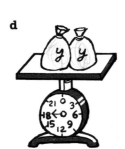

(1 weight missing)

c

Use both pictures to find the weight of the dog.

A straw model kit

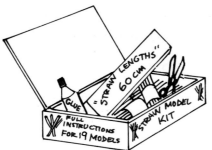

The problem: Make the triangular prism using one 60 cm length of straw.
Straws needed: 6 of x cm, and 3 of $2x$ cm (see sketch in book).

$$= 6x \text{ cm} + 6x \text{ cm}$$
$$= 12x \text{ cm}$$

Equation: $12x = 60$
$$x = 5$$

You need: 6 straws each 5 cm long, and 3 straws each 10 cm long. (Total 60 cm)

EXERCISE 1C

Make an equation for each model and solve it to work out how the 60 cm of straw provided should be cut up.

1 Cube

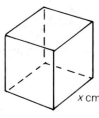

(all edges x cm)

2 Tetrahedron

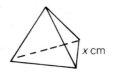

(all edges x cm)

3 Pentagonal pyramid

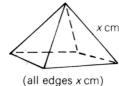

(all edges x cm)

4 Square pyramid

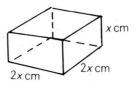

(all edges x cm)

5 Octahedron

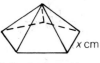

(all edges x cm)

6 Cuboid

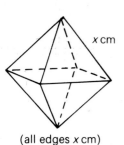

7 Triangular prism

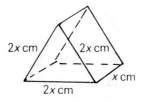

$2x$ cm $2x$ cm x cm $2x$ cm

8 Pentagonal pyramid

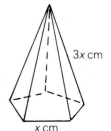

$3x$ cm
x cm

9 Octagonal prism

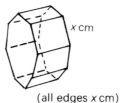

x cm

(all edges x cm)

10 Hexagonal pyramid

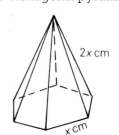

$2x$ cm
x cm

11 Cube and square pyramid

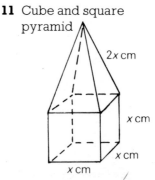

$2x$ cm
x cm
x cm
x cm

12 Dodecahedron

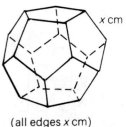

x cm

(all edges x cm)

PRACTICAL PROJECT

Use straws to make some of the skeleton models in Exercise 1C.

EXERCISE 2A

Use the 'cover up' method to solve these equations.

1 a $x + 9 = 18$ **b** $y - 3 = 7$
  c $k - 5 = 7$ **d** $m + 11 = 22$

2 a $6 - x = 2$ **b** $9 - y = 0$
  c $15 + n = 20$ **d** $9 + k = 17$

3 a $2 \times a = 18$ **b** $6 \times b = 30$
  c $3 \times c = 27$ **d** $7 \times d = 28$

4 a $5x = 30$ **b** $4y = 32$
  c $8t = 56$ **d** $9u = 27$

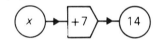 makes the equation
$x + 12 = 18$,
with solution $x = 6$.

Make equations for these, and then solve them.

5 a 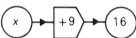   **b**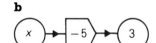

  c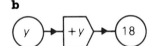

6 a 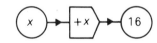   **b**

  c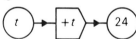

7 a 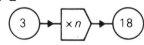   **b**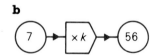

  c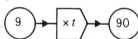

8 a 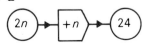   **b**

  c

These scales are balanced. Make an equation for each and solve it.

9 a    **b**

  c    **d**

10 a    **b**

  c 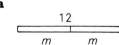   **d**

Extensions for paint rollers come in various lengths.

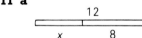

Describe each of these with an equation, then solve the equation.

11 a   **b**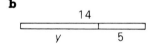

  c 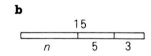   **d**

12 a 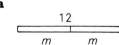   **b**

  c 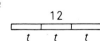   **d**

THINKING IT OUT

Each bag contains x weights

From the picture, $3x + 2 = 14$
To solve the equation, we have to find the number x stands for:

$$3x + 2 = 14$$
$$3x = 12$$
$$x = 4$$

$x = 4$ is the **solution** of the equation. There are four weights in each bag.

EXERCISE 2B

Make an equation for each picture, and solve it to find the number of weights in each bag.

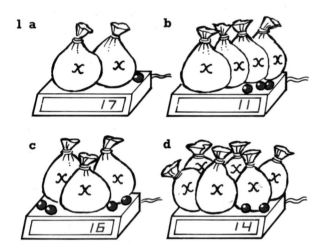

1 a

b

c

d

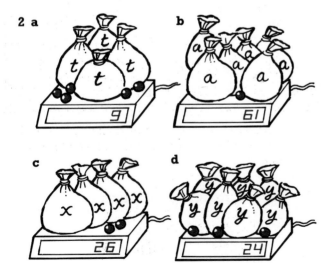

2 a

b

c

d

3 a

b

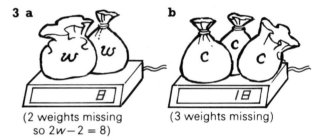

(2 weights missing so $2w - 2 = 8$)

(3 weights missing)

c

d

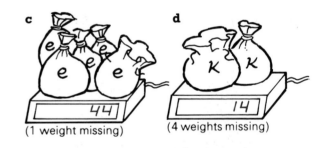

(1 weight missing)

(4 weights missing)

In questions **4–7**, make equations and solve them. Then write down the length of each object.

4 a

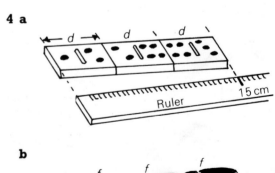

Ruler   15 cm

b

72 cm

5 a

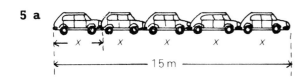

b

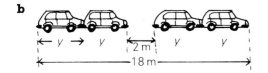

6 a

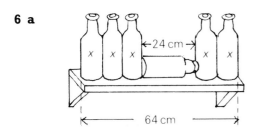

b

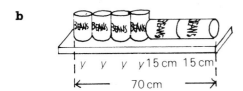

7 a

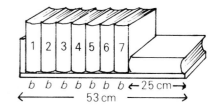

b

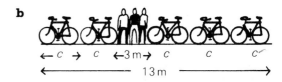

More practice! Solve these equations:

8 a $2x+1 = 5$ **b** $2a+7 = 9$ **c** $2t+3 = 15$
d $2s+3 = 3$ **e** $2n-1 = 5$ **f** $3m-4 = 14$
g $2p-3 = 11$ **h** $3q-7 = 2$

9 a $4x+1 = 25$ **b** $4g-2 = 10$ **c** $4z-4 = 0$
d $5k+1 = 26$ **e** $1+2a = 9$ **f** $3+6b = 9$
g $5+8c = 5$ **h** $12+4d = 28$

10 a $3x+x+4 = 12$ **b** $4y-y+1 = 13$
c $2z+2z-5 = 15$ **d** $5n-3n-1 = 15$
e $7t+2t+6 = 24$ **f** $8u-5u-7 = 20$

EXERCISE 2C

1

The numbers on the two sets of cards add up to the same total. Make an equation, and find the hidden number (x) and suit of the card.

2 The numbers on the two groups of dominoes have the same total.

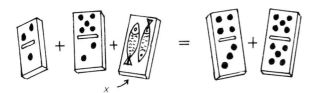

a Make an equation, and find the hidden number (x).
b List all the dominoes with this number of dots.
c Look again at the dominoes. What is the mystery one, exactly?

3 a Lee gave his uncle a puzzle. 'Five times my age, plus 10 years, makes 70 years. How old am I?' Make an equation and solve it. How old is Lee?

b His uncle replied. 'Four times my age, less 10 years, is 130.' Make an equation, and find his age.

4

I'VE THOUGHT OF A NUMBER, MULTIPLIED IT BY 3, ADDED 9, AND GET 33.

Take x for the number Sally thought of. Make an equation, and solve it to find her number.

Still more practice.

$$48 - 7p = 13$$

$$7p = 35$$

$$p = 5$$

Solve the equations in questions **5** and **6**.

5 a $15 - 4x = 3$ **b** $20 - 3y = 5$ **c** $47 - 6p = 5$
  d $8 - 2x = 4$ **e** $9 = 2a - 1$ **f** $31 = 2b + 15$
  g $27 = 3 + 4w$ **h** $9 = 5 + 4y$

6 a $0 = 36 - 4k$ **b** $19 = 11 + 2p$
  c $3q - 4 = 17$ **d** $6r - 13 = 17$
  e $5x + 2x - 3 = 18$ **f** $8y + 2 - 2y = 44$
  g $2z + 9 - z = 9$ **h** $5a - 7 - a = 9$

7 In a spreadsheet the entry in row n is $4n - 2$. Find:
  a the entry in row 10
  b the row in which the entry is 34.

8 In another spreadsheet the entry in row k is $5k - 3$. Find:
  a the entry in row 8
  b the row in which the entry is 32.

9 Find x in each puzzle. Remember this idea?

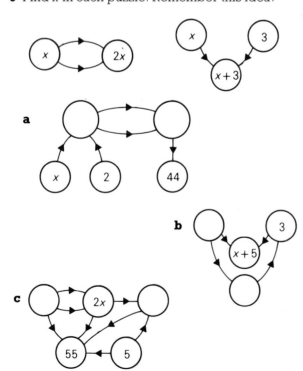

10 Here is a price list for mail-order stamp collecting:

Stamp number	1	2	3	4	5	6	7
Cost (each)	5p	3p	7p	6p	11p	15p	13p

Make an equation for each order below, and then solve it to find the number of stamps ordered.
  a x No. 1 stamps, totalling 45p
  b y No. 4 stamps, totalling 24p
  c t No. 3 stamps, with 20p postage, for 55p
  d w No. 6 stamps, with 30p discount, for 30p
  e n No. 2 stamps, with 25p postage, for 61p
  f k No. 7 stamps, with 25p discount, for 40p

BRAINSTORMERS

1 *Think of a number, double it, add 6, halve the result, then take away the number you first thought of. Explain why the answer is always 3.*

2

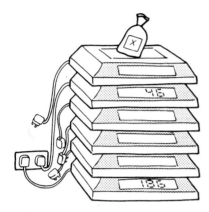

In this tower of weighing machines, each one will weigh everything that is piled on top of it. But only two machines are plugged in. How many 1 kg weights are in the bag marked x?

3

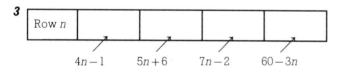

Row n				

$4n-1$ $5n+6$ $7n-2$ $60-3n$

Only one of these spreadsheet rows fits the model above. Which one? Give reasons for rejecting each of the others.

a

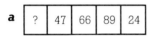

?	47	66	89	24

b

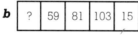

?	59	81	103	15

c

?	31	51	54	36

d

?	11	21	19	48

4 *A factory's current stock of parts is:*

Item 1: 300
Item 2: 93
Item 3: 116
Item 4: 47

QUICK-SHELF KIT
CONTENT LIST

Item 1 : 13 Screws
Item 2 : 4 Brackets
Item 3 : 5 Wood strips
Item 4 : 2 Glue tubes

a *x kits were produced, leaving only one screw in stock. Make an equation, and solve it to find the number of kits produced.*
b *How many of the other items were left in stock?*

INVESTIGATION

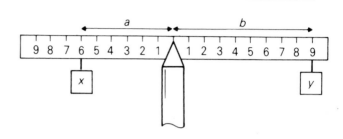

a *Try to hang weights x and y so that the beam is balanced.*
Calculate $x \times a$ and $y \times b$.
Make a table of results for different values of x, y, a and b.

x	a	y	b	$x \times a$	$y \times b$

b *Put $y = 2$ at $b = 9$, and find x at $a = 6$ to balance. Check, using the equation $6x = 9 \times 2$.*
c *Repeat **b** for:*
(i) $a = 6, b = 9, y = 4$ (ii) $a = 10, b = 4, y = 5$
(iii) $a = 5, b = 10, y = 3$ (iv) $a = 8, b = 4, y = 10$
d *Investigate values of a and b which balance the beam when $x = 3$ and $y = 6$. Check, using equations.*
e *Repeat **b** for weight x on the left side of the beam and weights y and z on the right side.*

CHECK-UP ON SOLVING EQUATIONS

1 Solve these equations by using the 'cover up' method:

a $x+7 = 12$ **b** $x-5 = 3$ **c** $x-6 = 8$
d $x+9 = 14$ **e** $a+1 = 30$ **f** $b-10 = 10$
g $c+8 = 15$ **h** $d-4 = 11$

2 Make equations for these pictures, and solve them to find x, y and k.

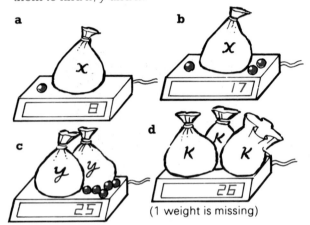

(1 weight is missing)

3 Use the patterns in the rows and columns to make as many equations as you can; then solve the equations.

	A	**B**	**C**	**D**
1	3	4	5	$x-1$
2	$a-8$	6	7	8
3	7	8	$c+9$	10
4	9	10	11	$d+5$

4 Make an equation for each balance, then solve it.

a

$x+8$ 12

b

$y-7$ 9

c

$t+12$ 20

d

$u-15$ 6

5 Make equations for these, then solve them:

a
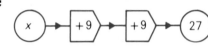

b
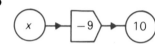

c
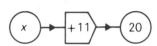

6 Solve:

a $2x+1 = 17$ **b** $3y-1 = 11$
c $4m+3 = 27$ **d** $5n-6 = 24$
e $3a+2a = 30$ **f** $4b-3b = 77$
g $c+c+c = 21$ **h** $d+d-d = 99$

7 x strawberry plants can be ordered by mail. They cost 80p each, and postage for any number is £1.20. If the total cost of the order is £6, how many plants were ordered?

8
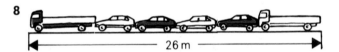
26 m

Each lorry is 5.5 m long, and each car is x m long. Make an equation and find the length of each car.

Solve the equations in questions **9** and **10**.

9 a $5k-7 = 13$ **b** $6t+3 = 39$ **c** $8u-2 = 54$
d $9v+16 = 16$ **e** $12-2c = 10$ **f** $25-3d = 10$
g $29 = 4x-7$ **h** $100 = 9x+19$

10 a $3x+2x+x = 42$ **b** $5y+y-2y = 36$
c $z+z+z-1 = 17$ **d** $v+2v+3 = 15$
e $5p+1+2p-1 = 21$ **f** $3q-4+q-4 = 40$
g $6r+7-r+7 = 19$

11 Explain why only one of these numbers could be entered in the space in the spreadsheet.

Row n	

$3n-2$

20 51 26 37 44

Many different units of length have been used in the past. Which of these have you heard of?

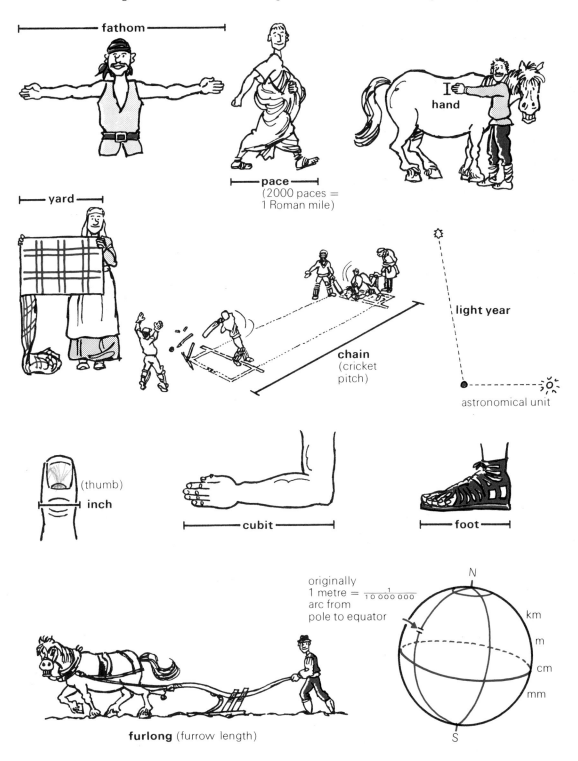

fathom

pace
(2000 paces =
1 Roman mile)

hand

yard

chain
(cricket
pitch)

light year

astronomical unit

(thumb)
inch

cubit

foot

originally
1 metre = $\frac{1}{10\,000\,000}$
arc from
pole to equator

N

km
m
cm
mm

S

furlong (furrow length)

New units for old

1 inch $\doteqdot$ $2\frac{1}{2}$ centimetres
1 yard $\doteqdot$ 1 metre
1 mile $\doteqdot$ $1\frac{1}{2}$ kilometres

($\doteqdot$ means 'is about to equal to')

Draw a straight line 3 inches long.
Measure its length in centimetres and tenths of a centimetre.
Then calculate the number of centimetres and tenths of a centimetre in 1 inch.
Repeat for lines 4 inches and 5 inches long.
Do you agree that 1 inch $\doteqdot$ $2\frac{1}{2}$ centimetres?

Use a dictionary or encyclopaedia to find more accurate relations between all the units.

LOOKING BACK

1

Ruler, tape measure, car mileometer, long tape measure, trundle wheel—which would you use to measure:
a the length of the playground
b the distance round your waist
c the length of a pencil
d the distance between two towns
e the width of the classroom
f the length of a fingernail?

2 Measure the lengths of the bicycle, car and bus models, in centimetres.

3 Draw pencils of lengths:
  a 5 cm **b** 7 cm **c** $9\frac{1}{2}$ cm

4 7 m 65 cm can be written 7.65 m. Write these lengths in the same way:
  a 3 m 12 cm **b** 5 m 80 cm **c** 12 m 6 cm
  d 85 cm

5

The thicknesses of these books are 2.5 cm, 3.3 cm, 1.7 cm, 2.6 cm, 1.2 cm and 0.8 cm. Calculate the height of the pile of books.

6 Nathan's new pencil was 17 cm long, but after a month it was only 14.3 cm long. What length had been used?

7 At the start of a journey a car's mileometer reads 126 574 km.

After the journey it reads 126 611 km.

a How long was the journey?
b The car travelled another 99 km. What was the mileometer reading then?

8 Draw a rectangle 12 cm long and 5 cm broad. Measure the length of its diagonal (from one corner, across the centre, to the other corner).

UNITS OF LENGTH

The **metre** is the standard unit of length in many countries.
We use millimetres (mm), centimetres (cm),
metres (m) and kilometres (km) to measure length.

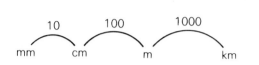

10 mm = 1 cm
100 cm = 1 m
1000 m = 1 km

EXERCISE 1A

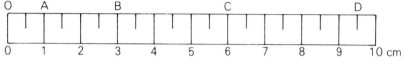

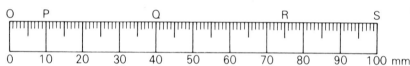

1 Write down the lengths shown on the first ruler
   in centimetres:
   a OA, OB, OC and OD   **b** AB, AC and AD
   c BC, BD and CD.

2 Write down the lengths shown on the second
   ruler in millimetres:
   a OP, OQ, OR and OS   **b** PQ, QR and RS.

3 How many millimetres are there in:
   a 1 cm   **b** 2 cm   **c** 3 cm   **d** 5 cm   **e** 10 cm?

4 The first ruler is 10 cm long. How many rulers
   like this would you need to put end to end to
   stretch one metre (100 cm)?

5 Measure the width of your desk, to the nearest
   centimetre. Is this more or less than one metre?

6 **a** Measure the length and breadth of this book,
   to the nearest centimetre.
   b Measure its thickness, in millimetres.

7 Look at the picture of the yacht.
   a *Guess* which is longer, the mast or the deck of
   the yacht.
   b Which *is* longer?
   c Is eyesight alone good enough for comparing
   lengths?

   d Are units of measurement necessary for
   comparing lengths?
   e When would you need to use units of
   measurement of length?

8 Which units—mm, cm, m or km—would you use
   to measure:
   a your height
   b the height of the school
   c the length of a pencil
   d the length of Britain (Land's End to John
   O'Groats)
   e the thickness of a book
   f the thickness of a fingernail
   g the distance to the school office
   h the distance to New York?

9 Estimate the lengths or distances in question **8**.

10 **a** Without using your ruler, draw a line
   'freehand' which you think is 3 cm long.
   b Measure its length with a ruler.
   c Write down the difference in length, in
   millimetres.

11 Repeat question **10** for lines of lengths:
   a 5 cm   **b** 8 cm   **c** 5 mm   **d** 12 mm

103

EXERCISE 1B/C

1

a Measure the width and the height of the opening in this doorway.

b Which of the doors below would you buy to fit the doorway?

c If you had to take one of the other doors, which one would you choose? Why?

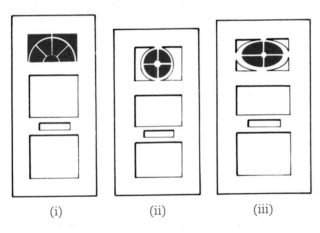

(i)   (ii)   (iii)

(iv)   (v)

2 The cost of placing an advert in a newspaper depends on what is being advertised, and the depth of the advertisement. The table below shows some of the charges.

Category	Cost per centimetre depth
Employment	£9.80
Property	£8.40
Entertainment	£8.25
Motor cars	£7.50
Charities	£3.00

Calculate the cost of placing each of these four ads.

a

b

c

d

3 The eleven members of a school team are training on a rectangular field 100 m long and 50 m broad. Make a scale drawing, using 1 cm to 50 m, and mark it as shown. AB = BC = ... = JK.

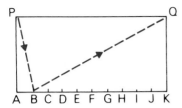

Team member A has to run from P to A to Q, member B from P to B to Q, and so on. Find the distance in metres that each member has to run. Which journey would the laziest member choose?

/ **PRACTICAL PROJECTS**

Try some of these.

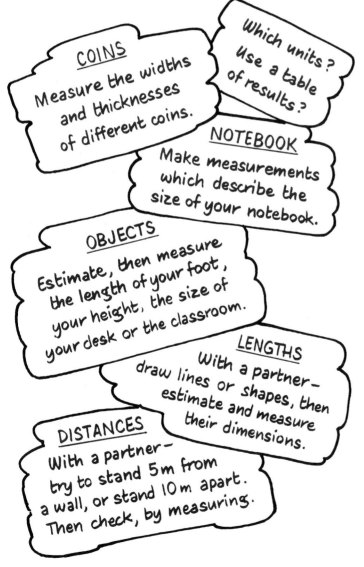

COINS
Measure the widths and thicknesses of different coins.

Which units? Use a table of results?

NOTEBOOK
Make measurements which describe the size of your notebook.

OBJECTS
Estimate, then measure the length of your foot, your height, the size of your desk or the classroom.

LENGTHS
With a partner — draw lines or shapes, then estimate and measure their dimensions.

DISTANCES
With a partner — try to stand 5 m from a wall, or stand 10 m apart. Then check, by measuring.

/ **INVESTIGATIONS**

1 Investigate the lengths of some of the units on page 101 in metric (mm, cm, m, km) or in Imperial (inch, foot, yard, mile) measures.

2 Investigate how your body measures up! Divide your height in cm by your wrist measurement in cm. Most people 'measure' about 10. The greater the value, the slimmer (?) fatter (?) you are. Which? Compare your value with those of your friends'.

/ **CHALLENGES**

1

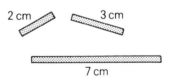

You are given rods 2 cm, 3 cm and 7 cm long. Here is how you can use them to measure 8 cm:

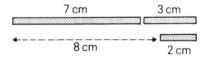

Draw sketches to show how you could use the rods to measure all lengths from 1 cm to 10 cm.

2 Show the relative heights of these famous buildings in a scale-drawing bar graph: Big Ben 96 m, Great Pyramid 146 m, Telecom Tower 177 m, Empire State Building 431 m, Canary Wharf Tower 244 m, St Paul's Cathedral 112 m, Nat West Tower 183 m.

PERIMETERS AND DIAMETERS

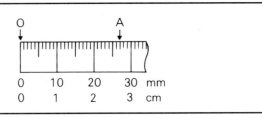

OA = 27 mm, or 2.7 cm in centimetres
and tenths of a centimetre.

EXERCISE 2A

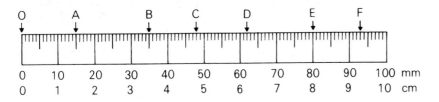

The diameter of a circle
A diameter, like AB,
passes through
the centre of
the circle.

1 Write down the lengths of OA, OB, OC, OD, OE
and OF in millimetres, and in centimetres and
tenths of a centimetre.

2 a Measure the length and breadth of each stamp
in millimetres.

b Calculate the perimeter of each stamp.

 The perimeter of a shape is the total distance round its edges.

3 a Measure the length and breadth of the cover of
this book, in centimetres and tenths of a
centimetre.
b Then calculate the perimeter of the cover.

4 Repeat question **3** for a page of your notebook.

5 Measure the diameters of these circles in
millimetres:

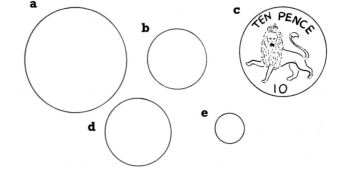

6 Measure the diameters of these circles in
centimetres and tenths of a centimetre.

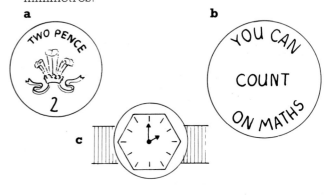

7 Draw a rectangle, square and triangle, each with
a perimeter of 24 cm.

8 Use compasses to draw circles with diameters
which measure:
a 4 cm   **b** 5 cm   **c** 60 mm   **d** 3.5 cm

EXERCISE 2B

A games company wants new designs for a pack of cards. Can you draw the four aces?

1 Ace of diamonds

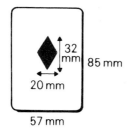

Draw the card first, a rectangle 57 mm by 85 mm. Find its exact centre, and draw the diamond symbol accurately.

2 Ace of hearts

Follow the diagram carefully to draw the heart symbol.

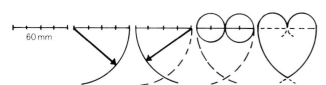

3 Ace of spades

Draw an upside down heart symbol. Then follow the diagram to make the spade symbol.

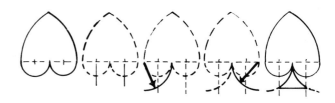

4 Ace of clubs

Follow the diagram and draw the club symbol.

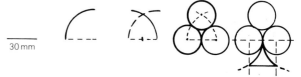

APPROXIMATION

a To one tenth of a centimetre, OA = 1.7 cm.
   To the nearest centimetre, OA = 2 cm.
b To one tenth of a centimetre, OB = 3.4 cm.
   To the nearest centimetre, OB = 3 cm.

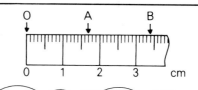

Remember the rule : If the next number is 5 or over, round up.

EXERCISE 2C

1 Round each length to the nearest centimetre:
   a 8.1 cm   **b** 6.6 cm   **c** 3.5 cm   **d** 4.4 cm
   e 6.6 cm   **f** 10.1 cm

2 (i) Write down the lengths of these pencils in centimetres and tenths of a centimetre.
   (ii) Now give each length to the nearest centimetre.

a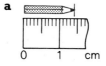

b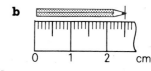

c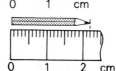

d

3 Find the diameters of these circular objects:
(i) in centimetres and tenths of a centimetre
(ii) to the nearest centimetre.

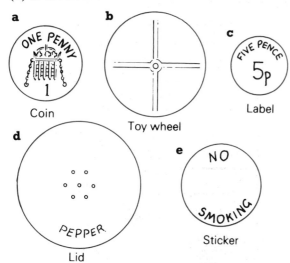

a Coin
b Toy wheel
c Label
d Lid PEPPER
e Sticker NO SMOKING

4 Which of these centipedes are 3 cm long, to the nearest cm?

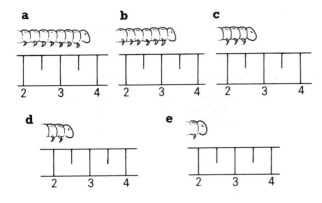

a   b   c
2 3 4   2 3 4   2 3 4

d   e
2 3 4   2 3 4

5 Which of these lengths would be rounded to 8 cm, to the nearest cm?
8.2 cm, 8.8 cm, 7.8 cm, 7.5 cm, 8.5 cm, 7.9 cm, 8.1 cm, 8.0 cm.

6 Which of these lengths would be rounded to 4 cm, to the nearest cm?
43 mm, 48 mm, 38 mm, 33 mm, 41 mm, 35 mm.

7 The leaf is 6 cm long, to the nearest centimetre. This means that its length is between 5.5 cm and 6.5 cm.

5.5 6 6.5

Between which lengths do these leaves lie?
a 5 cm long **b** 3 cm long **c** 1 cm long
d 10 cm long

8 a Calculate the perimeter of this TV screen, using the measurements shown.
b Round the length and breadth to the nearest centimetre, and calculate the perimeter again.
c Which is more accurate?

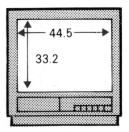

44.5
33.2

9 A birdbox should have a circular hole of diameter 4 cm, but an error of 0.5 cm is acceptable. Draw the largest acceptable hole, and inside it the smallest acceptable hole.

PRACTICAL PROJECTS

1 Estimate the perimeter of the school grounds in metres. Can you think of any easy way to make a rough measurement of the distance?

2 A cuboid has three dimensions —length, breadth and height.

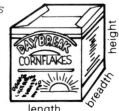

Choose some objects which are in the shape of cuboids, and complete a table like this.

Object	Length	Breadth	Height

Include the units—mm, cm or m.

3 a Use a tape measure, or a ruler and string, to measure the diameters and circumferences of a variety of cylindrical tins.

circumference   diameter

Complete a table like this:

Object	Diameter	Circumference

b Investigate the connection between the length of the diameter and the circumference of each top.

EXERCISE 3A

1

Alexander, Jack and Hassan took part in the triple jump event at the school sports.
a The three parts of Alexander's jump measured 1.3 m, 1.3 m and 1.5 m. What total length did he cover?
b Jack's results were 1.2 m, 1.3 m, 1.4 m. Hassan managed 1.4 m, 1.4 m, 1.2 m. Work out the total length of each of their jumps.
c Who won?

2 Kathy bought a strip of seven stamps, each 21 mm wide. How long was the strip?

3 Sarah is 164 cm tall, and Helen is 149 cm. How much taller than Helen is Sarah?

4

Dawn's small sister has a 'concertina' book. Each page has one letter of the alphabet, and is 83 mm wide. How long is the book when it is opened out:
a in mm **b** in cm?

5 Outside a factory new cars of the same type are parked bumper to bumper. A line of six cars takes up a space of 28.8 m. How long is each car?

6 Distances on the map are in kilometres.

a Calculate the distance from Ambleside to Greenodd.
 (i) through Coniston
 (ii) through Windermere.
b Find the shortest distance by road from Coniston to Morecambe.

7 Robert sees this road sign at Greenock.

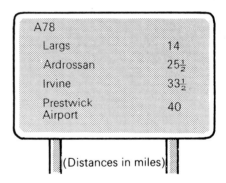

How far is it:
a from Greenock to Prestwick Airport
b from Largs to the Airport
c between Ardrossan and Irvine?

8 Not counting the covers, the thickness of a book is 30 mm. The book has 600 pages. How thick is each sheet of paper in the book? (Careful! There's a catch in this question.)

EXERCISE 3B

1 A botany class was doing a study of plants and flowers. Keith measured some foxglove plants. Their heights were: 56 cm, 57 cm, 61 cm, 62 cm, 60 cm and 64 cm.

a Add up the heights.
b Divide the total by the number of plants.
c Then write your answer: average height of foxgloves = . . . cm.

2 Diana decided to measure some primroses. Here are their heights: 5 cm, 6 cm, 7 cm, 4 cm, 4 cm, 3 cm, 6 cm, 5 cm, 3 cm and 7 cm. Calculate the average height of these primroses.

3 Some books on wild flowers describe the heights of plants like this:

Tall	60 cm and over
Medium	30 cm and less than 60 cm
Short	10 cm and less than 30 cm
Low	Less than 10 cm

Use this system, and Keith and Diana's results, to describe:
a the foxglove   **b** the primrose.

4 Copy and complete this table of some other plants studied by the botany class.

5 'KIRSTY' dolls are made one-sixth of life-size. Furniture for KIRSTY dolls will also be one-sixth life-size. The picture shows the sizes of an actual table and chair.

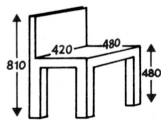

All measurements are in millimetres.

The back of a chair is 810 mm high. So the KIRSTY doll's chair will have a back which is $810 \div 6 = 135$ mm high.
a Scale down the other sizes given for the chair in the same way.
b Calculate, to the nearest millimetre, the length, breadth and height of the doll's table.
c Draw a picture of the doll's table and chair, and mark in their measurements.

Name of plant	Height (in cm)						Average height (to nearest 0.1 cm)	Description
Dandelion	13	12	11	10	13	13		Short
Daisy	5	5	6	4	4	5		
Poppy	35	37	35	36	36	37		
Buttercup (meadow)	27	33	29	31	28	27		

EXERCISE 3C

1 Jill's job in her youth club's project on the weather is to measure the rainfall. To do this she collects the rain in a jar. Each day she measures the depth of water in the jar, and every Saturday night she empties the jar.

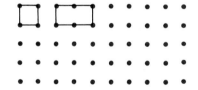

a Copy and complete this table.

Day	Reading	Rainfall
Sunday	7 mm	7 mm
Monday	15 mm	8 mm
Tuesday	20 mm	
Wednesday	26 mm	
Thursday	32 mm	
Friday	44 mm	
Saturday	44 mm	

b Calculate the average daily rainfall, to the nearest millimetre, for the week shown.
c Which days had rainfall above the average for the week?
d What was the weather like between Friday and Saturday?

2 Mr and Mrs Johnstone often use the ferry. This drawing of their car and caravan has a scale of 1 cm to 1.5 m.

Calculate the cost of:
a a single crossing for Mr Johnstone alone, with the car
b a return trip for Mr and Mrs Johnstone, with the car and the caravan.

	Driver/ Passenger (each)	Overall length not exceeding:		
		4.5 m	5.0 m	7.5 m
Single	£8.40	£44.30	£49.30	£65.85
Return	£15.35	£63.20	£70.40	£105.30

3 a How many spaces, each 2.5 m wide, are there in section A of the car park?

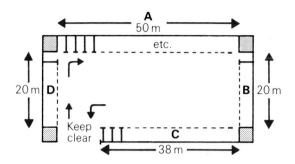

b How many cars can park in sections A, B, C and D altogether?
c Design your own car park in a rectangle of ground 45 m by 30 m. Allow 4 m by 2.5 m for each car. The spaces can be at right angles to the sides, or angled.

/ **CHALLENGE**

It is easy to make rectangles on a pinboard.

Investigate the number, and the dimensions, of different rectangles that can be made with perimeters of 4, 6, 8, 10, . . . units. Complete a table like this, and continue it as far as you can.

Perimeter	Number of rectangles	Dimensions
4	1	1,1
6	1	
8	2	1,3; 2,2
10	2	

Can you find a rule?

CHECK-UP ON MEASURING LENGTH

1 Estimate:
   a the length and the thickness of a matchstick
   b the length, breadth and depth of a video cassette case
   c the width of a pavement and of a main road
   d the distance from Edinburgh to London.

2 Draw rectangles 45 mm by 22 mm, and 6.5 cm by 3.5 cm. Measure the lengths of their diagonals (corner to corner).

3 a Estimate the length and breadth of the page you are writing on.
   b Then measure its length and breadth, and calculate the errors in your estimates.

4 Measure the diameter of the washer, and the perimeters of the chew and the ear-ring:
  (i) in millimetres
  (ii) in centimetres and tenths of a centimetre.

  a

Washer

  b

Chew

  c

Ear-ring

5 A piece of elastic is 93 cm long. By how much would you have to stretch it to reach 1 m?

6 Twelve encyclopaedias, side by side, take up 40.8 cm of shelf space. Calculate the thickness of each book.

7 1000 cards make a pile 1 m high.
  a Calculate the thickness of one card, in mm.
  b How many cards would be needed to make a pile 1 cm high?

8 A charity raises money by collecting 1 km of one penny coins, placed side by side in a straight line. The diameter of one penny is 2 cm.
  a How much money does the charity collect?
  b Investigate this fund-raising idea for different coins.

10 TILING AND SYMMETRY

LOOKING BACK

1 Congruent squares can form a tiling pattern.

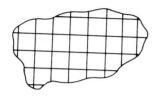

a Which of these shapes can make a tiling?

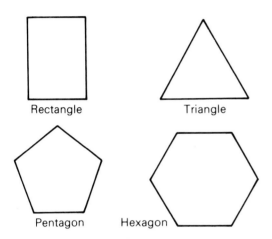

Rectangle   Triangle

Pentagon   Hexagon

b Draw a tiling of those that do. The easiest way to do this is to trace the shape and move the tracing about.

2 a Which of these shapes have line symmetry?

b Draw or trace the outlines of the symmetrical shapes, and show the line of symmetry in each by a dotted line.

3 Use tracing paper to copy and complete these pictures, so that they are symmetrical about the dotted lines.

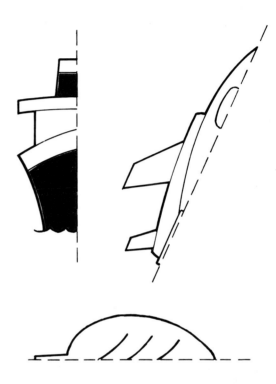

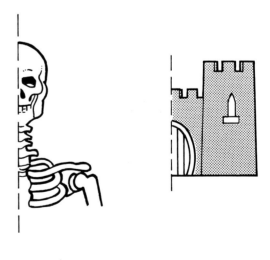

4 Draw some other shapes or patterns which are symmetrical, like the ones you have completed in question **3**.

113

TILINGS

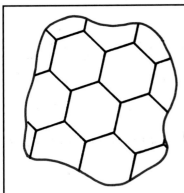

To make a tiling:
(i) Use sets of **congruent** tiles
   (ones that have **the same shape and size**).
(ii) Don't leave any gaps.
(iii) Don't have any overlaps.

EXERCISE 1A

1 Copy and extend these tiling patterns on squared paper, then colour them if you wish.

a

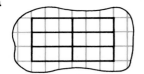   One tile

b   **c**

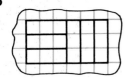   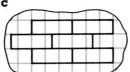

2 Copy these patterns on squared paper, or on tracing paper. Colour the sets of congruent shapes.

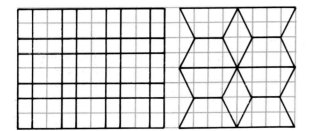

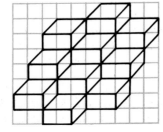

3 a Use tracing paper, or a cut-out template, to draw tilings based on these shapes.

(i)   (ii)

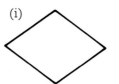

(iii)   (iv)

b Make your own wolf tiling, based on 2 by 4 rectangles on squared paper, like this.

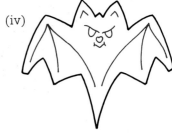

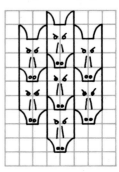

PROJECT

Collect pictures from magazines which show tilings in everyday life. Try to find enough to make a classroom poster.

EXERCISE 1B/C

1 Copy these floor shapes on squared paper or on tracing paper, and show how each can be tiled using the tile above it.

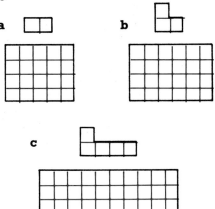

2 A tile made from five squares joined together, like the third one in question **1**, is called a **pentomino**. Peter has made four different pentominoes, and has thought of a fifth.

But his attempts to tile with his pentominoes do not produce repeating patterns.

Try making your own tilings based on these two pentominoes.

3 There are twelve different possible pentominoes. Can you sketch all of them and then produce a few tilings based on some of them?

4 Semi-regular tilings are made of two or more regular shapes.
  a Copy and extend this diagram to make a tiling of squares and hexagons.
  b Now try to make tilings based on:
    (i) squares and equilateral triangles
    (ii) hexagons, squares and equilateral triangles.

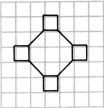

INVESTIGATION

a *Use tracing paper to draw tilings of each of the shapes in question 1 on page 113, if possible.*
b *Deduce the sizes of the equal angles round a point in each tiling.*
c *Explain why some regular shapes can be used to form tilings, while others cannot.*

BRAINSTORMERS

1 *One domino covers two squares of this chessboard.*
  a *Can dominoes be used to tile the chessboard?*
  b *If you take away two of the diagonally opposite corner squares, can the board still be tiled using dominoes?*

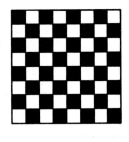

  c *If you take away two of the corner squares on one side of the board can the board be tiled using dominoes?*

2 a *Copy this tiling pattern on squared paper, and extend it.*
You have to colour the tiles so that:
    (i) *no two tiles with an edge in common are the same colour.*
    (ii) *as few colours as possible are used.*
  b *What is the smallest number of colours needed to colour countries in an atlas in this way?*

3 *It is possible to fit all twelve different pentominoes on a 10 by 6 grid of squares. Can you do this?*

LINE SYMMETRY

CLASS DISCUSSION

1 Look at these pictures. What is special about all of them? Why have dotted lines been drawn in some of them? Could this have been done in the other pictures?

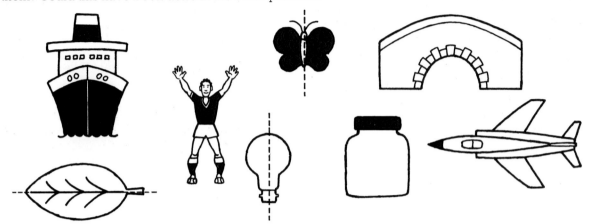

2 If you traced the butterfly, leaf and light bulb, and turned them over, would they still fit their outlines? Would this be true for the other pictures?
Each picture is 'balanced' about a line, the **line of symmetry** or **axis of symmetry**.

3 The star shape is **symmetrical** about the x-axis and the y-axis.

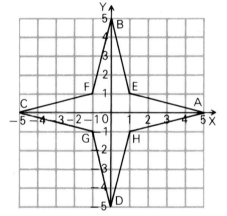

   a A is the point (5, 0). What are the coordinates of C?
   b B is the point (0, 5). What are the coordinates of D?
   c What do you notice in each case?
   d E is (1, 1). What are the coordinates of F, G and H? (Is there more than one route to G?)

EXERCISE 2A

---

1 Which of these pictures have line symmetry?

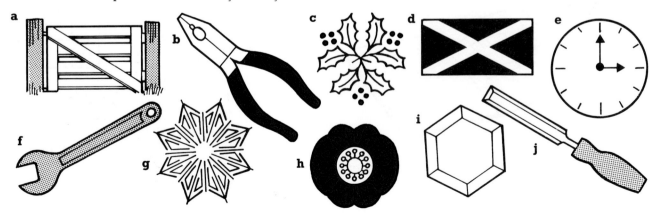

2 Copy these shapes on squared paper or on tracing paper. Draw in axes of symmetry, or cut out and fold the shapes to find the axes of symmetry. How many can you find for each shape?

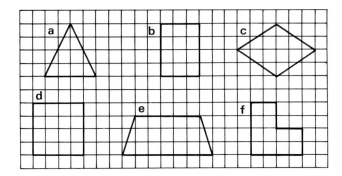

3 How many lines of symmetry can you find for each of the shapes below? If in doubt, trace and fold them.

4 Which of these road signs have line symmetry?

a
T-junction

b
Low flying aircraft

c
Cattle

d
End of speed limit

e
Keep right

f
Turn left

5 The *y*-axis is an axis of symmetry for each of these three shapes. Write down the coordinates of the pairs of points A and B, C and D.

a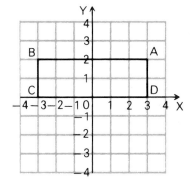

b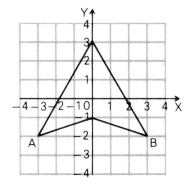

c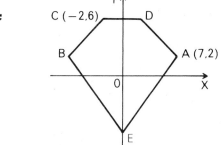

6 In this question the *x*-axis is an axis of symmetry for each shape. Write down the coordinates of the pairs of points A and B, C and D.

a

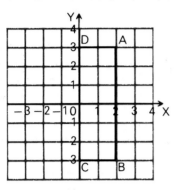

b

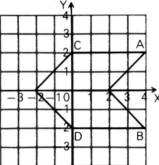

c

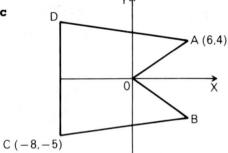

7 a Using squared paper or tracing paper, show how to fit together two shapes like the one shown to make a new shape which has an axis of symmetry.

b Try to do this in several different ways.

8 Repeat question **7** for each of these shapes.

9 The *x*-axis and the *y*-axis are *both* axes of symmetry for these shapes. Find the coordinates of all the vertices.

a

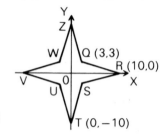

b

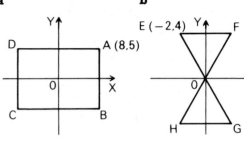

c

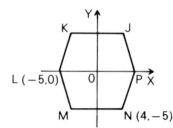

d

10 Fit each of these pairs of different pentominoes together to make a shape with an axis of symmetry. Try to find several ways of doing this for each pair of shapes.

a   **b**

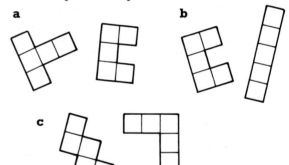

c

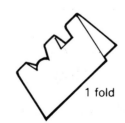

INVESTIGATION

Investigate the variety of symmetrical designs you can obtain by folding a sheet of paper one or more times, cutting out different shapes across the folds, and then unfolding the paper.

1 fold   2 folds

ON REFLECTION

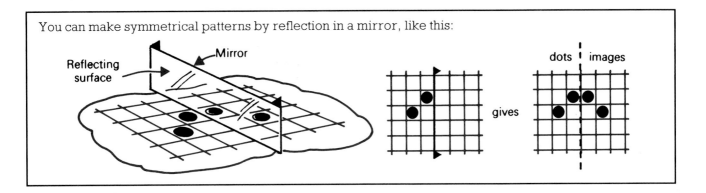

You can make symmetrical patterns by reflection in a mirror, like this:

Reflecting surface — Mirror — gives — dots ¦ images

EXERCISE 2B

1 Copy these dots and axes of symmetry on squared paper, or on tracing paper. Mark the images of the dots after reflection in the mirrors.

a 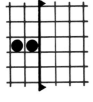   **b**

c    **d**

e 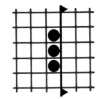   **f**

g   **h**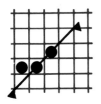

2 Here now are some harder diagrams.

a 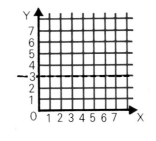   **b**

c   **d**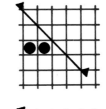

e 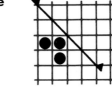   **f**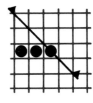

g 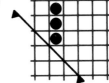   **h**

In questions **3** and **4**, plot the points on squared paper. Reflect them in the mirrors (the dotted lines). Then list the coordinates of their images.

3

Point	Image
(2, 1)	(2, 5)
(5, 2)	
(3, 0)	
(0, 0)	
(4, 2)	
(6, 1)	
(3, 3)	
(0, 2)	

Which coordinate stays the same?

4

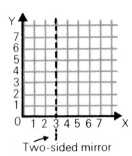

Point	Image
(2, 1)	
(4, 2)	
(5, 4)	
(0, 3)	
(3, 3)	
(6, 5)	
(1, 3)	

Two-sided mirror

Which coordinate stays the same?

5 A computerised lathe is programmed to make the cutting tool move from point to point while the object is spinning. The points (2, 5), (2, 8), (3, 6), (5, 6), (6, 8), (6, 5) produce the bobbin shown in the sketch.

Follow the same steps to produce sketches of:

a two wheels and an axle: (1, 5), (1, 8), (2, 8), (2, 6), (6, 6), (6, 8), (7, 8), (7, 5).

b a spinning top: (1, 5), (3, 10), (5, 6), (7, 6), (8, 8), (9, 6), (9, 5).

c a goblet: (1, 5), (2, 8), (4, 8), (5, 6), (9, 6), (11, 8), (11, 5).

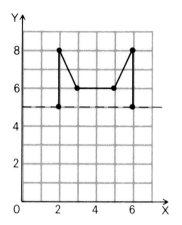

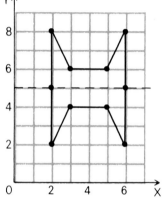

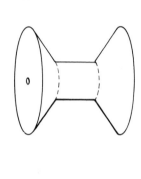

EXERCISE 2C

In questions **1–3**, copy the diagrams on squared paper or on tracing paper. Then complete them so that the dotted lines are axes of symmetry. You can check your results by folding along the axes of symmetry.

1

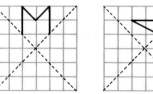

2

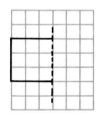   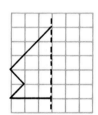

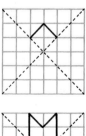

3

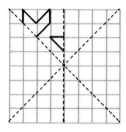

In questions **4** and **5**, plot the points on squared paper. Mark their images under reflection in the dotted lines, and list the coordinates of the images.

4

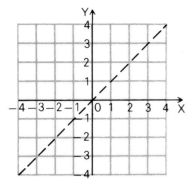

a

Point	(3, 1)	(4, 3)	(2, 0)	(−4, −2)	(2, −4)
Image					

b Write down the image of (a, b).

5

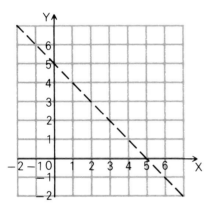

a

Point	(2, 1)	(4, 3)	(0, 0)	(3, 2)	(2, −2)	(−1, 5)
Image						

b What do you notice about the y-coordinate of each point and the x-coordinate of its image?

6

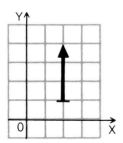

Investigate the image of this arrow after reflection in:
a the x-axis and then the y-axis
b the y-axis and then the x-axis.

Many 3-dimensional objects have **planes of symmetry**, often for very practical reasons. This motorbike has a plane of symmetry along its centre, so that it will be balanced in action.

1 Describe, or use tracings to show, the positions of planes of symmetry in these objects.

2 Investigate planes of symmetry in these solids. Describe them, or show them in tracings. Use actual solids, if possible.

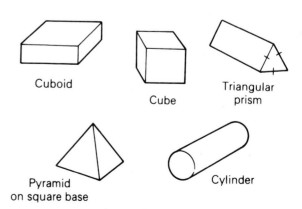

Cuboid

Cube

Triangular prism

Pyramid on square base

Cylinder

TURN SYMMETRY, OR ROTATIONAL SYMMETRY

Trace each shape below. Keep the tracing over the shape, and put the point of your pencil on the dot. Give the tracing a half-turn. Notice that the tracing fits the original shape. This is because the shape has **half-turn symmetry** about the dot. The dot is called the **centre of symmetry**.

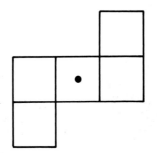

Use tracings to see that the shapes below have **quarter-turn symmetry** as well as half-turn symmetry.

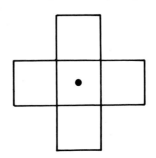

EXERCISE 3A

1 Which of these drawings have half-turn symmetry, and which have quarter-turn symmetry? Use tracing paper to help you to decide, if necessary.

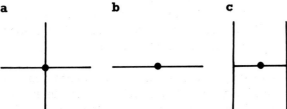

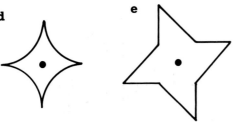

2 Decide whether each shape has $\frac{1}{4}$-turn symmetry, $\frac{1}{2}$-turn but not $\frac{1}{4}$-turn symmetry, or neither.

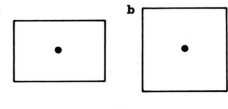

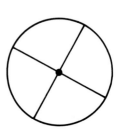

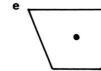

3 Repeat question **2** for these designs.

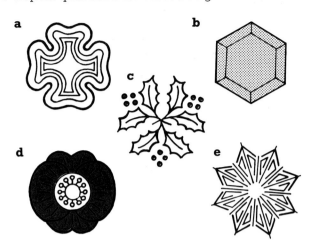

a b c d e

4 Copy the drawings below on squared paper, or trace them.
Then complete the drawings so that the dot becomes the centre of half-turn symmetry in each one.

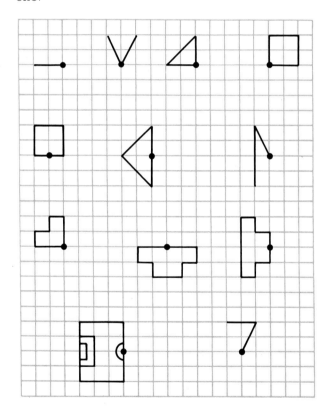

5 AOB is symmetrical about the origin.

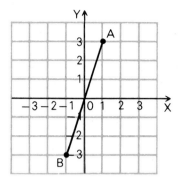

a Write down the coordinates of:
   (i) A
   (ii) B, the image of A after a half-turn about the origin.
b OA is extended to C so that OC = 2 × OA.
   Write down the coordinates of:
   (i) C
   (ii) the image of C after a half-turn about the origin.

6 ABCD has half-turn symmetry about the origin.

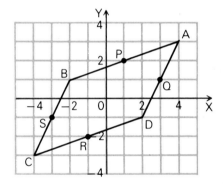

a Write down the coordinates of A, and of its image C after a half-turn about the origin.
b Repeat **a** for the points B, P, Q and their images after half-turns about the origin.

7 This shape has quarter-turn symmetry about O, and A is the point (2, 6). AB is parallel to the *x*-axis. Write down the coordinates of B, C, D, E, F, G and H.

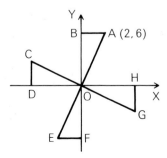

The number of ways in which a shape will fit its outline when turned once about its centre of symmetry is called its **order of symmetry**.

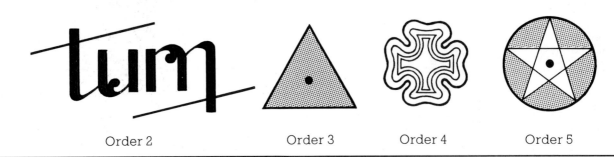

Order 2   Order 3   Order 4   Order 5

EXERCISE 3B/C

1 Write down the order of symmetry of each of these shapes.

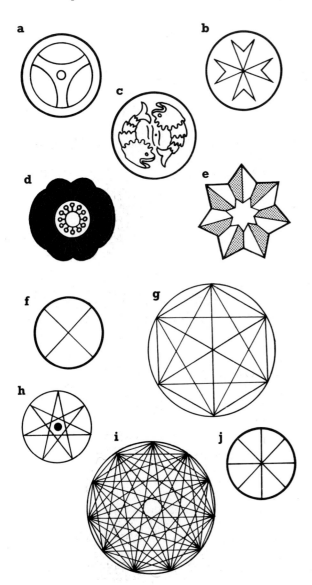

2 All the shapes in question **1** have centres of symmetry. The centre of half-turn symmetry, C in this diagram, is found by joining each point to its image, or 'partner'.

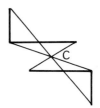

Use tracing paper to check that C is the centre of symmetry, and to help you find the centre of half-turn symmetry in each shape below.

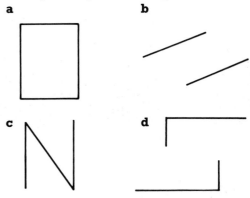

3 A parallelogram ABCD has its centre of symmetry at the origin. A is the point (2, 3) and B is (6, 1). Find the coordinates of:
a C **b** D
c M, the half-turn image of the midpoint of AB.

4 An octagon PQRSTUVW has order 4 symmetry about the origin. P is the point (0, 4), Q is (3, 3) and R is (4, 0). Find the coordinates of S, T, U, V and W.

5 Stars rotate around the Pole Star. With the Pole Star at the origin, the stars of the constellation called The Plough are at $(3, 3)$, $(4, 5)$, $(6, 2)$, $(6, 4)$, $(7, 1)$, $(9, 0)$ and $(11, 1)$.

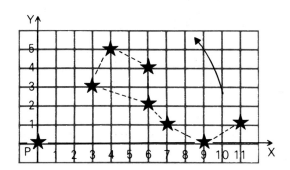

Find the coordinates of the stars after:
a a half-turn about P
b a quarter-turn about P.

6 a Draw pentominoes which have:
 (i) half-turn symmetry
 (ii) quarter-turn symmetry.
b Repeat **a** for pairs of pentominoes, placed together.

CHALLENGES

1 *Make up lists of the capital letters of the alphabet that should land in each barrel.*

2 *Old for new*

Squaring the circle

Can you devise words which can be read upside down also?

BRAINSTORMER

True or false?

a *If a shape has $\frac{1}{4}$ turn symmetry then it has $\frac{1}{2}$ turn symmetry.*
b *If a shape has $\frac{1}{2}$ turn symmetry then it has $\frac{1}{4}$ turn symmetry.*
c *If a shape has a centre of symmetry then it has line symmetry.*
d *If a shape has line symmetry then it has $\frac{1}{2}$ turn symmetry.*
e *A shape can have both a centre of symmetry and an axis of symmetry.*
f *No shape can have $\frac{1}{3}$ turn symmetry.*
g *A shape can have 3 lines of symmetry.*
h *A shape that does not have $\frac{1}{2}$ or $\frac{1}{4}$ turn symmetry does not have a centre of symmetry.*

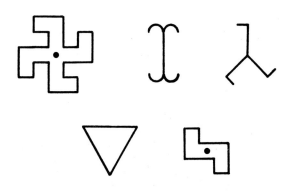

CHECK-UP ON TILING AND SYMMETRY

1 Copy and extend these tiling patterns on squared paper or on tracing paper. Colour them if you wish.

One tile

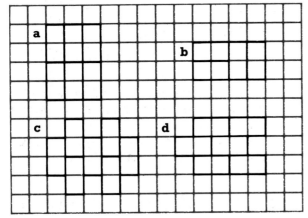

2 How many lines of symmetry does each shape have? Tracing paper may help.

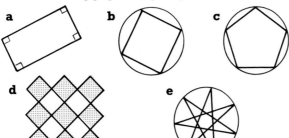

3 Shapes **a** and **b** below are symmetrical about both the *x* and *y*-axes. Write down the coordinates of all of their vertices.

a

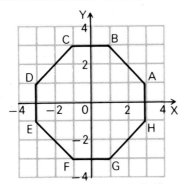

b

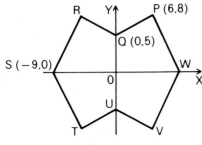

4

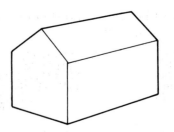

Sketch or trace the solid house shape above. Draw any planes of symmetry you can see.

5 Copy the dots and axes of symmetry on squared paper, or on tracing paper. Then mark the images of the dots under reflection in the axes of symmetry.

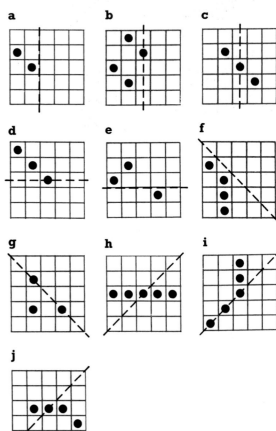

6 a Plot the points A (3, 1), B (−1, 4), C (−2, −2) and D (5, −3) on squared paper.
  b List their images under reflection in:
   (i) the *x*-axis   (ii) the *y*-axis.

7 List the images of points A, B, C and D of question **6** under reflection in the line *y* = *x*, which passes through the points (5, 5) and (−5, −5).

8 Find out whether each shape below has $\frac{1}{4}$-turn or only $\frac{1}{2}$-turn symmetry.

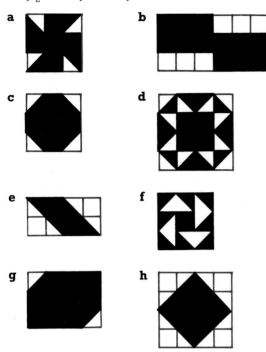

a

b

c

d

e

f

g

h

9 The arrangement of the four blades in a fan has symmetry of order 4. ABCDEF shows one of the blades in more detail.

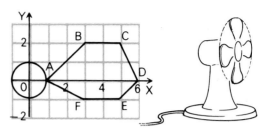

a Copy the diagram on squared paper, and complete it to show the symmetry of the four-blade system.

b List the coordinates of the images of A, B, C, D, E and F after quarter, half and three-quarter anti-clockwise turns.

10 For each design (**a**–**j**) in question **1** of Exercise 3B/C on page 124, find:
  (i) its number of axes of symmetry
  (ii) whether it has: $\frac{1}{4}$-turn symmetry; $\frac{1}{2}$-turn but not $\frac{1}{4}$-turn symmetry; neither.

MEASURING AREA

Washing an elephant takes longer than washing a dog because an elephant's skin has a greater **area** than a dog's skin.

LOOKING BACK

1 Mr Sim needs a new window.

  a What measurements should he take?
  b What will the cost of the glass depend on?

2 Count the number of squares in each of these shapes.

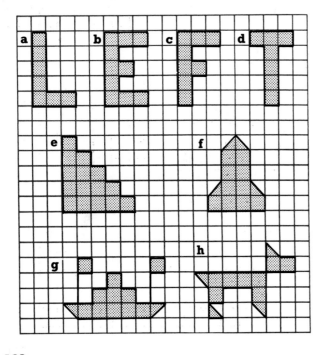

3 Estimate the area of each shape by counting squares.

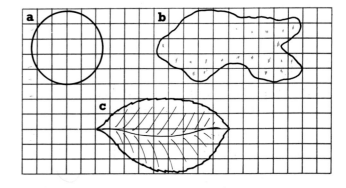

4 The square has an area of 36 square centimetres.
  a Write down the areas of the other shapes, which are made from parts of the square.

(i)

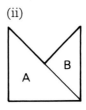

(ii)

(iii)

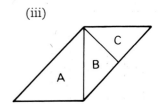

  b Show in diagrams how the parts A, B and C can fit together to make a triangle or a rectangle. What is the area of each one?

THE MEANING OF AREA

/ *CLASS DISCUSSION* /

Steve needs a new barred window for his
workshop. He looks at a few different shapes and
wonders which would let in most light.
Does this depend on the length or height of the
window, or the number of square panes in it? Write
down the length, height and number of panes for
each of the three windows shown.
Which window should Steve buy?

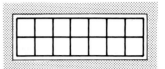

> The number of squares gives a measure of the
> **area** of each window, or the amount of surface
> of each window.

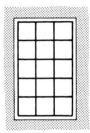

EXERCISE 1A

1 Find the areas of these windows, in squares. List
them in order, largest to smallest.

a 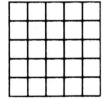   **b**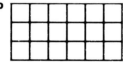

c 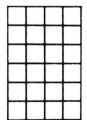   **d**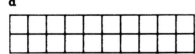

e

2 These paved areas all use the same size of slabs.
How many slabs are in each? Which covers the
largest area?

a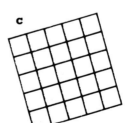

b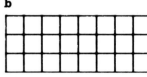

c 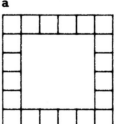   **d**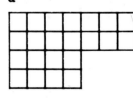

e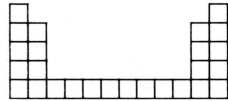

Areas are often measured in square centimetres, or cm².

The area of this rectangle is 6 cm².

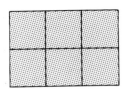

= 1 cm²

3 Estimate the number of square centimetres in the area of each shape below:

a [rectangle]

b
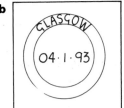

c
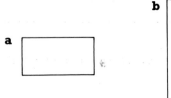

LONDON-PARIS
RETURN TICKET

d BY AIR MAIL
PAR AVION

e
f
g

4 Trace the shapes in question **3** onto centimetre squared paper, or use a transparent grid of centimetre squares to find the area of each shape. Count half squares or more as one square.

5 Find the areas of these four triangles in square centimetres by counting squares and half squares.

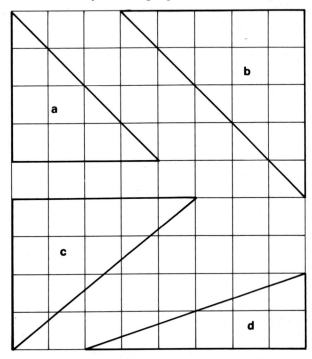

6 Plot these points on squared paper, join them in order, and find the area of each shape in square units:
  a O (0, 0), A (6, 0), B (6, 4), C (0, 4), O (0, 0)
  b D (3, 2), E (7, 2), F (7, 6), D (3, 2)
  c G (5, 3), H (−2, 3), I (−2, −1), J (5, −1), G (5, 3)
  d K (4, 0), L (0, 8), M (−4, 0), K (4, 0)
  e P (2, 0), Q (4, 0), R (6, 2), S (6, 4), T (4, 6), U (2, 6), V (0, 4), W (0, 2), P (2, 0)

/ **PRACTICAL PROJECT**

Place your hand, with fingers closed together, on top of centimetre squared paper, and draw round its edge. Count squares to find the area of your hand. Compare it with others in the class.

THE AREA OF A RECTANGLE

CLASS DISCUSSION

1 How can you find the area of this rectangle without counting the squares one by one?

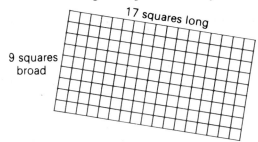

17 squares long

9 squares broad

2 Now calculate the areas of these windows without counting squares.

a

b

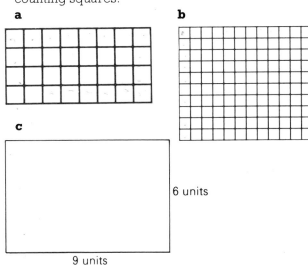

c

6 units

9 units

To calculate an area:
a count squares
   or
b use **area of rectangle = length × breadth.**
   Formula: $A = \ell \times b$, or $A = \ell b$

A b

ℓ

Finding area means finding the number of squares.

Types of square:
1 square millimetre (1 mm²),
1 square centimetre (1 cm²),
1 square metre (1 m²),
1 square kilometre (1 km²).

1 square millimetre, or 1 mm²

3 Which type of square would you use to measure the area of:
   a a page of this book
   b the letter O
   c the classroom floor
   d Scotland
   e your desk top
   f the blackboard
   g an insect's wing
   h the Atlantic Ocean
   i a sports field
   j a footprint
   k a calculator key
   l a compact disc?

EXERCISE 1B

1 Find the area of each object below. Remember to include the units of area in your answers.

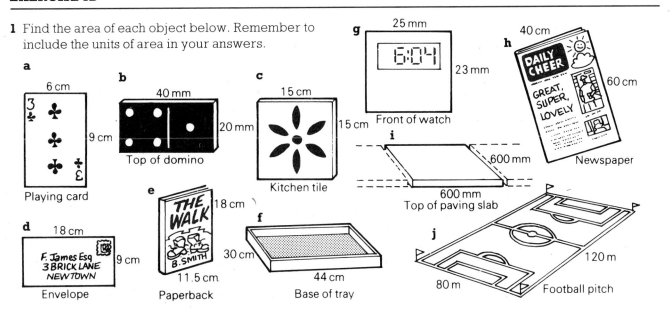

a
6 cm
9 cm
Playing card

b
40 mm
20 mm
Top of domino

c
15 cm
15 cm
Kitchen tile

g
25 mm
6:04
23 mm
Front of watch

h
40 cm
60 cm
DAILY CHEER
GREAT, SUPER, LOVELY
Newspaper

i
600 mm
600 mm
Top of paving slab

d
18 cm
F. James Esq
3 BRICK LANE
NEW TOWN
9 cm
Envelope

e
THE WALK
B. SMITH
18 cm
11.5 cm
Paperback

f
30 cm
44 cm
Base of tray

j
120 m
80 m
Football pitch

2

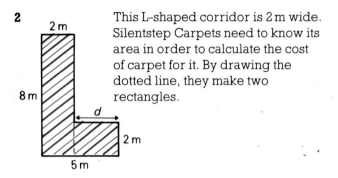

This L-shaped corridor is 2 m wide. Silentstep Carpets need to know its area in order to calculate the cost of carpet for it. By drawing the dotted line, they make two rectangles.

a What length is *d*, in metres?
b Calculate:
  (i) the area of each rectangle
  (ii) the total area of carpet required.

3 To check Silentstep's method, sketch the corridor and draw another dotted line which gives two different rectangles. Use these to calculate the area.

4 Another method would be to draw two dotted lines on the outside, to complete an 8 m by 5 m rectangle. Then calculate the area of the corridor by subtracting the area of a rectangle.

5 Repeat the calculations in questions **2–4**, for this corridor:

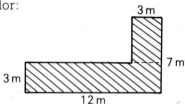

EXERCISE 1C

1 Sketch three different rectangles, each of which has an area of 12 cm². (All sides must be a whole number of centimetres: 2, 3, 4 etc.)

2 Calculate the lengths of these objects:

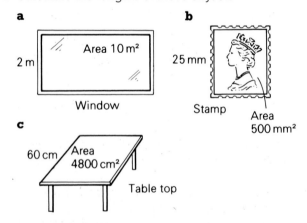

a Window — Area 10 m², 2 m

b Stamp — 25 mm, Area 500 mm²

c Table top — 60 cm, Area 4800 cm²

3 This square garden has a square pond in the middle with sides 4 m long.

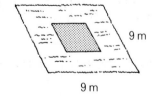

Calculate the area of:
a the whole garden
b the pond
c the lawn area around the pond.

4 Calculate the areas of these shapes by sketching them, and dividing them into suitable rectangles.

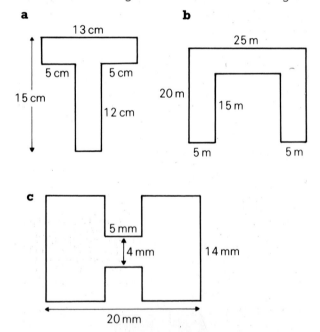

a 13 cm, 5 cm, 5 cm, 15 cm, 12 cm

b 25 m, 20 m, 15 m, 5 m, 5 m

c 5 mm, 4 mm, 14 mm, 20 mm

5 Copy and complete this table of rectangle calculations.

Length (cm)	7	5		8		
Breadth (cm)	9		12		40	
Perimeter (cm)		16	52			30
Area (cm²)				80	2000	50

Large areas, like farm fields, are measured in **hectares**. 1 hectare = 10 000 m².
Very large areas, like whole countries, are measured in **square kilometres**.

6 A rectangular sports field is 300 m long and 200 m broad. Calculate its area in:
a m²   **b** hectares.

7 Some maps have 10 km square grids on them.
   a Calculate the area of one square in km².
   b Write down the length and breadth of a square in metres.
   c Calculate the area of a square in:
      (i) m²   (ii) hectares.

PRACTICAL PROJECTS

Choose some of the following, or some other objects if you prefer. Estimate their areas. Then measure, or calculate, the areas. Use appropriate units, and round off where necessary. Compile a report, and include a comparison of your estimates with the actual areas.

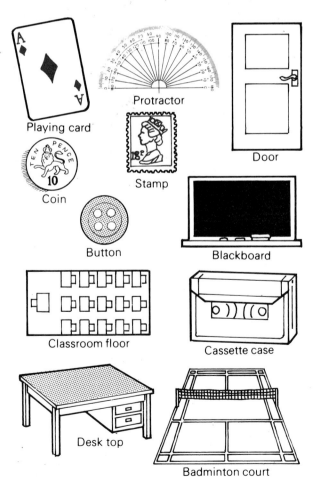

Playing card

Protractor

Door

Stamp

Coin

Button

Blackboard

Classroom floor

Cassette case

Desk top

Badminton court

BRAINSTORMER

1 *Find the area, in squares, of each triangle.*

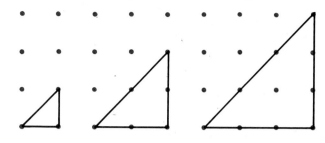

2 *Copy and complete the table.*

Length of side of triangle	1	2	3	4	5	6		10		n
Area of triangle (squares)										

INVESTIGATION

This diagram shows shapes with perimeters of 3 and 4 units that can be drawn on dotty paper.

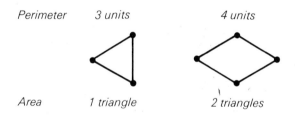

Perimeter	3 units	4 units
Area	1 triangle	2 triangles

1 *Investigate all the shapes, and their areas, that can be drawn with 5, 6, 7 and 8 unit perimeters.*

2 **a** *Find the shape in each group that has the greatest area, in triangles.*
   b *Then, find the shape with the smallest area, in triangles, in each group—can you see a rule?*

3 *Does an odd number of units in the perimeter mean there will be an odd number of units of area? Does an even number give an even number?*

4 *Investigate for shapes with larger perimeters.*

EXERCISE 2A

1 The paving stones for these patterns are 1 m by 1 m squares, and cost £8 each. Calculate:
  (i) the area of each path
  (ii) the cost of the paving stones.

a

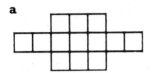

b

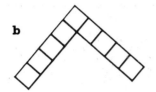

c

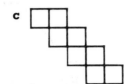

2 Paving stones of the same size which cost £12 each are used for these garden patios. Calculate:
  (i) the area of each patio
  (ii) the cost of paving it.

a

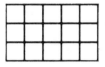

b

c

d

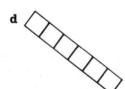

3 Cora is tiling part of her kitchen. Each tile is 10 cm by 5 cm.

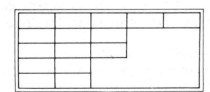

  a How many tiles does she need altogether for the area shown?
  b What is the length and breadth of the area she is tiling?

4 a How many tiles would Cora need for a section eight tiles long and six tiles high?
  b How many tiles would fit into 1 square metre, 100 cm by 100 cm?

5

CARPET SALE

50% wool – £9.99 per m²
80% wool – £16.75 per m²

The area of Mary's bedroom floor is 20 m². How much would it cost to cover it with:
  a 50% wool carpet   **b** 80% wool carpet?

6 Mary's living room is 7 m long and 5 m broad. How much would each type of carpet cost for this room?

7 Carpet comes in rolls 1 m wide.

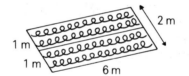 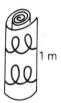

  a What length is needed to cover this floor?
  b How much would it cost in total if the carpet is £18 per square metre?

8 a Sketch two different ways of laying the 1 m wide carpet on this floor. Which method is better?

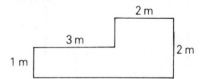

  b Calculate the cost at £18 per m².

EXERCISE 2B/C

1

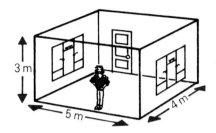

Jan Summers wants to paint her dining room. First she takes a few measurements, to the nearest metre.

If the room could be 'opened out' it would look like this:

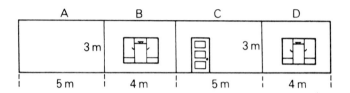

a Calculate the area of all four walls. (Don't worry about the windows and door at this stage.)

b The door is 2 m high and 1 m wide. Each window is 1.5 m high and 2 m wide. Calculate the area of the door and the two windows.

c What area has to be painted?

d A tin of paint covers 35 m². How many tins should Jan buy?

e She decides to paint the ceiling too, using the same paint. Will she have to buy more tins? Explain your answer.

2 Later, Jan decides to buy new fitted carpets for her house. Calculate the cost for the dining room (see question **1**) at £21.75 per m², and for these rooms:

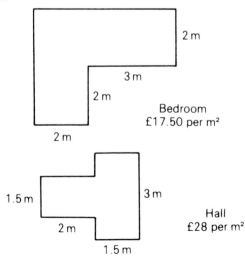

Bedroom
£17.50 per m²

Hall
£28 per m²

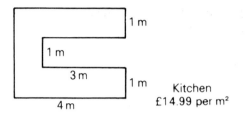

Kitchen
£14.99 per m²

3 Jan employs Mr Green to put a new lawn in her garden. He can either lay turf or sow grass seed.

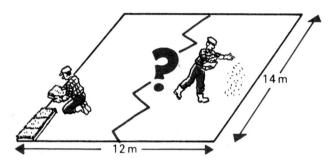

A turf is a square section of grass which measures ½ m by ½ m, like the one shown.

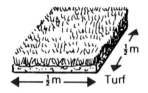

a How many pieces of turf does he need to cover one square metre?

b The lawn will be a 12 metre by 14 metre rectangle. What is its area?

c How many pieces of turf does he need to buy?

d If each turf costs 50p, how much will it cost to lay the lawn?

4 Grass seed is sold in boxes which contain enough seed for 10 m². Each box of seed costs £4.75.

a How many boxes of seed would Mr Green need?

b What would the cost be?

c Which method is cheaper—turf or seed? By how much?

d Why might someone choose the dearer method?

1 Which of these two shapes has the greater area?

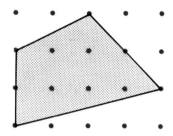

2 The dots are 1 cm apart. What is the area of this shape?

Nina is making place-mats for the dinner table. She takes strips of material like this:

and weaves them like this:

into a square-shaped mat like this:

a What area of material does she use?
b What is the area of the mat?
Explain the difference between your answers.

1 You have a closed loop of rope 16 m long, four pegs and a hammer. Your task is to peg out the rectangle with the largest possible area.

a Copy and complete this table.

Length (m)	1	2	3	4	5	6	7
Breadth (m)	7	6	5				
Area (m²)	7						

Which dimensions would you choose?
b Repeat the task for ropes of length:
(i) 18 m   (ii) 20 m.
c Describe the rectangle with perimeter x metres, and largest possible area.

2 a The side of a square courtyard is exactly 10 m long. What is its area?
b If the sides are 10 m long, to the nearest metre:
  (i) write down the range of length of each side, to 0.1 metre
  (ii) calculate the least and greatest areas of the courtyard.

Investigate the area of paper used in different newspapers, magazines or books. Are the prices of the publications related to the areas of paper used?

THE AREA OF A TRIANGLE

Right-angled triangles

Rachel and Marc were talking about how to calculate area. Rachel said that rectangles were easy—'just length × breadth'. Marc then said that right-angled triangles were easy too—'half the area of the rectangle'.

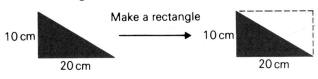

Make a rectangle

Area of rectangle = 20 × 10 cm²
= 200 cm²
So area of triangle = $\frac{1}{2}$ × 200 cm²
= 100 cm²

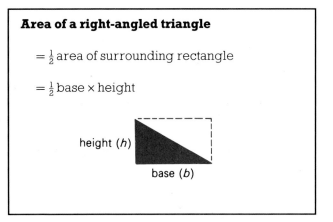

Area of a right-angled triangle

= $\frac{1}{2}$ area of surrounding rectangle

= $\frac{1}{2}$ base × height

height (*h*)

base (*b*)

EXERCISE 3A

1 Jan makes wooden triangle shapes from squares and rectangles. Calculate the area of:
  (i) each square or rectangle
  (ii) each triangle.

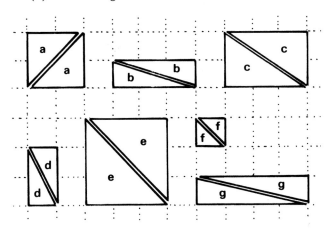

2 Copy these right-angled triangles on squared paper, and complete a rectangle for each one. Then calculate the areas of the triangles.

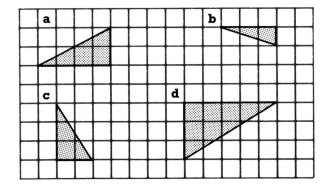

3 Calculate the area of each shaded right-angled triangle.

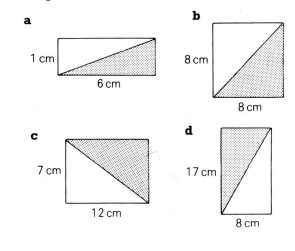

a 1 cm   6 cm

b 8 cm   8 cm

c 7 cm   12 cm

d 17 cm   8 cm

4 Calculate the areas of these right-angled triangles.

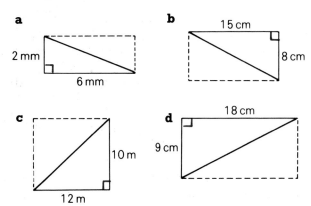

a 2 mm   6 mm

b 15 cm   8 cm

c 10 m   12 m

d 18 cm   9 cm

5 Calculate the area of each sail.

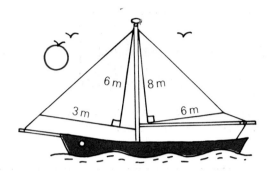

6 What area has to be painted below the stairs?

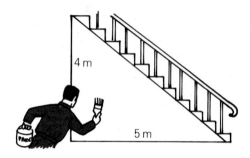

7

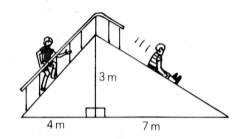

Calculate:
a the area of each triangle
b the total area below the slide.

8 Find the *total* wing area of the plane.

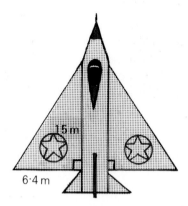

9 A machine has been programmed to cut out a triangle of metal.
  a Plot the vertices of the triangle on squared paper: (1, 1), (7, 1), (7,6).
  b Calculate the area of metal cut out.

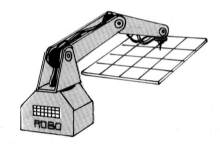

10 The machine has now to cut out a square.
  a Plot its vertices: A (2, 5), B (6, 1), C (10, 5), D (6, 9)
  b Join AB, BC, CD, DA. Then join AC and BD, crossing at M.
  c Write down the lengths of AC and MD.
  d Calculate the area of:
    (i) △ ACD
    (ii) square ABCD.

Area of any triangle

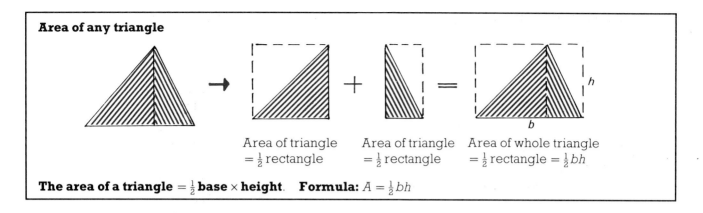

Area of triangle = ½ rectangle

Area of triangle = ½ rectangle

Area of whole triangle = ½ rectangle = ½ bh

The area of a triangle $= \frac{1}{2}$ **base** $\times$ **height**.   **Formula:** $A = \frac{1}{2}bh$

EXERCISE 3B/C

1 Aruna has made six triangles from pairs of right-angled triangles. Calculate the area of each of the six large triangles.

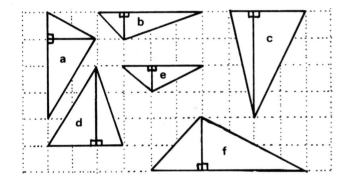

2 Calculate the areas of the large triangles below.

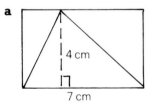

3 Calculate the areas of these triangles:

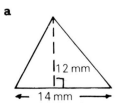

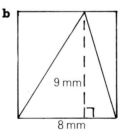

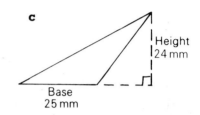

c

Height 24 mm

Base 25 mm

4 Arrange the following triangles in order, smallest area first:

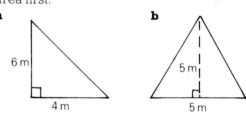

a

6 m

4 m

b

5 m

5 m

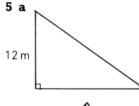

c

3 m

7 m

5 a

12 m

Area of triangle = 60 m². Calculate the length of its base.

b

8 m

Area of triangle = 84 m². Calculate the length of its base.

c

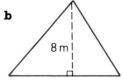

30 m

Area of triangle = 225 m². Calculate its height.

139

6 a On squared paper draw the triangle ABC, where A is the point (1, 1), B is (3, 4) and C is (4, 2).

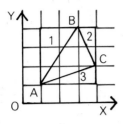

b Draw the rectangle around it with its sides parallel to the *x* and *y*-axes.
c (i) What is the area of the rectangle?
  (ii) What are the areas of triangles 1, 2 and 3?
  (iii) What is the area of triangle ABC?

7 Use the same method to find the area of the triangle PQR, where P is $(-2, -1)$, Q is $(3, 0)$ and R is $(2, 2)$.

8 Find the area of the 'boomerang' shape with corners D $(-3, -1)$, E $(-1, 0)$, F $(1, -1)$ and G $(-1, 1)$.

BRAINSTORMER

Two roads cross at right angles at A. A path runs in a straight line BC from one road to the other.

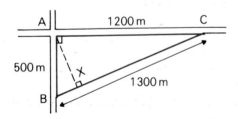

Find:
a *the area of ground in triangle ABC*
b *the shortest distance AX, to the nearest metre, from the cross-roads to the path.*

TANGRAMS

Copy this square and all the lines in it onto a sheet of paper. Cut along the lines to get seven pieces. You can put these together to make lots of different pictures, called tangrams.

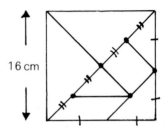

a *Make the pictures below, or some others of your own.*

b *Calculate the area of each of the seven pieces.*

CHECK-UP ON MEASURING AREA

1 Estimate the areas of these shapes in square centimetres. Then find the areas by tracing, or using a transparent centimetre squared grid.

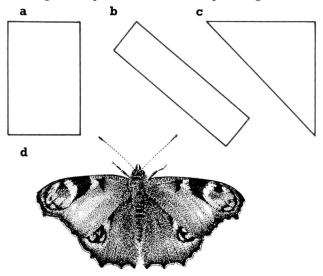

a   **b**   **c**

d

2 Find the area of each rectangular object. Remember to include the units of area (mm², cm² or m²) in your answers.

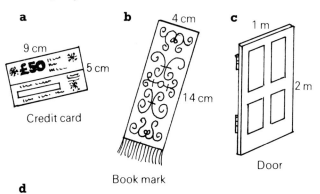

a
9 cm
£50
5 cm
Credit card

b
4 cm
14 cm
Book mark

c
1 m
2 m
Door

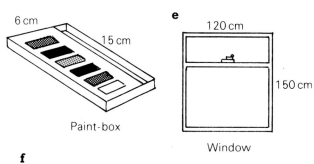

d
6 cm
15 cm
Paint-box

e
120 cm
150 cm
Window

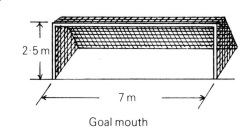

f
2·5 m
7 m
Goal mouth

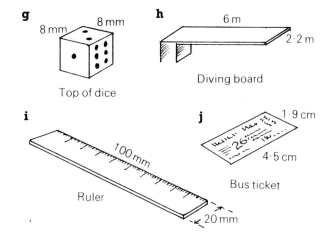

g
8 mm   8 mm
Top of dice

h
6 m
2·2 m
Diving board

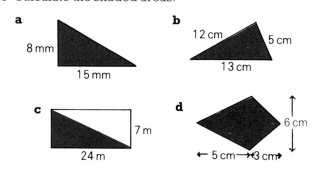

i
100 mm
20 mm
Ruler

j
1·9 cm
26
4·5 cm
Bus ticket

3 Calculate the shaded areas.

a
8 mm
15 mm

b
12 cm
5 cm
13 cm

c
7 m
24 m

d
6 cm
← 5 cm → 3 cm →

4 a Calculate the area of the triangle ABC where A is the point (1, 3), B is (6, 1) and C is (6, 5).
   b D is the point (4, 3). Calculate the area of ABDCA.

5 The roof of a shed is 4 m long, and its sloping edge is 3 m long.
   a What length of felt 1 m wide is needed to cover it?
   b The cost is £66. How much does the felt cost per square metre?

6 In **a** and **b**, calculate the area of △ ABC. In **c**, calculate the height of △ ABC. Units are cm.

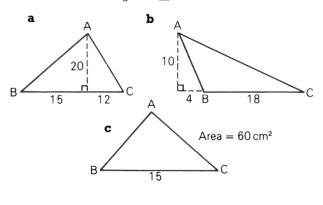

a
A
20
B   15   12   C

b
A
10
4   B   18   C

c
A
B   15   C
Area = 60 cm²

141

1 Find the missing numbers:
  a $\square + 8 = 15$ **b** $7 \times \square = 28$
  c $2 \times \square + 3 = 13$ **d** $5 \times \square - 6 = 9$

2 Which numbers do the letters stand for in these sequences?

  a $4, 8, 12, x, \ldots$ **b** $4, 8, 16, y, \ldots$
  c $100, k, 98, 97, \ldots$ **d** $81, 27, 9, n, 1, \ldots$

3 Write down a fourth term for each sequence:
  a $2 \times 1, 2 \times 2, 2 \times 3, \ldots$ **b** $3 + 1, 4 + 1, 5 + 1, \ldots$
  c $4 \times 1 + 5, 4 \times 2 + 5, 4 \times 3 + 5, \ldots$

4 Which numbers are missing from the sequences of numbers in column A?

a

	A
1	4
2	8
3	12
4	
5	

b

	A
1	7
2	14
3	21
4	
5	

c

	A
1	3
2	6
3	9
4	
5	

d

	A
1	4
2	7
3	10
4	
5	

5 Copy and complete the rows and columns of numbers in the sequences in these spreadsheets.

a

	A	B	C	D
1	3	4	5	
2	6	8		
3			15	18
4	12	16		24
5	15	20	25	

b

	A	B	C	D
1	3	5		9
2	6		14	
3		15		27
4		20	28	
5	15			45

6 How can you work out the numbers in column A from the row numbers in these examples?

a

	A
Row 1	2
Row 2	3
Row 3	4
Row 4	5
Row 5	6

b

	A
1	2
2	4
3	6
4	8
5	10

c

	A
1	6
2	7
3	8
4	9
5	10

d

	A
1	7
2	14
3	21
4	28
5	35

7 a 3 bicycles.
How many wheels?

b 4 cars.
How many wheels?

c 8 dogs.
How many legs?

d 12 hands.
How many fingers
and thumbs?

e  12 stamps.
How many pounds?

f  15 stamps.
How many shillings?

LETTERS AND NUMBERS

Given $m = 5$ and $n = 2$, find the values of:

a $m+3$ **b** $4n$ **c** $2m+2n$

a $m+3$
$= 5+3$
$= 8$

b $4n$
$= 4 \times 2$
$= 8$

c $2m+2n$
$2 \times 5 + 2 \times 2$
$= 10 + 4$
$= 14$

EXERCISE 1A

1 $m = 5$. Calculate the values of:
a $m+4$ **b** $m-1$ **c** $m+9$ **d** $m-5$ **e** $11+m$

2 $n = 2$. Calculate the values of:
a $n+3$ **b** $n-1$ **c** $6+n$ **d** $n+9$ **e** $2-n$

3 $x = 10$. Calculate the values of:
a $2x$ **b** $3x$ **c** $4x$ **d** $5x$ **e** $10x$

4 $y = 2$. Calculate the values of:
a $5y$ **b** $5y+1$ **c** $7y$ **d** $7y-1$ **e** $9y$

5 $t = 3$. Calculate the values of:
a $4t$ **b** $2t+1$ **c** $3-t$ **d** $5t$ **e** $3t-5$

6 $m = 4$ and $n = 1$. Calculate the values of:
a $m+n$ **b** $m-n$ **c** $2m$ **d** $2n$ **e** $2m+2n$

7 $u = 6$ and $v = 3$. Find the values of:
a $u+v$ **b** $u-v$ **c** $2u+2v$ **d** $3u-3v$
e $4u+5v$

Copy and complete the tables.

8

x	2	3	5	10
$x+1$	3			

9

x	1	4	6	9
$x-1$	0			

10

y	5	1	9	7
$2y$	10			

11

t	0	1	5	10
$3t$				

12

t	1	2	3	4
$3t+1$				

13

c	2	1	6	8
$2c-1$				

14

m	3	5	6	15
n	2	1	5	10
$m+n$				
$m-n$				

15

u	1	4	3	5
v	1	2	3	9
$2u$				
$2u+v$				

If the perimeter of the hexagon is P, then
$P = a + a + a + a + b + b$
$\quad = 4a + 2b$
$P = 4a + 2b$ is a *formula* for the perimeter of the hexagon.
If $a = 3$ and $b = 5$, then $P = 4 \times 3 + 2 \times 5$
$\qquad\qquad\qquad\qquad = 12 + 10$
$\qquad\qquad\qquad\qquad = 22$
If the units are centimetres, the perimeter is 22 cm.

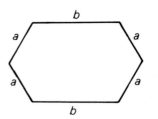

EXERCISE 1B

In questions **1–12**:
a Make a formula for the perimeter P of each shape.
b Use the formula to calculate the perimeter for the given lengths. All lengths are in centimetres.

1

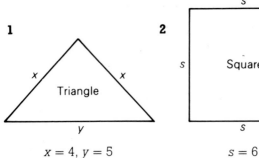

$x = 4, y = 5$

2

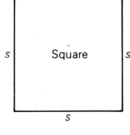

$s = 6$

7

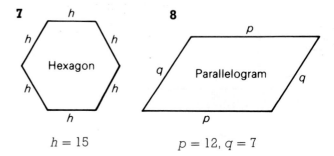

$h = 15$

8

$p = 12, q = 7$

3

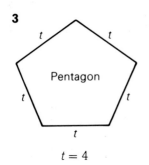

$t = 4$

4

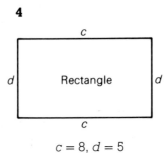

$c = 8, d = 5$

9

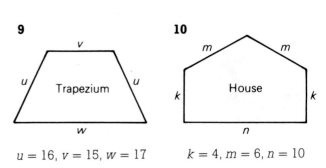

$u = 16, v = 15, w = 17$

10

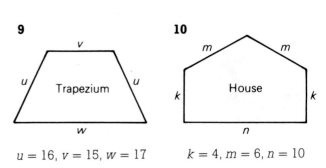

$k = 4, m = 6, n = 10$

5

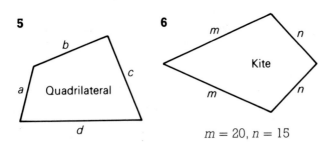

$a = 4, b = 5, c = 6, d = 7$

6

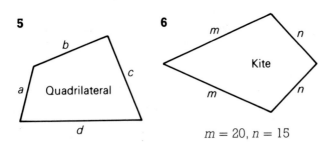

$m = 20, n = 15$

11

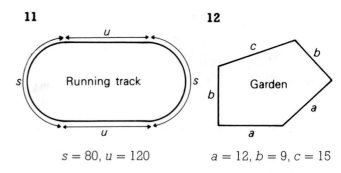

$s = 80, u = 120$

12

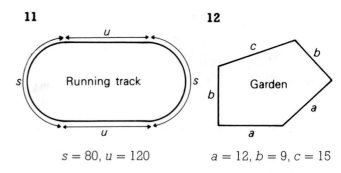

$a = 12, b = 9, c = 15$

EXERCISE 1C

Copy and complete these tables:

1

x	1	2	3	4
$2x+1$	3			

2

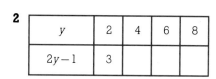

y	2	4	6	8
$2y-1$	3			

3

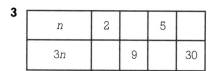

n	2		5	
$3n$		9		30

4

b	0	2	5	9
$3b+2$				

5

d	2	3	4	10
$3d-4$				

6

c	0		4	
$12c$		12		84

7

x	0	2	4	
$6-x$				0

8

u	7	6
v	5	8
$u+v$		
$2u+3v$		

9

y	1	2	4	5
$10-2y$				

10

z			5	9
$2z+1$	1	7		

11

k		4		10
$3k-1$			5	8

12

a	2	5	4		
b	1	2		3	
$a+b$	3		6		12
$a-b$	1			5	4

13

$p+q$				10	18
p	2	3	4	5	
q	3	1	2		5
$2p+q$					

14

	12	14	40		18	12	
	8	10	21	16			22
a	6	7	20	14			
b	2	3	1		6		
	4	4	19		13	6	12
	6	9	3			15	

SEQUENCES

Examples

1 How can you obtain each number in column A from its row number?

Each number in column A is 3 times its row number.

2 Find the missing entries in column A.

The missing entries are $3 \times 20 = 60$
$3 \times 21 = 63$
$3 \times n\ = 3n$

	A
1	3
2	6
3	9
4	12
5	15
20	
21	
n	

EXERCISE 2A

In questions **1** and **2**: (i) Explain how to get each number in column A from its row number.
(ii) Find the missing numbers in column A.

1 a

	A
1	2
2	4
3	6
4	8
5	10
8	
9	
n	

b

	A
1	5
2	10
3	15
4	20
5	25
10	
11	
n	

c

	A
1	4
2	8
3	12
4	16
5	20
23	
24	
n	

2 a

	A
1	10
2	20
3	30
4	40
5	50
13	
14	
n	

b

	A
1	7
2	14
3	21
4	28
5	35
17	
18	
n	

c

	A
1	9
2	18
3	27
4	36
5	45
30	
31	
n	

3

How many leaves are there on:
a 1 plant   **b** 2 plants
c 3 plants   **d** 4 plants
e 10 plants   **f** 100 plants
g x plants   **h** y plants?

6

How many fingers and thumbs are there on:
a 3 hands   **b** 8 hands
c h hands   **d** d hands?

4

How many prongs are there on:
a 1 fork   **b** 2 forks
c 3 forks   **d** 4 forks
e 10 forks   **f** 100 forks
g m forks   **h** n forks?

7

How many wheels are there on:
a 5 cars   **b** 500 cars
c x cars   **d** y cars?

5

How many legs if there are:
a 6 dogs   **b** 10 dogs
c k dogs   **d** t dogs?

8

Find the number of:
a faces on $1, 2, 3, \ldots, m$ cubes
b corners on $1, 2, 3, \ldots, n$ cubes
c edges on $1, 2, 3, \ldots, t$ cubes
d right angles on $1, 2, 3, \ldots, k$ cubes.

EXERCISE 2B/C

In questions **1** and **2**:
(i) Explain how to get each number in column A
   from its row number.
(ii) Find the missing entries in column A.

1 a

	A
1	3
2	4
3	5
4	6
5	7
10	
11	
x	

b

	A
1	7
2	8
3	9
4	10
5	11
20	
21	
n	

c

	A
1	2
2	3
3	4
4	
5	
17	
18	
k	

d

	A
1	5
2	6
3	7
4	
5	
91	
92	
m	

e

	A
1	10
2	11
3	12
4	
5	
124	
125	
t	

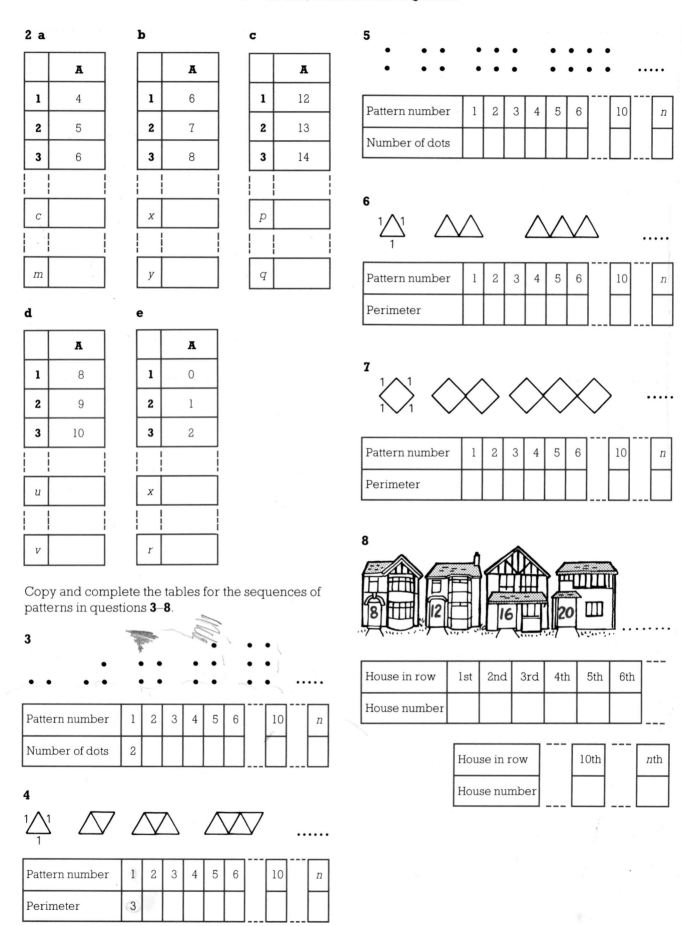

2 a

	A
1	4
2	5
3	6
⋮	
c	
⋮	
m	

b

	A
1	6
2	7
3	8
⋮	
x	
⋮	
y	

c

	A
1	12
2	13
3	14
⋮	
p	
⋮	
q	

d

	A
1	8
2	9
3	10
⋮	
u	
⋮	
v	

e

	A
1	0
2	1
3	2
⋮	
x	
⋮	
r	

Copy and complete the tables for the sequences of patterns in questions **3–8**.

3

Pattern number	1	2	3	4	5	6		10		n
Number of dots	2									

4

Pattern number	1	2	3	4	5	6		10		n
Perimeter	3									

5

Pattern number	1	2	3	4	5	6		10		n
Number of dots										

6

Pattern number	1	2	3	4	5	6		10		n
Perimeter										

7

Pattern number	1	2	3	4	5	6		10		n
Perimeter										

8

House in row	1st	2nd	3rd	4th	5th	6th	
House number							

House in row		10th		nth
House number				

Examples

1 Find the missing entries in column A.

Each number in column A is 7 times its row number.
So the missing entries are:
$7 \times 4 = 28, 7 \times 5 = 35, 7 \times 10 = 70, 7 \times n = 7n$

2 If the nth entry is 56, find n.

$7n = 56$
So $n = 8$

	A
1	7
2	14
3	21
4	
5	
10	
n	

EXERCISE 3A

1 For **a–c** below:
  (i) find the missing entries in column A
  (ii) if the nth entry in each column is 30, find n each time.

a

	A
1	2
2	4
3	6
4	
5	
10	
n	

b

	A
1	3
2	6
3	9
4	
5	
10	
n	

c

	A
1	5
2	10
3	15
4	
5	
10	
n	

2 For **a–c** below:
  (i) find the missing entries in column A
  (ii) if the nth entry in each column is 800, find n each time.

a

	A
1	4
2	8
3	12
4	
5	
10	
n	

b

	A
1	20
2	40
3	60
4	
5	
10	
n	

c

	A
1	25
2	50
3	75
4	
5	
10	
n	

3

How many bananas on 1, 2, 3, . . . , *x* bunches?

4

How many white stripes on 1, 2, 3, . . . , *y* flags?

5

How many holes in 1, 2, 3, . . . , *b* buttons?

6

s stars
How many points?

7

b bunches
How many grapes?

8

w weights
How many grams?

9

n loads
How many sacks?

10

d wheels
How many spokes?

11

m insects
How many legs?

12

r notices
How many: **a** letters
        b vowels?

13

c coins
a How many letters?
b How much money?

14

n gears
How many: **a** teeth
        b chain links?

Examples

1 Find the missing entries in column A.

	A
1	2
2	5
3	8
4	11
⋮	⋮
10	
⋮	⋮
n	

The entries differ by 3, like multiples of 3: 3, 6, 9, 12, . . .
Comparing entries with multiples of 3:

$$2 = 3 \times 1 - 1$$
$$5 = 3 \times 2 - 1$$
$$8 = 3 \times 3 - 1$$

So the 10th entry is $3 \times 10 - 1 = 29$
and the nth entry is $3 \times n - 1 = 3n - 1$

2 a Make a table for the number of matchsticks in patterns 1, 2, 3, 4, 10 and n.
   b Calculate the number of matchsticks in the 25th pattern.

Pattern number	1	2	3	4	10	n
No. of matches	5	9	13	17		

4 4 4

a The entries differ by multiples of 4, and $5 = 4 \times 1 + 1$
$$9 = 4 \times 2 + 1$$
$$13 = 4 \times 3 + 1$$

So the 10th entry is $4 \times 10 + 1 = 41$
and the nth entry is $4 \times n + 1 = 4n + 1$

b The 25th pattern has $4 \times 25 + 1 = 101$ matchsticks

EXERCISE 3B/C

For each part of questions **1** and **2**:
 (i) find the missing entries in column A
 (ii) for the value of the nth term under each table,
    find n.

1 a

	A
1	1
2	3
3	5
4	
5	
10	
n	

nth term = 15

b

	A
1	3
2	5
3	7
4	
5	
10	
n	

nth term = 29

c

	A
1	4
2	6
3	8
4	
5	
10	
n	

nth term = 20

d

	A
1	4
2	7
3	10
4	
5	
10	
n	

nth term = 37

e

	A
1	5
2	8
3	11
4	
5	
10	
n	

nth term = 26

2 a

	A
1	3
2	7
3	11
4	
5	
10	
n	

nth term = 27

b

	A
1	5
2	9
3	13
4	
5	
10	
n	

nth term = 49

c

	A
1	6
2	11
3	16
4	
5	
10	
n	

nth term = 76

d

	A
1	4
2	10
3	16
4	
5	
10	
n	

nth term = 118

e

	A
1	7
2	10
3	13
4	
5	
10	
n	

nth term = 40

For questions **3–10** opposite:

a make tables like the one shown for the matchstick designs

Pattern number	1	2	3	4		10		n
Number of matches								

b calculate the number of matches in the 25th pattern of each square.

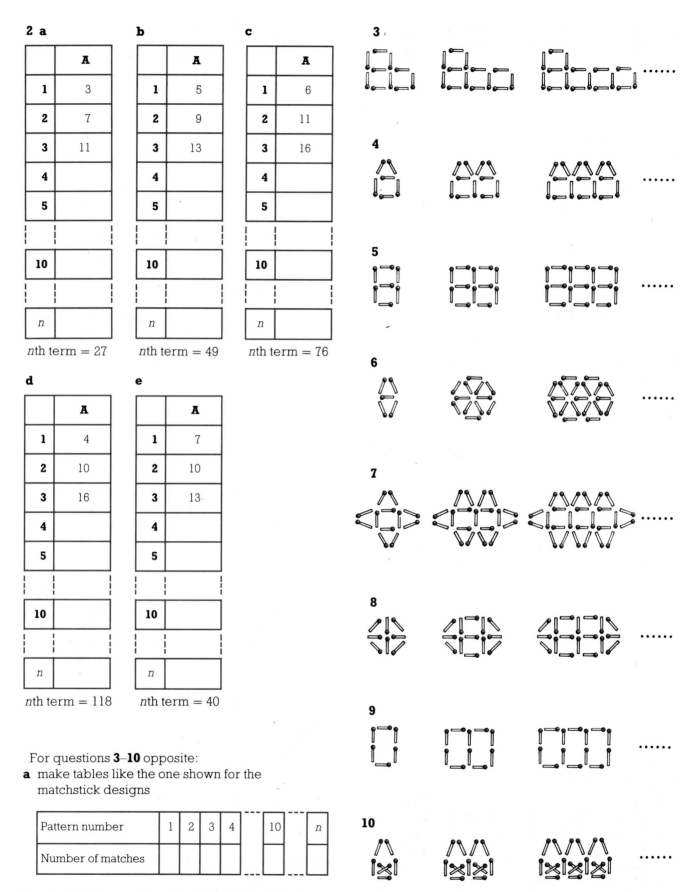

3

4

5

6

7

8

9

10

11 1 table, 4 chairs   2 tables, 6 chairs   3 tables, 8 chairs

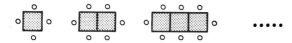

x tables. How many chairs?

12 1 table, 6 chairs   2 tables, 8 chairs   3 tables, 10 chairs

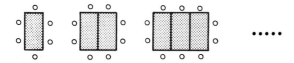

y tables. How many chairs?

13 1 table, 6 chairs   2 tables, 10 chairs   3 tables, 14 chairs

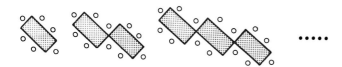

z tables. How many chairs?

14 Plan some arrangements using one or both of these tables. In each case, calculate the number of seats for x tables.

CHALLENGES

1 In a 3 by 3 magic square, each number from 1 to 9 is used once, and the numbers in each row, column and diagonal have the same total.

  a Complete as many different magic squares as you can. Which number is always in the same place?

  b Take $a = 5$, $b = 4$ and $c = 1$, and calculate the values of the entries in the following square. Is it a magic square?

$a-b$	$a+b-c$	$a+c$
$a+b+c$	a	$a-b-c$
$a-c$	$a-b+c$	$a+b$

    Investigate the result for other values of a, b and c. Take a larger than b, b larger than c.

  c Add the letters in each row, column and diagonal. What do you find?

2 a Investigate the number of 'inside' matches in each pattern in questions **3–10** of Exercise 3B/C. Find the number of 'inside' matches in the nth term of each sequence.

Inside matches

  b Repeat **a** for the number of 'outside' matches.

  c Compare your answers with those for the complete patterns. What do you find?

INVESTIGATION

1 Investigate the results of these computer programs when N is replaced by the given numbers. (Line numbers have been left out.)

  a FOR N = 1 TO 5
    PRINT 2*N+1
    NEXT N

  b FOR N = 1 TO 10
    PRINT N*N
    NEXT N

  c FOR N = 1 TO 6
    PRINT N*(N+1)
    NEXT N

  d FOR N = 1 TO 5
    PRINT 100−3*N
    NEXT N

2 Write programs that print out:

  a 1, 3, 5, 7, 9

  b 3, 7, 11, 15, 19, 23, 27

  c 13, 21, 29, 37

CHECK-UP ON LETTERS, NUMBERS AND SEQUENCES

1 Find the missing entries in column A.

a

	A
1	5
2	10
3	15
17	
18	
n	

b

	A
1	3
2	6
3	9
43	
44	
x	

c

	A
1	2
2	3
3	4
30	
t	

d

	A
1	11
2	12
3	13
w	
k	

2
c clocks.
How many hands?

3
s stars.
How many points?

4
h houses.
How many windows?

5
n cars. How many:
a wheels **b** headlights?

6
t elephants.
How many:
a legs
b legs on the ground?

7 $x = 5$ and $y = 2$. Find the values of:
a $x+7$ **b** $2x$ **c** $3x+1$ **d** $6y$ **e** $y-2$ **f** $4y+12$

8 Copy and complete these tables.

a

a	2	5	8	10
$5a$				

b

b	1	2	4	6
$b \times b$				

c

c	0	3	6	9
$2c+1$				

9

Copy and complete this table for the sequence of triangles of matches.

Number of triangles	1	2	3	4	5	6	n
No. of matches in perimeter							
No. of matches in shape							

10 Fruit trees cost £15 each.
  a If post and packing is £1 per tree, find the cost of:
    (i) 1 tree   (ii) 5 trees   (iii) n trees.
  b If post and packing is £5 per order, find the cost of:
    (i) 1 tree   (ii) 2 trees   (iii) 3 trees
    (iv) n trees.

11 Find the missing entries in column A.

a

	A
1	8
2	13
3	18
4	23
5	28
⋮	
69	
70	
⋮	
w	

b

	A
1	4
2	13
3	22
4	31
5	40
⋮	
56	
57	
⋮	
r	

c

	A
1	15
2	23
3	31
4	39
5	47
⋮	
28	
29	
⋮	
k	

d

	A
1	24
2	41
3	58
4	75
5	92
⋮	
123	
124	
⋮	
t	

e

	A
1	13
2	32
3	51
4	70
5	89
⋮	
107	
108	
⋮	
c	

1 The world is full of shapes of all kinds. Name the ones below.

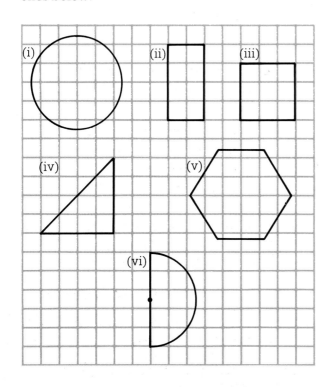

2 Which shape or shapes in question **1** have:
  a four sides
  b a curved edge
  c at least one right angle
  d most sides and angles
  e line symmetry
  f half-turn symmetry about their centres?

3 List LOGO instructions (Forward 2, etc) for drawing shapes (ii), (iii) and (iv) in question **1**, starting at the bottom left-hand corner of each.

4 Make a table like this of 2-dimensional shapes that you can see in the classroom:

Shape	Object

5 In the real world, all of the objects in the pictures at the top of the page are 3-dimensional, but their surfaces are 2-dimensional. Which 2-dimensional shapes would you see if you were standing beside them?

6 Draw these shapes on squared paper:
  a a rectangle with sides 2 cm and 4 cm long
  b a square with sides 3 cm long
  c a triangle with two of its sides 4 cm long, and a right angle between them.

THE RECTANGLE—SIDES AND SYMMETRY

Cut out a rectangle from squared paper.
Fold it so that the two parts match exactly.
Open it out, and fold it in a different way to match.

Do the parts match when you fold it along a diagonal?
How many axes of symmetry have you found?

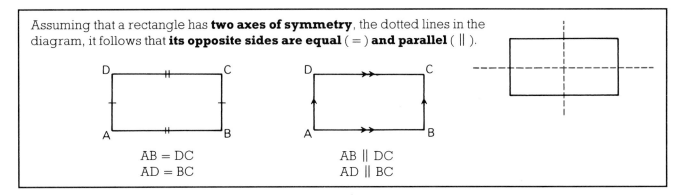

Assuming that a rectangle has **two axes of symmetry**, the dotted lines in the diagram, it follows that **its opposite sides are equal** (=) **and parallel** (‖).

AB = DC
AD = BC

AB ‖ DC
AD ‖ BC

EXERCISE 1A

1 The cover of this book is a rectangle. Write down the lengths of the top and the left-hand side (SR and PS).

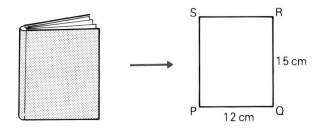

2 Write down the lengths of the unmarked sides of these rectangles, in this form, DC = 12 cm.

a

D   12 cm   C

8 cm

A   B

b

H   G

E   14 m   F   7 m

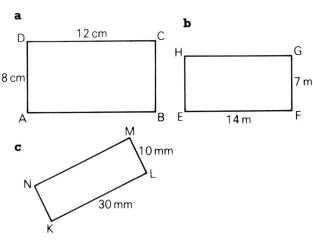

c

M
10 mm
L
N
30 mm
K

3 In the rectangles in question **2**, name the sides that are parallel to:
a AD   **b** HG   **c** (i) KL   (ii) KN.

4 Calculate the perimeter of each of these rectangles (the total distance round its edges).

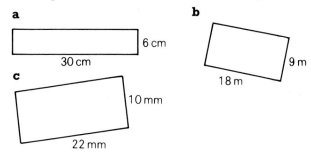

a

30 cm   6 cm

c

22 mm   10 mm

b

18 m   9 m

5 a Copy this diagram on squared paper.

Y
4
3   D
2
1   A

0 1 2 3 4 5 6 7 8 X

b Complete rectangle ABCD so that the dotted line is an axis of symmetry.
c Write down the coordinates of B and C.

6 a Measure the width of your notebook page in three places.
b Why do these measurements suggest that the opposite edges are parallel?

7 Draw a rectangle ABCD, and mark pairs of parallel sides with arrows.

157

8 a Why must railway lines always be the same distance apart?

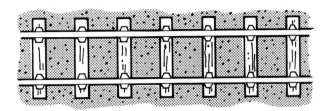

   b Are these railway lines parallel?
   c Are the railway sleepers parallel?

9 a AD = 3 units. Write down the names and lengths of the other sides of the rectangle.

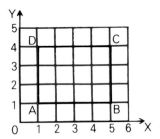

   b Name the pairs of parallel sides.

10 On squared paper draw the rectangle PQRS with P(2, 1), Q(5, 1) and R(5, 7).
   a What are the coordinates of S?
   b Which pairs of sides are equal?
   c What are the lengths of the sides?

11 Repeat question **10** for the rectangle OQRS, where O is the origin, Q is the point (6, 0) and R is (6, 5).

12 a Why are doors rectangular?

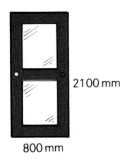

   b All the wooden parts of the door are 150 mm wide. Calculate the width and height of the two congruent glass panels.

13 a Find the total length of wood needed to make the goalposts and bar across the top.

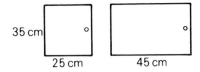

   b The goalkeeper can reach up to 2.3 m with his feet on the ground. How high must he jump to reach the bar?

14 Smoothline Kitchen Cabinets come in two different sizes:

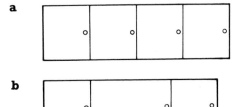

Find the total lengths of the combinations shown below.

   a

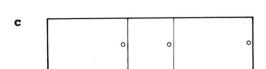

   b

   c

15 The frame of the box kite is made of wire rectangles.

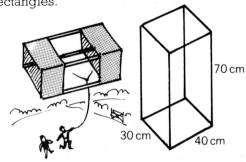

   a How many rectangles are there in the frame altogether?
   b Copy the frame, and fill in the lengths of all the wire edges.
   c Then calculate the total length of wire in the frame.

EXERCISE 1B/C

1 a Calculate the length of the safety rail right round the top of this block of flats.

b What height is each flat?

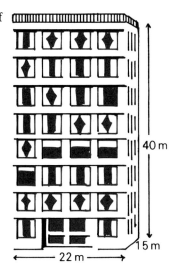

40 m

15 m

22 m

2 E is the point (3, 3) and G is (8, 5). EFGH is a rectangle with EF parallel to the *x*-axis and EH parallel to the *y*-axis.
Draw the rectangle on squared paper. Write down:
a the coordinates of F and H
b the names and lengths of the sides
c the names of the parallel sides.

3 Repeat question **2** for points E(−2, −1) and G(2, 3).

4 Calculate the perimeters of the rectangles in questions **2** and **3**.

5 Plot the points K(2, −1) and L(2, 2). There are two possible rectangles KLMN which have perimeter 16 units. Find the coordinates of M and N for each rectangle.

6 A sheep farmer has 30 metres of fencing. He plans to use it to make a rectangular sheep pen. Find all possible lengths and breadths he could choose, keeping to whole numbers of metres.

7 ABCD is a rectangle. A is the point (0, 2), B is (2, 0) and C is (7, 5). Find the coordinates of D, and of the point E where the diagonals cross.

8 a Keep folding a rectangular piece of paper, so that the parts match each time, until you see how to fill in this table. Copy and complete it.

Number of folds	0	1	2	3	...
Number of rectangles	1				...

b How many rectangles would there be after:
 (i) 7 folds
 (ii) 10 folds
 (iii) *n* folds?

/ **CHALLENGE** /

Trace these shapes, and mark the letters on them as shown. Cut them out of your tracing paper, or transfer them onto card.

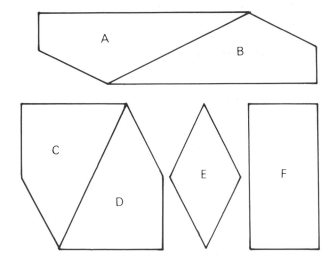

1 *Fit parts A, B, C, D and E together to form a rectangle, with the diamond E in the middle.*

2 *Fit parts A, B, C, D and F together to form a diamond, with the rectangle F in the middle.*

ANGLES

From the tiling of congruent rectangles you can see that there are equal angles at each of the four corners.

a What is the sum of the angles round a point?
b What is the size of each angle?

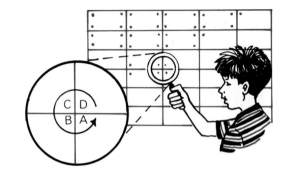

> **All the angles of a rectangle are right angles.**

EXERCISE 2

1 Copy these rectangles, and fill in the sizes (in degrees) of all the unmarked angles.

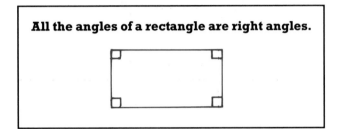

a

b

c

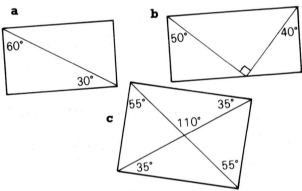

2 Draw a rectangle ABCD. Mark:
   a pairs of equal sides   **b** pairs of parallel sides
   c all the right angles.

3 What is the sum of the four angles of a rectangle, in degrees?

4 Name each unmarked angle in the rectangle KLMN, and give its size, in degrees.

5 Calculate the size of the unmarked angles at R, S, T and U. What kind of shape is RSTU?

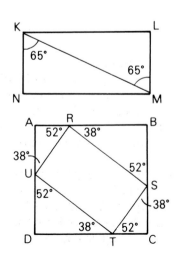

6 a How many right angles are there on this side view of a brick wall?

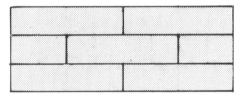

   b How many rectangles can you see? (There are a lot more than 7!)

7 a Copy this gate, and fill in as many angles as you can.

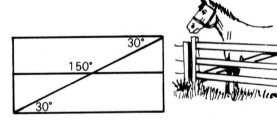

   b What shapes help to make the gate strong?

8 Rectangle ABCD rotates 20° clockwise about A. Find the sizes of the angles marked $a°$, $b°$ and $x°$.

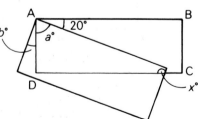

9 Rectangular windows open in many different ways. Describe some of these ways, with the help of sketches.

DIAGONALS

If rectangle ABCD is folded about the dotted line of symmetry, then A → B and C → D.
So AC → BD,
and AC = BD.

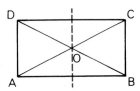

The diagonals of a rectangle are equal, AC = BD.

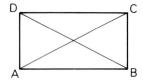

If rectangle ABCD is folded about its lines of symmetry, then OA → OB → OC → OD.
So OA = OB = OC = OD.

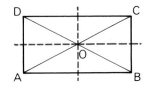

The diagonals of a rectangle bisect each other (cut each other in half).

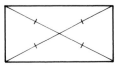

EXERCISE 3A

1 Find the lengths of all the lines named below each rectangle.

a

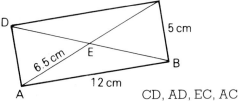

CD, AD, EC, AC

b

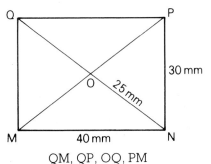

QM, QP, OQ, PM

c

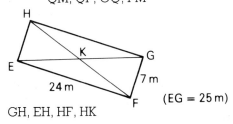

(EG = 25 m)

GH, EH, HF, HK

2 a Draw a rectangle PQRS, and join PR and QS, crossing at O.
  b Mark PQ = 8 cm, QR = 6 cm and PR = 10 cm
  c Write down the lengths of OP, OQ, OR, OS.

3

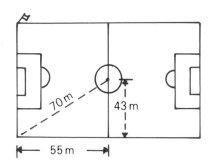

Calculate:
a the length and breadth of the pitch
b the distance from the centre to:
    (i) a corner flag   (ii) a goalmouth
c the shortest and the longest straight line distances between two of the corner flags.

4 Draw several pairs of equal lines AB and CD which cross at their midpoint O. Join AC, CB, BD and DA, to see the different shapes of rectangles you can get.

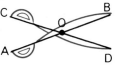

5 Use careful measurement to arrange these rectangles in order, using:
  (i) their lengths
 (ii) their breadths
(iii) their diagonals.

Make three lists, shortest to longest for each measurement. Assume 'length' greater than 'breadth'.

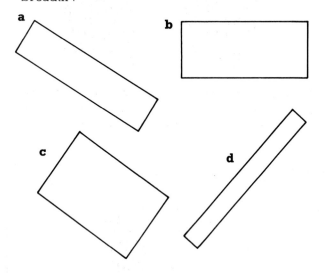

a

b

c

d

6 A(1, 1) and C(5, 3) are opposite corners of rectangle ABCD, with AB parallel to the x-axis and AD parallel to the y-axis.
  a Draw the rectangle and its diagonals crossing at E.
  b Write down the coordinates of B, D and E.

7 Repeat question **6** for A(-2, -4) and C(2, 4).

8

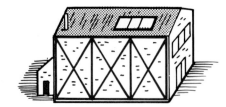

A warehouse has scaffolding on one side. Each rectangular part of it is 4 m wide and 7.5 m high, and has a diagonal strut 8.5 m long. Calculate the total length of the scaffolding poles.

9 Sketch the front of a television set, and show what is meant by 'a 51 cm screen'. What other common sizes are there?

EXERCISE 3B/C

1 D(2, 1) and F(-4, -3) are opposite corners of rectangle DEFG, which is named in a clockwise order.
  a Draw the rectangle and its diagonals crossing at H.
  b Write down the coordinates of E, G and H.

2 P(0, 4), Q(2, 2) and R(6, 6) are corners of a rectangle PQRS.
  a Draw the rectangle and its diagonals crossing at T.
  b Write down the coordinates of S and T.

3

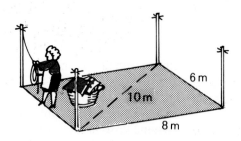

Mrs Jones needs a new washing line. Find the shortest length of rope, in one piece, that she needs to join all four poles, round the sides and across both diagonals of her rectangular lawn. Allow 1 metre extra for loops and knots.

4 A jogging circuit is laid out round a rectangular park ABCD. The park is 400 m long and 300 m broad, and has diagonal paths 500 m long. Calculate two possible lengths of the circuit
A → B → C → D → A → C → D → B → A.

5 Use the axes of symmetry to help you to write down the sizes of the angles marked x° and y° in these rectangles:

a

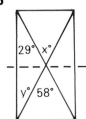

30°   x°   y°

b

29° x°

y° 58°

c

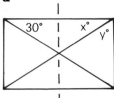

60°   x°

y°

d

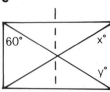

50°

x°

y°

6 An engineering company has to cut diamond shapes from metal sheets which have rectangular grids on them.

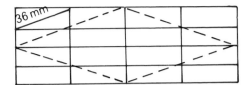

Calculate:
a the perimeter of one of the diamond shapes
b the fraction of each metal sheet that is used.

7 KLMN is a rectangle whose diagonals bisect at P. K is the point $(-7, -2)$, P is $(-2, -1)$ and N is $(-3, -6)$. Find the coordinates of L and M.

The sides and base of this clear plastic tank are rectangles.

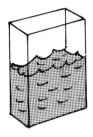 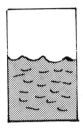

Without measuring, how could you pour out some of the water, to leave the tank half full? Would the same method work for a cylindrical jar?

COMPUTER GRAPHICS

Laura is using her computer to draw on the screen. There is a square grid on the screen, and a flashing dot which tells her where she is at any time.
When she types MOVE (2, 1), the dot moves to the point (2, 1).
When she types DRAW (2, 4), the dot draws a line from (2, 1) to (2, 4).

EXERCISE 4

1 Use a computer and screen, or imagine you are the computer and obey the instructions on squared paper.

MOVE (2, 1)
DRAW (2, 4) } These are shown on the diagram.
DRAW (7, 4)
DRAW (7, 1)
DRAW (2, 1)

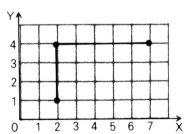

What shape have you drawn?

2 On squared paper draw the rectangle with corners (2, 2), (2, 8), (6, 8) and (6, 2). List instructions for drawing the rectangle by computer.

3 Repeat question **2** for the rectangle with corners (0, 0), (5, 0), (5, 2) and (0, 2).

4 Duncan decided to try drawing on the screen. He began by drawing the diagonals of his rectangle, which he had worked out on squared paper. Follow his instructions on computer or on squared paper.

MOVE (3, 3)
DRAW (5, 9)
MOVE (1, 5)
DRAW (7, 7)

Write out the list of instructions needed to draw his rectangle.

5 Laura typed in these instructions:
MOVE (1, 1)   DRAW (1, 5)   DRAW (7, 5)
a Follow these instructions on computer or on squared paper.
b Laura was trying to draw a rectangle. Complete the instructions, and draw the rectangle.

6 To draw one of the diagonals Laura typed
MOVE (1, 1) DRAW (7, 5).
- **a** Give instructions for drawing the other diagonal.
- **b** What instruction would move the dot to the point where the diagonals cross?

7 a On the same diagram as question **5**, draw three more rectangles congruent to Laura's, with bottom left-hand corners (7, 1), (1, 5) and (7, 5).
- **b** List computer instructions for the first one.
- **c** Join the four points where the diagonals intersect in each rectangle.
- **d** What is special about the shape you've drawn?

8 Pamela made a sketch of the rectangle she wanted to draw on the screen.

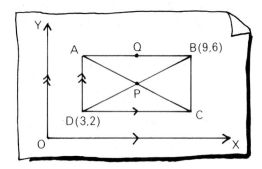

- **a** What are the coordinates of A, C and P?
- **b** She wanted to draw rectangles which formed a brick wall tiling. List the instructions for drawing the rectangle which has its bottom left-hand corner at Q.

9 Draw a sports pitch or court of your choice on a 16 by 16 squared grid. List instructions for drawing all the lines by computer.

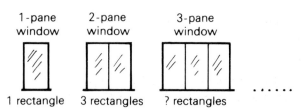

BRAINSTORMER

1-pane window — 1 rectangle
2-pane window — 3 rectangles
3-pane window — ? rectangles

......

a *Copy and complete the table:*

Number of panes	1	2	3	4	5	6
Number of rectangles	1	3				

b *Find a systematic way to count the rectangles. Then calculate the number of rectangles in a 7-pane, 10-pane and n-pane window.*

THE SQUARE—A SPECIAL RECTANGLE

The square is a special rectangle.
It is a rectangle with all its sides equal.

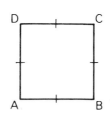

$AB = BC = CD = DA$

EXERCISE 5A

1 Look at shapes **a–j**.

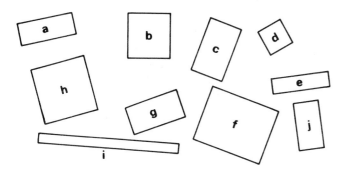

(i) How many squares do you see?
(ii) How many rectangles do you see that are not squares?
(iii) How many rectangles are there altogether?

2 PQRS is a square.
What can you say
about its:
a sides
b angles
c diagonal lengths?

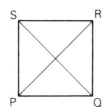

3 a Draw a square ABCD with AB 2 cm long.
b Mark:
  (i) the length of all its sides
  (ii) the size of all its angles.

4

This chequered flag is a tiling of congruent squares.
Can you think of two more examples of square tilings in real life?

5 A cycle race is to be held on a track laid out round some squares in a city centre. Each square is 75 m long. Calculate the length of each lap, from A back to A. Ignore the width of the roads.

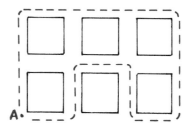

6 a Copy this diagram on squared paper.

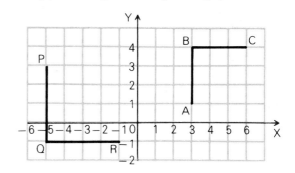

b Complete square ABCD, and write down the coordinates of A, B, C and D.
c Complete square PQRS, and write down the coordinates of P, Q, R and S.

7 A square has two opposite corners at O(0, 0) and S(6, 6). Find the coordinates of its other corners, and the point where its diagonals intersect.

8 a Cut out or trace a large square, using squared paper.
b Fold it in different ways to discover all the axes of symmetry. (You know two of them already. Why?)
c Draw the lines of symmetry as dotted lines.

A square has four axes of symmetry.

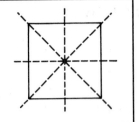

The diagonals of a square:
  (i) bisect the angles of the square
 (ii) bisect each other at right angles.

9 a PQ is an axis of symmetry. Calculate the size of each marked angle.

b PQ is an axis of symmetry. Calculate the size of each angle marked with a cross.

c RS is an axis of symmetry. Write down the size of each marked angle in the square.

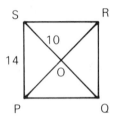

d AC and BD are diagonals, and also axes of symmetry. Name a line equal to:
  (i) AO   (ii) DO.

10 Sketch this square, in which lengths are given to the nearest cm. Fill in the lengths of all the lines and the sizes of all the angles.

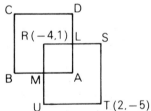

11 A square has corners A(3, 0), B(6, 3), C(3, 6) and D(0, 3). Draw it on squared paper. Write down the lengths of the diagonals and the coordinates of the point where they cross.

EXERCISE 5B/C

1 E(2, 1), F(4, 3), G(2, 5) and H are corners of a square. Find the coordinates of H, and of the point of intersection of its diagonals.

2 K is the point (4, 4) and L is (7, 4). KLMN is a square. Find the coordinates of the two possible positions of M and N.

3 PQRS is a square. P is the point (−1, 1) and R is (1, −3). Find the coordinates of the other two vertices, and of the point of intersection of the diagonals.

4 a Copy this 'nest' of squares on squared paper.
b If the side of each small square in the grid is *x* cm long, calculate the perimeter of the largest square.
c If the diagonal of each small square is *y* cm long, calculate the perimeter of the second largest square.
d Calculate the sum of the perimeters of all four squares in the nest, in its simplest form.

5 Two congruent squares intersect as shown to form a square RLAM. RS is parallel to the x-axis, and L is the midpoint of RS. Find the coordinates of:
a S and U
b A, B, C and D
c the centre of half-turn symmetry of the figure.

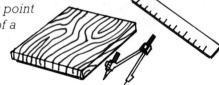

PUZZLES

1 Explain, with the help of drawings, how you could balance a square sheet of wood horizontally on:
a a compass point
b the edge of a ruler.

2 Fold a rectangular piece of paper to make the largest possible square. Which properties of the square helped you to do this?

COMPUTER SQUARES

EXERCISE 6

1 Helen was working at the computer, and started
to draw a square.
MOVE (1, 1).
This plots the point (1, 1).
DRAW (1, 8).
This draws a straight
line from (1, 1) to (1, 8).
DRAW (8, 8).

a On squared paper, or
on the screen, complete
the square.

b List the rest of the
instructions for
drawing the square
on the screen.

2 **a** Draw the diagonals in Helen's square.

b List the instructions for drawing the diagonals
on the screen.

3 Helen is trying to draw
a picture frame. Its outside
edge is the square she has
already drawn. She wants
the frame to be one unit
wide all round.

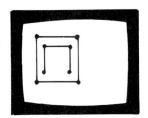

a Draw the complete frame on squared paper or
on a screen.

b List the instructions for drawing the inner
square on the screen.

4 Sam is planning a square
tiling on the screen, with
the sides of the tiles
parallel to the sides of the
screen. Each tile is three
units long, and the point
(8, 9) is the bottom left-
hand corner of one of the
tiles.

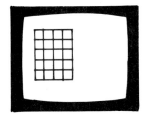

a On squared paper, or on a screen, draw the
four tiles around the point (8, 9).

b What larger shape is formed by these tiles?

c List instructions for drawing this larger shape
on the screen.

5 Sam plans another square tiling, with its diagonals
parallel to the sides of the screen, and four units
long. (8, 9) is still a point where four corners meet.

Repeat questions **4a**, **b**
and **c** for this tiling.

/ **PRACTICAL PROJECT**

*On paper or card draw a
square with sides 10 cm
long.
Mark each side in
centimetres (1–10).
Draw and colour, or stitch
in wool, patterns of straight
lines like the ones shown.
Investigate other designs
of your own.*

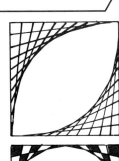

/ **CHALLENGE**

*Trace these shapes, and mark the letters on them as
shown.*

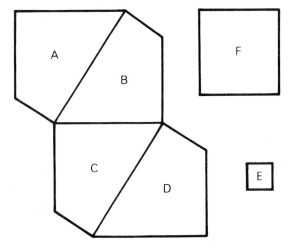

*Cut them out of your tracing paper, or transfer them
onto card.*

a *Fit parts A, B, C, D and E together to make a
square, with the square E in the middle.*

b *Fit parts A, B, C, D and F together to make a
square, with the square F in the middle.*

INVESTIGATION

a *You see rectangular shapes everywhere— windows, doors, books, newspapers, carpets, pictures . . . . Did you ever notice that some rectangular shapes looked better than others? Artists have agreed for many years that one particular rectangle pleases the eye more than any other. They call it the 'Golden Rectangle'. Can you pick it out from these?*

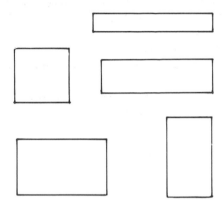

b *Carry out these instructions for constructing a golden rectangle.*

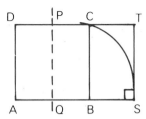

(i) *Draw a square ABCD of side 5 cm.*
(ii) *Draw an axis of symmetry PQ.*
(iii) *With centre Q, and radius QC, draw an arc to cut AB produced to a point S.*
(iv) *Complete the golden rectangle ASTD. Was this the shape you chose?*

c *An Italian mathematician, Fibonacci, who lived in the thirteenth century, used the sequence: 1, 1, 2, 3, 5, 8, 13, . . . in solving a problem.*
(i) *Write down four more terms of the sequence.*
(ii) *There is a surprising connection between this sequence and the lengths of the sides of a golden rectangle. Can you find the connection?*

Making sure

A **rectangle** has two axes of symmetry.

Its opposite sides are equal and parallel.

All its angles are right angles.

Its diagonals are equal, and bisect each other.

In addition for a **square**:
All its sides are equal.

It has four axes of symmetry.

Its diagonals bisect at right angles.

CHECK-UP ON TWO DIMENSIONS: RECTANGLE AND SQUARE

1 Draw these shapes, and mark their axes of symmetry:
a a rectangle **b** a square.

2 Draw a rectangle ABCD, with its diagonals crossing at O.
a Name a line equal in length to:
  (i) AB (ii) BC (iii) AC.
b Name three lines equal in length to OA.

3 In rectangle PQRS, name:
a two pairs of parallel lines
b four right angles.

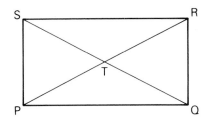

4 Copy the rectangle below, and fill in the lengths of as many lines, and the sizes of as many angles, as you can.

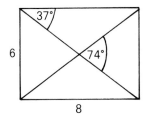

5 Plot the points A(6, 0) and B(6, 3). ABCD is a square. Find two possible sets of coordinates for C and two for D.

6 Copy these squares, and fill in the lengths of as many lines and the sizes of as many angles as you can.

a 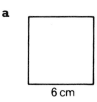   6 cm

b 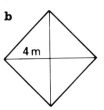   4 m

7 Draw rectangle OPQR on squared paper. O is the origin, P is the point (5, 0) and Q is (5, 8). Write down:
a the coordinates of R
b the length and breadth of the rectangle.

8 The diagram shows two rectangles which overlap at right angles.

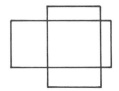

Count the total number of:
a right angles **b** rectangles.

9 Say whether each of the following is true or false for: (i) all rectangles (ii) all squares.
a All the angles are right angles.
b All the sides are equal.
c Opposite sides are parallel.
d Diagonals bisect each other.
e Diagonals bisect the angles.
f Has half-turn symmetry.
g Has quarter-turn symmetry.
h Has only two axes of symmetry.
i Diagonals are axes of symmetry.
j Pairs of sides are perpendicular.

10 Rectangle EFGH has its sides parallel to the x and y-axes. E is the point (2, 4), and the diagonals cross at (4, 5). Find the coordinates of F, G and H.

11 P is the point (3, 4) and R is (3, 10). If PQRS is a square, find the coordinates of Q and S.

14 MEASURING VOLUME

LOOKING BACK

1 Copy the scale on this jar, and mark arrows at:
 a $\frac{1}{2}$ litre **b** $\frac{1}{4}$ litre **c** $\frac{3}{4}$ litre.

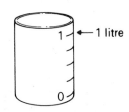

2 The jar in question **1** is $\frac{1}{4}$ full. How much liquid has to be poured in to fill it to the 1 litre mark?

3 Which of these units are used to measure volume?

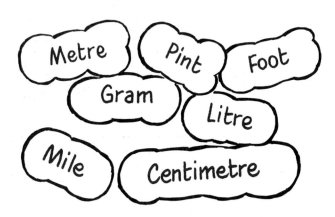

4 **a** When full, which container holds:
 (i) most liquid (ii) least liquid?

 b How many cartons of milk could be poured into the petrol can?

5 **a** How much liquid is in each of these?

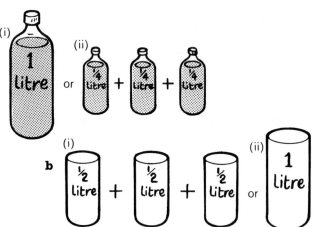

 b What happens if all the liquid in (i) is poured into the jar (iii).

6 In each pair of pictures below which bottles or cans hold more juice—(i) or (ii)?

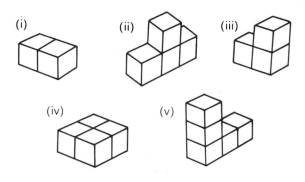

7 These solids are made of centimetre cubes.

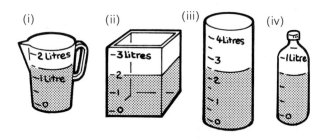

Which take up:
 a most space **b** least space **c** the same space?

8 Sketch different solids made of four cubes like those in question **7**.

Here are two boxes of sugar cubes. Which box is larger?

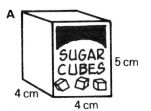

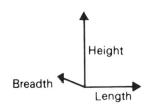

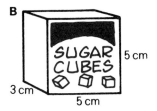

1 Which box is: **a** longer   **b** broader   **c** taller?

2 Which has the larger front face?

3 Which has the larger base?

But which box holds more sugar cubes?

To find out, fill each box with sugar cubes, like this:

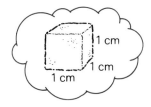

4 For box A:
   a Put in one layer. How many cubes?
   b How many layers will it hold?
   c How many cubes will it hold?

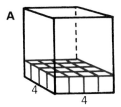

5 Repeat question **4** for box B.

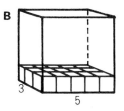

6 a Which box holds more cubes, A or B?
   b So which box is larger?

The number of cubes gives a measure of the **volume** of each box, or the amount of space in each box.

This cube has a volume of 1 cubic centimetre, or 1 cm³.

Calculation

1 The volume of box A
   = 4 × 4 × 5 cubic centimetres
   = 4 × 4 × 5 cm³
   = 80 cm³

2 What is the volume of box B?

EXERCISE 1A

In this exercise, all the cubes are centimetre cubes.

1 Count the number of cubes in each solid, then write down its volume in cm³.

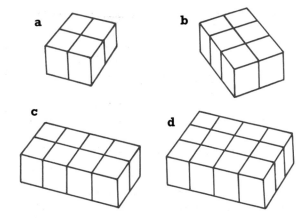

a

b

c

d

Copy and complete the calculations in question **2–6**.

2 a Number of cubes in each layer = ____ .

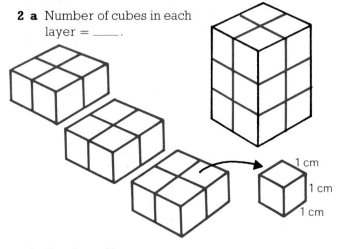

1 cm
1 cm
1 cm

  b Number of layers = __ __ .
  c Number of cubes in box = ____ .
  d Volume of box = ____ cm³.
  e Check by counting the cubes.

3 a Number of cubes in each layer = ____ .
  b Number of layers = ____ .
  c Number of cubes in box = ____ .
  d Volume of box = ____ cm³.
  e Check by counting the cubes.

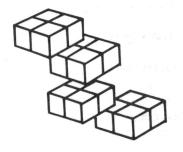

4 cm
2 cm
2 cm

4

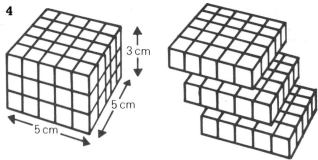

3 cm
5 cm
5 cm

  a Number of cubes in each layer = ____ .
  b Number of layers = ____ .
  c Number of cubes in box = ____ .
  d Volume of box = ____ cm³.

5

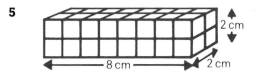

2 cm
8 cm
2 cm

Volume of box = 8 × ____ × ____ = ____ cm³.

6

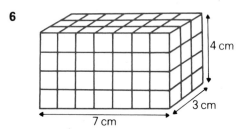

4 cm
3 cm
7 cm

Volume of box = ____ × ____ × ____ = ____ cm³.

7 Calculate the volumes of these cuboids, in cubic centimetres.

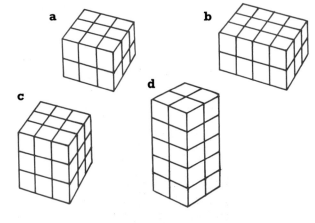

a

b

c

d

8 Sketch these cuboids, and then calculate their volumes:
  a 2 cubes long, 2 cubes broad (from back to front) and 2 cubes high
  b 3 cubes long, 2 cubes broad, 1 cube high
  c 6 cubes long, 3 cubes broad, 2 cubes high.

To calculate the volume of a cuboid (box), multiply its length by its breadth by its height.
   Formula: $V = \ell \times b \times h$, or $V = \ell bh$.

UNITS OF VOLUME

The units of volume include the cubic millimetre (mm^3),
                              the cubic centimetre (cm^3),
                              the cubic metre   (m^3).

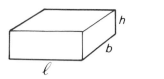

1 m³ (each edge 1 m)
1 cm³ (each edge 1 cm)
1 mm³ (each edge 1 mm)

EXERCISE 1B

1 Calculate the volume of each box. Measurements are in centimetres.

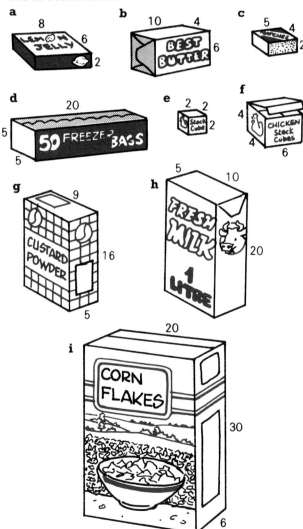

a 8 6 2

b 10 4 6

c 5 4 2

d 20 5 5

e 2 2 2

f 4 4 6

g 9 16 5

h 5 10 20

i CORN FLAKES 20 30 6

2 Why are so many packets in the shape of cubes and cuboids?

3 Calculate the volumes of these objects. Remember to give units in your answers—mm^3, cm^3 or m^3.

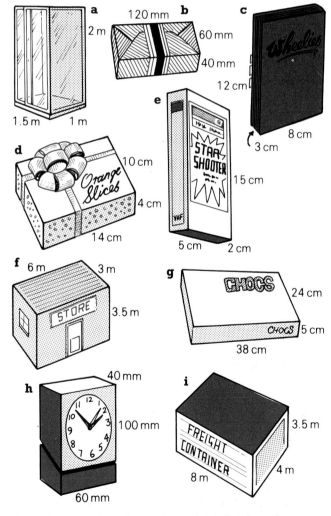

a 2 m 1.5 m 1 m

b 120 mm 60 mm 40 mm

c 12 cm 8 cm 3 cm

d 10 cm 4 cm 14 cm

e 15 cm 5 cm 2 cm

f 6 m 3 m 3.5 m

g 24 cm 5 cm 38 cm

h 40 mm 100 mm 60 mm

i 3.5 m 4 m 8 m

4 a Measure the dimensions of this book to the nearest centimetre, and calculate its volume.
   b Repeat **a** for measurements in millimetres.

EXERCISE 1C

1 Calculate the volumes of these objects:

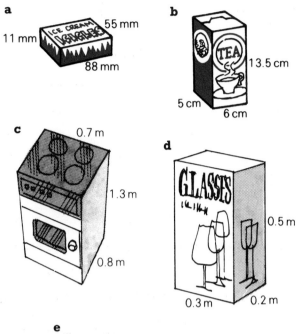

a 55 mm 11 mm 88 mm

b 13.5 cm 5 cm 6 cm

c 0.7 m 1.3 m 0.8 m

d GLASSES 0.5 m 0.3 m 0.2 m

e

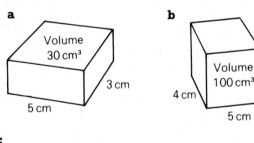

CREAM CRACKERS 20 cm 7.5 cm 7.5 cm

2 A fish tank is 50 cm long, 30 cm broad and 20 cm high.
  a Calculate its volume:
    (i) in cm³   (ii) in litres (1 litre = 1000 cm³).
  b The tank contains 10 litres of water. What depth is the water?

3 Calculate the height of each cuboid:

a Volume 30 cm³ 3 cm 5 cm

b Volume 100 cm³ 4 cm 5 cm

c Volume 200 cm³ 8 cm 10 cm

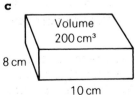

4 Calculate the volumes of these prisms by adding or subtracting the volumes of two or more cuboids. The units are centimetres.

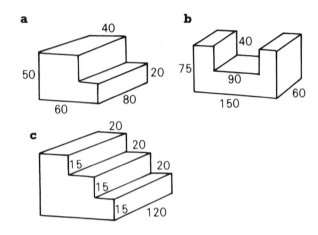

a 40 50 20 60 80

b 40 75 90 150 60

c 20 20 15 20 15 15 120

5 A factory makes plastic cubes. A block of plastic 30 cm by 20 cm by 10 cm is melted down. How many solid cubes can be made of side length:
  a 2 cm   **b** 5 cm   **c** 10 cm?

6 How many matchboxes, each 5 cm by 4 cm by 2 cm, can be packed into a cubical box with sides 1 metre long?

/ CHALLENGES

1 a *How many different cuboids can you make with twelve 1 cm cubes? Draw each shape in two dimensions—dotty paper is useful for this.*
  b *What is the volume of each shape you made?*
  c *Repeat parts **a** and **b** for 24 cubes.*

2 *The sum of the length, breadth and height of a cuboid is 9 cm.*
  a *List all its possible whole number lengths, breadths and heights.*
  b *Calculate all the volumes. Which shape has the greatest volume?*

/ PRACTICAL PROJECTS

1 *Calculate the volume of your classroom, to the nearest cubic metre. How much space does each pupil have?*

2 *Choose some everyday containers in the shape of cubes or cuboids. Estimate their volumes. Then measure them and calculate their volumes.*

Liquids are often measured in litres, or millilitres.

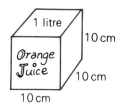

$$1\text{ litre} = 1000\text{ ml} = 1000\text{ cm}^3$$
$$1\text{ ml} = 1\text{ cm}^3$$

EXERCISE 2A

1 How many millilitres are in each jug?

a   **b**

c   **d**

2 How many 200 ml glasses can be filled from a 1 litre carton of orange juice?

3 a How many 10 ml spoonfuls of cough mixture does the bottle hold?
  b How many 5 ml spoonfuls?

4 An apple juice carton is 10 cm long, 5 cm broad and 20 cm high.

  a Calculate its volume: $10 \times 5 \times 20 \text{ cm}^3 = \ldots \text{ cm}^3$.
  b Write down the dimensions of a pack of four, and calculate its volume.
  c The pack costs £3. What is the cost of one carton?

5 How many millilitres does each bottle hold?

  a   **b**   **c**

6 A fish tank is 25 cm long, 12 cm broad and 10 cm high.
  a Calculate its volume:
     $25 \times \ldots \times \ldots \text{ cm}^3 = \ldots \text{ cm}^3$.
  b Write down its volume in millilitres and in litres.

Remember: $1\text{ cm}^3 = 1\text{ ml}$

7 a Copy and complete:
     Volume of oil can
     $= 25 \times 20 \times 10 \text{ cm}^3$
     $= \ldots \text{ cm}^3$
  b 1 litre = 1000 ml. How many litres of oil will the can hold?
  c 1 litre of oil costs £1.20. How much is the can of oil?

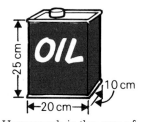

8 A petrol tank is 40 cm long, 30 cm broad and 20 cm high.
  a What is the capacity of the tank in:
     (i) cm^3 (ii) litres?
  b What is the cost of filling it with petrol at 50p per litre?

9 Using the label from the spring water bottle, calculate:
  a the weight of calcium in a glass which holds:
     (i) $\frac{1}{2}$ litre   (ii) 250 ml
     (iii) 100 ml
  b the most you can drink without consuming more than
     (i) 2 mg magnesium
     (ii) 1 mg sodium.

1 Litre
SPRING
WATER
Contains —
Calcium 24 mg
Magnesium 4 mg
Sodium 10 mg

10 A large container in the shape of a cube has sides one metre long. Calculate its capacity in:
  a cubic centimetres   **b** millilitres   **c** litres.

EXERCISE 2B

When fridges and freezers are advertised we are often told their **cubic capacity**. This means the amount of space inside them. The larger the capacity, the more food they will hold.

1 Look at this chest freezer.

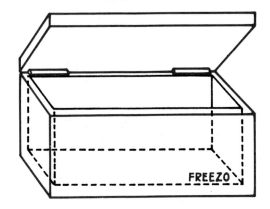

Its inside is a box like this:

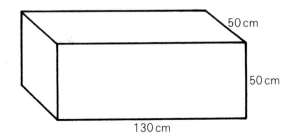

50 cm
50 cm
130 cm

Calculate the capacity of the freezer in:
a cubic centimetres **b** litres.

2 Here are two different fridge/freezers.

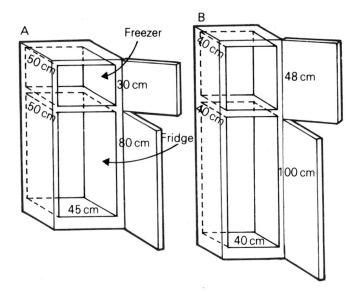

A Freezer B
50 cm 30 cm 40 cm
50 cm 48 cm
80 cm Fridge 40 cm
45 cm 100 cm
40 cm

a Which do you think has the greater:
(i) freezer capacity   (ii) fridge capacity?
b Calculate the capacities of both freezers and fridges in cubic centimetres and in litres.
c Which freezer, and which fridge, has the larger capacity in litres, and by how much?

EXERCISE 2C

The size of central heating radiator required for a room depends on the volume of the room.

Radiator	Volume of room
size 1	Less than 65 m³
size 2	From 65 m³ to 99 m³
size 3	More than 99 m³

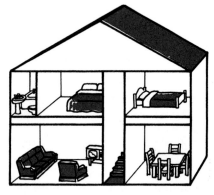

The dining room in this house has a height of 4 metres. Its length is 5 metres and its breadth is also 5 metres.
So its volume = $4 \times 5 \times 5$ m³ $= 100$ m³.
From the chart, you can see that a size 3 radiator is the best one for this dining room.

1 List the volumes of, and suitable radiators for, these rooms. Dimensions are in metres.

Room	Length	Breadth	Height	Volume	Radiator size
Main bedroom	5	5	3		
Small bedroom	5	4	3		
Bathroom	4	4	3		
Kitchen	4	4	4		
Lounge	6	5	4		
Hall (and stairs)	5	2	7		

2 The following information is known about the house next door.

Room	Length	Breadth	Height	Radiator size
Bedroom		4	2.5	1
Lounge		5	3.6	3
Dining room	5		4	2

For the given sizes of radiator, calculate:
a the maximum length of the bedroom
b the minimum length of the lounge
c the maximum and minimum lengths of the dining room.

BRAINSTORMER

Using these pairs of jars, how could you measure out the volumes of liquid given below them?

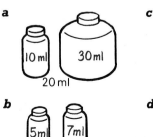

a

b

(i) 2 ml   (ii) 3 ml

c

d

(i) 2 ml   (ii) 5 ml
(iii) 4 ml (any more?)

INVESTIGATION

Check that these two cartons have the same volume.

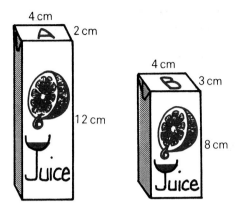

They both hold the same amount of juice, but the area of special card needed to make them is not the same.

1 Copy and complete this table:

	Carton A		Carton B	
Face	$l \times b$ (cm²)	Area (cm²)	$l \times b$ (cm²)	Area (cm²)
Left	2 × 12	24		
Right	2 × 12			
Top	2 × 4			
Bottom				
Front				
Back				
Total area of card				

2 Which carton needs less card?

3 Find another carton, with the same volume, that needs even less card.

4 Design a carton, using the least amount of card, to hold 216 ml of juice.

5 Repeat **4** for volumes of 343 ml and 512 ml.

CHECK-UP ON MEASURING VOLUME

1 The juice in this glass comes
from a full 1 litre bottle.

   a How much is in the glass?
   b How much is left in the bottle?
   c How many refills of this size
   can be poured from the bottle?

2 Another bottle holds 2.5 litres.
   a How many millilitres is this?
   b How many 100 ml drinks will it provide?

3 Calculate the volumes of these cuboids. Each
small cube has sides 1 cm long.

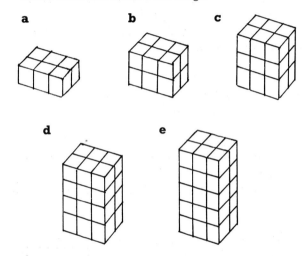

a   **b**   **c**

d   **e**

4 A fishtank is 40 cm long, 20 cm broad and 20 cm
high.
   a How many litres of water can it hold?
   b 6 litres of water are put into the empty tank.
   What depth is the water?

5 Calculate the volumes of these objects.

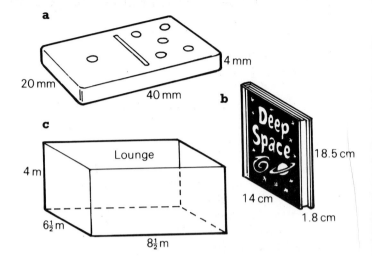

a

20 mm   40 mm   4 mm

b Deep Space   18.5 cm   14 cm   1.8 cm

c Lounge   4 m $6\frac{1}{2}$ m $8\frac{1}{2}$ m

6 A carton is 10 cm long and 5 cm broad. If it holds 1
litre of juice, calculate its height.

7 a How many litres of liquid does a tank 90 cm by
40 cm by 40 cm hold?
   b Another tank has the same capacity, and the
   area of its base is 4000 cm². Calculate its height.

8 A plastic strip is 1 m long, 1 cm broad and 1 mm
thick.

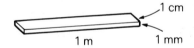

1 cm   1 m   1 mm

   a (i) Write down its length, breadth and depth in
   centimetres.
   (ii) Calculate its volume in cubic centimetres.
   b Repeat **a**, using millimetres and cubic
   millimetres.

LOOKING BACK

1 Write down all the fractions you can see in these pictures.

33⅓ rpm

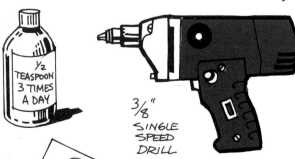

2 a How full are these three jars?

(i) (ii) (iii)

b What fraction of each jar is empty?

3 Write down the fraction used in each of these in number form, for example $\frac{1}{5}$.
a Half price sale **b** Three-quarter length coat
c One-third full moon.

4 Calculate:
a $\frac{1}{2}$ of £10 **b** $\frac{1}{4}$ of £8 **c** $\frac{1}{3}$ of £18
d $\frac{1}{5}$ of £15 **e** $\frac{1}{10}$ of £100

5 a Mark, Gayle and Shalim share a bar of chocolate equally. What fraction should each have?
b The bar is 12 cm long. What length should each have?

6 a What fraction of this square is:
  (i) shaded horizontally
  (ii) shaded vertically
  (iii) unshaded?

b What is the sum of the three fractions?

7 Arrange these in pairs of equal fractions:
$\frac{1}{2}, \frac{1}{3}, \frac{1}{5}, \frac{2}{10}, \frac{2}{4}, \frac{2}{6}$

8 Arrange these in order, smallest to largest:
$\frac{1}{2}$ of 10 cm, $\frac{1}{3}$ of 6 cm, $\frac{1}{5}$ of 20 cm, $\frac{1}{10}$ of 30 cm.

9 Make four copies of this rectangle and the squares inside it and label them (i)–(iv).

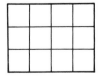

a Now shade: (i) $\frac{1}{2}$ (ii) $\frac{3}{4}$ (iii) $\frac{1}{6}$ (iv) $\frac{2}{3}$
b Use your diagrams to arrange the fractions in order, smallest to largest.

THE MEANING OF A FRACTION

Four people sat their driving tests.
3 out of 4 passed; $\frac{3}{4}$ of them passed.
1 out of 4 failed: $\frac{1}{4}$ of them failed.
In the fraction $\frac{1}{4}$, 1 is the **numerator** and 4 is the **denominator**.

EXERCISE 1A

1 What fraction of each bottle is filled with juice?

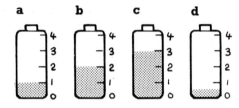

2 Each shape is divided into equal parts. Copy or trace the shapes, and shade the fractions shown below them.

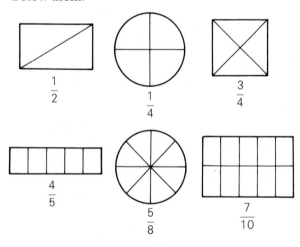

3 a How many days are there in a week?
b How many start with S?
c What fraction of the days start with S?

4 a How many months are there in a year?
b What fraction of them are summer months (June, July, August)?

5 a How many fingers and thumbs are on two hands?
b What fraction of them are:
(i) fingers   (ii) thumbs?

6 What fraction of these shapes are:
a triangles   **b** circles   **c** rectangles?

7 Write these fractions in number form, for example $\frac{3}{4}$.
a One quarter   **b** two thirds   **c** seven tenths
d one twelfth   **e** four fifths.

8 Copy and complete this table for the six diagrams below.

Shape	a	b	c	d	e	f
Fraction shaded						
Fraction unshaded						

a   **b**   **c**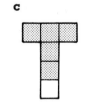

d   **e**   **f**

9 How many slices of cake are cut if it is divided into:
a quarters   **b** eighths   **c** halves
d fifths   **e** tenths?

10 What fraction of the normal price do you have to pay during this sale?

SALE
⅓ OFF ALL PRICES

11 What fraction of the keys on this keyboard are:
a black   **b** white?

12 Sketch a car's petrol gauge.
Mark: E (Empty), $\frac{1}{4}$, $\frac{1}{2}$, $\frac{3}{4}$, F (Full).
Draw the pointer at $\frac{3}{4}$. What fraction of a tankful of petrol has been used?

EXERCISE 1B

1 1, 3, 5, 7, ... are odd numbers, and 2, 4, 6, 8, ... are even. What fractions of the numbers in these collections are odd?
a 1, 2, 4, 6, 7   **b** 1, 3, 6, 9
c 4, 5, 6, 7, 8, 9, 10   **d** 5, 10, 15, 20

2 A class has 12 boys and 13 girls. What fraction of the pupils are boys?

3 What fraction of the eggs has been used in each tray?

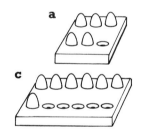
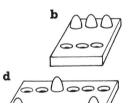

4 How many slices of the circle are needed to make up these fractions of it?
a $\frac{1}{8}$ **b** $\frac{1}{4}$ **c** $\frac{1}{2}$
d $\frac{3}{4}$ **e** $\frac{7}{8}$ **f** $\frac{8}{8}$

5 Chris carried out a survey to find the number of pupils who travelled to school in various ways. What fraction of the pupils:
a travel by bus   **b** cycle
c don't cycle?

Walk	13
Cycle	9
Car	7
Bus	21

6 Write, as fractions, the sizes of the parts when:
a a 2 metre length of ribbon is cut into five equal lengths
b a 3 metre plank of wood is cut into eight equal lengths
c two bars of chocolate are divided equally between three people
d the £200 cost of a holiday is shared equally by eight friends.

7 What unit is:
a $\frac{1}{10}$ cm   **b** $\frac{1}{100}$ m   **c** $\frac{1}{1000}$ kg   **d** $\frac{1}{7}$ week
e $\frac{1}{60}$ hour   **f** £$\frac{1}{100}$?

8 What fraction of a year (not a leap year) is:
a a week   **b** a day   **c** an hour
d a minute   **e** a second?

9 What fraction of a pack of playing cards is:
a red   **b** black   **c** hearts   **d** aces?

10 The pie chart shows the number of teams that scored 0, 1, 2, 3 and 4 goals one Saturday.

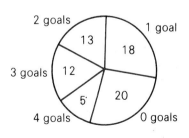

a What was the most common score?
b How many teams scored 3 goals?
c How many teams are there altogether?
d What fraction of teams scored:
    (i) 0 goals   (ii) more than 2 goals?

EXERCISE 1C

1 Alan ate $\frac{1}{4}$ of this bar of chocolate, then Bernard had $\frac{1}{3}$ of the bar. What fraction was left for Charles?

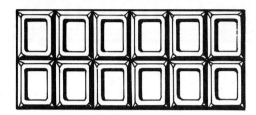

2 Next time, Alan ate $\frac{1}{4}$ of the bar, then Bernard had $\frac{1}{3}$ *of what was left*. What fraction did Charles get this time?

3 Try questions **1** and **2** again, using the fractions $\frac{1}{2}$ and $\frac{1}{3}$.

4 Show how to break up a bar of chocolate so that it is easy to give away these fractions of the bar:
a $\frac{1}{2}$ and $\frac{1}{3}$ **b** $\frac{1}{2}$ and $\frac{1}{8}$ **c** $\frac{1}{3}$ and $\frac{1}{5}$.

5 Copy these flags, and show how to divide them up in order to shade the given fractions.

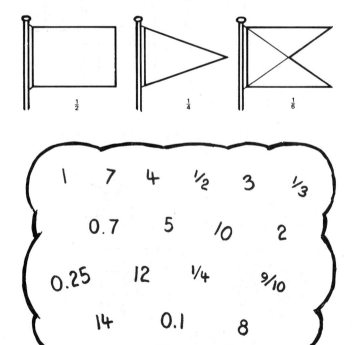

6 What fraction of the numbers in the collection above are:
a even whole numbers **b** odd whole numbers
c decimal fractions **d** other fractions
e greater than 7 **f** less than 3?

CHALLENGES

1 *Decimal fractions*
a $\frac{1}{2} = 1 \div 2 = 0.5$, an exact decimal fraction.
$\frac{2}{3} = 2 \div 3 = 0.6666\ldots$ *Check this on your calculator.*
Use your calculator to investigate which fractions can be expressed as exact decimal fractions. Be systematic. Try to find rules for exact decimal fractions and write up a report.

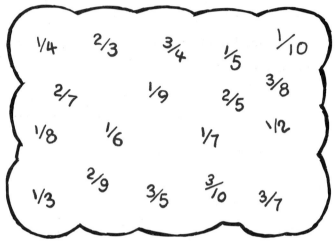

b *Investigate the pattern of numbers in the decimal equivalents of $\frac{1}{7}, \frac{2}{7}, \frac{3}{7}, \frac{4}{7}, \ldots$. Can you find another set of fractions with a repeating pattern?*

2 *Calculate the fraction of your week that is spent:*
a *sleeping* **b** *at school*
c *watching TV* **d** *doing mathematics.*

PRACTICAL PROJECT

Find ways of folding a rectangular sheet of paper into:
a *halves* **b** *quarters* **c** *eighths* **d** *thirds*
e *sixths* **f** *twelfths.*

EQUAL FRACTIONS—EASIER FRACTIONS

In the theatre

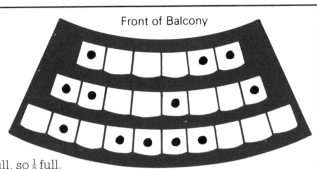
Front of Balcony

Front row   3 out of 6 seats taken. $\frac{3}{6}$ full, or $\frac{1}{2}$ full.

Second row   4 out of 8 seats taken. $\frac{4}{8}$ full, or $\frac{1}{2}$ full.

Third row   5 out of 10 seats taken. $\frac{5}{10}$ full, or $\frac{1}{2}$ full.

In the whole balcony, 12 out of 24 seats are taken. $\frac{12}{24}$ full, so $\frac{1}{2}$ full.
So $\frac{1}{2} = \frac{3}{6} = \frac{4}{8} = \frac{5}{10} = \frac{12}{24}$. The **simplest** of these equal fractions is $\frac{1}{2}$.

To get equal fractions, multiply or divide the numerator and denominator by the same number.

Examples

a $\dfrac{1}{2} = \dfrac{1 \times 5}{2 \times 5} = \dfrac{5}{10}$ **b** $\dfrac{12}{24} = \dfrac{12 \div 12}{24 \div 12} = \dfrac{1}{2}$,   *or* $\dfrac{\cancel{12}^{1}}{\cancel{24}_{2}} = \dfrac{1}{2}$.

EXERCISE 2A

1 Which two equal fractions are shaded in each pair of diagrams?

a

b

c

2 Copy and complete these calculations for the pairs in question **1**.

a $\dfrac{1}{2} = \dfrac{1 \times}{2 \times} = \dfrac{2}{4}$ **b** $\dfrac{1}{2} = \dfrac{1 \times}{2 \times} = \dfrac{3}{6}$

c $\dfrac{3}{4} = \dfrac{3 \times}{4 \times} = \dfrac{6}{8}$

3 Find the simplest form of each fraction (**a–h**).
For example, $\dfrac{\cancel{5}^{1}}{\cancel{10}_{2}} = \dfrac{1}{2}$ (dividing 'top' and 'bottom' by 2.)

a $\frac{2}{4}$ **b** $\frac{2}{6}$ **c** $\frac{2}{8}$ **d** $\frac{3}{6}$ **e** $\frac{3}{9}$ **f** $\frac{2}{10}$ **g** $\frac{4}{8}$ **h** $\frac{10}{30}$

4 Simplify each fraction. For example, $\dfrac{\cancel{8}^{2}}{\cancel{12}_{3}} = \dfrac{2}{3}$ (dividing 'top' and 'bottom' by 4).

a $\frac{6}{8}$ **b** $\frac{6}{9}$ **c** $\frac{9}{12}$ **d** $\frac{8}{10}$

e $\frac{10}{15}$ **f** $\frac{15}{20}$ **g** $\frac{20}{30}$ **h** $\frac{18}{20}$

5 a Write down the fractions of these rectangles that are shaded.

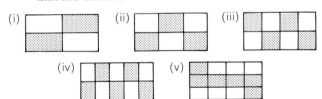

(i)   (ii)   (iii)

(iv)   (v)

b Show that each fraction is equal to $\frac{1}{2}$.

6 Find, in their simplest form, the fractions shaded in these shapes:

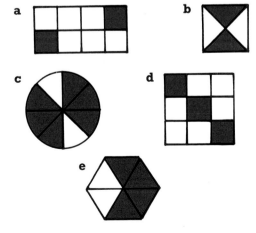

7 What fraction of the months of the year, in simplest form, begins with:
a A . **b** J?

8 Copy and complete the following table, giving each answer in its simplest form.

Sum of money	50p	20p	25p	60p	75p	10p
Fraction of £1	$\frac{1}{2}$					

9 Write as fractions of an hour, in their simplest form:
   a 30 minutes   **b** 15 minutes
   c 20 minutes   **d** 45 minutes

10 What fraction of a 400 metre track is the 100 metre track?

11 What fractions of 90°, in their simplest form, are:
   a 10° **b** 30° **c** 45° **d** 60°?

12 Kris is paying for his bicycle in 16 weekly instalments. What fraction has he paid after 12 weeks, and what fraction has he still to pay?

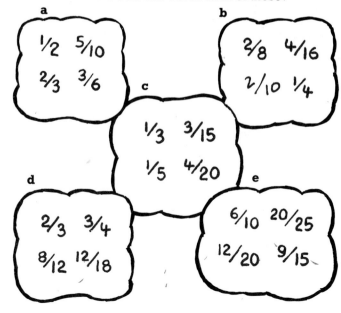

EXERCISE 2B/C

1 Copy and complete:
   a $\frac{1}{2} = \frac{}{8}$ **b** $\frac{1}{3} = \frac{}{9}$ **c** $\frac{1}{5} = \frac{2}{}$ **d** $\frac{1}{8} = \frac{3}{}$
   e $\frac{1}{4} = \frac{5}{}$ **f** $\frac{1}{10} = \frac{}{100}$

2 Simplify each fraction. For example, $\dfrac{\cancel{18}^{3}}{\cancel{24}_{4}} = \dfrac{3}{4}$.
   a $\frac{6}{9}$ **b** $\frac{4}{10}$ **c** $\frac{8}{12}$ **d** $\frac{18}{20}$
   e $\frac{10}{100}$ **f** $\frac{5}{40}$ **g** $\frac{24}{30}$ **h** $\frac{32}{40}$

3 Find the shaded fractions, in simplest form:

a   **b**   **c**

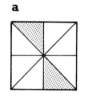

d   **e**

4 35 girls and 15 boys go on a school trip. What fraction, in simplest form, is:
   a girls **b** boys?

5 a 16 out of 20 girls in a Ranger Guide company completed the Duke of Edinburgh gold award. What fraction of the company was this?
   b 35 pupils in a school worked for the silver award, and 21 were successful. What fraction was this?

6 Sheila's school has six periods each day, Monday to Friday. Calculate the fraction one period is of:
   a a school day **b** a school week

7 A working week, Monday to Friday, is split into 10 equal shifts. What fraction of the week is worked by someone who is employed for:
   a two shifts **b** five shifts **c** eight shifts?

8 In garages, the mechanics sometimes measure in thousandths of an inch ('thou'). Write down the simplest form of 20 'thou'.

9 Pam has run 625 m of a 1000 m race. What fraction, in simplest form, has she:
   a run **b** still to run?

10 Which is the odd one out in each of these?

a ½ 5/10 ⅔ 3/6

b 2/8 4/16 2/10 ¼

c ⅓ 3/15 ⅕ 4/20

d ⅔ ¾ 8/12 12/18

e 6/10 20/25 12/20 9/15

11 You should have the following teeth in each of your upper and lower jaws: 4 incisors, 2 canines, 4 premolars and 6 molars.
What fraction, in simplest form, should you have of each kind of tooth in each jaw?

12 Simplify:
a $\frac{12}{16}$ **b** $\frac{24}{36}$ **c** $\frac{15}{50}$ **d** $\frac{18}{30}$

e $\frac{49}{56}$ **f** $\frac{27}{45}$ **g** $\frac{32}{64}$ **h** $\frac{65}{100}$

13 Copy and complete:
$$\frac{2}{3} = \frac{2 \times}{3 \times} = \frac{}{12}, \text{ and } \frac{3}{4} = \frac{3 \times}{4 \times} = \frac{}{12}$$

Which is larger, $\frac{2}{3}$ or $\frac{3}{4}$?

14 a Repeat question **13** for the fractions $\frac{3}{4}$ and $\frac{5}{6}$.
b Arrange $\frac{2}{3}, \frac{3}{4}$ and $\frac{5}{6}$ in order, largest first.

15 Use the same method to arrange these fractions in order:
a $\frac{3}{5}, \frac{2}{3}, \frac{11}{15}$ **b** $\frac{5}{8}, \frac{3}{4}, \frac{9}{16}$.

FRACTION SNAP

A game for two or more players

List all the halves, quarters, eighths and sixteenths which are equal to each of $\frac{1}{8}, \frac{2}{8}, \frac{3}{8}, \frac{4}{8}, \frac{5}{8}, \frac{6}{8}, \frac{7}{8}, \frac{8}{8}$. For example, $\frac{2}{8} = \frac{1}{4} = \frac{4}{16}$. You should get 22 fractions altogether.
Put each fraction on a card, or a small rectangle of paper. Play 'Snap' like this. Share out the cards. Take turns to place one, face up, on the desk. If the fraction is equal to the previous one, call 'Snap', and take all the cards in the pile. Continue until one player has all 22 cards.

CHALLENGES

1 a *Use equal fractions to find a route from START to FINISH. Write down the fractions in order.*

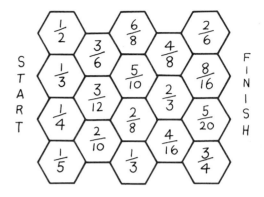

b *Try to find a different route.*
c *Copy the grid and make up your own set of equal fractions from START to FINISH.*

2 *You have to move from one stepping stone to another by going to a smaller fraction each time.*

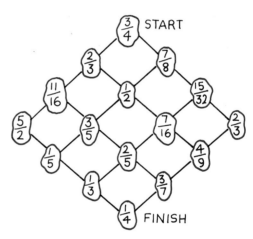

List the fractions on your route, in order. Can you find a different route?

USING FRACTIONS

Example

The area of the rectangular fence = length × breadth

$$= 8 \times \tfrac{3}{4}\,\text{m}^2$$
$$= \tfrac{8}{1} \times \tfrac{3}{4}\,\text{m}^2$$
$$= \tfrac{24}{4}\,\text{m}^2$$
$$= 6\,\text{m}^2$$

EXERCISE 3A

1 Calculate these. For example,
$8 \times \tfrac{1}{4} = \tfrac{8}{1} \times \tfrac{1}{4} = \tfrac{8}{4} = 2$.
a $8 \times \tfrac{1}{2}$ **b** $6 \times \tfrac{1}{2}$ **c** $6 \times \tfrac{2}{3}$ **d** $4 \times \tfrac{3}{4}$
e $10 \times \tfrac{1}{2}$ **f** $12 \times \tfrac{1}{4}$ **g** $12 \times \tfrac{3}{4}$

2 Calculate these. For example,
$\tfrac{2}{3}$ of $12 = \tfrac{2}{3} \times \tfrac{12}{1} = \tfrac{24}{3} = 8$.
a $\tfrac{1}{2}$ of 10 **b** $\tfrac{1}{3}$ of 18 **c** $\tfrac{1}{4}$ of 20 **d** $\tfrac{1}{8}$ of 24
e $\tfrac{2}{5}$ of 25 **f** $\tfrac{3}{4}$ of 16 **g** $\tfrac{2}{3}$ of 9

3 a A football match lasts 90 minutes. How long is the first half?

b A rugby match lasts 1 hour 20 minutes. How many minutes does the first quarter last?

4 Brian has 45p, but he owes $\tfrac{1}{5}$ of it to Peter. How much is this? How much has he left?

5 $\tfrac{3}{10}$ of a class of 30 pupils are absent. How many are absent? How many are present?

6 42 cars are in the car park. $\tfrac{1}{3}$ of them are blue. How many is this?

7 Calculate the area of a rectangular carpet 15 m long and $\tfrac{3}{5}$ m broad.

8 A shop window needs a new pane of glass 3 m by $\tfrac{2}{3}$ m. What is the area of the glass?

9 Calculate these, in pence. For example,
$\tfrac{2}{5}$ of £1 = $\tfrac{2}{5} \times 100\text{p} = \tfrac{200}{5}\text{p} = 40\text{p}$.
a $\tfrac{1}{10}$ of £1 **b** $\tfrac{3}{10}$ of £2 **c** $\tfrac{3}{4}$ of £1 **d** $\tfrac{1}{2}$ of £5
e $\tfrac{1}{5}$ of £2 **f** $\tfrac{2}{3}$ of £1.50

10 In a test, $\tfrac{1}{5}$ of the pupils will be given an A grade, $\tfrac{1}{2}$ a B grade, $\tfrac{1}{4}$ a C grade, and the rest a D grade. Out of a group of 40 pupils, how many will get each grade?

11 A tank holds 1600 litres of oil when it is full. If it is $\tfrac{1}{4}$ full, how many litres have been used?

12 Calculate:
a $\tfrac{2}{3}$ of 12 cm **b** $\tfrac{3}{4}$ of 20 pupils
c $\tfrac{2}{5}$ of 30 grams **d** $\tfrac{7}{8}$ of 24 days

13 How many minutes are there in:
a $\tfrac{1}{2}$ hour **b** $\tfrac{1}{4}$ hour **c** $\tfrac{3}{4}$ hour
d $\tfrac{1}{3}$ hour **e** $1\tfrac{1}{2}$ hours?

14 Calculate the sale prices of these items:

a

b

EXERCISE 3B/C

1 Calculate:
a $\frac{3}{4}$ of £100   **b** $\frac{1}{10}$ of £120   **c** $\frac{3}{8}$ of £40
d $\frac{2}{5}$ of £35   **e** $\frac{2}{3}$ of £27

2 How many degrees are in:
a $\frac{2}{3}$ of a right angle   **b** $\frac{3}{4}$ of a straight angle?

3 $\frac{2}{3}$ of a person's weight is water. Jean weighs 63 kg. How much of this is water?

4 On the moon things weigh $\frac{1}{6}$ of their weight on the earth. How much will a 72 kg astronaut weigh on the moon?

5 Calculate the length of tape needed to record two TV programmes, each lasting $\frac{3}{4}$ hour.

6 Calculate:
a $\frac{3}{10}$ of 240 m   **b** $\frac{2}{3}$ of 210 kg   **c** $\frac{3}{5}$ of 600 pupils
d $\frac{5}{8}$ of 120 cm   **e** $\frac{9}{10}$ of £1000

7 Calculate the areas of these rectangles:

a

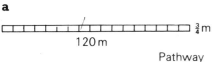
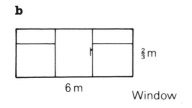

120 m
$\frac{3}{4}$ m

Pathway

b

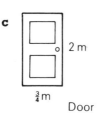

6 m
$\frac{2}{3}$ m
Window

c

2 m
$\frac{3}{4}$ m
Door

8 Calculate, to the nearest penny, with the help of a calculator:
a $\frac{1}{7} \times £5$ **b** $\frac{5}{12} \times £11$ **c** $\frac{5}{16} \times 89p$
d $\frac{4}{9} \times 75p$ **e** $\frac{4}{15} \times £26$

9 An aircraft flying at 1800 km per hour reduces its speed by half, and then by a further three-quarters for landing. Calculate its landing speed.

10 To prepare for a sale, a shop assistant has to reduce the price of all items over 50p by $\frac{1}{10}$.

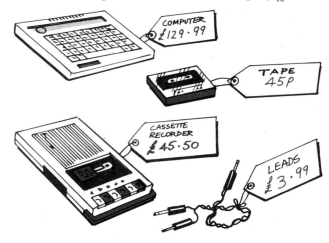

a Reprice the items shown above, using the flow chart. Again, a calculator should be used.

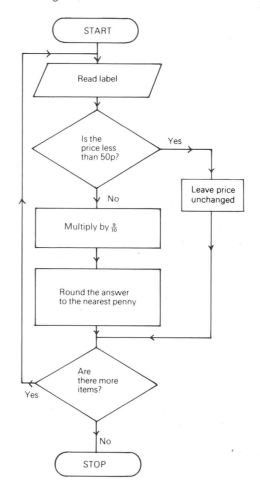

START

Read label

Is the price less than 50p?   Yes

Leave price unchanged

No

Multiply by $\frac{9}{10}$

Round the answer to the nearest penny

Are there more items?

Yes

No

STOP

b Why did he multiply by $\frac{9}{10}$?
What fraction would he use if the sales reduction was:
(i) $\frac{1}{5}$ (ii) $\frac{1}{3}$ (iii) $\frac{1}{4}$ (iv) $\frac{1}{2}$?

PER CENT—A VERY SPECIAL FRACTION

Per cent means **per hundred.** 1 per cent, or 1%, means **1 per hundred.** $1\% = \frac{1}{100}$

Examples
a $3\% = \frac{3}{100}$ **b** $87\% = \frac{87}{100}$ **c** $123\% = \frac{123}{100}$ **d** $100\% = \frac{100}{100} = 1$

EXERCISE 4A

1 Write down the meaning of each of these. For example, $5\% = \frac{5}{100}$
  a 1%   **b** 10%   **c** 9%   **d** 19%
  e 60%   **f** 100%

2 Write each of these as a fraction. For example, $15\% = \frac{15}{100}$
  a 12%   **b** 35%   **c** 80%   **d** 5%
  e 7%   **f** 50%

3 Each figure has 100 small squares. 10 shaded squares represent $\frac{10}{100}$ or 10%.

(i) 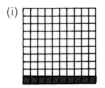   (ii)   (iii)

(iv)   (v)

Which figure shows:
  a 10%   **b** 25%   **c** 50%   **d** 75%   **e** 100%?

4

| A | B | C | D E | F | G | H I |

0% 10% 20% 30% 40% 50% 60% 70% 80% 90% 100%
Start   **Finish**

The edge of the swimming pool is divided into 100 equal parts. When Nick swims to A, he has covered 10%, or $\frac{10}{100}$ of the total length. Copy and complete this table for the distances marked.

Distance	A	B	C	D	E	F	G	H	I
Percentage	10								
Fraction	$\frac{10}{100}$								

5 The Smith family's monthly income is usually spent like this:
food—20%, clothes—10%, fuel bills—15%, house costs—25%, car costs—10%, bank standing orders—15%.
What percentage of their income is left for holidays?

6 100 pupils were asked to choose their favourite school snacks. Here are the results.

Filled roll	Salad	Beans on toast	Curry	Fish fingers	Baked potato
20	22	10	13	14	21

a Write the results as percentages.
b List the snacks in order of popularity. Which is your favourite?

7 Arrange these percentages in order, largest first:

1%   9%   7½%   5.8%   8.5%   11%   3½%

8 Write these percentages as fractions in their simplest form. For example,

$$35\% = \frac{\cancel{35}^{\,7}}{\cancel{100}_{\,20}} = \frac{7}{20}$$

a 10%	**b** 25%	**c** 50%	**d** 75%
e 100%	**f** 70%	**g** 90%	**h** 15%
i 5%	**j** 4%	**k** 8%	**l** 88%

9 Look at this diagram of all the different costs you have if you own a car.

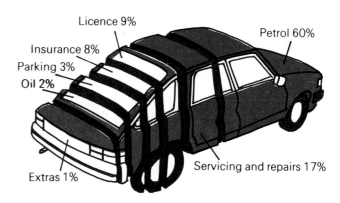

Licence 9%
Insurance 8%
Parking 3%
Oil 2%
Petrol 60%
Servicing and repairs 17%
Extras 1%

a Add up the percentages. Did you expect this answer? Explain why.
b Arrange the costs in order, from largest to smallest.

10 Write these as fractions in their simplest form. For example, $48\% = \frac{\cancel{48}^{\,12}}{\cancel{100}_{\,25}} = \frac{12}{25}$.

a 30%	**b** 70%	**c** 60%	**d** 20%
e 40%	**f** 55%	**g** 80%	**h** 1%
i 200%	**j** 150%	**k** 2%	**l** 500%

Worth remembering

$10\% = \frac{1}{10}$	$25\% = \frac{1}{4}$	$50\% = \frac{1}{2}$	$75\% = \frac{3}{4}$	$100\% = 1$

EXERCISE 4B/C

1 Each figure has 100 small squares. Write down the fraction of 100, and the percentage, of each figure that is shaded.

2 Write these fractions as percentages.
a $\frac{38}{100}$ **b** $\frac{95}{100}$ **c** $\frac{121}{100}$ **d** $\frac{273}{100}$ **e** $\frac{7}{100}$ **f** $\frac{1}{100}$

3 Write these as fractions, simplifying them where possible. For example,

$$44\% = \frac{\cancel{44}^{\,11}}{\cancel{100}_{\,25}} = \frac{11}{25}.$$

a 33% **b** 36% **c** 77% **d** 6%
e 56% **f** 100%

a   b   c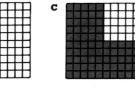

d   e   f

4 List these in order, from the smallest to the largest percentage.

only 5pc   167% higher   9.05%   9.25%   0.8%   14.64%   9.50%   8.375%   0.008%   4%   9.52%   9.5%   10.25%   12%

5 Per cent means per hundred. In order to see the percentage, therefore, the denominator of the fraction must be 100. For example,

$$\frac{17}{20} = \frac{17 \times 5}{20 \times 5} = \frac{85}{100} = 85\%.$$

Find out what percentage each fraction below represents:

a $\frac{11}{20}$ **b** $\frac{16}{25}$ **c** $\frac{7}{10}$ **d** $\frac{49}{50}$

e $\frac{3}{5}$ **f** $\frac{10}{40}$ **g** $\frac{40}{80}$ **h** $\frac{24}{60}$

6

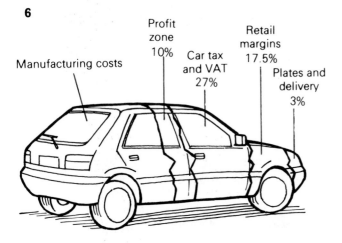

Profit zone 10%   Car tax and VAT 27%   Retail margins 17.5%   Plates and delivery 3%

Manufacturing costs

Where the money goes! Calculate the percentage of the car's purchase price which pays for the manufacturing costs.

7 In a tray of 20 eggs, two are broken.
  a What fraction is broken?
  b What percentage is broken?

8 Petra leaves home at 8 am and returns at 2 pm.
  a What fraction of 24 hours is she away?
  b What percentage is this?

9 Look at Penny's report card.

Subject	Mark
ENGLISH	15/20
MATHS	35/50
FRENCH	18/30
HISTORY	32/40
SCIENCE	50/75

  a Calculate all her marks as percentages.
  b List her subjects in order, from best to worst.

10 By changing these fractions to percentages, find which is the larger in each pair.
  a $\frac{4}{5}, \frac{3}{4}$ **b** $\frac{1}{4}, \frac{3}{10}$ **c** $\frac{7}{10}, \frac{17}{25}$ **d** $\frac{13}{50}, \frac{4}{16}$ **e** $\frac{9}{75}, \frac{6}{50}$

11 The diagram shows the number of people treated in one day in a hospital accident unit.

Broken bones	Sprains	Eye injuries	Cuts	Head injuries

(pictogram)

= 1 patient

  a What was the total number of people treated?
  b Calculate the percentage treated for:
    (i) broken bones
    (ii) sprains
    (iii) eye injuries
    (iv) cuts
    (v) head injuries
  c Add up all the percentages. What should the total be?

USING PERCENTAGES

Example
Dorothy buys the watch marked £20.
How much does she get off the marked price?

(i) *Without a calculator*
15% of £20 = $£\frac{15}{100} \times \frac{20}{1} = £\frac{300}{100} = £3$

(ii) *With a calculator*
15% of £20 = £15 ÷ 100 × 20 = £3
or, using 15% = $\frac{15}{100}$ = 0.15, 15% of £20 = 0.15 × £20 = £3
She gets £3 off the marked price.

EXERCISE 5A

Try these questions without using a calculator.

1 Calculate 10% of each of these.

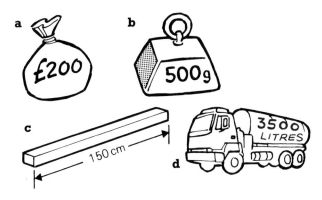

a £200

b 500 g

c 150 cm

d 3500 LITRES

2 Calculate:
  a 50% of £10   **b** 10% of £80   **c** 50% of £70
  d 10% of £50   **e** 25% of £60   **f** 20% of £100
  g 75% of £40   **h** 30% of 50p   **i** 40% of 10p
  j 5% of 80p

3 Calculate 8% of each of these:

a 200 marbles

b 2000 people

c 150 LPs

d 25 books

4 At a sale 25% is given off all prices. How much does Mike save on:
  a a notebook priced £2   **b** a pencil priced 60p
  c a book priced £10?
  How much does he pay for each?

5 To boost sales, a firm offers 20% extra with each package of its goods. How much extra would you get in each of these?

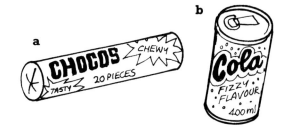

a CHOCDS CHEWY TASTY 20 PIECES

b Cola FIZZY FLAVOUR 400 ml

c BonBons Traditional 250 g

d THE WORLDS LONGEST CHEWY 15 cm long

6 Calculate:
  a 3% of £200   **b** 5% of £120
  c 20% of £50   **d** 30% of £70
  e 1% of 2500 m   **f** 60% of 200 kg
  g 100% of 500 people **h** 150% of £8

7 It's January, so the sales are on. Most shops are giving discounts on their prices. For each item shown, calculate the discount, and the price you would have to pay.

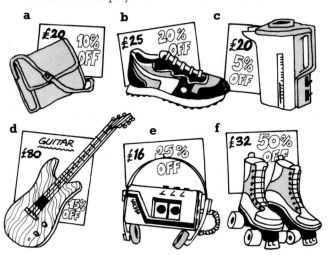

8 The pie chart shows the percentage of space in a magazine given to advertisements and stories.
  a What percentage of space is used for pictures?
  b There are 64 pages in the magazine. How many are taken up by pictures?

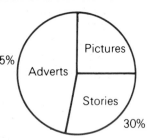

9 Now try to answer the questions in this exercise again, with the aid of a calculator. But first, have you noticed that $15\% = \frac{15}{100} = 0.15$, $7\% = \frac{7}{100} = 0.07$, $40\% = \frac{40}{100} = 0.4$, and so on? Write these as decimal fractions, for practice, and then answer questions **1–8** again.
  a 12%   **b** 25%   **c** 80%   **d** 20%
  e 5%   **f** 9%   **g** 66%   **h** 1%

EXERCISE 5B/C

A calculator will be useful in this exercise.

1 Calculate:
  a 25% of £80   **b** 50% of £26   **c** 75% of £100
  d 20% of £5   **e** 13% of £70   **f** 28% of £80
  g 36% of £120   **h** 4% of £5   **i** 5% of £30
  j 1% of £1

2 A TV company provides 20 hours of viewing daily.
  a 5% of the time is for News. How much time is this?
  b Four hours' viewing is for children. What percentage of time is this?

3 2000 people were asked 'If there were to be a General Election tomorrow, which party would you vote for?' The pie chart shows the results.
  a How many replied:
    (i) Labour
    (ii) Green party?
  b How many would not vote Labour?
  c What percentage is 'Other'?

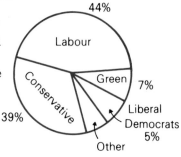

4 In a Cash and Carry, items are priced without VAT. This is added on at the check-out.
  a Calculate:
    (i) the VAT at 17.5% on each Cash and Carry item

	Cash and Carry (ex. VAT)	High St. Shop (inc. VAT)
Beans	20p	24p
Coffee	£1.80	£1.99
Cereal	80p	97p
Loaf	60p	77p

    (ii) the cost of each Cash and Carry item with VAT added on.
  b Which items are now cheaper at the Cash and Carry, and by how much?

5 If you put £500 into the National Savings Account you would receive interest of 12% of £500 after one year. Calculate a year's interest for each account below.

  a

  b

  c

6 a If a discount of 20% is offered, what percentage of the price has to be paid?

b Calculate the amount to be paid for each of these:

(i) tennis racquet, usually £35; discount 15%

(ii) tracksuit, usually £85; discount $12\frac{1}{2}$%

(iii) sports shoes, usually £28.50; discount 5%.

7 a Mr Big got a 3% increase in his salary of £25 500. Calculate his increase.

b Mr Small was given 9% on his salary of £8500. Calculate his increase.

c Even without doing the calculations you should be able to see that the increases must be the same. Why?

8

This clock radio sells for £22, plus 17.5% VAT. Calculate:

a the VAT   **b** the total cost of the radio.

9 The salaries in a company range from £9500 to £19 000. Would it be fair to give all the employees an increase of 4%? What would the range of salaries be after an increase of 4%?

10 Tim's father bought a used car for £5000, and sold it three years later for £2400. Owing to inflation the price of new cars rose by 10%, 8% and 5% during these three years. How much money would his father have to find to exchange his old car for a new one?

INVESTIGATION

Each time, this ball bounces to a height of 70% of the height of its previous bounce.

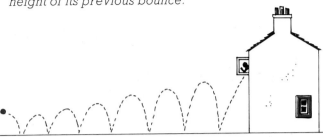

a *It is dropped from a height of 400 cm. How high will it rise after 1, 2, 3 and 4 bounces?*

b *Will it ever stop bouncing?*

c *Use your calculator to help you to explain what will happen eventually.*

BRAINSTORMER

The old and new sizes of FAB PHOTO prints are drawn to scale.

Is FAB's claim for a 50% increase in area correct?

FAB PHOTOS 50% INCREASE IN AREA

FREE

CHECK-UP ON FRACTIONS AND PERCENTAGES

1 What fraction of each shape is shaded?

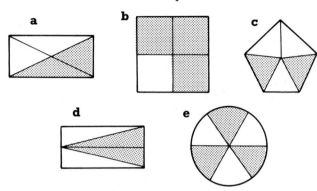

a   **b**   **c**

d   **e**

2 What do we call:
  a $\frac{1}{12}$ of a year   **b** $\frac{1}{60}$ of a minute

  c $\frac{1}{24}$ of a day   **d** $\frac{1}{100}$ of a dollar?

3 Simplify these fractions:
  a $\frac{6}{8}$ **b** $\frac{10}{20}$ **c** $\frac{10}{15}$ **d** $\frac{12}{16}$ **e** $\frac{30}{100}$ **f** $\frac{40}{100}$ **g** $\frac{64}{72}$

4

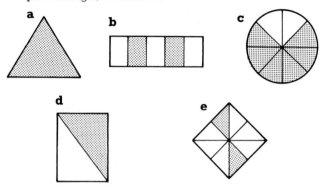

JUNE

S	M	T	W	T	F	S
		1	2	3	4	5
6	7	8	9	10	11	12
13	14	15	16	17	18	19
20	21	22	23	24	25	26
27	28	29	30			

Look at this calendar and find, in simplest form, the fraction of the days in June that are:
  a Sundays   **b** Wednesdays
  c weekends   **d** week days.

5 Calculate:
  a $\frac{1}{10}$ of £1   **b** $\frac{3}{10}$ of £2   **c** $\frac{4}{5}$ of £1

  d $\frac{1}{2}$ of £5   **e** $\frac{7}{10}$ of £80

6 A car park can hold 180 cars.
  a How many cars are in it when it is one quarter full?
  b There are 120 cars in it. What fraction of the spaces are:
    (i) used   (ii) free?

7 In each shape below what fraction, and what percentage, is shaded?

a   **b**   **c**

d   **e**

8 Calculate:
  a 5% of £200   **b** 10% of £120   **c** 25% of £60
  d 60% of £25   **e** 1% of £1000

9 600 patients were admitted to a hospital one month. 90% were treated successfully. How many was this?

10 a How much reduction will there be on a carpet marked £160?
  b What is its sale price?

CARPETS
SALE 15% OFF ALL CARPETS

11 Arrange these dominoes to match each other in a straight line.

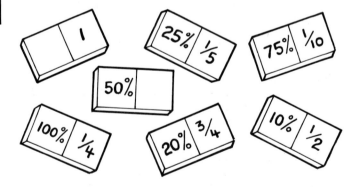

12 60 000 tickets are sold for a football match. Each of the two clubs is allocated 15 000 tickets. What percentage of tickets:
  a does each club get
  b is available for others?

16 SOLVING MORE EQUATIONS

1 Which numbers go into these boxes?
 a $\square + 8 = 17$ **b** $10 - \square = 3$ **c** $4 \times \square = 32$
 d $3 \times \square + 1 = 7$

2 Write down:

 a the number of weights   **b** the total weight

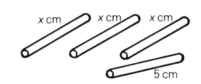

 c the amount of cash   **d** the total length.

3 Simplify:
 a $2x + x$ **b** $2x - x$ **c** $3y - 3y$ **d** $5p + 3p$
 e $3q - 2q$ **f** $3x + 2x + x$

4 Solve these equations:
 a $x + 3 = 6$ **b** $y + 4 = 10$ **c** $t - 2 = 8$
 d $p - 7 = 0$ **e** $2n = 14$ **f** $5k = 20$
 g $2x + 1 = 5$ **h** $2y - 1 = 3$

5 If $x = 7$, how many weights are in each picture?

 a   **b**   **c**   **d**

                                          1 weight
                                          missing

6 What goes into each OUT space below?

 a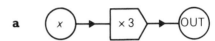

 b

 c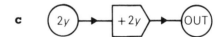

 d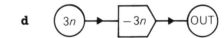

7 Find the missing entries in the sequences in these three tables:

 a

	A
1	2
2	4
3	6
4	8
5	
17	
18	
x	

 b

	A
1	3
2	4
3	5
4	6
5	
27	
28	
n	

 c

	A
1	4
2	7
3	10
4	13
5	
33	
34	
k	

SOLVING THE EQUATION $2x+3=7$

The weights on the balance illustrate the equation $2x+3=7$.
We can find x by solving the equation

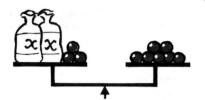

$$2x+3=7$$
$$2x=4$$
$$x=2$$

EXERCISE 1A

Use the 'cover up' method to solve these equations.

1 $x+3=6$ **2** $x+8=11$ **3** $y+1=11$
4 $y+7=14$ **5** $a-2=5$ **6** $b-1=3$
7 $c-3=6$ **8** $d-5=10$ **9** $x+8=14$
10 $x-3=7$ **11** $y+3=10$ **12** $t-2=9$
13 $2x=8$ **14** $3y=9$ **15** $5t=45$

16 $8u=56$ **17** $2x+1=11$ **18** $2k-1=7$
19 $2p+3=5$ **20** $2t-4=0$ **21** $a+9=18$
22 $3b-9=0$ **23** $c+12=15$ **24** $d-8=15$
25 $3x+2=11$ **26** $4y+1=5$ **27** $2k-3=7$
28 $4t-3=1$ **29** $3t-1=8$ **30** $2u+8=8$
31 $5v+2=27$ **32** $8w-1=23$

EXERCISE 1B

Write down an equation for each picture, then solve it.

1
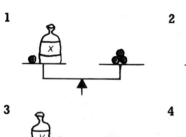

2

3
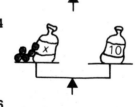

4
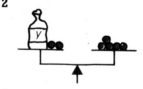

5

6
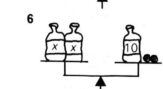

7
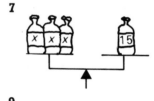

8

9
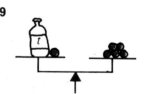

10

11

12
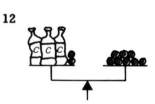

EXERCISE 1C

Solve these equations:

1 $5x+6=16$ **2** $3y-5=10$ **3** $7a+6=20$
4 $8b-7=9$ **5** $10-x=2$ **6** $7+y=7$
7 $8-p=0$ **8** $6+k=15$ **9** $10=4+3y$

10 $15=4x-1$ **11** $20=14+3n$ **12** $18=5m+3$
13 $8+2p=14$ **14** $12-3q=9$ **15** $16+5t=26$
16 $18-6u=0$ **17** $29=3q-13$ **18** $91-7h=0$
19 $49+12t=97$ **20** $55-7x=20$

ADDING AND SUBTRACTING

Study these two boxes carefully:

Situation	Number of weights
(two bags labelled x, x with 3 weights)	$2x + 4$
Action: Take away 2 bags	$-2x$
Result: (tray with weights)	4

Situation	Number of weights
(two bags labelled x, x with 1 weight)	$2x + 1$
Action: Add 1 bag	$+x$
Result: (three bags labelled x, x, x)	$3x + 1$

EXERCISE 2A

Add and subtract in questions **1–7**.

1 a $\begin{array}{r} 6 \\ +6 \\ \hline \end{array}$ **b** $\begin{array}{r} 6 \\ -6 \\ \hline \end{array}$ **c** $\begin{array}{r} 10 \\ -5 \\ \hline \end{array}$ **d** $\begin{array}{r} 8 \\ +5 \\ \hline \end{array}$ **e** $\begin{array}{r} 12 \\ -7 \\ \hline \end{array}$

2 a $\begin{array}{r} 3x \\ +2x \\ \hline \end{array}$ **b** $\begin{array}{r} 3x \\ -2x \\ \hline \end{array}$ **c** $\begin{array}{r} 2y \\ +2y \\ \hline \end{array}$ **d** $\begin{array}{r} 2y \\ -2y \\ \hline \end{array}$ **e** $\begin{array}{r} 4y \\ +3y \\ \hline \end{array}$

3 a $\begin{array}{r} 4a \\ +2a \\ \hline \end{array}$ **b** $\begin{array}{r} 4a \\ -2a \\ \hline \end{array}$ **c** $\begin{array}{r} 3b \\ +b \\ \hline \end{array}$ **d** $\begin{array}{r} 3b \\ -b \\ \hline \end{array}$ **e** $\begin{array}{r} 5c \\ +5c \\ \hline \end{array}$

4 a $\begin{array}{r} x \\ +x \\ \hline \end{array}$ **b** $\begin{array}{r} x \\ -x \\ \hline \end{array}$ **c** $\begin{array}{r} y \\ +y \\ \hline \end{array}$ **d** $\begin{array}{r} y \\ -y \\ \hline \end{array}$ **e** $\begin{array}{r} 2y \\ -y \\ \hline \end{array}$

5 a $\begin{array}{r} d \\ +2d \\ \hline \end{array}$ **b** $\begin{array}{r} 3d \\ +5d \\ \hline \end{array}$ **c** $\begin{array}{r} 2e \\ -2e \\ \hline \end{array}$ **d** $\begin{array}{r} f \\ +f \\ \hline \end{array}$ **e** $\begin{array}{r} 6g \\ -5g \\ \hline \end{array}$

6 a $\begin{array}{r} 2x+1 \\ +2x \\ \hline \end{array}$ **b** $\begin{array}{r} 3y-1 \\ +2y \\ \hline \end{array}$ **c** $\begin{array}{r} x+1 \\ +x \\ \hline \end{array}$ **d** $\begin{array}{r} y-1 \\ +y \\ \hline \end{array}$

7 a $\begin{array}{r} x+4 \\ -x \\ \hline \end{array}$ **b** $\begin{array}{r} 2y+3 \\ -2y \\ \hline \end{array}$ **c** $\begin{array}{r} 3n-4 \\ -n \\ \hline \end{array}$ **d** $\begin{array}{r} 4m+1 \\ -2m \\ \hline \end{array}$

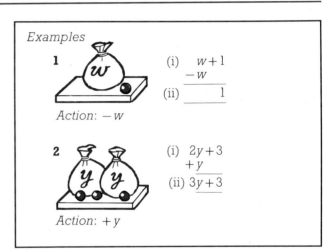

Examples

1 (bag labelled w with 1 weight)
   (i) $\begin{array}{r} w+1 \\ -w \\ \hline \end{array}$
   (ii) $\quad 1$

Action: $-w$

2 (two bags labelled y, y with weights)
   (i) $\begin{array}{r} 2y+3 \\ +y \\ \hline \end{array}$
   (ii) $3y+3$

Action: $+y$

In questions **8–11**, write down:
(i) the number of weights on each tray
(ii) the number after the given action.

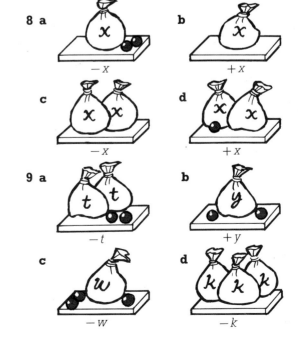

8 a (bag x) $-x$ **b** (bag x) $+x$
c (two bags x, x) $-x$ **d** (two bags x, x) $+x$

9 a (two bags t, t) $-t$ **b** (bag y) $+y$
c (bag w) $-w$ **d** (three bags k, k, k) $-k$

10 a
$+x$

b
$+2m$

11 a
$-s$

b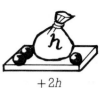
$+2h$

c
$-2c$

d
$-2n$

c
$-3p$

d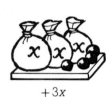
$+3x$

EXERCISE 2B/C

Simplify:

1 a $m+m-3$ **b** $2n-n+2$ **c** $5t-2t-1$
  d $7x+3x-5$ **e** $2y-2y+4$

2 a $5w+3-w$ **b** $6n+13+n$ **c** $8x+9-4x$
  d $7m+1-3m$ **e** $4y+3-4y$

3 a $7+3a-a$ **b** $5-b+b$ **c** $1-2c+2c$
  d $4+3x-2x$ **e** $6+x-x$

In questions **4** and **5**, write down:
 (i) the number of weights on each tray
 (ii) the number after the given action.

> (2 weights missing)
> *Example*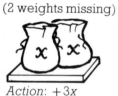
> (i) $2x-2$
> (ii) $2x-2+3x$
> $=5x-2$
> *Action:* $+3x$

4 a (2 weights missing) **b** (1 weight missing)

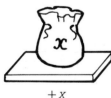
$+x$

$+2y$

c (4 weights missing) **d** (3 weights missing)

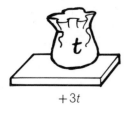
$+3t$

$+c$

5 a (2 weights missing) **b** (1 weight missing)

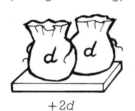
$+2d$

$+y$

c (1 weight missing
from each bag) **d** (2 weights missing
from each open bag)

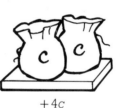
$+4c$

$+3x$

Copy each of the following (**6** and **7a–j**), then:
 (i) show the action you would take to 'cancel out',
   or eliminate, the x-term.
 (ii) write down the result.

> *Examples* **1** $2x+5$ **2** $1-3x$
>   (i) $\underline{-2x}$ (i) $\underline{+3x}$
>   (ii) $\underline{5}$ (ii) $\underline{1}$

6 a $x+5$ **b** $2x+3$ **c** $5x+1$ **d** $4x+1$ **e** $7x+2$
  f $4x$ **g** $2x$ **h** x **i** $1-x$ **j** $3-2x$

7 a $2-x$ **b** $4-2x$ **c** $1-3x$ **d** $8x+2$
  e $8-2x$ **f** $3x+4$ **g** $4-3x$ **h** $x+5$
  i $5-x$ **j** $10x+10$

KEEPING YOUR BALANCE

Study these two boxes carefully:

Balance	Equation
![balanced scale with marbles] (balanced)	$6 = 6$
Remove 1 weight from right side. ![unbalanced scale] (unbalanced)	-1 $6 \neq 5$ (not an equation)

For balance, the same must be added to, or subtracted from, each side.

Balance	Equation
![balanced scale with bags x x x and x] (balanced)	$3x = x + 4$
Remove x weights from each side. ![scale with two x bags] (still balanced)	$-x \quad -x$ $2x = 4$ (still an equation) $x = 2$

Rule. Eliminate the x-term from one side by adding or subtracting the same term on each side of the equation.

Examples
Solve these equations:

1 $4x = \quad x + 9$
  $-x \quad -x$ ... to eliminate x from right side
  $3x = 9$
  $\quad x = 3$

2 $3x = 4 - x$
  $+x \quad +x$ ... to eliminate $-x$
  $4x = 4$
  $\quad x = 1$

EXERCISE 3A

1 Copy these equations, and solve them using the hints given.

a $2x = \quad x + 6$ **b** $2y = \quad y + 3$ **c** $3a = a + 8$
  $-x \quad -x$ $-y \quad -y$ $-a \quad -a$

d $4b = \quad b + 9$ **e** $2x = 6 - x$ **f** $3y = 8 - y$
  $-b \quad -b$ $+x \quad +x$ $+y \quad +y$

g $4m = 5 - m$ **h** $\quad t = 10 - t$
  $+m \quad +m$ $+t \quad +t$

2 Write down an equation for each balance (**a**–**d**). Then use the hints to solve the equations.

a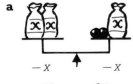
  $-x \qquad -x$

b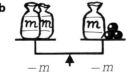
  $-m \qquad -m$

c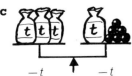
  $-t \qquad -t$

d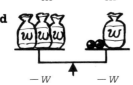
  $-w \qquad -w$

3 Solve these equations:
  a $3m = m + 2$ **b** $4n = n + 9$ **c** $5k = k + 16$
  d $6p = p + 5$

4 Solve:
  a $3x = 8 - x$ **b** $4y = 15 - y$ **c** $5t = 12 - t$
  d $6u = 21 - u$

5 Solve:
  a $3x = x + 8$ **b** $4y = y + 6$ **c** $5a = a + 12$
  d $6b = b + 10$ **e** $2s = 9 - s$ **f** $3t = 12 - t$
  g $5u = 6 - u$ **h** $2v = 18 - v$

6 Solve:
  a $5x = 30$ **b** $x + 8 = 15$ **c** $2x + 3 = 11$
  d $x - 6 = 9$ **e** $3y + 4 = 10$ **f** $2y - 12 = 0$
  g $8y = 48$ **h** $10y + 1 = 21$ **i** $2t = t + 7$
  j $3t = 20 - t$ **k** $4u = u + 18$ **l** $5v = 60 - v$

Example   Solve: $5x = 2x + 18$

$$5x = 2x + 18$$
$$-2x -2x$$
$$3x = 18$$
$$x = 6$$

An alternative setting:

$$5x = 2x + 18$$
$$5x - 2x = 2x + 18 - 2x$$
$$3x = 18$$
$$x = 6$$

EXERCISE 3B

1 Solve these equations:

a $2x = x + 10$ **b** $3x = x + 6$ **c** $5y = 2y + 3$
d $8n = 3n + 15$ **e** $2k = 12 - k$ **f** $4t = 50 - t$
g $u = 10 - u$ **h** $3v = 16 - v$ **i** $4x - 3 = x$
j $3y - 15 = 2y$ **k** $9p = 2p + 49$ **l** $6s = 3s + 30$

2 Make an equation for each of these pairs of equal straws. Solve the equation, and find the lengths of the straws.

a

| $2x$ cm |
| $x + 4$ cm |

b

| $3x$ cm |
| $2x + 5$ cm |

c

| $6x$ cm |
| $2x + 20$ cm |

d

| $5x$ cm |
| $3x + 4$ cm |

e

| $3x - 6$ cm |
| x cm |

f

| $4x - 10$ cm |
| $2x$ cm |

g

| $4x - 6$ cm |
| $3x$ cm |

h

| $8x - 15$ cm |
| $3x$ cm |

3 A parking space can hold three cars, or one car, a trailer and a van.

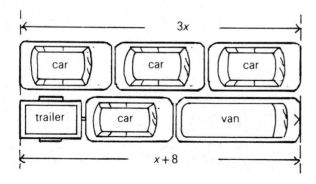

a Make an equation, where x metres is the length of a car.
b Solve it to find the length of a car, in metres.
c Calculate the length of the parking space.

4 The shelf can hold four cartons, or two cartons with a 30 cm space left.

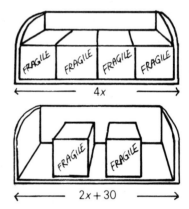

a Make an equation, where x cm is the width of a carton.
b Solve it to find the width of one carton, in cm.
c Calculate the length of the shelf.

5 Eric is making breadboards. From a plank of wood he can cut five boards exactly, or two boards with 90 cm over.

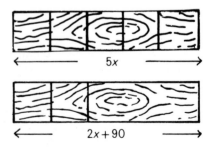

a Make an equation, where x cm is the length of a board.
b Solve it to find the length of one breadboard, in cm.
c Calculate the length of the plank of wood.

EXERCISE 3C

1 Make equations for **a**–**d** below, and solve them to find x. Check that the scales are still balanced!

a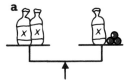

b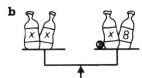

c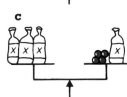

d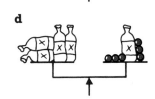

2 In each pair of columns, the numbers in the nth row are equal. Find which row this is, by solving an equation.

a

	A	**F**
1	3	10
2	6	12
3	9	14
n	$3n$	$= 2n+8$

b

	A	**F**
1	6	22
2	12	26
3	18	30
n	$6n$	$= 4n+18$

c

	A	**F**
1	8	32
2	16	36
3	24	40
n	$8n$	$= 4n+28$

3 Solve these equations:

a $5x = 21-2x$ **b** $7x+4 = 60$ **c** $6x = 2x+36$
d $7x-1 = 6x$ **e** $12 = 18-y$ **f** $12 = 16-2y$
g $3y = 28-y$ **h** $6y = 54-3y$

4

For 50p I can buy four pencils and get 2p change. If a pencil costs x pence, make an equation and find the cost of a pencil.

5

For 80p I can buy three bars of chocolate and two penny chews. Make an equation, and find the cost of a bar of chocolate.

6 With the money I have in my pocket I can buy three bars of chocolate and two penny chews, or one bar of chocolate and twenty penny chews. Make an equation, and find the cost of a bar of chocolate. How much money do I have?

SOLVING THE EQUATION $4x+2=2x+8$

Balance	Equation
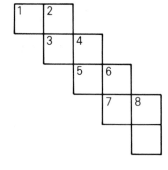	$4x+2=2x+8$
Remove $2x$ weights from each side.	$-2x \quad -2x$ $2x+2=8$ $x=3$

EXERCISE 4A

1 Solve these equations:

  a $\begin{array}{l}2x+1=\ \ x+3\\ -x\ \ \ \ \ \ \ \ -x\end{array}$ **b** $\begin{array}{l}2x-3=6-x\\ +x\ \ \ \ \ \ \ \ +x\end{array}$

  c $\begin{array}{l}3y+2=\ \ y+14\\ -y\ \ \ \ \ \ \ \ -y\end{array}$ **d** $\begin{array}{l}3y-1=7-y\\ +y\ \ \ \ \ \ \ \ +y\end{array}$

2 Solve:

  a $2x+3=x+7$ **b** $2x-1=2-x$
  c $3y-2=y+4$ **d** $3y+5=13-y$
  e $2k-1=k+7$ **f** $4t-3=t+9$
  g $5m+1=13-m$ **h** $3n-2=6-n$

3 Write down an equation for each balance below. Then solve the equation.

  a

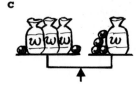

  b

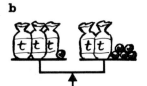

  c

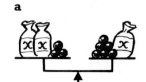

  d

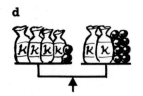

  e

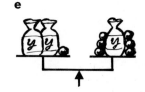

  f

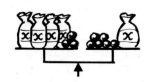

4 Copy and complete this cross-number puzzle. Solve the equations to find the entries in the puzzle. Check Across and Down.

Across
1 $2x=24$
3 $2x+2=x+16$
5 $2x-1=x+31$
7 $3x=x+102$

Down
2 $x+9=30$
4 $2x+3=x+46$
6 $2x-1=49$
8 $3x+5=x+25$

5 Solve these equations:

  a $7x=42$ **b** $3x+5=5$ **c** $5x-1=9$
  d $10-x=7$ **e** $3a=a+8$ **f** $2b=12-b$
  g $5c=c+12$ **h** $4d=20-d$ **i** $3x=2x+5$
  j $4y=2y+10$ **k** $3x=30-2x$ **l** $6y=40-2y$

6 Solve:

  a $\begin{array}{l}5a-2=\ \ 2a+10\\ -2a\ \ \ \ \ \ \ \ -2a\end{array}$ **b** $\begin{array}{l}4b+3=\ \ 2b+27\\ -2b\ \ \ \ \ \ \ \ -2b\end{array}$

  c $\begin{array}{l}3c-3=12-2c\\ +2c\ \ \ \ \ \ \ \ +2c\end{array}$ **d** $\begin{array}{l}2d+5=5-2d\\ +2d\ \ \ \ \ \ \ \ +2d\end{array}$

  e $5x-2=3x+10$ **f** $4y+3=y+15$

  g $4k-3=17-k$ **h** $6p+1=8-p$

EXERCISE 4B

1 Make an equation for each pair of equal canes. Solve the equation, and find the length of each cane (in centimetres).

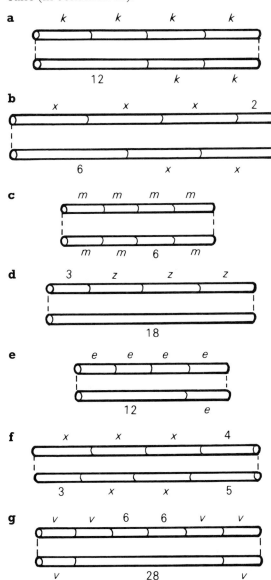

a

k   k   k   k

12   k   k

b

x   x   x   2

6   x   x

c

m   m   m   m

m   m   6   m

d

3   z   z   z

18

e

e   e   e   e

12   e

f

x   x   x   4

3   x   x   5

g

v   v   6   6   v   v

v   28   v

2 Copy and complete the cross-number puzzle.

Across
1 $4y + 2 = y + 41$
2 $2y + 17 = 71$
3 $5y - 2 = 4y + 32$
4 $10y + 30 = 5y + 135$

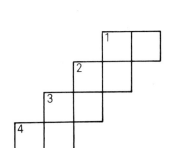

Down
1 $3y = y + 34$
2 $6y - 3 = 3y + 69$
3 $3y + 17 = 2y + 48$
4 $8y = 3y + 130$

3 For each picture (**a**–**i**) make up an equation, and solve it to find the number of weights in each bag. Then check your solution with the picture, making sure the weights are balanced.

a
2 weights missing

b
1 missing

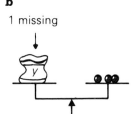

c
3 missing

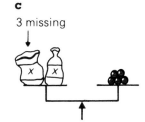

d
3 missing

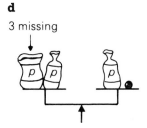

e
1 missing

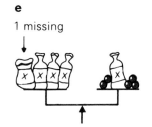

f
3 missing

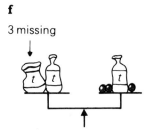

g
5 missing

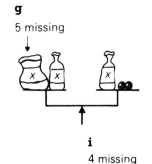

h
1 missing

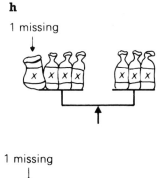

i
4 missing   1 missing

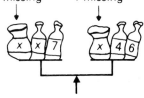

4 Solve:
  a $9x = x + 24$ **b** $8x - 6 = 7x$
  c $5x - 3 = 7 - 5x$ **d** $7x + 2 = 18 - x$
  e $8 - x = 3x$ **f** $12 - x = 4x - 13$
  g $x + 10 = 3x + 2$ **h** $2x + 5 = 5x + 2$
  i $3x - 2 = 14 - x$ **j** $2x + 10 = 5x + 7$
  k $8 - x = 12 - 2x$ **l** $3 - 2x = 3 - 4x$

EXERCISE 4C

1 Find an expression for the *n*th entry in each sequence. Then make an equation and solve it to find the row in which the *n*th entries of each pair of sequences are equal.

a

	A	F
1	2	21
2	4	22
3	6	23
4	8	24
5	10	25
n		= $n+20$

b

	A	G
1	4	52
2	7	53
3	10	54
4	13	55
5	16	56
n	$3n+1$	=

c

	A	H
1	2	80
2	5	81
3	8	82
4	11	83
5	14	84
n		=

2 Make an equation for each pair of pictures below. Solve it to find *x*, and check your solution.

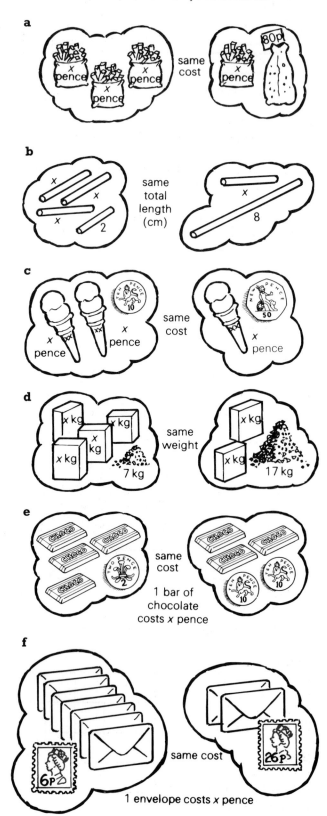

a   same cost

b   same total length (cm)

c   same cost

d   same weight

e   same cost

1 bar of chocolate costs *x* pence

f   same cost

1 envelope costs *x* pence

3 Make an equation, and solve it. What is the volume of the tank?

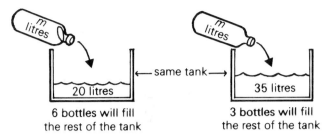

←— same tank —→

20 litres

35 litres

6 bottles will fill
the rest of the tank

3 bottles will fill
the rest of the tank

4 a Meg reads eight pages of a book per minute.
  (i) How many pages does she read in four minutes?
  She finishes the book in x more minutes. How many pages does she read:
  (ii) in x minutes   (iii) altogether?

  b Rashid reads five pages per minute.
  (i) How many pages does he read in seven minutes?
  He too finishes the book in x more minutes. How many pages does he read:
  (ii) in x minutes   (iii) altogether?

  c Make an equation, and solve it. How many pages has the book?

5 David: Travels 60 km   He has travelled
                each hour.   for three hours.

   Heather: Travels 50 km   She has travelled
                each hour.   for four hours.

If each now takes x hours to finish the same journey, what is the length of the journey in km?

CHALLENGES

1 Solve this cross-number puzzle.

Across
1 $2n+1 = n+15$
4 $5x = 3x+242$
6 $2y = y+210$
7 $7k+3 = 4k+54$

Down
2 $3t = t+822$
3 $3m-1 = m+61$
5 $10c = 9c+201$
6 $5g+3 = 3g+61$

2 a The numbers on these five houses increase by two each time. If the lowest number is x, write down all five numbers in terms of x.

If the sum of the numbers is 120, make an equation and solve it to find the house numbers.

  b Repeat part **a** for five house numbers which increase by: (i) 3   (ii) 4   (iii) 5
  c Investigate further. Can you find any patterns? How far can you go?

3 Solve these equations in the order shown. Then apply the code $1 \to A, 2 \to B, 3 \to C, \ldots$, to the solutions, and fill in the secret message below:
———––/——————————/——/———––– .

The problem is: 'Is the message true or false?'

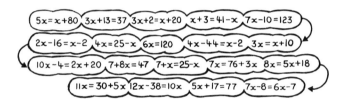

$5x = x+80$ $3x+13 = 37$ $3x+2 = x+20$ $x+3 = 41-x$ $7x-10 = 123$

$2x-16 = x-2$ $4x = 25-x$ $6x = 120$ $4x-44 = x-2$ $3x = x+10$

$10x-4 = 2x+20$ $7+8x = 47$ $7+x = 25-x$ $7x = 76+3x$ $8x = 5x+18$

$11x = 30+5x$ $12x-38 = 10x$ $5x+17 = 77$ $7x-8 = 6x-7$

BRAINSTORMER

The king's problem

A powerful King receives his taxes in gold coins from his four regions. Each coin weighs 100 g, but a spy tells him that one of his Regional Governors is cheating him by melting down the coins and mixing in a lighter, worthless metal. All the coins from this region weigh 90 g.
Unfortunately the King has only a very, very old weighing machine and only one old penny left to make the machine speak. Using only one weighing, how can the King find out which Governor is cheating him?

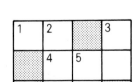

CHECK-UP ON SOLVING MORE EQUATIONS

1 Solve these equations:
  a $x+5 = 13$ **b** $7x = 28$ **c** $2y+2 = 14$
  d $3y-5 = 7$

2 Write down:
  (i) the number of weights on each tray
  (ii) the number after the action shown is taken.

a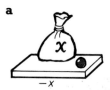

b

c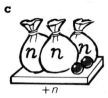

d

3 Simplify:
  a $t+2$ **b** $2-u$ **c** $3m+1$ **d** $1-k$
     $\underline{-t}$ $\underline{+u}$ $\underline{-m}$ $\underline{+k}$

4 Solve these equations:
  a $2n = n+4$ **b** $2p = 12-p$ **c** $3m = 2m+7$
  d $4x = x+15$ **e** $5y = 12-y$ **f** $3b = 20-b$
  g $5c = 4c+10$ **h** $6t = t+10$

5 Make an equation for each pair of equal canes, and solve it. Write down the lengths of the canes (in centimetres).

a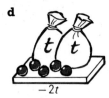

b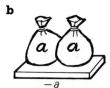

c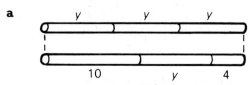

6 Solve:
  a $4x-1 = 3x+1$ **b** $7t+1 = 6t+5$
  c $8k-2 = 6k+10$ **d** $3m-1 = 7-m$

7 Make an equation for each picture, and solve it. Check your solution.

a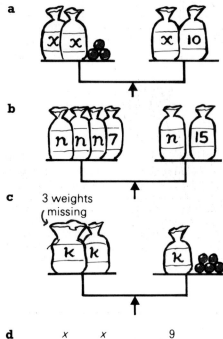

b

c 3 weights (missing)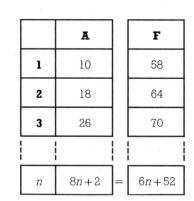

d
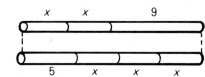

Find x.

e

	A	**F**
1	10	58
2	18	64
3	26	70
n	$8n+2$	$=$	$6n+52$

The numbers in row n are equal.
Find n.

f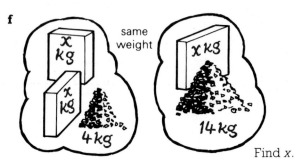

same weight

Find x.

LOOKING BACK

Mrs Adams has been out shopping. She has put all the things she bought on the table. There are items of various shapes and sizes. Some of these 3-dimensional shapes have special names.

1 Name each of the shapes below.

a  **b** **c**

d  **e** **f** **g**

2 Copy this table, and list each of the items Mrs Adams bought, under the correct shape heading.

Cube	Cuboid	Cone	Cylinder	Pyramid	Triangular prism
	Crackers				

3 Were you able to pick out the cuboids because of:
   a their colour   **b** their size
   c the writing on them   **d** their rectangular faces?

4 a What shape is a dice?

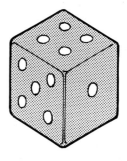

   b Why is this a good shape for it?
   Try to think of more than one reason.

5 What shapes are the faces of:
   a a cube   **b** a cuboid
   c a square pyramid   **d** a triangular prism?

6 List some everyday objects whose shapes are based on those in question **1**.

3-DIMENSIONAL SOLIDS

 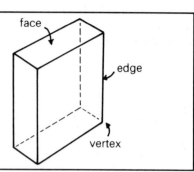

The packet of Flakes is in the shape of a **cuboid**.
All of its faces are rectangles.

EXERCISE 1A

Describe one difference between the cuboid above and each of the solids below. Each question gives a clue to the answer required.

1 Cube

The shapes of the faces.

2 Triangular prism

The number of vertices.

3 Square pyramid

The number of edges.

4 Cone

The number of faces.

5 Sphere

The number of vertices.

6 Cylinder

The number of edges.

7 Copy and complete this table for the solids in questions **1–6**.

	Number of faces	Number of edges	Number of vertices
Cube			
Triangular prism			
Square pyramid			
Cone			
Sphere			
Cylinder			

8 a Why is a cuboid a good shape for bricks used to build a wall?

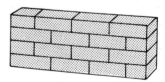

b Why are pyramids and prisms not so suitable?

EXERCISE 1B/C

In questions **1–9** name the shape of:
a each 3-dimensional object
b each 2-dimensional face shown by an arrow.

10 John makes models from simple 3-dimensional shapes. Which shapes are used in each of these models?

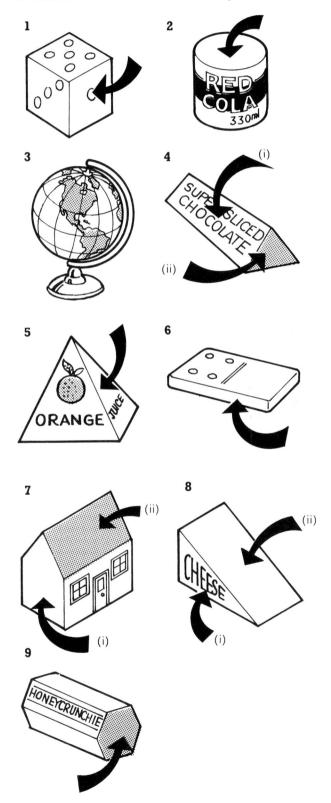

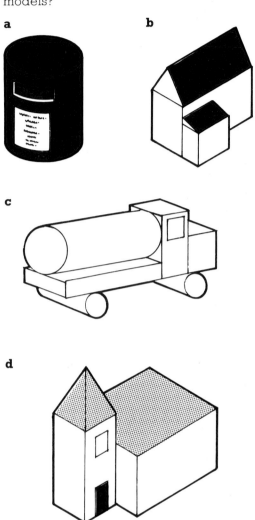

11 Which solids might these phrases describe?
  a It has six square faces.
  b It has only one face.
  c It has only one vertex.
  d It has exactly six edges.
  e It has two triangular and three rectangular faces.
  f It has one square and four triangular faces.
  g Its surface includes two circular faces.

12 Which of these are 2-dimensional (with length and breadth only), and which are 3-dimensional (with length, breadth and height):
  a rectangle **b** cuboid **c** circle **d** pyramid
  e sphere **f** triangle **g** prism **h** square?

DRAWING CUBES AND CUBOIDS

EXERCISE 2A

1 Sandra found an easy way to draw cuboids. Try it. On squared paper draw the rectangle in *Stage 1*. Then complete *Stage 2*, and *Stage 3*.

Stage 1 One rectangle

Stage 2 Another congruent rectangle.

Stage 3 Join the vertices.

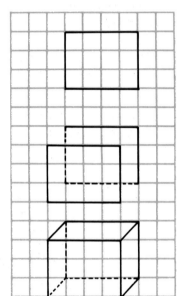

2 Copy the square and the two rectangles. Then complete the cuboids.

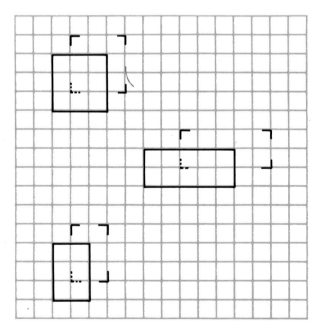

3 Draw two cuboids of your own on squared paper.

4 Copy and complete the shapes below to draw prisms of different shapes.

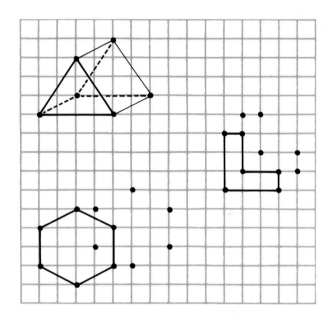

5 June preferred using 'dotty' paper, like this:

Copy the diagrams below onto dotty paper, and complete the cuboids.

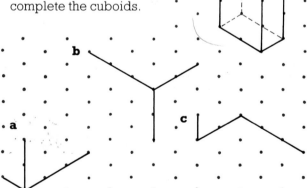

6 The dimensions of the given cuboid in question **5** are 2 by 1 by 3 units. What are the dimensions of cuboids **a**, **b** and **c**?

7 Draw cuboids on dotty paper with dimensions:
a 4 by 3 by 2   **b** 5 by 3 by 1   **c** 4 by 4 by 4.

EXERCISE 2B/C

1 These solids are made up of congruent wooden cubes. How many cubes are in each one?

a

b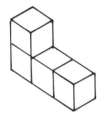

c

d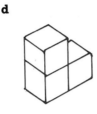

e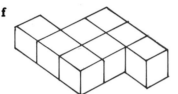

f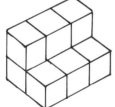

g

h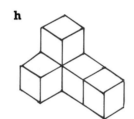

2 In the complete solid in question **1a** you should be able to see three faces, seven vertices and nine edges. Check this. How many (i) faces (ii) vertices (iii) edges can you see in each of the other complete solids (**b**–**h**)?

3 Make a solid of your own, using cubes. Then draw a diagram of it, and answer the questions asked in **2**.

4 Draw 2-dimensional diagrams of a cube or cuboid on a computer screen, using LOGO.

AN OPTICAL ILLUSION—NOW YOU SEE IT, NOW YOU DON'T!

This block of wood has had a piece cut from one corner. But the piece is still there! If you don't believe it, turn your page upside down.

MAKING CUBES AND CUBOIDS

EXERCISE 3A

1

Jack has popped out of his box but the sides of the box have fallen flat on the table. Can they be folded up again to form a box? How many squares are there?

The diagram of squares on the table is called the **net** of the cube they will make.

2 Kate thinks that the net she has drawn could be used to make a dice.

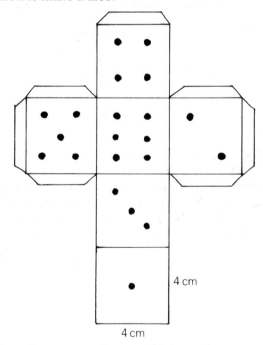

4 cm

4 cm

Draw it on squared paper. Make each square 4 cm long, and mark in the dots.

If you are going to glue the edges, draw the flaps.

If you are going to tape the edges, leave out the flaps.

Cut out the shape, and see if Kate is right.

3 a What is the area of each square in the net in question **2**?

b So what is the total surface area of the cube?

4 Calculate the total surface area of a cube where each edge is: **a** 3 cm long **b** 5 cm long.

5 What is always the sum of the dots on two opposite sides of a dice?

6 Here are the nets for five dice. Copy them, and fill in the missing dots.

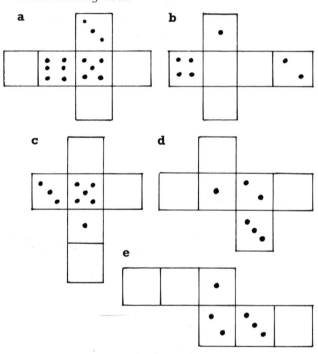

7 Kate's friend Ruth thought that these four nets could be used to make cubes. Draw them on squared paper, making each square 2 cm long. Cut them out, and find out if Ruth was correct.

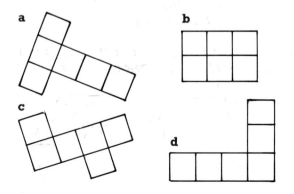

EXERCISE 3B

1 The diagram shows the net of a tray.

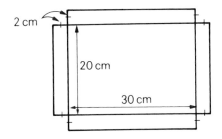

a Each part at the corners is 2 cm long. Why must they all be the same length?

b Calculate the area of:
(i) each rectangle   (ii) the net.

c If the tray is changed to a closed box, what would the length and breadth of the lid be? Where could you draw the lid on the net?

2 This is the net of a scale model of the box of soap powder Mrs Adams bought at the start of this chapter.

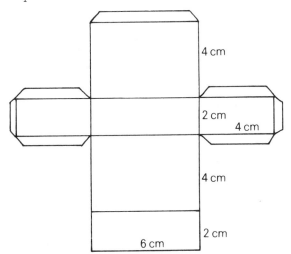

a Draw the net on squared paper, cut it out, and make the box.

b Calculate:
(i) the total area of the net (ignoring the flaps used for glueing)
(ii) the volume of the box.

3 a A manufacturer sells 'Junior' packs of cards in boxes like this. Draw a net of the box on squared paper.

b Calculate the area of card used to make the box (ignoring flaps).

c Write down the volume of the box.

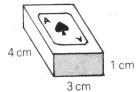

4 Is it possible to make cuboids from the following card rectangles? Sketch them, if possible.
a Two rectangles 10 cm by 8 cm, two 8 cm by 4 cm and two 10 cm by 4 cm.
b Four rectangles 5 cm by 3 cm, and two squares 3 cm by 3 cm.

5 Can you find the length, breadth and height of four *different* cuboids which all have a volume of 60 cm³? Their edges must be an exact number of centimetres long. Make one of them.

PRACTICAL PROJECT

Collect some empty packets of household goods like cereals and detergents. Take them apart carefully, and open them out flat in order to see the different nets used and the ways in which the sides have been glued together. Sketch some of the nets.

BRAINSTORMER

A fly decides to fly across this box from A to B.

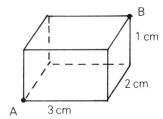

a *Copy the diagram, and draw the line which shows its shortest possible flight.*

b *The fly returns from B to A by crawling round the surfaces of the box. What is its shortest route now? Hint. Draw the net, and mark the points A and B on it.*

EXERCISE 3C

1 Mr Ferguson wants to make a toy-box with a lid that has a hinge at one side. The front of the box will be 100 cm by 50 cm, and the side of the box will be 50 cm by 60 cm. A DIY shop will cut the wood for him.

a List the details of the wood he will need.
b Draw a net for the box, measuring 1 cm on your drawing for 10 cm on the box.

2 A cereal carton has to have a base 4 cm by 5 cm, and a volume of 240 cm³.
a Calculate its height.
b Sketch a net for it, and calculate the area of the net.

3 Mr Barr is a designer. He has been asked to design small boxes to hold sweets. He decides to make them cube-shaped so that the empty boxes can be used as Alphabet Bricks. Each edge is 3 cm long.

a Draw this net, cut it out and make one of the boxes. The lid of the box must have a flap to keep it shut.
b Calculate the area of material needed (excluding the flap), and the volume of the box.
c The nets are stamped out of rectangular sheets of card 36 cm by 18 cm. Plan the best way to do this for minimum waste.

NETS OF PRISMS AND PYRAMIDS

EXERCISE 4

1

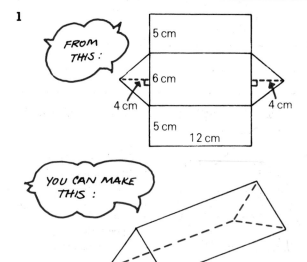

a Draw the net on squared paper. Put flaps on every second edge, cut it out, and make the prism.
b How many faces, edges and vertices does the prism have?

2 a Draw this net on squared paper. Cut it out, and make a prism.

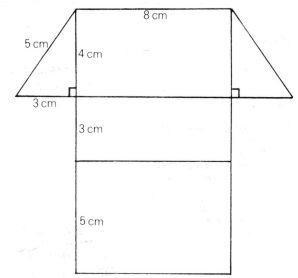

b If you put the two triangles on the net together, could you make a rectangle? Calculate the area of the net.

3 Draw a net for this tent. Remember that you won't need any material for the base!

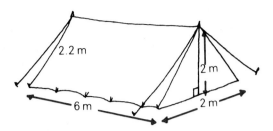

4 Both nets (**a** and **b**) opposite make pyramids. Draw them, and cut them out to make the pyramids. How many faces, edges and vertices does each one have?

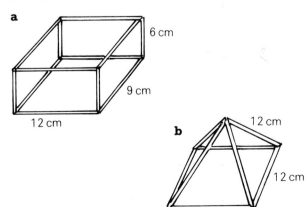

a *Square pyramid net*

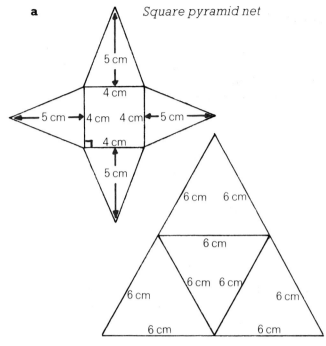

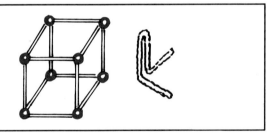

b *Triangular pyramid* or *tetrahedron net*

SKELETON MODELS

Alan and Mark noticed a wire model of a molecule of salt in the science lab. Alan decided to make his own model, using 12 pieces of straw and 8 pieces of wire pipe cleaner bent in the shape shown.
Mark made a model too, using thin canes and plasticine joints.

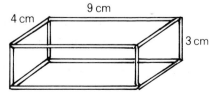

EXERCISE 5A

1 Make a list of the lengths and numbers of straws or canes needed to make each of these skeleton models.

a

6 cm

9 cm

12 cm

b

12 cm

12 cm

12 cm

2 Calculate the length of wire needed to make each of these cuboids.

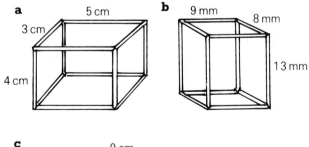

a

5 cm

3 cm

4 cm

b

9 mm

8 mm

13 mm

c

9 cm

4 cm

3 cm

215

3 a Add together the length, breadth and height of the cuboid in question **2a**. Multiply your answer by four, and compare this to the length of wire you found you would need in **2a**. Explain why the answers are the same.

b Check your answers to questions **2b** and **2c** in the same way.

4 Calculate the total length of the rods used for these skeleton models:

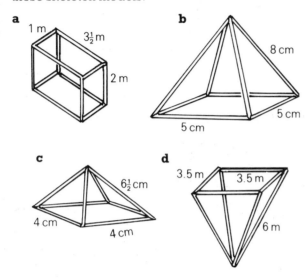

a
1 m
$3\frac{1}{2}$ m
2 m

b
8 cm
5 cm
5 cm

c
$6\frac{1}{2}$ cm
4 cm
4 cm

d
3.5 m
3.5 m
6 m

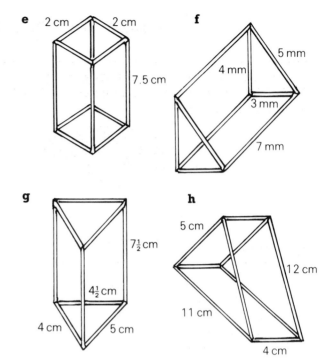

e
2 cm 2 cm
7.5 cm

f
5 mm
4 mm
3 mm
7 mm

g
$7\frac{1}{2}$ cm
$4\frac{1}{2}$ cm
4 cm 5 cm

h
5 cm
12 cm
11 cm
4 cm

5 Moya used the whole of a cane 160 cm long to make a skeleton cuboid. The base was 12 cm long and 10 cm broad. What was the height of her cuboid?

EXERCISE 5B/C

---

1 Meena was given a kit for making a box-kite for her birthday. When put together, the kite had a frame of thin wooden canes, rigidly fixed at the joints. Cloth was wrapped round the sides, leaving the square top and bottom ends open.

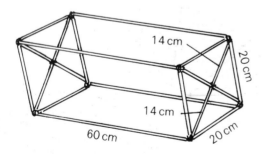

14 cm
20 cm
14 cm
60 cm
20 cm

a Make a list of the canes that were part of the kit.
b What is the total length of cane needed to make the kite?
c Calculate the length, breadth and area of cloth in the kit.

2 A children's playhouse is made of a wire frame covered with painted plastic roof and walls.

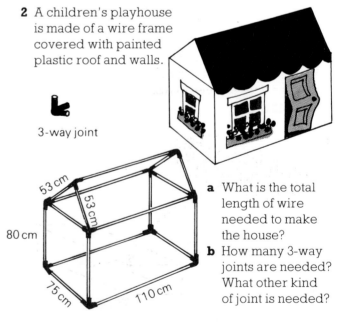

3-way joint

53 cm
53 cm
80 cm
75 cm
110 cm

a What is the total length of wire needed to make the house?
b How many 3-way joints are needed? What other kind of joint is needed?

c The triangular parts of the ends are left open to let light in. What area of plastic cover is needed for the roof and four walls of the house?
d The manufacturer of the playhouse has to put a list of contents on the box. Make out this list.

NAMES FOR POINTS, LINES AND ANGLES

It is often useful to label points, lines and angles in a diagram. If this cassette is represented by the cuboid ABCDEFGH, no mathematical information is lost, but it is easier to describe the faces, edges, vertices and angles of the cassette.

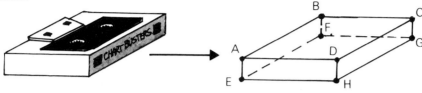

EXERCISE 6A

1 In the cassette cuboid above, name:
   a the four top corners
   b the base
   c the four shortest edges
   d the angle on top at corner D
   e a line equal in length to AB
   f the rectangle congruent to CDHG.

2

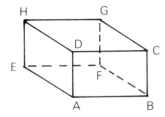

In this cuboid, name:
   a three lines parallel to AB
   b three lines parallel to AD
   c three lines parallel to AE.

3

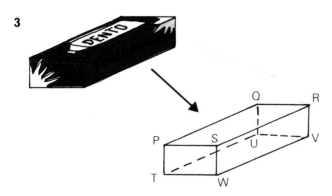

Name:
   a the face which is congruent to PQRS
   b three edges equal in length to PS
   c three edges parallel to VR
   d three right angles at corner S.

4 In this drawing, KNRO is a square.

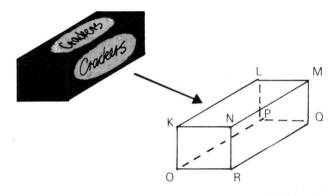

   a Is KLMNOPQR a cube?
   b Name three edges parallel to KL.
   c Name three faces congruent to KLMN.
   d Name seven lines equal to OR.

5 This box of tissues is sitting on a horizontal table.

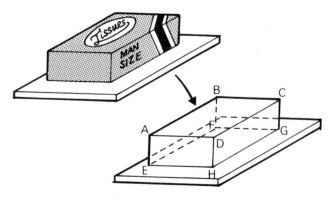

   a Name four vertical edges.
   b Are vertical lines always parallel?
   c What can you say about the four vertical edges?
   d Name two sets of horizontal parallel edges.
   e How many sets of four parallel edges are there on a cuboid?

EXERCISE 6B

1 A new energy-efficient house has been designed in the shape of a triangular prism. The sloping sides and the base are rectangles.

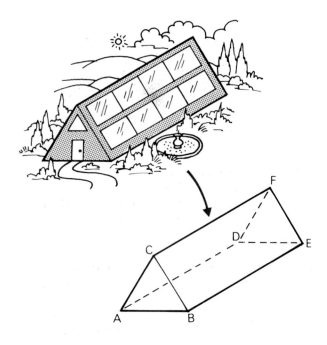

a Name:
 (i) the base
 (ii) the two triangular ends
 (iii) an edge equal to AC
 (iv) an angle equal to ∠EDF
 (v) the right angles at B.
b The side BCFE faces south. What direction does the front door face?

2 Jolly Juice are using square pyramid cartons for their Sunshine juice. The four sloping sides are congruent triangles.

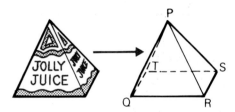

a Name:
 (i) three edges equal to PT
 (ii) four right angles
 (iii) two triangles, each of which has PS as one side.
b What line would you draw to find the height of P above the base?

3 Rain and wind don't affect the new Tetra Tents. These tents are in the shape of tetrahedrons, with all edges the same length.

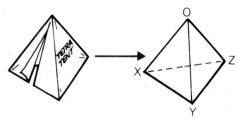

a Name all of its:
 (i) vertices
 (ii) edges
 (iii) faces.
b (i) Which edge is hidden?
 (ii) Which faces are hidden?
c Name all the angles at vertex O. What size is each angle?
d Explain why the shape is good for bad weather, but not so good for living in.

EXERCISE 6C

1

> RT and RW are two of the **face diagonals** of the cuboid.

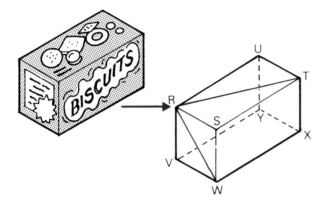

a Name two face diagonals on:
(i) STXW   (ii) VWXY.
b Name three face diagonals which are equal to:
(i) RT   (ii) RW.
c Name a face diagonal which is parallel to:
(i) RT   (ii) RW.

2 In the cuboid in question **1**, which of these angles are acute, right or obtuse?
a ∠URV   **b** ∠URT   **c** ∠URW
d ∠VWX   **e** ∠VWS   **f** ∠TRW.

3

> AG and BH are **space diagonals** of the cuboid.

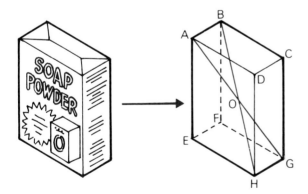

a Name the other two space diagonals in this cuboid.
b If the space diagonals all cross at O, name all the lines equal to OA.

4

> KLQR is a **diagonal plane** of cuboid KLMNOPQR.

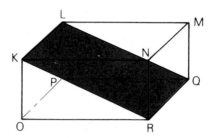

a What size is each angle of KLQR?
b What shape is KLQR?
c Name a diagonal plane congruent to KLQR.
d Name two other pairs of congruent diagonal planes.

5 The diagonal plane KLQR in question **4** divides the cuboid into two congruent 3-dimensional shapes.
a Name each, using the letters in the diagram.
b What name is given to each of these shapes?

6

> PQRS is a vertical **plane of symmetry** of the cuboid, passing through the midpoints of the sides.

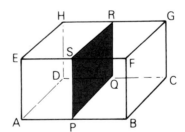

a Sketch the cuboid, and draw another vertical plane of symmetry in it. (Think of slicing it again into two equal parts.)
b How many horizontal planes of symmetry does the cuboid have?

7 A cube has four vertical planes of symmetry. Show them in separate diagrams.

8 Now draw diagrams to show the vertical planes of symmetry of:
a a triangular prism in which all the sides of the triangles are equal
b a square pyramid.

INVESTIGATION—A COLLAPSING CUBOID AND A POP-UP PERSON

1   Use a rectangular strip of paper or card to make an open-sided box ABCDEFGH which can change shape like this:

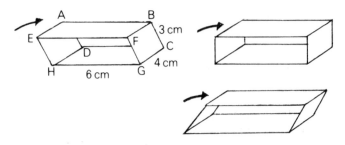

Glue the base onto the left-hand page of your notebook, with GC along the fold between the pages. Glue FBCG onto the right-hand page, and crease this page so that it stays open without pulling the box flat.

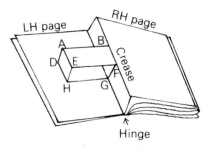

By moving the right-hand page, you should now be able to 'swing' the cuboid about its base CDHG. Investigate:
a   which faces change shape
b   which angles change size
c   which edges change direction
d   which face diagonals and space diagonals change length.

2   A picture glued onto face AEHD will pop up as your notebook opens. Investigate the maximum height the pop-up figure can be if it just disappears when you close your notebook.

3   Design a greetings card based on this pop-up cuboid idea.

CHALLENGES

1   How many cubes are there in this structure?

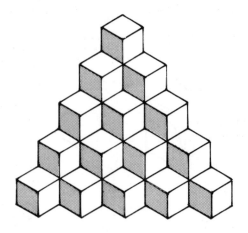

2   Draw a 5 by 3 grid of squares like the one below. Divide it into three parts, each of which is the net of an open-top cube.

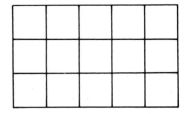

3   Sketch, and then construct, a skeleton model made from six straws, each 8 cm long. What shape is your 3-dimensional model?

CHECK-UP ON THREE DIMENSIONS

1 Which of these solids have:
a 6 faces   **b** 5 faces   **c** 9 edges   **d** 5 vertices?

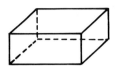

Cuboid
(all its faces
are rectangles)

Cube
(all its faces
are squares)

Square
pyramid

Cone   Cylinder   Triangular
prism

2 True or false for a cuboid?
   a It has 3 right angles at each corner.
   b It has 8 edges.
   c Its net is made up of 6 rectangles.

3

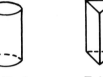

For any one of these cubes, what is the greatest
number of each of the following that you can see
at any one time:
a faces   **b** edges   **c** vertices?

4 Calculate the total length of wire needed to make
these skeleton models.
   a Cuboid   **b** Cube

3 cm

5 cm   6 cm   4 cm

5 Draw nets of the cuboid and cube in question **4**.

6 Calculate the total surface areas, and the
volumes, of the cuboid and cube in question **4**.

7

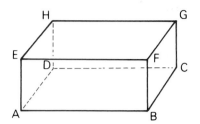

In this cuboid, name:
   a three lines parallel to AB
   b four lines perpendicular to base ABCD
   c three face diagonals through A
   d the space diagonal through A
   e three right angles at A.

8 This pyramid is on a square base of edge 6 cm.
The height of each side is 6 cm.

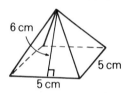

6 cm

5 cm

5 cm

   a Draw a net of the pyramid.
   b Calculate the surface area of the pyramid.

9 Which skeleton shape can you make with:
   a eight straws, each 6 cm long
   b eight straws 6 cm long, and four straws 10 cm
   long?

10 The volume of a cube is 2744 cm³. Calculate the
length of its edge, and its total surface area.

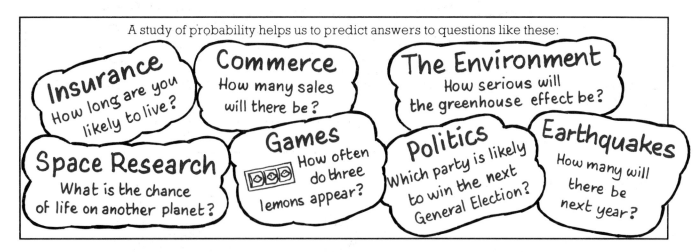

A study of probability helps us to predict answers to questions like these:

Insurance How long are you likely to live?

Commerce How many sales will there be?

The Environment How serious will the greenhouse effect be?

Space Research What is the chance of life on another planet?

Games How often do three lemons appear?

Politics Which party is likely to win the next General Election?

Earthquakes How many will there be next year?

LOOKING BACK

1

Joel and Gavin are trying to decide who will take the first turn in a game. Which of these ways are fair, and which are unfair? Give reasons for your answers.
- **a** Tossing a coin. Joel starts if it's heads.
- **b** Rolling a dice. Joel starts if an odd number comes up.
- **c** Rolling a dice. Gavin starts if a number less than 3 results.

2

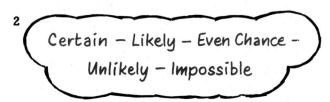

Certain – Likely – Even Chance – Unlikely – Impossible

Which would you choose to describe each event?
- **a** Tuesday is the day after Monday.
- **b** Big Ben will still be chiming 20 years from now.
- **c** You will grow to be over 3 metres tall.
- **d** If you roll a dice, you will score 6.
- **e** A pupil in the school chosen at random will be a boy.
- **f** An odd number multiplied by an odd number will produce an odd number.

3 Tina asked all the girls in her class how they travelled to school.

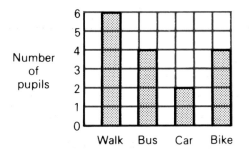

- **a** How many girls are in her class?
- **b** What fraction of them travel to school:
  (i) by car   (ii) by bus   (iii) on foot?

4 You are allowed to take one sweet from each packet. For each pair of packets, which one gives you a better chance of taking a red sweet?

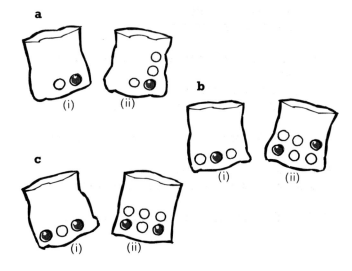

Class discussion

It will <u>probably</u> rain today.

The <u>odds</u> are against Sonia being on time.

It is <u>likely</u> that our friends will come today.

Sarah has a <u>good chance</u> of getting the job.

Terry has an <u>even chance</u> of winning.

Success and failure are <u>equally likely</u>.

Can you think of other situations where words like 'probable', 'odds', 'likely', 'chance', 'equally likely', 'even chance', are used?

All of these have a common theme—**chance**, or **probability**.

Why is a game often started by—

Tossing a coin?

Rolling a dice?

Drawing a card?

What other ways can you think of?

EXERCISE 1

Impossible   Unlikely   Even chance   Likely   Certain

Choose the best words from those above to describe the events in questions **1–12**.

1 This afternoon the weather will be:
  a very cold   **b** very hot   **c** very wet.

2 On tossing a coin you will get:
  a heads   **b** heads or tails.

3 You will leave school:
  a next week   **b** some day.

4 In your next mathematics test or examination you will score:
  a less than half marks
  b more than half marks   **c** full marks.

5 A pupil chosen at random will be left-handed.

6 On rolling a dice you will score:
  a 6   **b** 7   **c** 1, 3 or 5   **d** a number from 1 to 6.

7 You will be late for school one day next week.

8 People will land on Mars within the next:
  a year   **b** ten years   **c** century.

9 On drawing a card from a pack of playing cards, Amy will get:
  a a red card   **b** a heart   **c** an ace.

10 On rolling a dice twelve times, Alan will score 6:
  a once   **b** twice   **c** four times
  d at least once.

11 This table shows the number of boys and girls in the upper and lower classes at Burnside School. A pupil chosen at random will be:
  a in the upper section   **b** a boy.

	Upper	Lower
Boys	110	210
Girls	125	195

12 A matchstick 4 cm long is dropped onto a grid of squares with 4 cm sides. The matchstick will not touch the sides of any square.

PREDICTING PATTERNS AND PROBABILITIES

PRACTICAL PROJECTS (CLASS, GROUP OR INDIVIDUAL)

1 Tossing a coin

a *If you toss a coin 10, 20 or 30 times, how many heads would you expect to get? What fraction of your throws would be heads?*

b *Try the experiment for 10 tosses, and fill in a table like this.*

	Tally	Number
Heads		
Tails		

c *Repeat **b** several times and add your results, or else add those in your group or class.*

d *Write a sentence about your predictions in **a**, and the results in **c**.*

2 Rolling a dice

*Repeat experiment **1** for throwing a dice. As well as filling in the table show your results in a bar graph or a pie chart.*

Score	Tally	Number
1		
2		

3 Drawing a card from a pack

*Repeat experiment **1** for drawing either:*
 (i) *a black or red card*
or (ii) *a heart, diamond, club or spade*
or (iii) *an Ace, King, Queen, . . .*
Use a well-mixed pack for each draw.

4 Dropping a drawing pin

*Repeat experiment **1** for dropping a drawing pin onto a horizontal surface.*

	Tally	Number
Pin up		
Pin down		

CALCULATING PROBABILITIES

In tossing a coin there are **two** possible results, heads and tails.
There is only **one** favourable result for Peter, 'Heads'.
He has one chance in two of calling correctly.
The probability of success for Peter is $\frac{1}{2}$, and we write P(Head) = $\frac{1}{2}$.
Where there are several equally likely results

$$\textbf{the probability of a favourable result} = \frac{\textbf{number of favourable results}}{\textbf{number of possible results}}$$

Example

Ten cards are numbered from 1 to 10. The cards are mixed, and one is drawn from the pack. Calculate the probability that:
a it is the 7   **b** it is an even number.

a Favourable result: 7.
  Possible results: 1, 2, 3, 4, 5, 6, 7, 8, 9, 10 (all equally likely).
$$P(7) = \tfrac{1}{10}.$$

b Favourable results: 2, 4, 6, 8, 10.
  Possible results: 1, 2, 3, 4, 5, 6, 7, 8, 9, 10.
$$P(\text{even number}) = \tfrac{5}{10} = \tfrac{1}{2}.$$

EXERCISE 2A

These cards are mixed, and placed face down.

1 a How likely are you to choose the 6—likely, even chance, or unlikely?
b In choosing a card, how many possible results are there?
c How many are favourable results (choosing a 6)?
d What is the probability of choosing the 6? P(6) = ...

2 Repeat question **1**, for choosing an even number.

3 Repeat question **1**, for choosing a number greater than 1.

Calculating the probability gives a more definite prediction than guessing 'likely', etc.

4 a List the possible results for tossing a coin.
b Calculate the probability of a 'tail'.

5

The four cards are shuffled, and placed face down. Campbell closes his eyes and picks a card.
a How many possible results are there?
b Calculate the probability that he picks the ace.

6 A pencil-case holds red, blue, green, black and yellow pencils—one of each. Hester chooses a pencil at random.
a How many possible results are there?
b Calculate the probability that she chooses the red one.

7 Eileen rolls a dice.
a How many possible results are there?
b Calculate the probability that she scores:
(i) 4 (ii) an odd number (iii) more than 4.

8 Tony, Alice and Nicole draw straws to see who does the washing-up. There are two long straws and one short one. Tony draws first.
a How many straws are there?
b What is the probability that Tony draws:
(i) the short straw (ii) a long straw?

9 Colin's game has a special pack of cards with all the letters of the alphabet. Each card has a different letter on it. Colin draws a card.
a How many possible results are there?
b What is the probability that he draws:
(i) Z   (ii) a letter in the word IN
(iii) a vowel?

10 a For spinner A, calculate P(1).
b For spinner B, calculate:
(i) P(1) (ii) P(even number).
c For spinner C, calculate:
(i) P(3) (ii) P(odd number)
(iii) P(whole number from 1 to 5).

11 Alison has a bag of marbles, 12 white, 6 red, 4 blue, 2 green. She chooses one at random. Calculate:
a P(white) **b** P(blue) **c** P(red or green)
d P(black).

12 Daniel has the black counter, and it is his turn to throw the dice.

What is the probability that he will:
a lose £200 **b** win £1000
c go to jail **d** land on a blank square?

PRACTICAL PROJECT

Plan and carry out one or more of the following surveys to find the probability that:
1 *a car chosen at random in a car park, or passing the school, will be red*
2 *a pupil chosen at random has a birthday in December*
3 *all numbers are equally likely to be chosen when pupils are asked to pick any number from 1 to 12 to reveal a sports personality.*

EXERCISE 2B

1 Lindsay's spinner has 1 to 8 marked on it. It is equally likely to stop at any number. Calculate the probability that it stops at:
a 1   **b** an odd number
c a number greater than 6.

2 Each letter of the word PROPORTION is written on a different card. The cards are shuffled, and one is chosen. Calculate the probability that the chosen letter is:
a T   **b** P   **c** O   **d** a vowel   **e** a consonant.

3 Pam is booking her seat for her flight to Canada.

a She thinks that the probability of getting a window seat is 0.2. Check her calculation. What assumptions is she making?
b Assuming no seats have been booked, what is the probability that she will be given a seat next to an aisle?

4 Mohammed drops 5 red beads and 15 blue beads, all the same size, into a bag. He shakes them around, and takes out one bead. What is the probability that it is:
a red   **b** blue?

5 There are 25 pupils in class 1B, including three sets of twins. What is the probability that a pupil in the class, chosen at random, will be a twin?

6 A bag contains 5 white, 3 black and 2 red marbles.
a What is the probability that one chosen at random will be white?
b A white marble *is* chosen, and not put back into the bag. What is the probability that the next marble chosen will be black?

7 The bar graph shows the number of pupils in Miss Jack's class with different colours of hair.

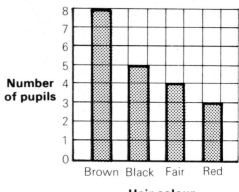

a Calculate the probability that a pupil chosen at random will have:
(i) red hair   (ii) brown hair.
b How would you choose a pupil at random?

8 Pat chooses a card from a pack of 52.

Calculate:
a P(king of hearts)   **b** P(a red king)
c P(a king)   **d** P(a heart)
e P(an ace, king, queen or jack).

9 Robin enters the lift on the fifth floor, closes his eyes and presses one of the buttons.

a Calculate the probability that the lift:
(i) stays where it is
(ii) goes down
(iii) goes up.
b What assumptions did you make?

EXERCISE 2C

1

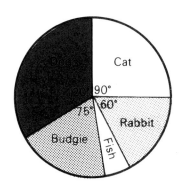

Rows

Columns

The soldiers are standing in three rows and eight columns. One is chosen at random. Calculate:
a P(he is in the front row)
b P(he is in the third column)
c P(he is in the second row and sixth column)
d P(he is in an odd row and even column).

2

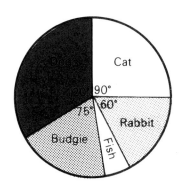

A class survey produces this pie chart of the popularity of different pets. If a class member is chosen at random and asked to choose his or her favourite pet, what is:
a P(cat)   **b** P(dog)   **c** P(rabbit)
d P(budgie)   **e** P(fish)?
Calculate the sum of the probabilities.

3 Nick and Kay are playing battleships on 10×10 grids of squares. Each has:

1 Submarine

1 Frigate

1 Aircraft-carrier

1 Battleship

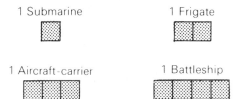

Nick fires first, choosing a square at random. Calculate the probability that he:
a hits the submarine   **b** hits the battleship
c misses all the ships.

4 Damien has to guess the day, hour and minute when the clock will stop showing the time.

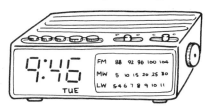

Calculate the probability, correct to three decimal places, that Damien guesses the correct:
a day   **b** hour (12-hour clock)   **c** minute.

5 One sweet is taken from each packet. For each pair of packets, which is more likely to give a red sweet?

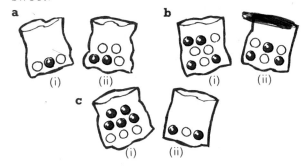

6 Ryan arrives for his exam and is given one of the empty seats. Calculate these probabilities:
a P(boy on each side)
b P(boy in desk in front)
c P(girl in desk behind)
d P(desk is in the second row from the front)
e P(boy on his left).

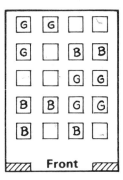

7 The diagram shows the Wilson family tree.

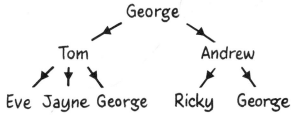

George has two sons, Tom and Andrew, who each have families of their own. George bought one raffle ticket for each family member, and one has won a prize. Calculate the probability that the prizewinner:
a is called George   **b** is a father
c has a brother   **d** has a sister.

1 *The full-time score is 'Rovers 2, United 2'. List all possible half-time scores, and find the probability that the score was a draw at half-time also.*

2 a *At noughts and crosses, Sandra plays X and Cathie plays O.*

   (i) Sandra starts, and places her first X at random. Calculate P (X in centre square).

   (ii) Sandra chooses the centre square, then Cathie plays at random. Calculate P (O in corner space).

   (iii) Cathie chooses a corner space, then Sandra plays again at random. Find the probability that she plays in such a way that Cathie has to stop a line of Xs with her next go.

b *In each of the following, find the probability that after Sandra's next go, Cathie is forced to stop a row of Xs.*

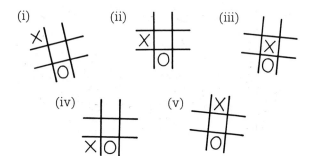

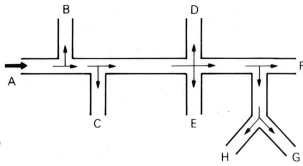

Cars entering this road system at A are equally likely to take any route at each junction. If 240 cars enter at A:

a *investigate the number likely to reach B, C, D, E, F, G, H*

b *calculate the probability that a car entering at A arrives at B, C, D, . . . , G.*

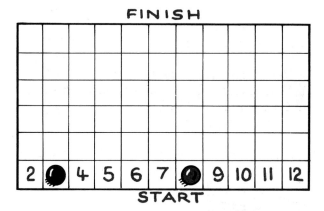

In this game each player chooses a number from 2 to 12, and puts his or her counter on it. The players then take turns to roll a pair of dice. If the numbers on the two dice total their chosen number, they move forward one square. The first person to reach the finish line wins. Investigate the probabilities of getting scores 2 to 12 to find whether this is a fair game.

CHECK-UP ON PROBABILITY

1 Choose the best word or words to describe the chance of each of these events taking place.

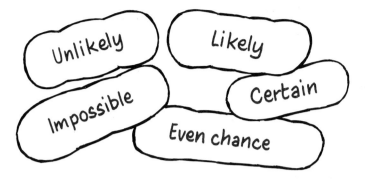

- **a** Everyone in the class will have porridge for breakfast tomorrow.
- **b** Someone in class has a birthday in May.
- **c** The sun will rise tomorrow.
- **d** The next baby to be born in Britain will be a girl.
- **e** Everyone will score more than the class average in the next maths test.

2 John rolls a dice sixty times, and gets twenty-five 3s.

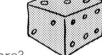

- **a** What fraction of 3s did he score?
- **b** What fraction of 3s would you have expected?
- **c** Does this suggest that there is something 'wrong' with the dice?

3 Elaine's TV set can receive BBC1, BBC2, Channel 3 and Channel 4. She selects one at random.

Calculate the probability that she gets:
a BBC1   **b** a BBC station   **c** Sky Satellite TV.

4 A letter is chosen at random from the letters of the word MISSISSIPPI. Calculate:
a P(I)   **b** P(vowel)   **c** P(consonant).

5 In a survey of 5000 homes, 2600 have central heating. Calculate the probability that a home chosen at random:
- **a** will have central heating
- **b** will not have central heating.

6 Ella rolls a dice. She needs a 3 or more to win. What is the probability that she wins?

7 The numbers in Bingo run from 1 to 100. What is the probability that the first number drawn is:
a 50   **b** an even number
c the square of a whole number?

8 A box contains 11 blue, 10 red, 5 yellow, 9 black and 15 white buttons. If one is taken out at random, calculate:
a P(red)   **b** P(yellow)   **c** P(white)
d P(green).

9 There are 28 dominoes in a 'sixes' domino set. What is the probability that a domino, chosen at random:
a is double 6   **b** is a double
c has a score of 6?

10 a Calculate the probability that if you play this game, you will:
(i) win 20p   (ii) lose 15p.
  b Who really won at the end of the day?

REVISION EXERCISES

REVISION EXERCISE ON CHAPTER 1: WHOLE NUMBERS IN ACTION

1 a Place the heights of these mountains in order, highest first:
Ben Nevis, 4406 feet; K2, 28 250 feet; Mont Blanc, 15 771 feet; Scafell, 3206 feet.
b Write the heights of K2 and Scafell in words.

2

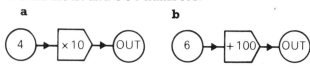

Swansea   Cardiff   Swindon Reading London
          73 km   109 km   66 km   58 km

a Calculate the rail distance from Swansea to London.
b Which journey is longer, and by how many km—London to Cardiff, or Reading to Swansea?

3 A factory packs calculators in cartons of 10 and boxes of 100.
a How many cartons, and how many boxes, would be needed to pack 800 calculators?
b How many of each would be needed for 7500 calculators?

4 There are 712 girls and 689 boys at Riverside High School.
a How many pupils are at the school?
b How many more girls than boys?

5 A box contains 24 chocolates.

a How many chocolates are needed to fill 12 boxes?
b How many boxes can be filled from a supply of 720 chocolates?

6 Find the IN and OUT numbers:

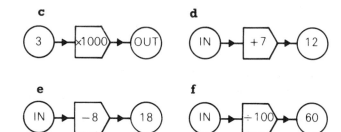

7 Find two more terms for each sequence, and explain the rule you have used:
a 7, 13, 19, 25, . . . **b** 2, 6, 18, 54, . . .
c 100, 98, 96, 94, . . . **d** 1, 3, 6, 10, . . .

8 A bank makes up bags of 1000 10p coins and 250 20p coins.

a What is the value of each bag?
b How many 50p coins would there be in bags of the same value?

9 In three throws of a dice, what sets of scores give a total of 12? (3, 4, 5 in any order is one set.)

10 Find the numbers behind the stars:

a	b	c	d	e
13	5*	*4*	3*	**2
+*8	+*3	+2*6	−*8	−6*
4*	*20	644	14	38

11 Round the heights of the mountains in question **1** to the nearest:
a 1000 feet **b** 100 feet **c** 10 feet.

12 In the City, Mrs Dawes earns £2870 each month and Mrs Morris earns £645 each week. Who earns more in a year? How much more?

REVISION EXERCISE ON CHAPTER 2: ANGLES AROUND US

1 Say whether each angle is acute, obtuse, right or straight.

a

b

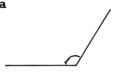

c

d

2 a Using a ruler and pencil only, try to draw angles of:
(i) 30°   (ii) 100°   (iii) 160°.

b Use a protractor to measure the angles. Write down the number of degrees you were out.

3 a Name an obtuse angle shown on this protractor. What size is it?

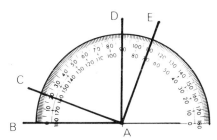

b Name an angle equal to ∠BAC. What size is it?

c Name two right angles.

4 How many degrees are there between the hands of a clock at:
a 9 am   **b** noon   **c** 4 pm   **d** 7 pm?

5 a How many degrees are there in the smallest angle between:
(i) N and S
(ii) NW and SW
(iii) S and SE
(iv) NE and S?

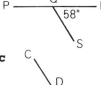

b A weather vane pointing east swings through an acute angle. Which of the eight compass points might it be facing now?

6 What size of angle must be:
a added to 280° to give a complete turn
b subtracted from 265° to give a straight angle?

7 Calculate the size of the angle, in degrees, between the spokes of:
a the front wheel
b the back wheel.

8 In one complete turn of a wheel, a bicycle travels two metres. How far does it travel when the wheel turns through:
a 720°   **b** 180°   **c** 270°?

9 The golfer is playing from A to B.

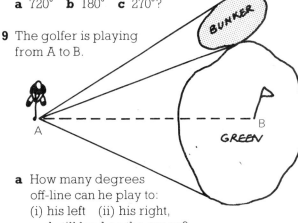

a How many degrees off-line can he play to:
(i) his left   (ii) his right,
and still land on the green?

b His ball lands in the bunker. What can you say about the number of degrees he is off line?

10 Name and calculate the size of each unmarked angle below.

a

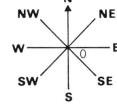

b

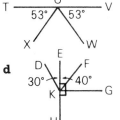

c

d

11 a On this swing, name all the:
(i) horizontal lines
(ii) vertical lines.

b Name two pairs of equal angles, apart from the right angles.

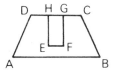

12 The pointer on a weighing machine makes a complete turn when a 20 kg weight is put on the scales. What angle will it turn through when four 3.5 kg parcels are weighed?

REVISION EXERCISE ON CHAPTER 3: LETTERS AND NUMBERS

1 Find y for each picture.

a

b
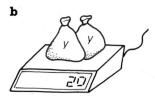

c
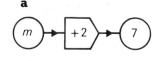

d

2 The numbers in each set (**a**–**e**) add up to 20. Find the number that each letter stands for:
a 2, 10, x **b** y, 1, 1 **c** t, t, 10 **d** k, 18, k
e 8, n, 12

3 Which numbers do these letters stand for?

a
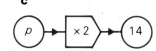

b
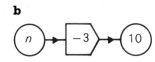

c
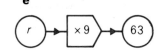

d
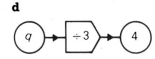

e
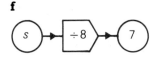

f

4 Write in a shorter form:
a $x+x+x$ **b** $2y+y$ **c** $3t-t$
d $4p-2p$ **e** $x+x+y-y$ **f** $2x-2x+3y-y$
g $5x-x+6$ **h** $3x-3x+4-4$

5 Which numbers do the letters stand for in the sequences in this spreadsheet?

	A	B	C	D	E
1	3	4	a	6	7
2	6	b	10	12	14
3	9	12	15	c	21
4	d	16	20	24	28
5	15	20	25	30	e

6 Give the total number of coins in each picture.

a

b
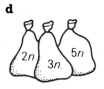

c

d

7 In question **6**, there are 20 coins in each picture. Find the numbers that x, t, y and n stand for.

8

Part of a keyboard

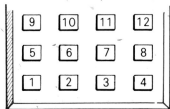

Copy and complete these parts of the keyboard.

a

b

c

9 Simplify:
a $t+t+t+t$ **b** $4n+3n+2n+n$
c $3k+2k+3+2$ **d** $m+1+m+1$
e $2p+3-p-2$ **f** $2x+y+x+2y$
g $3c+d-c-d$ **h** $2u-v+2v-u$

REVISION EXERCISE ON CHAPTER 4: DECIMALS IN ACTION

1 a Write in figures:
 (i) ten point five
 (ii) two hundred and fifty point two one.
 b Write in words:
 (i) 20.6 (ii) 407.9 (iii) 0.01

2 Greg Louganis scored 710.91 points for highboard diving in the Olympic Games. What figure shows:
 a hundreds **b** hundredths **c** tenths?

3 Arrange in order, smallest first: 1.09, 1.1, 8.9, 1.01, 1.3.

4 Write these amounts of money in figures:
 a three pounds eighty pence
 b twenty pounds nine pence.

5 Which numbers are the arrows pointing to?

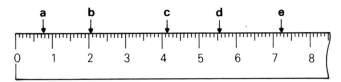

6 In a gymnastics competition, Dawn scored 9.9 and Sharon scored a maximum 10 points. Gill's score was halfway between these. What was it?

7 Ten pencils cost £1.20. At the same rate, calculate the cost of:
 a 100 pencils **b** 1000 pencils **c** 1 pencil.

8 Calculate the perimeter of this L-shape. The lengths are in centimetres.

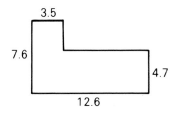

9 A unit of electricity costs 5.76 pence.
 a Estimate the cost of:
  (i) 8 units (ii) 23 units (iii) 77 units.
 b Calculate the actual costs, to the nearest penny.
 c How many whole units can be bought for £50?

10 Calculate:
 a 24.5×3.14 **b** $15.64 \div 2.3$ **c** 0.35 of £5.

11 Write in decimal form:
 a $3\frac{3}{10}$ **b** $2\frac{25}{100}$ **c** $25\frac{1}{100}$

12

Diagram of a fishplate for joining rails together. Lengths in millimetres.

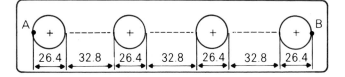

 a Calculate the distance from A to B in the diagram above.
 b The plate is 260 mm long. A and B are equal distances from the two ends of the plate. Calculate this distance.

13 Donald bought two different makes of golf ball. One cost £1.35 each, the other cost £1.40 each. He received 40p change from £10. How many of each type did he buy?

14 Joan looks at the exchange rates of £s for American dollars: $1.7375 for £1.
 a How much should she get for £250, to the nearest cent (hundredth of a dollar).
 b Later she changed $25 back to £s at the same rate. How much did she receive, to the nearest 10p?

REVISION EXERCISE ON CHAPTER 5: FACTS, FIGURES AND GRAPHS

1 This pictogram illustrates the entries in the local flower show.

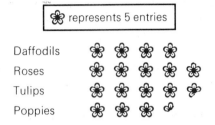

✿ represents 5 entries

Daffodils	✿ ✿ ✿ ✿
Roses	✿ ✿ ✿ ✿ ✿
Tulips	✿ ✿ ✿ ✿ ✿
Poppies	✿ ✿ ✿ ✿

  a How many daffodil entries were there?
  b Which flower had most entries?
  c How many entries were there altogether?

2 36 pupils were asked about the number of children in their family.

Number of children in family	1	2	3	4	5
Number of families	6	9	14	4	3

  a Draw a bar graph.
  b What fraction of the pupils had no brothers or sisters?

3 Penny went on a diet, and kept a weekly chart of her weight.

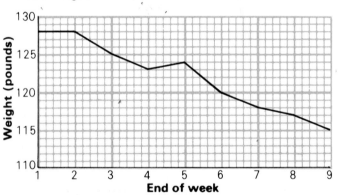

  a How much weight had she lost after 9 weeks?
  b What did she weigh after 7 weeks?
  c During which week did she gain weight?

4 A recent report on houses built by Happyhomes plc is shown in the table.

Year	1987	1988	1989	1990	1991	1992
No. of houses built	86	70	58	50	40	44

  a Draw a line graph of the report.
  b Write a sentence about the figures.

5 A survey of favourite crisp flavours produced this pie chart.

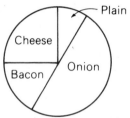

  a List the crisps in order, with the most popular first.
  b What fraction of people preferred:
    (i) onion (ii) cheese (iii) other flavours?

6 This is how the Russell family spend their money each week: food £60, fuel £45, council tax £25, clothes £30, other £20. Draw a pie chart to show their average weekly expenditure.

7 The Growmore Building Society's receipts and withdrawals for the first six months of last year are shown in the graphs.

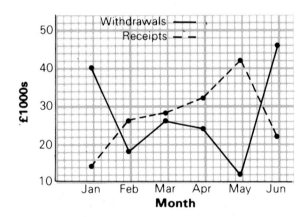

  a In which month were withdrawals at their peak? How much was withdrawn then?
  b During which month was the difference between receipts and withdrawals greatest? What was the difference?
  c How much money did the Society take in altogether over this six-month period?

8 1A's marks in a class test:
   5 10 12 8 15 19 14 13 18
   17 12 20 9 12 15 19 13 7
   17 16 10 9 18 16 13 15 15
  a Put the marks in class intervals 1–5, 6–10, etc.
  b Draw a bar graph of the marks.

REVISION EXERCISE ON CHAPTER 6: MEASURING TIME AND TEMPERATURE

1 Which month:
  a has the fewest number of days
  b is the first month in the year with 30 days
  c is the last month with 30 days?

2 How many days are there in:
  a a fortnight **b** July **c** a leap year?

3 a April 28th is a Tuesday. What day is May 7th?
  b How many days are there from 28th April to 7th May, including both given dates?

4 a Classes begin at 8.50 am and end at 12.05 pm. How long is this?
  b Afternoon classes start at 12.50 pm and last 2 hours 30 minutes. When do they end?

5 Write down the time on each clock, using am or pm time.

a  **b**

c  **d**

6 How long is it from the time on:
  (i) clock **a** to clock **b** (ii) clock **c** to clock **d**?

7 Write down the times on the clocks in question **5** in 24 hour time.

8 Which is the fastest, and which is the slowest train journey from Seaton to Sandy Bay?

Seaton	08 50	11 25	13 10	14 55	17 48
Sandy Bay	10 20	13 00	14 35	16 40	19 05

9 The temperature in London is 16°C and in Glasgow 9°C.
  a Which city is warmer? By how many degrees?
  b The temperature in Glasgow rises 4°C. What is the new temperature?

10 Write these temperatures in order, coldest first:
  3°C, −4°C, 1°C, 0°C, −9°C, 8°C

11 John's temperature was taken at 9 am, and again at 6 pm, as shown on the thermometers.

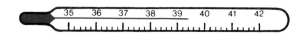

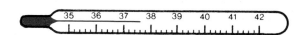

  a How many degrees was each temperature above normal (37°C)?
  b How many degrees did his temperature fall during this time?

12

Moscow = −6°C
Athens = 12°C
Helsinki = −12°C

  a Which city has:
   (i) the highest temperature
   (ii) the lowest temperature?
  b What is the difference in temperature between the highest and lowest?

13

Euston	depart	22 30
Inverness	arrive	09 35

Inverness	depart	19 30
Euston	arrive	06 49

  a Which journey is quicker?
  b By how much?

REVISION EXERCISE ON CHAPTER 7: COORDINATES: X MARKS THE SPOT

1 Margaret has a picture puzzle, but the pieces are all mixed up (Picture 1), and she has to rearrange them to look like Picture 2. A4 → B3 moves the piece at A4 to its correct place at B3. Help her to solve the puzzle by moving all the parts in the same way.

Picture 1

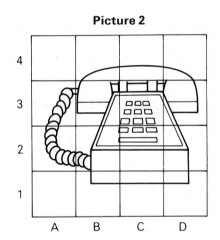

Picture 2

2 Join these points in the given order to draw a pentagon and its diagonals:
A(-6, 6), C(2, 6), E(-5, -1), B(-2, 8),
D(1, -1) → A → B → C → D → E → A.

3

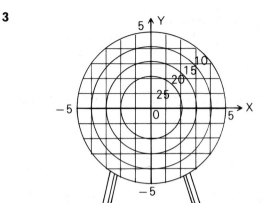

a Mandy fires three arrows at the target. They land at (-2, 4), (2, -1) and (1, 3). Find her total score.

b James' arrows hit (-3, 1), (-1, 1) and (-2, -3). What is his score?

c In the next round, Mandy hits (1, 1), (4, 2) and (-2, -4). James hits (-2, -1), (1, -2) and (2, -3). Who won this round?

4 A(1, 1), B(4, 1), C(4, 4) and D(1, 4) are vertices of the front face of a cube. Other vertices are at E(6, 2), F(6, 5), G(3, 5) and H. Draw the cube on squared paper, and write down the coordinates of the hidden vertex H.

5 a Draw a pair of coordinate axes, and then draw lines through all the points with:
   (i) x-coordinate 4   (ii) x-coordinate 8
   (iii) y-coordinate 2.

   b Draw two lines parallel to the x-axis, each of which completes a square with the three lines in **a**.

   c Write down the equations of these two lines.

6 a Draw the hexagon formed by P(-2, 2), Q(2, 4), R(6, 2), S(6, -4), T(2, -6) and U(-2, -4).

   b Draw the diagonals and write down the coordinates of the point where they cross.

REVISION EXERCISE ON CHAPTER 8: SOLVING EQUATIONS

1 Solve these equations.
 a $y+9 = 11$ **b** $t-3 = 4$ **c** $x+4 = 4$
 d $r-6 = 6$ **e** $w+1 = 17$ **f** $4+k = 8$
 g $8-x = 2$ **h** $10-c = 10$

2 Make an equation for each picture (**a**–**d**), and then solve it.

a

b

c

d
4 weights missing

3 Use the sequences in the rows and columns to make as many equations as you can. Then solve them.

	A	**B**	**C**	**D**
1	2	3	$y+1$	5
2	5	6	7	$2t$
3	$x-3$	9	10	11
4	11	12	$7y-1$	14

4 Solve:
 a $2y-1 = 7$ **b** $4x+2 = 10$ **c** $3t-5 = 10$
 d $8c+2 = 18$ **e** $7d-5 = 23$ **f** $6f+7 = 49$
 g $12x-2 = 10$ **h** $13m+12 = 12$

5 Make equations for these pictures, and solve them.

a

b

c

d

(1 weight is missing from the open bag.)   (3 weights are missing from each open bag.)

6 The edges of a cuboid are x cm, $2x$ cm and $4x$ cm long.
 a What is the total length of the edges, in terms of x?
 b If the total length is 56 cm, make an equation and find x.
 c Write down the lengths of the sides of the cuboid.

7 Make equations for these pictures, and solve them.

a

b

c
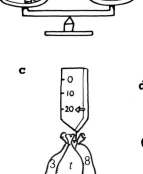

d

8 Solve these equations:
 a $18-2x = 8$ **b** $17+3x = 26$
 c $17 = 3y-4$ **d** $20 = 5t+15$
 e $41 = 12+29m$ **f** $40-3x = 1$
 g $5m-3m+7 = 15$ **h** $4t-t+10 = 31$
 i $8+7k+8k-3 = 80$ **j** $6r+5r-r = 100$
 k $5x-3-2x+7x = 147$

REVISION EXERCISE ON CHAPTER 9: MEASURING LENGTH

1 Which metric unit would you use to measure:
  a the height of a lamppost
  b the distance from London to Paris
  c the thickness of a compact disc
  d the width of a TV screen?

2 Write down the lengths of the lines OA, OB and AB in:
  a mm **b** cm.

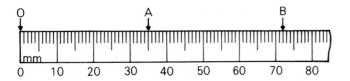

3 The top of a matchbox measures 5.3 cm by 3.7 cm.
  a Draw an accurate rectangle for the top. Measure the length of its diagonal.
  b Calculate the perimeter of the rectangle.

4 Measure the diameters of these circles in:
  a millimetres **b** centimetres.

5 Mrs Jackson lives 24 km from the school where she works. How far does she drive, to and from work, in a five day week?

6 In 1991 the women's triple jump record was 14.52 m, and the men's record was 17.97 m. How much longer was the men's record jump?

7 Each brick is 20 cm long and 8 cm high. The cement between each brick is 0.5 cm thick.

Calculate:
  a the height of the wall
  b the number of bricks in the top row of a wall 102 cm long.

8 Measure the front of your calculator, and find its perimeter, correct to the nearest centimetre.

9 A racing circuit is 6.5 km long.
  a How far will a car have travelled after 50 laps?
  b One car covers 416 km in a race. How many laps did it complete?

10 Two ladders are 3.85 m and 2.67 m long.
  a Estimate the difference in their lengths, and their total length if laid end to end.
  b Calculate the lengths in **a**.

11 £1 gift stamps 15 mm long come in rolls 3 m long. How much would a roll cost?

12 The lengths, in kilometres, of road resurfaced each day by Renew Road Repairs are listed here.

Calculate:
  a the total length of road resurfaced that week
  b the length that must still be done to complete 10 km.

Monday	... 1.275
Tuesday	... 1.850
Wednesday	... 1.425
Thursday	... 1.645
Friday	... 1.930

REVISION EXERCISE ON CHAPTER 10: TILING AND SYMMETRY

1 Draw each of these shapes on squared paper, and show how to make tilings based on them.

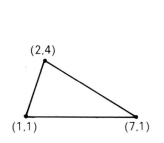
(2,4)
(1,1)   (7,1)

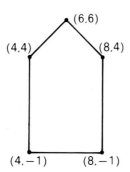
(6,6)
(4,4)   (8,4)
(4,−1)   (8,−1)

2 a Plot each set of points below on squared paper, and join them up in order.
(i) $(2, 0), (0, 4), (-2, 0), (0, -1)$
(ii) $(2, 3), (-2, 3), (-2, -3), (2, -3)$
(iii) $(2, 0), (1, 2), (-1, 2), (-2, 0), (-1, -2),$
    $(1, -2)$
(iv) $(3, 0), (1, 1), (0, 3), (-1, 1), (-3, 0),$
    $(-1, -1), (0, -3), (1, -1)$

b How many axes of symmetry does each shape have?

c Through how many degrees, up to 360°, can you turn each shape about the origin to make it fit its outline?

3 State whether each shape below has:
(i) line symmetry   (ii) turn symmetry
(iii) neither type of symmetry.

a   **b**

c   **d**

e   **f**

g   **h**

4 Plot the following points, joining them in the order given.
$(1, 1), (2, 1), (2, 3), (3, 3), (3, 4), (2, 4), (2, 5), (4, 5),$
$(4, 6), (1, 6), (1, 1)$
a The shape is reflected in the y-axis. Draw the image, and list the coordinates of its vertices.
b The shape is reflected in the x-axis. Draw the image, and list the coordinates of its vertices.
c Find the coordinates of the image of the original shape after reflection in the x-axis and then in the y-axis.

5 Each of the following shapes has rotational symmetry about its centre. State the order in each case.

a   **b**

c   **d**

e   **f**

g   **h**

REVISION EXERCISE ON CHAPTER 11: MEASURING AREA

1 Find the area of each shape (**a**–**d**) by counting squares.

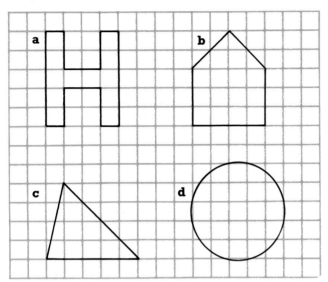

2 Calculate the area of each object below. Include the units in your answers.

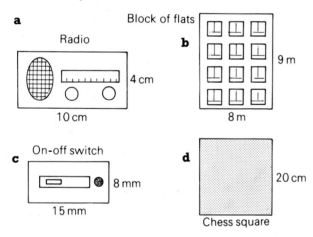

3 Fran wants to pave round the edges of her garden, leaving a 4 m by 3 m rectangular flower bed in the middle.

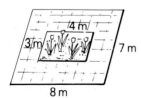

  a Calculate the area of:
   (i) the whole garden   (ii) the flower bed
   (iii) the paved part.
  b What would be the cost of paving at £5 per square metre?

4 Calculate the areas of the triangles below.

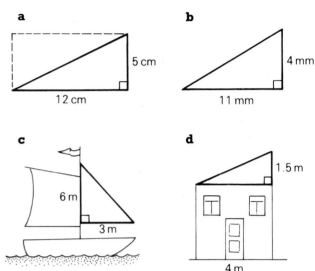

5 Calculate the breadth of:
  a a postcard 17 cm long, with an area of 204 cm²
  b a stamp 40 mm long, with an area of 300 mm².

6 Calculate the areas of these shapes, which are all made up of rectangles and right-angled triangles.

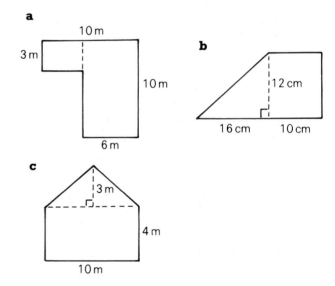

7 a Find the dimensions of all possible rectangles that can be made with 24 square paving stones 1 metre long. The stones must not be broken up.
   b Which has:
    (i) the greatest perimeter
    (ii) the smallest perimeter?

REVISION EXERCISE ON CHAPTER 12: LETTERS, NUMBERS AND SEQUENCES

1 Find the missing entries in these spreadsheets.

a

	A
1	7
2	14
3	21
12	
13	
x	

b

	A
1	6
2	7
3	8
19	
20	
n	

c

	A
1	4
2	8
3	12
23	
24	
t	

2 a

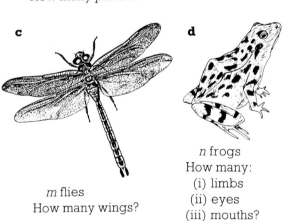

x packets
How many pencils?

b

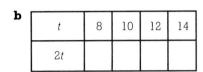

y weights
How many grams?

c

m flies
How many wings?

d

n frogs
How many:
  (i) limbs
  (ii) eyes
  (iii) mouths?

3 Find the value of:
  a $2x$, when $x = 3$ **b** $4y - 1$, when $y = 6$
  c $y + 4$, when $y = 7$ **d** $7t + 1$, when $t = 5$
  e $10 - x$, when $x = 4$ **f** $6 + 3m$, when $m = 2$

4 Copy and complete these tables:

a

y	1	2	3	4
$y - 1$				

b

t	8	10	12	14
$2t$				

c

m	5	8	11	14
$3m + 1$				

5 a One 50p coin and t 10p coins. How many pence altogether?

  b t triangles and s squares. How many sides altogether?

6

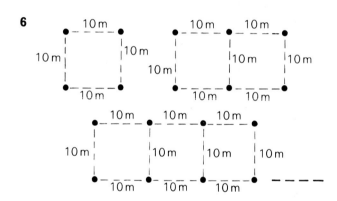

Copy and complete this table:

Number of enclosures	1	2	3	4	5		20		n
Number of posts									
Total length of fence (m)									

7 A rectangle has sides a cm, a cm, b cm and b cm long.
  a Write down a formula for its perimeter P cm.
  b Calculate P when $a = 15$ and $b = 12$.

REVISION EXERCISE ON CHAPTER 13: TWO-DIMENSIONS— RECTANGLE AND SQUARE

1 Draw a rectangle ABCD and a square PQRS. In each one, mark:
   a the sizes of the angles   **b** the equal sides
   c the parallel sides (use arrows)
   d the axes of symmetry (use dotted lines).

2 The Scottish Saltire flag is a blue rectangle with a white cross from corner to corner.

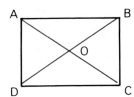 

   a What are the lines AC and BD called?
   b AC = 180 cm. What are the lengths of:
      (i) BD   (ii) AO   (iii) OB?
   c ∠ODC = 40°. What are the sizes of:
      (i) ∠ODA   (ii) ∠OCD?

3 VWXY is a square. Copy the diagram, and fill in the lengths of as many lines, and the sizes of as many angles as you can.

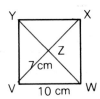

4 R(3, 2), S(7, 2), T(7, 6) are vertices of a square RSTU. Find the coordinates of:
   a U
   b the point of intersection of its diagonals.

5 A house 15 m long and 12 m wide is built in the centre of a rectangular plot 45 m long and 27 m wide, with its sides parallel to the sides of the plot. Draw two possible sketches of the house and plot, and calculate the widths of the sections of garden around the house in each case.

6 How many axes of symmetry has each face of this dice?

  a   **b**   **c**

7 Draw a rectangle with diagonals 10 cm long, crossing at an angle of 60°. Measure the length and breadth of the rectangle.

8 a Draw the line from K(5, 6) to L(5, 1), then complete two possible squares KLMN.
   b Give the coordinates of the two possible positions of M and N, and of the centre of each square.

9   (i)      (ii)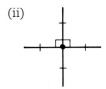

   (iii)   (iv)

Which of these pairs of lines could be the diagonals of:
   a a square   **b** a rectangle?

10 Towns A, B, C, D lie at the corners of a rectangle, and town E is at the midpoint of AC.

A●   ● B

          ● E

D●   ● C

   a Copy and complete the table of distances shown.

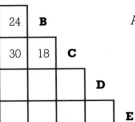

A to B = 24 km

   b What is the length of a bus journey from A → B → C → D → E → A?

REVISION EXERCISE ON CHAPTER 14: MEASURING VOLUME

1 Which unit would you use to measure the volume of:
a a box of cereal **b** a room **c** a matchstick?

2 Which metric unit would you use for the capacity of:
a a petrol tank **b** a spoonful of medicine?

3 Marjory buys a 2-litre bottle of fabric conditioner for her washing machine.

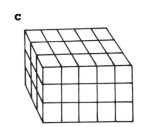

a How many millilitres is this?
b How many 50 ml capfuls will she get from it?

4 How many cubes are there in each solid below?

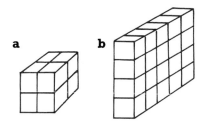

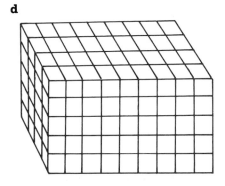

5 Calculate the volume of each container. Include units in your answers.

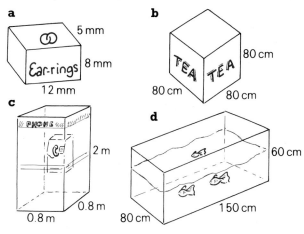

6 Find the volume of the fish tank in **5d** above in:
a millilitres **b** litres.

7

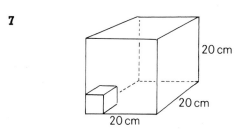

Tim has a number of toy cube bricks which are stored in this box. The edges of the bricks are all 5 cm long. How many bricks will fit:
a along one edge of the box **b** in one layer
c in the box?

8 a

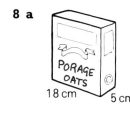

Volume = 2250 cm³
What is the height of the box?

b

Volume = 980 cm³
The ends are square.
What are the dimensions of the ends?

9 Rachael needs a new freezer. The Icicle is 100 cm by 50 cm by 40 cm, and costs £180. The Arctic is 70 cm by 60 cm by 50 cm, and costs £195.
a Which has the larger capacity in litres?
b Which gives more freezing space per £1 of purchase price?

REVISION EXERCISE ON CHAPTER 15: FRACTIONS AND PERCENTAGES

1 What fraction of each shape is shaded?

a 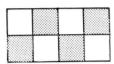 **b**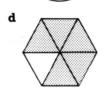

c **d**

2 Now copy the shapes in question **1**, but in **a** shade $\frac{3}{4}$, **b** $\frac{1}{5}$, **c** $\frac{5}{8}$ and **d** $\frac{1}{3}$.

3 What fraction of the numbers in the bag are:
a even **b** odd **c** greater than 6?

4 Simplify:
a $\frac{5}{10}$ **b** $\frac{4}{6}$ **c** $\frac{9}{12}$ **d** $\frac{6}{14}$ **e** $\frac{60}{100}$ **f** $\frac{32}{36}$

5 What fraction of £1, in simplest form, is:
a 10p **b** 15p **c** 48p **d** 75p?

6 Calculate:
a $\frac{1}{2}$ of £3 **b** $\frac{1}{5}$ of £15 **c** $\frac{2}{3}$ of £12 **d** $\frac{3}{10}$ of £40.

7

How much would you pay for a pair of:
a shoes **b** boots?

8 What fraction is each term in the sequence of the term before it?
a 16, 8, 4, 2, . . . **b** 27, 9, 3, . . .
c 10 000, 1000, 100, . . .

9 Calculate the area of a floor 8 m long and $2\frac{1}{2}$ m broad.

10 Stefan has 120 p. He spends $\frac{1}{2}$ of it on magazines, $\frac{1}{3}$ of the remainder on sweets and $\frac{1}{4}$ of what is now left on his bus fare. How much has he left?

11 Express as fractions:
a 7% **b** 10 per cent **c** 100%

12 Write as percentages:
a $\frac{9}{100}$ **b** $\frac{3}{10}$ **c** $\frac{3}{4}$ **d** $\frac{7}{20}$ **e** $\frac{21}{25}$

13 Calculate:
a 10% of £80 **b** 25% of £20 **c** 20% of £9
d 15% of £420

14

20% off all items

£150   £385   £45

a What discount would be given on each of the three items?
b How much would you pay for each one?

15 a Change all Peter's marks to percentages.

English $^{14}/_{20}$ French $^{21}/_{30}$
Maths $^{37}/_{50}$ History $^{54}/_{75}$

b List his subjects in order, best first.

16 Calculate the cost of this restaurant bill.

	£
3 Soups at £1·20 each	
2 Salads at £4·25 "	
1 Haddock at £4·50 "	
3 Coffees at 80p "	
SUB TOTAL	
VAT at 15%	
TOTAL COST	

17 A piece of elastic 20 cm long is stretched to double the length. Calculate:
a the increase in length
b the fractional increase in length
c the percentage increase.

18 The pie chart shows where the village sports club makes its profits.
Calculate:
a the percentage made from putting
b the actual profit from each, if the total is £18 000.

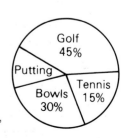

REVISION EXERCISE ON CHAPTER 16: SOLVING MORE EQUATIONS

1 Solve these equations.
  a $w-5=7$ **b** $2t=16$ **c** $4x-2=14$
  d $3m-7=14$ **e** $12-n=8$ **f** $17=2x+5$
  g $3t+4-2t=9$ **h** $7-x+3x=27$

2 What entries go into the empty boxes or circles below?

a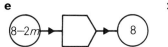

b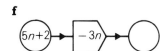

c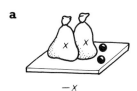

d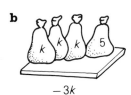

e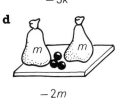

f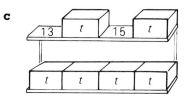

3 Find the number of weights on each tray after the given action.

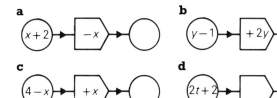

a $-x$ **b** $-3k$

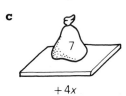

c $+4x$ **d** $-2m$

4 Solve these equations.
  a $4x=3x+2$ **b** $2r=9-r$ **c** $5m=2m+9$
  d $5t=4t+6$ **e** $8k=35+3k$ **f** $4n=n+18$
  g $4c-15=c$ **h** $6p=14-p$

5 Make an equation for each picture, and solve it. Check your solution.

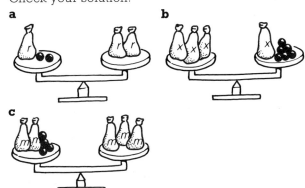

6 Make an equation for each *pair* of shelves, and solve it. Then find the length of each shelf. Units are centimetres.

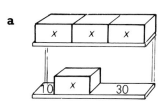

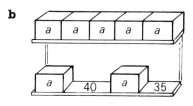

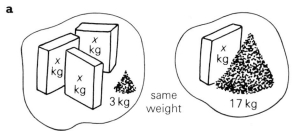

7 Solve:
  a $2x+1=x+8$ **b** $4y-2=2y+10$
  c $4t-4=t-1$ **d** $5m+6=18-m$
  e $5-n=10-2n$ **f** $7+3k=35-k$
  g $9c+7=5c+11$ **h** $12e+12=7e+22$

8 Make an equation for each pair of pictures, and solve it. Remember to check your solution.

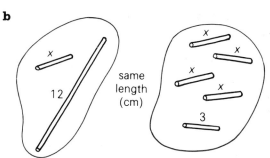

REVISION EXERCISE ON CHAPTER 17: THREE DIMENSIONS

1 Sophie was looking at some games and puzzles.

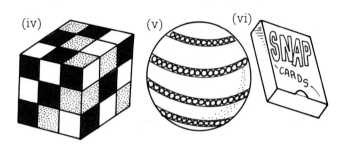

a Which ones contain cubes and cuboids?
b What other shapes are there?

2

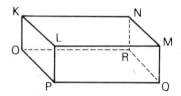

This fish tank is in the shape of a cuboid. Name:
a three edges parallel to PQ
b four edges at right angles to PQ
c four edges perpendicular to the base
d the face congruent to PLKO.

3 a Draw the net of a dice with edge 2 cm long.
b Calculate the surface area and the volume of the dice.

4 The top, bottom and two sides of a shoe box are rectangles 30 cm long and 10 cm wide. What are the dimensions of the ends of the box?

5 A block of flats is shaped like a cuboid. Name:
a the vertical edges
b the horizontal edges
c the face parallel to PQRS
d three right angles at W
e two horizontal faces
f the space diagonals.

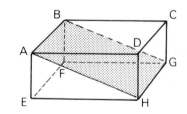

6 What length of wire would be needed to make a skeleton model of the block of flats in question **5**, if you used 1 cm of wire for 1 m on the flats?

7 a Draw a net for this brass coal box. Use a scale of 1 cm for 10 cm on the box.

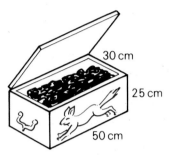

b Calculate:
(i) the volume
(ii) the surface area of the box.

8 Which skeleton models can be made with:
a 12 straws 5 cm long
b 4 straws 10 cm long and 4 straws 15 cm long
c 6 straws of 8 cm and 3 straws of 6 cm?

9 The technical department made ramps by sawing wooden cuboids in half along a diagonal plane.

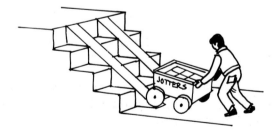

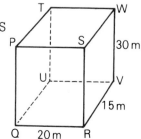

a What name is given to:
(i) AH (ii) AG?
b Name three lines equal to:
(i) AH (ii) BH.
c How many cuboids had to be cut to make a ramp for these stairs?

10 Draw the net of a pyramid with a rectangular base.

REVISION EXERCISE ON CHAPTER 18: PROBABILITY

1 Choose the best word or words to describe the chance of these events taking place.

a If you add two odd numbers you will get an even number.

b If you multiply two odd numbers you will get an even number.

c Theo will get an odd number when he rolls a dice.

d There will be a General Election in Britain this year.

e In two tosses of a coin, you will get at least one 'head'.

2

Stacey chooses an apple at random. One of them is bad. What is the probability that she chooses:
a the bad one   **b** a good one?

3 Toby made a tally table of the lunch arrangements of 40 pupils. Calculate the probability that a pupil chosen at random:
a goes home
b has school lunch
c brings a packed lunch.

School lunch	ЖГ ЖГ ЖГ
Packed lunch	ЖГ ЖГ II
Go home	ЖГ III
Other	ЖГ

4 In a game, Melissa wins if she scores more than 4 with a dice. What is the probability of her winning when she rolls a dice?

5 Geoff uses this spinner in a cricket game. He scores the number the spinner stops at. W means he loses a wicket. What is the probability that on the next spin, he:
a loses a wicket
b scores 1
c scores more than 1?

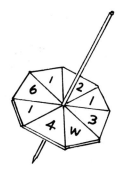

6 A letter is chosen at random from the word INVESTIGATIONS. Find:
a P(I)   **b** P(T)   **c** P(vowel)
d P(letter in second half of alphabet).

7 Kerry rolls a dice. She needs a 6 to win! Jonathan tosses a coin. He needs a 'head' to win! Who is more likely to win? Why?

8 There are 240 girls and 160 boys on the roll of St Andrews Academy. A pupil is chosen at random to make a prize draw. What is the probability that a girl is chosen?
Give your answer as a percentage.

9 A ball is chosen at random from each bag. From which bag are you more likely to choose a white ball? Explain.

a   **b**

ANSWERS

1 WHOLE NUMBERS IN ACTION

Page 1 Looking Back

1 37 **2** 1080 km **3** 100; 10
4a 1, 7 **b** 10, 50, 90
5a 80 miles **b** 190 miles **c** 440 miles
6a 100 miles **b** 200 miles **c** 400 miles
7a 0 **b** 18 **c** 480 **d** 1100 **e** 5 **f** 90 **g** 20
8a 4 = 4+0 = 3+1 = 2+2 = 1+3 = 0+4
b 7 = 7+0 = 6+1 = 5+2 = 4+3 = 3+4 = 2+5 = 1+6 = 0+7
c 10 = 10+0 = 9+1 = 8+2 = 7+3 = 6+4 = 5+5 = 4+6 = 3+7 = 2+8 = 1+9 = 0+10
9a 22, 28 **b** 23, 20 **c** 27, 81 **d** 2, 1
10a 48 **b** 9 **c** 6 **d** 28
11a (i) 406 (ii) 380 **b** 118
12 £105 **13a** 30 **b** 20 **c** 15 **d** 12 **e** 10 **f** 7 **g** 6
h 4 **14** £3.06

Page 2 Exercise 1A

1a 3 **b** 31, 11, 24 miles **2a** 33 miles **b** 22 miles
c 11 miles **3** 55 miles
4 The scores are doubled and trebled
5a (i) 8 (ii) 14 (iii) 21 (iv) 9 (v) 24 (vi) 30
(vii) 36 (viii) 36 (ix) 42 (x) 38 (xi) 51 (xii) 57
b 60 **6** Robert: 1+double 3, or 3+double 2, or
5+double 1; Liz: 1+double 4, or 3+double 3, or
5+double 2, or 7+double 1

Page 3 Exercise 1B/C

1 W-N35; W-CC31; W-S43; S-CC38; S-E42; N-CC28;
N-E51; CC-E29 **2** Karen 82, Bobby 106, Wendy 108
3 Karen 50, Bobby 62, Wendy 55
4 Bobby £152; Wendy £123
5a Via Newbury, then back to the motorway at
junction 13 **b** 39 miles
c To avoid possible traffic jams

Page 4 Exercise 2

1a 15 **b** 15 **c** 15. They are equal
2 Rows: **a** 2, 7, 6; 9, 5, 1; 4, 3, 8 **b** 8, 1, 6; 3, 5, 7; 4, 9, 2
c 8, 3, 4; 1, 5, 9; 6, 7, 2 **d** 2, 9, 4; 7, 5, 3; 6, 1, 8
4 Their bases are 6, 9, 4; 2, 7, 5; 5, 8, 3
5 Rows: **a** 8; 6, 1, 5; 7, 3, 4, 2, 9 **b** 8; 5, 3, 4; 7, 2, 6, 1, 9
c 8; 3, 4, 2; 7, 6, 1, 5, 9

Page 5 Exercise 3A

1a 1 **b** 10 **c** 100 **d** 1000
2a 3512 **b** 6040 **c** 7008
3a Subtract 70 **b** Subtract 5000 **c** Add 2 **d** Add 22
4a 8005, 7895, 6480, 3905, 1050, 995
b Eight thousand and five, nine hundred and
ninety-five **5a** 2, 5 **b** 20, 80 **c** 200, 600
6 7, 25, 700 **7** 5, 50, 12 **8a** Amy, 132 **b** 4850
9a 50 **b** 56 **c** 4
10a 7, 5 **b** 2, 3 **c** 6, 2 **d** 7, 2 **e** 9, 6 **f** 9, 5

Page 6 Exercise 3B

1a a-Radio 4, b-Radio 5, c-Radio Wales, d-Radio 3
b One thousand, two hundred and fifteen
2 54321, 12345; 41976
3 Rows: **a** 1, 3, 3; 4, 6; 10 **b** 5, 7, 9; 12, 16; 28
c 2, 1, 12; 3, 13; 16 **d** 6, 4, 7; 10, 11; 21
4 21 Mar 55 039, 14 Feb 41 223, 21 Feb 28 622,
7 Mar 28 239, 14 Mar 28 134, 28 Feb 27 971
5a 15 **b** 8 **c** 40 **6** 8 **7** £46.80
8a 3, 9, 1 **b** 5, 7, 1 **c** 2, 7, 1 **d** 4, 8 **e** 6, 2 **f** 1, 2

Page 7 Exercise 3C

1 Nearly 4 **2a** Madrid, Athens, Berlin, Paris
b Three million, one hundred and eighty-eight
thousand **3a** 40, 55, 31 miles **b** 32, 56, 16 km
4a 15°C, 100°C **b** 50°F, 167°F
5a 3, 3, 2 **b** 1, 8, 2 **c** 7, 11, 12 **d** 11, 4, 31

Page 8 Exercise 4A

1 1, 3, 5 . . . Add 2 **2a** Add 3; 14 **b** Add 5; 21
c Subtract 1; 6 **d** Add 20; 80 **e** Subtract 5; 85
f Add 1; 104 **g** Add 9; 34 **h** Subtract 7; 25
3a 1, 4, 7, 10; 13, 16 **b** 1, 5, 9, 13; 17, 21
c 1, 3, 5, 7; 9, 11 **d** 1, 4, 9, 16; 25, 36
4a 25; add 5 **b** 10; subtract 2 **c** 9; add 3
d 14; add 7 **e** 24; subtract 12 **f** 28; add 9
g 90; add 10 **h** 39; subtract 5
5a 9th, 16th, 23rd, 30th **b** 6th, 13th, 20th, 27th

Page 9 Exercise 4B

1a 8, 10 **b** 20, 25 **c** 31, 41 **d** 24, 21
2a Multiply by 3 **b** Multiply by 2 **c** Divide by 10
d Divide by 4 **3a** 25 **b** 0 **c** 110 **d** 63
5 1, 5, 10, 10, 5, 1; 1, 6, 15, 20, 15, 6, 1; 1, 7, 21, 35, 35, 21, 7, 1
6a 20, 30, 40, 50, 60, 70; 20, 45, 80, 125, 180, 245; 40, 75,
120, 175, 240, 315 **b** No. It is 3 times, or more

Page 9 Exercise 4C

1a Add 2 **b** Subtract 1 **c** Multiply by 3
d Divide by 2 **e** Add 1, then 2, then 3, . . .
f Add 3, then 5, then 7, . . . (or squares)
g Odd terms are all 1; even terms 2, then add 1, . . .
h For every fourth term add 1, then follow by zero;
for other terms, subtract 1
2 3, 5, 7, . . . ; 2, 2, . . .
3 1, 2, 4, 7, 11, . . . ; 1, 2, 3, 4, . . . ; 1, 1, 1, . . .
4 1 000 000; 60; 15, 12; 4
5a 1; 1, 1; 1, 2, 1; 1, 3, 3, 1; 1, 4, 6, 4, 1
b Each row starts and ends with 1. Each term is the
sum of the two nearest terms above it.
c 1, 2, 4, 8, 16, . . . add 1, 2, 4, 8, . . .
6a Add the two preceding terms; 13, 21, 34, . . .
b Next term is the product of terms in the sequences
1, 3, 5, . . . and 3, 4, 5, . . . ; 9×7, 11×8, 13×9, . . .

Page 11   Exercise 5A

1 Each answer zero.
2a 10 **b** 170 **c** 660 **d** 1010 **e** 53 210
3a 800 **b** 8000 **c** 23 400 **d** 100 **e** zero
4a 23 000 **b** 1000 **c** zero **d** 100 000 **e** 1 000 000
5a 940 **b** 3800 **c** zero **d** 85 000 **e** 1000 **f** 5000
g 2040 **h** 91 000 **i** 10 000 **j** zero
6a 30 **b** 42 **c** 64 **d** 45 **e** 49 **f** 63 **g** 40 **h** 32
i 27 **j** 81 **k** 162 **l** 1620 **m** 16 200 **n** 162 000
o zero

Page 11   Exercise 5B/C

1a 10 000 **b** zero **c** 2400 **d** 20 400 **e** zero
2a 90 **b** 81 **c** 132 **d** 420 **e** 384 **f** 497 **g** 280
h 288 **i** zero **j** 615 **k** 188 **l** 1880 **m** 18 800
n 188 000 **o** zero
3a 34 **b** 340 **c** 3400 **d** zero **e** zero **f** 310
g 296 **h** 456 **i** 496 **j** 599 **k** 1640 **l** 3800
m 3240 **n** 2310 **o** 10 560
4a 70 **b** 240 **c** 190 **d** 340 **e** 10 000 **f** 1600
g 570 **h** 1700 **i** 3300 **j** zero **k** 4100 **l** zero
5a 8 **b** 56 **c** 10 **d** 70 **e** 104
6a 6 **b** 9 **c** 120 **d** 38 **e** 145
7a 3 **b** 75 **c** 80 **d** 1 **e** 1000
8a 9 **b** 1 **c** 12 **d** 100 **e** 23 **f** 29 **g** 31 **h** 18
i 87 **j** 61 **k** 111 **l** 69 **m** 73 **n** 78 **o** 234
p 102 **q** 62 **r** 101 **s** 66 **t** 334

Page 12   Exercise 6A

1 921 **2** 6184 **3** 2160; 36 **4** 28 **5** 1363 **6** 28
7a 216 **b** 15 **8** £22.80
9a 64, 9, 26, 0, 16 years **b** 51 years **c** Georges
10a 5 **b** 19

Page 13   Exercise 6B

1a 800 m, 1100 m, 1900 m, 2700 m, 3200 m **b** 3510 m
2a £426 **b** £1676 **3a** (i) 511 miles, 149 miles   (ii) 660 miles
b (i) 393 miles, 107 miles   (ii) 500 miles **4** 24
5 £15.22 **6** 20 **7a** Cannot be as accurate as this.
191 000, 174 000, 420 000, 766 000 **b** (i) 1 186 000
(ii) 592 000 **8a** £411.60 **b** 2178

Page 14   Exercise 6C

1a 239 000, 80 000, 386 000, 94 000 tonnes
b 799 000 tonnes **c** 306 600 tonnes **2** £18.75, £750
3 Yes. 21 **4** 52 kg **5** 212 km **6** £1200

Page 15   Check-up on Whole Numbers in Action

1a Super Prize **b** Top Prize **c** One hundred and
five thousand pounds; nine thousand, nine hundred
pounds **2a** 9 **b** 20 **c** 450 **d** 8000 **e** 100 000
3a 9 **b** 700 **c** 41 **d** 530 **e** 9 **f** 4 **g** 6000 **h** 7
4 700 **5** £360 **6a** 2, 7, 6; 9, 5, 1; 4, 3, 8
b 6, 7, 2; 1, 5, 9; 8, 3, 4
c 20, 70, 60; 90, 50, 10; 40, 30, 80
7a 1, 3, 6, 10, 15 **b** 1, 4, 7, 10, 13, 16
8a 8, 10. Add 2 **b** 25, 31. Add 6 **c** 67, 59. Subtract 8
d 243, 729. Multiply by 3. **9a** 840, 8400, 84 000
b 3700, 370, 37; 1000 **10** 988 **11a** 77 366 **b** 22 634
12a 7, 4 **b** 2, 5 **c** 7, 6, 5 **d** 3, 6, 1 **e** 2, 7
f 8, 3 **13** £2.50 **14** 15p

ANGLES AROUND US

Page 16   Looking Back

1 Right angle **2a** (i) and (iv) **b** acute
3a 90° **b** 180° **4** Obtuse
6a Acute **b** obtuse **c** right **d** acute **e** straight
7a 32° and 58° **b** 32° and 148° **8a** 130° **b** 55°
9a Three **b** Two acute, one obtuse
10 No. Each is less than 90°

Page 19   Exercise 1A

1a Obtuse **b** obtuse **c** acute **d** acute **e** obtuse
f right, acute **g** acute **h** acute **i** obtuse **j** obtuse
3 e, a, b, c, d
4a 40° **b** 90° **c** 140° **d** 180° **e** 20°
5a 90° **b** 180° **c** 360°
6a Two **b** four **c** five **7** 3 o'clock and 9 o'clock
8a 90° **b** 120° **c** 60°
9a 360° **b** 720° **c** 180° **d** 6°

Page 20   Exercise 1B

1 68° acute, 90° right, 145° obtuse, 89° acute, 156° obtuse
2a 90° **b** 180° **c** 360° **3a** 90° **b** 3600° **c** 1080°
4 Acute, straight, acute, obtuse, right, obtuse
6a 90° **b** 90°, 90°, 180° **c** 60° **d** 18° **e** 30° **f** 120°
7a 72° **b** 360° **c** 144° **d** 216°
8a Yes **b** Yes **c** No; the smallest obtuse angle is
over 90°

Page 21   Exercise 1C

3 $\frac{1}{2}, \frac{1}{4}, \frac{1}{6}, \frac{1}{8}, \frac{1}{360}$ **4** 360°, 1440°, 270°, 180°
5 6, 8, 9, 10, 12, 18; 60°, 45°, 40°, 36°, 30°, 20°
6a 45° **b** 9 **7a** 30° **b** 6° **c** $\frac{1}{2}$° **8** 12 000
9a No; smallest obtuse angle is over 90° **b** Yes
c Yes

Page 22   Exercise 2A

1a ∠ABC, B, BA, BC **b** ∠PQR, Q, QP, QR
c ∠CRO, R, RC, RO **d** ∠SKE, K, KS, KE
3 ∠s DEF, EFD, FDE; ∠s PQR, QRS, RSP, SPQ
4 50° **5** 60° **6** 120°
7a ∠s KMN, DEF **b** ∠s ABC, JHG
8 ∠s WVX, XVY, WVY
9a ∠CBD = 45° **b** ∠GFH = 90° **c** ∠PKJ = 50°
d ∠QSR = 80°

Page 23   Exercise 2B/C

1a ∠s AOC, COD, DOB **b** ∠s AOD, BOC, AOB
2a ∠s WXY, XYW, XYZ **b** ∠s YWZ, YWX, WYZ, WYX
3 240° **4a** 47° and 37° **b** 28° **c** 18°
5a ∠AOD **b** ∠s AOB or COD **6** 75° **7** 55°
8 114°, 66°, 114°, 66°; 59°, 121°, 59°, 121°;
125°, 55°, 125°, 55° **9** 23°, 77°, 92°, 168°
10 ∠KON = 120°, ∠KOM = 60°; so ∠PON = 60° and
∠MOP = 120°. Then ∠MOP = 2 ∠PON
11a 60°, 30° **b** 55°, 35° **c** 63°, 27°
12a 90° **b** (1 + 2 + 3) + (1 + 2 + 3) = 180°,
so 1 + 2 + 3 = 90°

Page 24   Exercise 3A

1 $\angle$ABC = 30°, $\angle$RST = 80°, $\angle$DEF = 110°,
$\angle$NKM = 90°, $\angle$GHK = 50°, $\angle$ZYX = 130°
2 $\angle$ABC = 30°, $\angle$DEF = 50°, $\angle$GHK = 120°,
$\angle$JKL = 90°, $\angle$PNM = 45°, $\angle$QRS = 100°
3a $\angle$ABC, $\angle$GHK   **b** $\angle$s ABC, DEF, PNM
c $\angle$s GHK, QRS
4a 60°   **b** 6   **c** 45° (8), 40° (9), 36° (10), etc
5 60°, 75°, 85°   **6** 90°, 90°, 37°, 37°, 53°, 53°

Page 25   Exercise 3B/C

1 $\angle$BAC = 40°, $\angle$ABC = 95°, $\angle$ACB = 45°,
$\angle$DEF = 90°, $\angle$EFG = 70°, $\angle$DGF = 90°,
$\angle$EDG = 110°
2a $\angle$RSU = 25°, $\angle$USV = 110°, $\angle$VST = 45°   **b** 180°
4a 215°   **b** 230°

Page 26   Exercise 4

4a (i) SE   (ii) NE   **b** 180   **c** (i) N, S   (ii) NE, SW
d (i) 90°   (ii) 45°   (iii) 135°   **5a** NE   **b** SE   **6** 90°
7b No, they are the same size   **c** No
10 6 cm, 6 cm, 2 cm, 2 cm, 30°, 30°, 30°, 90° (or 270°)

Page 29   Exercise 5

2 Horizontal: top and bottom of blackboard, top and
bottom edges of coin, surface of milk, rim of light
shade. Vertical: side edges and surface of blackboard,
sides of coin, cord holding light
3a Horizontal: AB and DC. Vertical: AD and BC
b AB, DC and AD, BC; AB, BC; BC, CD; CD, DA;
DA, AB   **4** Cube: 8, 2, 4, 4. Pyramid: 4, 1, 0, 0
5a PQ, QR; QR, RS; RS, SP; SP, PQ
b AB, FE; BC, GF; CD, HG; DE, AH
6 True: **a**, **b**, **c**. False: **d**
7 Cone: 1, 1, 0, 0. Prism: 6, 2, 3, 3. Cuboid: 8, 2, 4, 4

Page 30   Check-up on Angles Around Us

1a Right   **b** obtuse   **c** straight   **d** acute
2 Acute: 10°, 89°. Obtuse: 170°, 110°, 98°. Right: 90°.
Straight: 180°
3a 60°, acute   **b** 90° right   **c** 140°, obtuse   **4** 180°
5a $\angle$s ABD, CBD, ABC, BCD
b Acute, acute, right, right   **6** $\angle$s QRS, PSR
7 $\angle$DEG = 45°, $\angle$HKP = 60°, $\angle$STU = 148°
8 $\angle$ABC = 25°, $\angle$XYZ = 130°
9a $\angle$AOB = 30°, $\angle$AOC = 80°, $\angle$AOD = 145°
b $\angle$COD = 65°, $\angle$BOD = 115°   **c** $\angle$s AOD, BOD
10 1080°   **11a** 320°   **b** 8   **12a** 60°   **b** 180°   **c** 240°
13 80°

3   LETTERS AND NUMBERS

Page 31   Looking Back

1a 5   **b** 5   **c** 2   **d** 4   **e** 5   **f** 4   **g** 100   **h** 9
2a 7, 9, 11   **b** 20, 25, 30   **c** 7, 6, 5   **d** 25, 20, 15
3a 8   **b** 10   **c** 16   **d** 81   **4a** Add 1   **b** Add 2
5a 5, 6, 7; 7, 8, 9; 9, 10, 11
b 8, 9, 10; 10, 11, 12; 12, 13, 14   **6a** 49   **b** 5   **c** 8

Page 32   Exercise 1A

1a $x = 10$ **b** $y = 12$ **c** $m = 50$ **d** $n = 47$
2a $x = 5$ **b** $c = 9$ **c** $d = 6$ **d** $t = 9$
3a $x = 8$ **b** $y = 40$ **c** $t = 2$ **d** $v = 6$
4a $k = 8$ **b** $p = 6$ **c** $q = 19$ **d** $w = 10$
5a $x = 1$ **b** $y = 0$ **c** $m = 100$ **d** $n = 9$
6 $a = 10, b = 11, c = 12, d = 17, e = 15,$
$f = 21, g = 20, h = 21$
7a $a = 7, b = 1, c = 3, d = 9$
b $e = 6, f = 4, g = 3, h = 7, i = 2$
c $j = 8, k = 5, m = 9, n = 3, t = 4$
d $p = 7, q = 9, r = 8, s = 3, t = 1$

Page 33   Exercise 1B

1a $x = 5$ **b** $y = 8$ **c** $t = 10$ **d** $x = 10$
2a $n = 7$ **b** $x = 7$ **c** $t = 7$ **d** $y = 3$
3a $x = 6$ **b** $c = 3$ **c** $x = 20$ **d** $x = 5$
4a $s = 20$ **b** $s = 40$ **c** $s = 60$
5a $x = 9, t = 24, y = 60, r = 36, d = 72, w = 192$
b 6, 480   **6** $n = 7$ **7** $x = 26$ **8** $y = 7$
9a 18, 17, 25   **b** 35, 40, 45, 60   **c** 90

Page 34   Exercise 1C

1a $x = 10$ **b** $y = 7$ **c** $x = 10$
2a $t = 7$ **b** $x = 9$ **c** $t = 8$
3a $x = 8$ **b** $m = 8$ **c** $x = 3$
4a 3, 4, 5; 6, 8, 10; 18, 21, 24; 72, 76, 80; 360, 365, 370
b 7
5a $x = 8, y = 11$ **b** $p = 9, q = 15, r = 21$
c $a = 7, b = 17, c = 27$

Page 35   Exercise 2A

1a $x+2$ **b** $y+3$ **c** $t+5$ **d** $x+5$
2a $a+2$ **b** $c+12$ **c** $x+10$ **d** $z+5$
3a $y-1$ **b** $n-4$ **c** $x-3$ **d** $m-10$
4a $a-2$ **b** $x+8$ **c** $t-4$ **d** $n+11$
5a 7   **b** $x+3$ **c** 3   **d** $y-2$ **e** x **f** y
6a 15, 17; 16, 18   **b** 77, 79, 81; 78, 80, 82
c $x, x+2, x+4; x+1, x+3, x+5$ **d** $y-1, y+1; y, y+2$
e $t-2, t; t-1, t+1$ **f** $u-2, u, u+2; u-1, u+1, u+3$

Page 36   Exercise 2B/C

1a $x+4$ **b** x **c** y **d** $c+1$ **e** $d+5$ **f** $n+1$
2a 10, 11, 12; 9, 8, 7   **b** $x+3, x+4, x+5; x+2, x+1, x$
3a 12, 10, 4
b Scheme 1

x	$x+1$	$x+2$	$x+3$
$x+7$	$x+6$	$x+5$	$x+4$
$x+8$	$x+9$	$x+10$	$x+11$

Scheme 2

x	$x+5$	$x+6$	$x+11$
$x+1$	$x+4$	$x+7$	$x+10$
$x+2$	$x+3$	$x+8$	$x+9$

Scheme 3

x	$x+1$	$x+2$	$x+3$
$x-1$	$x-2$	$x-3$	$x-4$
$x-8$	$x-7$	$x-6$	$x-5$

Page 37   Exercise 3A

1a 10   **b** 21   **c** $3n$ **2a** $2x$ **b** $2y$ **c** $3z$
3a $4m$ **b** $x+5$ **c** $y+2$ **4a** $x+9$ **b** $2a$ **c** $b+1$
5a $2t+3$ **b** $2s+1$ **c** $u+12$
6a $2v+7$ **b** $3x+1$ **c** $3x+5$ **7** 1B, 2A, 3D, 4C
8 1D, 2A, 3B, 4C   **9** 1F, 2C, 3D, 4H, 5B, 6A, 7E, 8G
10a 14   **b** 18   **c** 5   **d** 36   **e** $2x$ **f** $2y$ **g** $3a$ **h** $4b$
11a $3c$ **b** $2d$ **c** $4t$ **d** $5k$ **e** $2x+5$ **f** $2y-1$
g $3m+4$ **h** $2n-2$

12a $3t+3$ **b** $2v-4$ **c** $4a+1$ **d** $3b-3$ **e** $2x+5$
f $2y+3$ **g** 0 **h** $8a+4$

Page 39   Exercise 3B

1 1A, 2B, 3A, 4 miss, 5C, 6B, 7D, 8C, 9A, 10B, 11C
2 Julie: x, $x+5$, $x+2$, $2x+2$, $2x$, $2x+10$.
Jamie: x, $2x$, $2x+8$, $4x+8$, $4x+2$, 2
3a $3x+2$ metres **b** $4x+1$ metres **c** $6x+3$ metres
4a $6m$ min **b** $9m$ min **c** 12 min **d** $15m+12$ min
5a $2x+4$ **b** $2y+1$ **c** $2p+3$ **d** $3r$ **e** $2x+1$
f $2a$ **g** $4a$ **h** $5x+8$
6a $3x+7$ **b** $2a+2b+9$ **c** $2y$ **d** $2x+2$ **e** $x+8$
f $2r+9$ **g** $4w+5t$ **h** $6a+3x$ **i** $2x+5$ **j** 1 **k** $w+3t$
l $2x+8y+11$

Page 40   Exercise 3C

1a 7 **b** x **c** x **d** $x+2$ **e** $x+1$ **f** $x+4$ **g** $2x$
h $2x+2y$ **i** $2x$ **j** $2x+4y$ **k** $2x+2$ **l** $2x+1$
2a $x=2$ **b** $y=6$
3a $2x+2y$ **b** $a+2b$ **c** $2c$ **d** $5e+6f$ **e** $7g+h$
f $m+n+3$ **g** $2p+q$ **h** $10r+14$
4a $s-t+3$ **b** $2u-3v+5$ **c** $5w+v+3$ **d** $8x-3y+2$
e $10a+3b$ **f** $2e$ **g** 0 **h** $2m+2n+20$
5a Simplifies to $10n$, always even
b Simplifies to $6n+1$, always odd

Page 42   Check-up on Letters and Numbers

1a $x=22$ **b** $x=17$ **c** $x=10$ **d** $x=11$
2a $m+2$ **b** $3n$ **c** $t-3$ **d** $2x+2$
3a $x+5$ **b** $y-5$ **c** $2m$ **d** $2n+1$
4a $2m+2$ **b** $2x+7$ **c** $3x+4$ **d** $4t$ **e** $2x+1$
f $5y+8$ **g** $3a$ **h** $x+3$
5a $3a-1$ **b** 1 **c** $6z$ **d** 0 **e** 1 **f** 0 **g** $2y+2z$
h $2n$
6a $6, 11, 16$ **b** (i) $x, x+1, x+2; x+2, x+3, x+4$
(ii) $t-4, t-3, t-2; t-2;, t-1, t; t, t+1, t+2$
7a (i) $x+1, x+3, x+5; x, x+2, x+4$
(ii) $x-4, x-2, x; x-5, x-3, x-1$ **b** $y+1$

4   DECIMALS IN ACTION

Page 43   Looking Back

1a $\underline{3}4$ **b** $7\underline{1}5$ **c** $60\underline{2}0$ **2** $9, 3$
3a £1.25 **b** £5.10 **c** £0.12 **d** £1.05
4a Three pounds sixty-five pence **b** Seven pence
c Thirteen pounds eighty pence
5a £2.40 **b** £20.09 **c** £0.60 **d** £0.08 **e** £1.10
6a 70 **b** 170 **c** 550 **d** 1050 **e** 9860
7a £8 **b** £3 **c** £46 **d** £52
8 David has most, Mike least **9** 85p, 15p
10a £6 **b** £4 **11a** Jim £1.70, Asher £1.15
b Jim. Any two **c** Yes

Page 44   Exercise 1

2a 50, 500, 5000 **b** 200, 2000, 20 000
c 1000, 10 000, 100 000
3a 2, 0.54 **b** 0, 0.914 **c** 4, 0.546 **d** 28, 0.35
e 453, 0.6 **f** 1, 0.76

4a 0.6, 1.3, 1.8, 2.1, 2.9, 3.5, 4, 4.4 **b** (i) 1.9, 2.1, 3.0
(ii) 0.6, 0.7, 0.9 (iii) 0.9, 1.1, 1.2 (iv) 2.5, 2.9, 3.1
(v) 3.09, 3.12, 3.21
5a £7.20, seven pounds twenty pence; £0.68,
sixty-eight pence; £4.09, four pounds nine pence;
£3.10, three pounds ten pence
b (i) Three hundred and forty-nine pounds
(ii) Two thousand and seventy-one pounds
(iii) Five pounds 43 (iv) Seventeen pounds 05
(v) One thousand two hundred and thirty-four
pounds 56

Page 45   Exercise 2A

1a 2.4 **b** 73.2 **c** 312.7
2a 5.6 **b** 31.2 **c** 0.3 **d** 20.5 **e** 100.4 **f** 0.01
3a 0.7 **b** 1.4 **c** 2 **d** 2.9 **e** 3.5 **f** 4.1
4

0	1	2	3	4	

5 Tenths: 3, 7, 0, 2, 0, 6
Hundredths: 5, 0, 4, 0, 8, 3
6a £5.65 **b** 2.1 m **c** 0.71 **d** 2.11 **e** £10.01
f 76.40 **g** 3.10 **h** 0.1
7a 0.7, 1.3, 2.5, 3.2, 3.8 **b** (i) 0.5 (ii) 2.2
8 A 1.3 m, B 1.29 m, C 1.17 m, D 1.08 m, E 0.98 m
9a Twelve pounds 52 **b** Twenty-two pounds 90
c One hundred and sixty pounds 05
10 14.28, 14.5, 14.75, 14.78, 14.93, 14.99, 15.01, 15.1

Page 46   Exercise 2B/C

1a 8.4 **b** 8.45 **c** 8.52 **d** 8.6 **e** 8.66
2 9.876, 9.95, 10, 10.004, 10.04, 10.104
3 One million, two hundred and thirty-four thousand,
five hundred and sixty-seven point eight nine nought
4a 98.4 **b** 3.6 **c** 0.05, 0.24 **d** 29.2, 29.75
5a 0.8, 0.35 litre **b** 0.2, 0.65 litre
6 57.2, 57 200 000; 78.63, 78 630 000; 248.84, 248 840 000;
1113.9, 1 113 900 000
7 Mil, iron, link, fathom, rod, chain, nautical mile

Page 47   Exercise 3

1 AX 6.2, AY 16, AZ 6.59; BX 7, BY 16.8, BZ 7.39;
CX 2.05, CY 11.85, CZ 2.44
2 AX 4.8, AY 5, AZ 4.41; BX 5.6, BY 4.2, BZ 5.21;
CX 0.65, CY 9.15, CZ 0.26
3a 0.9, 0.8, 1.4, 0.5; 1.7, 2.2, 1.9; 3.9, 4.1; 8
b 3.3, 4.9, 0.5, 0.5; 8.2, 5.4, 1; 13.6, 6.4; 20
c 1.8, 0.6, 1.9, 0.7; 2.4, 2.5, 2.6; 4.9, 5.1; 10
4a 1.1 **b** 3.8 **c** 10 **d** 0.9
5 Reading across: 27.57; 8.18, .34; 9, .1, 3; .9, .2, 7;
9.2, 18.2; 540.7

Page 48   Exercise 4A

1a £2.90 **b** £2.10 **2a** 0.15 m **b** 3.29 m
3a £19.05 **b** £3.25 **4a** £70 **b** 125.5 litres **5** £3.35
6a 11.5 cm **b** 36.2 cm **c** 30.2 cm
7a 239.4 s, or 3 min 59.4 s **b** 0.6 s
8 Gary, by 0.30 point

Page 49   Exercise 4B/C

1 60 107.2   **2a** £153.96   **b** £845.94
3a (i) 0.31 m (ii) 0.09 m   **b** 0.16 m   **4** £9.06
5a 44.8 cm   **b** 106.9 cm   **6** 15.4 m
7a 26.5 s, 27.5 s, 27.6 s   **b** the first one
8a 13.985 km   **b** 6.97 km

Page 50   Exercise 5

1a AW 234, AX 2.34, AY 2340, AZ 0.234; BW 8,
BX 0.08, BY 80, BZ 0.008; CW 52, CX 0.52, CY 520,
CZ 0.052   **2a** £2   **b** £0.80   **c** £1.20   **d** £23.50   **e** £53
3a £32.50   **b** £2703   **c** £8.50   **d** £0.62   **e** £127.50
4a 250 kg   **b** 80 kg   **c** 1350 kg   **d** 6.5 kg   **e** 1525 kg
5a £36, £3.60   **b** 18.5, 1.85 m   **c** 2.35, 0.235 s
d 104.7, 10.47 kg
6a 94.4, 944, 9440 Fr   **b** 197.1, 1971, 19710 Sch
c 2408, 24 080, 240 800 Esc   **d** 21 050, 210 500,
2 105 000 L
7a (i) 100   (ii) 240   (iii) 68   (iv) 502   **b** (i) 1000
(ii) 2400   (iii) 680   (iv) 5020

Page 51   Exercise 6

1 AX 21, 21.6; AY 42, 43.2; AZ 63, 64.8; BX 3, 1.62;
BY 6, 3.24; BZ 9, 4.86; CX 63, 64.8; CY 120, 129.6;
CZ 180, 194.4
2 AX 2, 2.4; AY 1, 1.2; AZ 1, 0.8; BX 0.2, 0.18;
BY 0.1, 0.09; BZ 0.1, 0.06; CX 7, 7.2; CY 4, 3.6; CZ 2, 2.4
3a 1.6, 4, 1.25; 6.4, 5; 32   **b** 1.2, 6, 1.5; 7.2, 9; 64.8
c 6, 1.5, 8; 9, 12; 108
4 Reading across: 2.9, 4.5; 61, 25; 3, .81, 0; 78, .84;
.35, 5.7; 6.4, 6
5 A 1, B 2, C 9, D 4, E 3, F 10, G 7, H 6, I 5, J 8

Page 52   Exercise 7A

1a 24p   **b** 16p   **c** 7p   **d** 50p   **e** 11p   **f** 96p
g £1.24   **h** £2.46   **i** £4.19   **j** £8.39   **k** £1.40
l £35.51   **2a** 2.64   **b** 6.28   **c** 0.81   **d** 0.20
3 £26.10   **4** 45p   **5a** £1.70   **b** £6.80   **c** £21.25
d £108.38   **6** £20.5   **7a** 73p   **b** £1.40   **c** £3.24
8 £21.04   **9** 120   **10a** £136.50   **b** 20
11 £39.43, £28.21

Page 53   Exercise 7B/C

1a $15.24   **b** $23.13   **c** $232.64   **d** $10 606.05
2 £122   **3** £6.90   **4** By cash. £5.79   **5** 94p
6a (i) £17.63   (ii) £17.60   (iii) £18   **b** (i) 42   (ii) 42.2
7 £36.55   **8a** 2.8, 3.2 ml   **b** 11.4, 12.2 ml
c 11.1, 14.3 ml   **d** 2.3, 2.1 g   **e** 0.6, 0.7, 0.8 g   **f** 6.5,
7.2, 9.2 g

Page 54   Check-up on Decimals in Action

1a 16.2   **b** 105.8   **c** 0.14
2a 10, 10.5, 11.2, 11.9, 12.6
b 0.01, 0.02, 0.05, 0.08
3a 15.6, 16, 16.1, 16.5, 17.0
b 9.68, 9.96, 10.81, 11.12   **4a** 6, 1   **b** 8.01, 3.33
5a 3.45   **b** 0.93   **c** 110.8   **6** 157.23, 154.08; 3.15
7 194.4 km   **8** 84.2 cm. Yes
9a 34, 340   **b** 125, 1250   **c** 10.9, 109   **d** 2345,
23 450   **e** 1, 10
10a 40, 39   **b** 27, 28.8   **c** 48, 49.6   **d** 150, 151.8
e 6, 5.67

11a 0.34, 0.034   **b** 1.25, 0.125   **c** 0.109, 0.0109
d 23.45, 2.345   **e** 0.01, 0.001
12a 5, 4.9   **b** 5, 5.3   **c** 5, 5.5   **d** 3, 2.6
e 0.5, 0.8
13a £5.63   **b** £1.25   **c** £0.09   **d** £7.13   **e** £3.20
14 £2.06   **15** £47.53   **16** 9 pence per km

5   FACTS, FIGURES AND GRAPHS

Page 55   Looking Back

1a 10, 9   **b** 19   **2a** Dark hair: ⦀⦀ IIII, 9;
Fair hair: ⦀⦀, 5; Red hair: ⦀⦀, 5
3

Dark hair   XXXXXXXXX

Fair hair   XXXXX

Red hair   XXXXX

4a Yellow   **b** Purple   **c** 24   **d** 80
5a Bars 6, 7, 5, 9, 3 boxes high   **b** Orange
c Orange, soda, cola, lime, lemon
6 Bars 4, 1, 7, 10, 8, 3, 5 units high

Page 56   Exercise 1A

1 7, 9, 4, 1, 3, 5, 1. Nick   **2** 10, 8, 5, 1, 1, 4. Simon
4

Colour	Blue	Brown	Grey	Green	Hazel
Tally	⦀⦀ ⦀⦀ I	IIII	⦀⦀ III	II	II
Number	11	4	8	2	2

5a (i) 30, 35, 40, 50, 55   (ii) 210
b The numbers rise fairly steadily, year by year, with
the largest increase in the 4th year

Page 57   Exercise 1B

1a To reduce the number of symbols he has to draw
b With head, 2 arms and leg
c Choir 30, chess 20, sports 24, drama 17

2 School lunch: XXXXXXX

Packed lunch: XXXXX

Cafe: XXXXX

Home: XXXXX

3a

Mark	0	1	2	3	4	5	6	7	8	9	10
Tally	II	III	III	IIII	HHT HHT I	HHT	I	I		I	I
Number	2	3	3	4	11	5	1	1	0	1	1

Mark	0	1	2	3	4	5	6	7	8	9	10
Tally	I	III	II	II	HHT	HHT	II	III	IIII	III	II
Number	1	3	2	2	5	5	2	3	4	3	2

b No. A2 has more high marks

4a

Result	Tally	Number
Won	HHT III	8
Drawn	IIII	4
Lost	HHT I	6
		18

b 20 **c** Yes. They won or drew most games

Page 57   Exercise 1C

1 1–10, 1; 11–20, 2; 21–30, 4; 31–40, 8; 41–50,5;
51–60, 8; 61–70,7; 71–80, 8; 81–90, 1; 91–100, 6
2 1–20, 3; 21–40, 12; 41–60, 13; 61–80, 15; 81–100, 7
3a 1–20, 3; 21–40, 13; 41–60, 13; 61–80, 10; 81–100, 11
b No; very similar overall
4 25–29, 6; 30–34, 6; 35–39, 9; 40–44, 9; 45–49, 5; 50–54, 1

Page 58   Exercise 2A

1a (i) Curry   (ii) Prawn   **b** (i) Curry 10, plain 5,
bacon 8, prawn 3, vinegar 7, cheese 9   (ii) 42
2b Plain, cheese, curry, beef, tomato, onion
3b $\frac{20}{40}$, or $\frac{1}{2}$. People were rash, or careless, and were
hit by the swings   **4a** $\frac{1}{2}$ **b** $\frac{1}{4}$ **c** $\frac{1}{2}$ **d** $\frac{3}{4}$ **e** $\frac{1}{8}$
5a $\frac{3}{4}$ **b** $\frac{1}{2}$ **c** $\frac{1}{3}$ **d** $\frac{1}{4}$ **6a** $\frac{1}{2}$ **b** $\frac{1}{4}$ **c** $\frac{2}{5}$ **d** $\frac{3}{4}$
7a $\frac{1}{2}$ **b** $\frac{1}{4}$ **c** $\frac{1}{8}$ **d** $\frac{1}{8}$
8a 2 kg   **b** (i) 4 kg   (ii) 8 kg   **c** 4 months
d He did not gain any weight
9a April   **b** May   **c** 43   **d** Jan 2, Feb 8, Mar 10,
Apr 12, May 6, Jan 5
10b Saturday. People not at work or school
c Sales peaks were on Wednesday and Saturday, with
lows on Monday and Thursday.

Page 61   Exercise 2B

1b The line graph. It suggests the continuous growth
of the plant
2a (i) USA   (ii) France   **b** USA 70, France 20,
Germany 30, Japan 40, UK 35, Italy 30
3a Wednesday, $39\frac{1}{2}°$ or 39.5°   **b** 5   **c** 37°
4a 1   **b** (i) $3\frac{1}{2}$ or 3.5 kg   (ii) 6 kg   (iii) 9 kg
c The sixth   **d** The fifth
5a No. There are more Japanese cars
b Cars made in other countries
c Japanese, British, Italian, German, Others
d (i) $\frac{1}{4}$ (ii) $\frac{1}{3}$

6 There were more strong swimmers, fewer
non-swimmers and poor swimmers.
7 The lowest temperatures of 4°C were in January
and February, and rose fairly steadily to their highest
value of 15°C in July and August, before falling again.

Page 62   Exercise 2C

1a Week 6, 64 000   **b** 4   **c** 10 and 11
d The sales rose steadily for 4 weeks, then peaked in
weeks 4 and 6, before falling steadily for 5 more weeks
2a 46–87   **b** 45–49, 2; 50–54, 4; 55–59, 8; 60–64, 8;
65–69, 13; 70–74, 6; 75–79, 6; 80–84, 2; 85–89, 1   **d** 13
3 180°, 120°, 60°   **5** 90°, 120°, 45°
6a 30   **b** 72°, 36°, 108°, 36°, 12°, 96°
7a 140 000 litres   **b** 912 000 litres   **c** $\frac{2}{9}$
d Sales of leaded petrol fell throughout the year as
sales of unleaded rose. Sales were equal during July.
The reasons for the changes include the environmental
benefit of unleaded, and the fact that it is cheaper
than leaded petrol.
8b 17 50 hours   **c** After   **d** Least between 11 00 and
12 00; most between 16 00 and 18 00

Page 65   Check-up on Facts, Figures and
Graphs

1a Thursday, 16   **b** Friday, 43   **c** 133   **2b** 19
3a 0–8, 1–11, 2–8, 3–7, 4–3, 5–1   **b** (i) 19   (ii) 11
4a 1–10, 3; 11–20, 5; 21–30, 12; 31–40, 3; 41–50, 2
b 21–30
5a Rent, food, travel, other, clothes
b (i) $\frac{1}{4}$ (ii) $\frac{1}{3}$ (iii) $\frac{1}{8}$
c Rent £40, food £30, travel £20; other £15, clothes £15
6b No   **c** (i) 136 cm   (ii) 161–162 cm. The line
advances fairly smoothly.

6   MEASURING TIME
AND TEMPERATURE

Page 66   Looking Back

1 April, May, June   **2** 1795, 1855, 1905, 1950, 2001
3 Sunday, Tuesday, Thursday
4a 3 o'clock   **b** 6 o'clock   **c** 10 o'clock   **d** 2.30
e 7.45   **5** 10.30, 10.45   **6** 25 minutes   **7** 12.15 am   **8** 5
9a 9.20 am   **b** 9.55 pm   **10a** 1, 8, 15, 22, 29   **b** Thursday

11 61   **12a** Seventeenth of August, nineteen ninety-nine   **b** 04.10.96   **13a** 09:05   **b** 10:45
14a 40   **b** 25   **c** 17   **15a** 21°C   **b** 6°

Page 67   Exercise 1A

1a 31   **b** 30   **c** 31   **2** 7   **3b** Saturday   **c** 20th
4 Wednesday   **5** Sunday
6a Saturday, Monday, Wednesday   **b** Wednesday, Saturday, Tuesday
7 Seventh of October, nineteen ninety-eight
8 303, 410, 1066, 1314, 1492, 1564, 1666, 1969
9 1996, 2000, 2004
10 Four $\frac{1}{4}$ days make the extra day in a leap year
11b Monday   **c** 27th

Page 68   Exercise 1B/C

1 91   **3a** Tuesday   **b** Wednesday
4 60; 60; 24; 7; 14; 28, 29, 30, 31; 365, 366; 52; 12; 10; 100   **5** 31   **6** 12+30+31+20 = 93   **7a** 55   **b** 52
8a 32   **b** 52   **c** 175   **9 b, d, f**
10 303–4th, 410–5th, 1066–11th, 1314–14th, 1492–15th, 1564–16th, 1666–17th, 1969–20th
11a 365 days = 52 weeks and 1 day; the extra day moves the day on from Friday to Saturday
b 1994, Sunday; 1995, Monday; 1996, Wednesday; 1997, Thursday; 1998, Friday; 1999, Saturday

Page 70   Exercise 2A

1a 8 am, 8 pm   **b** 6 am, 6 pm   **c** 9.30 am, 9.30 pm
d 11.20 am, 11.20 pm
2a   **b**   **c**   **d**

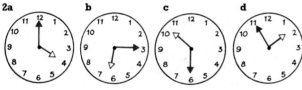

3a 1.30 pm   **b** 2.20 pm   **c** 2.45 pm   **d** 4.35 pm
4a Five thirty in the morning
b Quarter to twelve at night
c Five past three in the afternoon
5a 2 hours   **b** 5 hours   **c** 6 hours   **d** 9 hours
e 10 hours   **f** 17 hours   **g** 10 hours   **h** 8 hours
6 25 min   **7** 8.45 pm   **8** 2.05 pm
9a 3.15 pm   **b** 3.30 pm   **c** 4.15 pm
10a 12 hours   **b** 1 hour 45 minutes
c 13 hours 45 minutes

Page 71   Exercise 2B/C

1a 1 h 55 min   **b** 10 min   **c** 40 min
2a The Natural World 7.15, 8.05   **b** Snooker 8.05, 9.40
c Not Mozart 9.40, 10.25
3a 95 min   **b** 4.35 pm   **c** 4.25 pm
4a 16 h 2 min   **b** 6 h 55 min
5a 8.10 am, 8.50 am   **b** 8.55 am, 9.35 am, 10.15 am
c 10.40 am   **6** The old second
7a 2×3–5 min   **b** 2×5–2×3 min   **c** 2×5–3 min

Page 72   Exercise 3A/B

1a 09 00   **b** 17 00   **c** 01 30   **d** 22 15
2a 9 am   **b** 5 pm   **c** 1.30 am   **d** 10.15 pm
3 04 00, 10 00, 14 00, 17 00; 3 am, 4 pm, 9 pm
4a 8 pm   **b** 8.51 am   **c** 11.04 pm   **d** 4.34 pm
5a 15:00   **b** 12:00   **c** 11:30   **d** 23:30
6 21 15 and 22 30   **7a** 6.45 pm   **b** 03 20

8a Haymarket, Falkirk, Larbert, Stirling, Perth
b 1 h 33 min   **9** 17 15   **10** 22 49   **11** 18 45
12a 4   **b** 11   **13 a** 2   **b** 6   **c** 5
14a Gleneagles   **b** Stirling and Falkirk
15a 1 h 14 min   **b** 1 h 33 min

Page 73   Exercise 3C

1 35 min + 1 h 10 min = 1 h 45 min   **2** 1 h 45 min
3 03 54 next day
4a 1 h 20 min   **b** 2 h 35 min   **c** 1 h 49 min
d 5 h 15 min   **5** 19 35 and 22 20
6a 1 h 55 min   **b** 3 h 10 min
c 14 05 hours from Heathrow

Page 74   Exercise 4A

1a Athens   **b** Sydney   **c** 19°C
2 Corfu, New Delhi, Rome, Athens
3a 12°C   **b** 7°C   **c** 0°C
4a 15, 20, 22, 19   **b** Noon   **c** 2°   **d** 8 am and noon
5a 7°   **b** 9°C   **6a** 38.5°C
b Indicates normal body temperature
c This is the range of body temperatures when alive.
7a 38.0°C   **b** 37.5°C   **c** 37.4°C   **d** 37.8°C

Page 75   Exercise 4B/C

1 3, 11, 8, 13   **2** 4, 88, 0.5, 15.7   **3** 0.8, 19.3, 0.6, 25.2
4a 26°C   **b** 22°C   **c** 48°C   **d** 34°C   **e** 34.5°C
f 34.2°C
5a 13°C   **b** 28°C   **c** 26°C   **d** 13°C   **e** 34°C   **f** 6°C
6 11°, 9°, 41°, 19°, 21°, 21°, 3.3° rise, 4.7° fall
7a 5   **b** 130°C   **c** (i) 180°C   (ii) 225°C   (iii) 110°C

Page 76   Exercise 5A

1

2

3a 5°   **b** 3°   **c** 0°   **d** −1°   **e** −4°   **f** −5°C
4a −2°   **b** −5°   **c** −3°   **d** −10°   **e** −6°   **f** −2°C
5a −8°C   **b** −11°C   **c** 3°C   **d** −1°C
6a 5°C, −10°C   **b** −3°C, −5°C
7a (i) −5, 10   (ii) −5   **b** (i) −5, 0   (ii) −5
c −4, −2   (ii) −4   **8a** 4°C   **b** −3°C

Page 77   Exercise 5B/C

1a (i) 2°C   (ii) 0°C   (iii) −4°C   (iv) −7°C
b (i) 5°C   (ii) 3°C   (iii) 0°C   (iv) −3°C
2a −3°, −1°, 0, 5°C   **b** −20°, −10°, 0°, 9°, 10°C
c −100°, −19°, −1°, 0°, 50°, 100°C
3a +18   **b** −12
4a (i) 4°, −2°C   (ii) 6°   **b** (i) 12, −12°C   (ii) 24°
c (i) 10°, −8°C   (ii) 18°   **5** −10°C   **6** 13°
7a 1°C   **b** D   **c** B and C   **d** D and E   **e** 3°C   **f** F
g 2°C   **h** −4°C   **8** −19.9°C
9a At 14 00 and 06 00 hours   **b** 11°
c (i) 10 00–12 00   (ii) 00 00–02 00

Page 79 Check-up on Measuring Time and Temperature

1a 7 **b** 31 **c** 365 **2** Tuesday **3** 47 **4** 1 h 15 min
5a 10 am **b** 6.15 pm **c** 4.45 am
6a 9 **b** 10 **c** 8 **7** 33
8 9.13 am and 10.43 am **9** 11.30 am Wednesday
10 17 00, 15 00, 8 am, 11 pm
11a 10 00 **b** 18 15 **c** 04 45
12 1 h 30 min, 2 h 15 min, 2 h, 1 h 30 min
13a 20 15–20 45, 22 00–23 50 **b** 40 min
14a 10.39 **b** 0.06s **15a** 40° **b** 15° **c** 7°
16 0°, 19°, 31°, 55°, 100°C **17** 5.6°
18a 14 **b** 22 **c** 0.9 **d** 25.4
19 −4°, −3°, −1°, 0°, 2°, 3°C
20a, b

c 6°

COORDINATES: X MARKS THE SPOT

Page 80 Looking Back

1a Gill **b** Tim **c** Habib **d** James **e** B1 **f** B3
g A3 **h** A2
2a C5 **b** J8 **c** F6 **d** F4 **e** London Rd and
Regent Rd **f** Princes St and Lothian Rd **g** A7 to F8
h F7 to J10 **3a** M, A, T, H, S **b** HELLO
c THIS IS EASY **d** ALL THE ALPHABET IN GRID
4a E2 **b** B3 **c** B1 **d** F3

Page 81 Exercise 1A

1 B(2, 2), C(7, 4), D(3, 7), E(2, 5), F(7, 7), 6, 7
2 E(8, 1), F(1, 1), G(5, 4), H(5, 6), J(0, 3), K(5, 0), L(7, 5),
M(0, 5) **5** Dog

Page 82 Exercise 1B

1a A(4, 2), B(6, 4), G(7, 0) **b** B(6, 4) and C(6, 6)
c F(0, 5) and D(3, 5) **d** C(6, 6) **e** F(0, 5) **f** G(7, 0)
2a S **b** T **c** A **d** M **e** P **f** S **g** Stamps
4b Yes **c** South 1 block, 3 west, 4 north, 6 east
d (2, 1)

Page 83 Exercise 1C

1c Inner, outer, inner **d** (3, 3)
2a,b

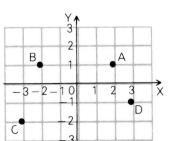

3a (5, −1) **b** (−4, 0) **4a** 4 west **b** 1 west, 3 south
c 6 east, 1 north **d** 1 east, 2 south **5** (−7, 1)

Page 84 Exercise 2A

1 A(4, 1), B(−3, 3), C(−2, −1), D(2, −4), E(0, 2),
F(−4, 0)
2a A(3, −1), B(3, 2), C(−1, 2), D(−1, −1)
b (i) E(2, 1), F(0, 2), G(−2, 1), H(0, −3)
(ii) J(2, 1), K(3, 3), L(−2, 3), M(−3, 1)
(iii) O(0, 0), P(−2, −2), Q(0, −4), R(2, −2)
3a L **b** V **c** N **d** M **4b** A star **c** (0, 0)

Page 85 Exercise 2B

1a A(2, 0), G(3, 0), E(6, 1), H(0, −1)
b Q(1, 1), V(−4, −4), Z(0, 3)
c K(1, −3), L(2, −4), N(8, −3)
d S(−3, −2), W(−2, −4)
2a (−4, −2) **b** (1, −2)
c (2, 0), (5, −4), (0, −4), (−3, 0)
3a P(−7, 5), Q(−2, 6), R(−2, 4), S(−7, 3)
b A(0, 1), B(6, 3), C(0, 5), D(2, 3)
c K(−5, 2), L(−3, −5), M(−7, −5)
d E(4, 1), F(6, 1), G(7, −2), H(6, −5), I(4, −5), J(3, −2)

Page 86 Exercise 2C

2a F **b** A, B **c** C, D, E, G **d** E **e** A, C, G
f B, D, F
3a A 1st, B 2nd, C 4th, D 3rd, G 4th **b** (i) Both positive
(ii) p negative, q positive (iii) both negative
(iv) p positive, q negative

Page 87 Exercise 3A

1a 2 **b** y-axis **2a** 2 **b** x-axis **c** (2, 2)
3a (0, 2), (2, 2), (4, 2), (6, 2) (8, 2), (10, 2) **b** x-axis
4a (2, 14), (2, 18), (2, 22) **b** Parallel to the y-axis
5a At 45° to the x or y-axis
b (0, 0), (2, −2), (4, −4), (6, −6), (8, −8) etc

Page 88 Exercise 3B/C

1a (1, 2), (3, 2), (5, 2), (7, 2), (9, 2), (11, 2), (19, 2) **b** 2
2a (1, 2), (2, 4), (3, 6), (4, 8), (5, 10), (6, 12) **b** Two
3a $y = 3x$ **b** $y = 4x$ **c** $y = \frac{1}{2}x$ **d** $y = x+1$
e $y = x+2$ **f** $y = -x$
4a (i) (1, 1), (2, 2), (3, 3), etc
b (i) (1, −1), (2, −2), (3, −3) **c** (i) (1, 2), (2, 4), (3, 6)
d (i) (1, −2), (2, −4), (3, −6) **e** (i) (1, 2), (2, 3), (3, 4)
f (i) (1, 0), (2, 1), (3, 2) **5a** Two
6a (6, −1), (8, −2): (−4, 4), (−6, 5) **b** $y = -\frac{1}{2}x+2$, or
$x+2y = 4$

Page 89 Check-up on Coordinates: X Marks the Spot

1a Earring **b** (i) D4 (ii) C4 **c** B3, C3, D3
d (i) They're at corners (ii) A5, E5
2b (i) A rectangle (ii) (5, 3)
3a Origin **b** x-axis **c** y-axis **d** C, D **e** I, E **f** y
g A cat? **4a** L **b** V **c** N **d** Z **e** M
5 (0, 2), (1, 2), (1, 1), (2, 1), (2, 3), (1, 3), (1, 4), (3, 4), (3, 1)
(4, 1), (4, 2), (5, 2), (5, 3), (4, 3), (4, 5), (5, 5)
6a (2, 1), (0, 1), (0, −1), (2, −1), (2, 1), (4, 1), (4, −1),
(2, −1), (2, −3), (0, −3), (0, −1), (−2, −1), (−2, 1),
(0, 1), (0, 3), (−2, 3), (−2, 1), (−4, 1), (−4, −1),
(−2, −1) **b** They start and finish at (2, 1) and
(−2, −1)

SOLVING EQUATIONS

Page 90 Looking Back

1a 4 **b** 18 **c** 9 **d** 28
2a $a = 11, b = 10, c = 13, d = 17, e = 15, f = 21$
3a $5y$ **b** x **c** $2t$
4a $3n$ **b** $5m$ **c** $3t$ **d** t **e** s **f** $6u$ **g** $2v$
h $2x+1$ **i** $3y-1$ **j** $z+5$
5a $x = 12$ **b** $y = 18$ **c** $k = 4$ **d** $n = 37$
6a $x = 17$ **b** $y = 9$ **c** $d = 11$ **d** $k = 6$
7a $x+2$ **b** $y+4$ **c** $2x+1$ **d** $2y-2$
8a 2 **b** $7x$ **c** $2a+b$

Page 91 Exercise 1A

1a $x = 3$ **b** $x = 8$ **c** $x = 7$ **d** $x = 0$
2a $y = 5$ **b** $y = 4$ **c** $y = 7$ **d** $y = 8$
3a $n = 4$ **b** $n = 3$ **c** $n = 4$ **d** $n = 1$
4a $k = 2$ **b** $k = 7$ **c** $k = 7$ **d** $k = 9$
5a $t = 8$ **b** $t = 6$ **c** $t = 8$ **d** $t = 14$
6a $u = 12$ **b** $u = 9$ **c** $u = 17$ **d** $u = 17$
7a $m = 1, n = 9, p = 1$ **b** $a = 9, b = 0, c = 3$
8a $s = 3, t = 3, u = 14$ **b** $d = 1, e = 13, f = 3$
9a $a = 9$ **b** $m = 11$ **c** $n = 3$ **d** $k = 7$
10a $x = 10$ **b** $y = 7$ **c** $a = 8$ **d** $t = 7$
11a $c = 6$ **b** $n = 6$ **c** $y = 9$ **d** $s = 9$
12a $x = 8$ **b** $t = 20$ **c** $n = 26$ **d** $w = 11$

Page 93 Exercise 1B

1a $x = 4$ **b** $y = 3$ **c** $z = 5$ **d** $k = 7$ **e** $m = 9$
2a $p = 6$ **b** $t = 8$ **c** $u = 9$ **d** $w = 10$ **e** $z = 5$
3a $x = 1$ **b** $y = 2$ **c** $a = 4$ **d** $b = 3$
4a $c = 1$ **b** $d = 0$ **c** $g = 5$ **d** $h = 6$
5a $t = 5$ **b** $z = 10$ **c** $x = 8$ **d** $y = 9$
6a $t = 6$ **b** $a = 4$ **c** $x = 2$ **d** $x = 3$
7a $x = 6$ **b** $x = 2$ **c** $8\,(x = 5)$

Page 94 Exercise 1C

1 $x = 5$, 12 straws 5 cm long
2 $x = 10$, 6 straws 10 cm long
3 $x = 6$, 10 straws 6 cm long
4 $x = 7.5$, 8 straws 7.5 cm long
5 $x = 5$, 12 straws 5 cm long
6 $x = 3$, 4 straws 3 cm long and 8 straws 6 cm long
7 $x = 4$, 3 straws 4 cm long and 6 straws 8 cm long
8 $x = 3$, 5 straws 3 cm long and 5 straws 9 cm long
9 $x = 2.5$, 24 straws 2.5 cm long
10 $x = 3\frac{1}{3}$ or $3.33\ldots$, 6 straws of $3\frac{1}{3}$ cm and 6 straws of $6\frac{2}{3}$ cm
11 $x = 3$, 12 straws 3 cm long and 4 straws 6 cm long
12 $x = 2$, 30 straws 2 cm long

Page 95 Exercise 2A

1a $x = 9$ **b** $y = 10$ **c** $k = 12$ **d** $m = 11$
2a $x = 4$ **b** $y = 9$ **c** $n = 5$ **d** $k = 8$
3a $a = 9$ **b** $b = 5$ **c** $c = 9$ **d** $d = 4$
4a $x = 6$ **b** $y = 8$ **c** $t = 7$ **d** $u = 3$
5a $x = 7$ **b** $x = 8$ **c** $x = 7$
6a $x = 8$ **b** $y = 9$ **c** $t = 12$
7a $n = 6$ **b** $k = 8$ **c** $t = 10$
8a $n = 8$ **b** $u = 15$ **c** $v = 9$
9a $x = 7$ **b** $y = 9$ **c** $t = 14$ **d** $u = 16$
10a $v = 15$ **b** $w = 16$ **c** $k = 3$ **d** $n = 38$

11a $x = 4$ **b** $y = 9$ **c** $k = 6$ **d** $s = 8$
12a $m = 6$ **b** $n = 7$ **c** $t = 4$ **d** $p = 7$

Page 96 Exercise 2B

1a $x = 8; 8$ **b** $x = 2; 2$ **c** $x = 4; 4$ **d** $x = 2; 2$
2a $t = 1; 1$ **b** $a = 10; 10$ **c** $x = 6; 6$ **d** $y = 3; 3$
3a $w = 5; 5, 3$ **b** $c = 7; 7, 7, 4$ **c** $e = 9; 9, 9, 9, 9, 8$
d $k = 9; 9, 5$
4a $d = 5, 5$ cm **b** $f = 18, 18$ cm
5a $x = 3, 3$ m **b** $y = 4, 4$ m
6a $x = 8, 8$ cm **b** $y = 10, 10$ cm
7a $b = 4, 4$ cm **b** $c = 2, 2$ m
8a $x = 2$ **b** $a = 1$ **c** $t = 6$ **d** $s = 0$ **e** $n = 3$
f $m = 6$ **g** $p = 7$ **h** $q = 3$
9a $x = 6$ **b** $y = 3$ **c** $z = 1$ **d** $k = 5$ **e** $a = 4$
f $b = 1$ **g** $c = 0$ **h** $d = 4$
10a $x = 2$ **b** $y = 4$ **c** $z = 5$ **d** $n = 8$ **e** $t = 2$
f $u = 9$

Page 97 Exercise 2C

1 $x = 4$, 4 of spades
2a $x = 7$ **b** $(6, 1), (5, 2), (4, 3)$ **c** $(6, 1)$
3a $x = 12$, 12 years **b** $y = 35$, 35 years **4** $x = 8$
5a $x = 3$ **b** $y = 5$ **c** $p = 7$ **d** $x = 2$ **e** $a = 5$
f $b = 8$ **g** $w = 6$ **h** $y = 1$
6a $k = 9$ **b** $p = 4$ **c** $q = 7$ **d** $r = 5$ **e** $x = 3$
f $y = 7$ **g** $z = 0$ **h** $a = 4$ **7a** 38 **b** 9th
8a 37 **b** 7th **9a** $x = 20$ **b** $x = 1$ **c** $x = 9$
10a 9 **b** 4 **c** 5 **d** 4 **e** 12 **f** 5

Page 100 Check-up on Solving Equations

1a $x = 5$ **b** $x = 8$ **c** $x = 14$ **d** $x = 5$ **e** $a = 29$
f $b = 20$ **g** $c = 7$ **h** $d = 15$
2a $x = 7$ **b** $x = 14$ **c** $y = 10$ **d** $k = 9$
3 $x = 7, a = 13, c = 0, d = 7$
4a $x = 4$ **b** $y = 16$ **c** $t = 8$ **d** $u = 21$
5a $x = 9$ **b** $x = 19$ **c** $x = 9$
6a $x = 8$ **b** $y = 4$ **c** $m = 6$ **d** $n = 6$ **e** $a = 6$
f $b = 77$ **g** $c = 7$ **h** $d = 99$ **7** 6 **8** $3\frac{3}{4}$ m
9a $k = 4$ **b** $t = 6$ **c** $u = 7$ **d** $v = 0$ **e** $c = 1$
f $d = 5$ **g** $x = 9$ **h** $x = 9$
10a $x = 7$ **b** $y = 9$ **c** $z = 6$ **d** $v = 4$ **e** $p = 3$
f $q = 12$ **g** $r = 1$
11 Only $3n - 2 = 37$ gives a whole number, 13, for n

 MEASURING LENGTH

Page 102 Looking Back

1a Trundle wheel **b** tape measure **c** ruler
d mileometer **e** long tape measure **f** ruler
2 2 cm, $3\frac{1}{2}$ cm, 6 cm **4a** 3.12 m **b** 5.80 m
c 12.06 cm **d** 0.85 m **5** 12.1 cm **6** 2.7 cm
7a 37 km **b** 126 710 km **8** 13 cm

Page 103 Exercise 1A

1a 1 cm, 3 cm, 6 cm, $9\frac{1}{2}$ cm **b** 2 cm, 5 cm, $8\frac{1}{2}$ cm
c 3 cm, $6\frac{1}{2}$ cm, $3\frac{1}{2}$ cm
2a 10 mm, 40 mm, 75 mm, 100 mm
b 30 mm, 35 mm, 25 mm
3a 10 **b** 20 **c** 30 **d** 50 **e** 100 **4** 10

6a 28, 22cm **b** about 13mm
7b The deck **c** No **d** No
e For recording an actual length
8a cm **b** m **c** cm **d** km **e** mm **f** mm **g** m
h km
9 *Examples*: **a** 130 cm **b** 20 m **c** 10 cm **d** 1000 km
e 35 mm **f** 1 mm **g** 80 m **h** 4000 km

Page 104　Exercise 1B/C

1a 23 mm, 46 mm **b** (iv) **c** (i) or (iii). They could be
cut or planed to size
2a £22.50 **b** £49.50 **c** £49 **d** £58.80
3 162, 154, 148, 144, 142, 141, 142, 144, 148, 154, 162 m.
P to F to Q

Page 106　Exercise 2A

1 15 mm, 1.5 cm; 35 mm, 3.5 cm; 48 mm, 4.8 cm; 62 mm,
6.2 cm; 80 mm, 8.0 cm; 93 mm, 9.3 cm
2a (i) 20 mm, 23 mm (ii) 40 mm, 29 mm
b (i) 86 mm (ii) 138 mm **3a** 27.6 cm, 21.6 cm **b** 98.4 cm
5a 25 mm **b** 31 mm **c** 20 mm
6a 2.8 cm **b** 1.6 cm **c** 2.4 cm **d** 1.8 cm **e** 0.8 cm

Page 107　Exercise 2C

1a 8 cm **b** 7 cm **c** 4 cm **d** 4 cm **e** 7 cm **f** 10 cm
2a (i) 1.4 cm (ii) 1 cm **b** (i) 2.5 cm (ii) 3 cm
c (i) 1.4 cm (ii) 1 cm **d** (i) 3.8 cm (ii) 4 cm
3a (i) 2.2 cm (ii) 2 cm **b** (i) 2.8 cm (ii) 3 cm
c (i) 1.6 cm (ii) 2 cm **d** (i) 3.4 cm (ii) 3 cm
e (i) 2.2 cm (ii) 2 cm **4 b, c, d**
5 8.2 cm, 7.8 cm, 7.5 cm, 7.9 cm, 8.1 cm, 8.0 cm
6 43 mm, 38 mm, 41 mm, 35 mm
7a 4.5 cm and 5.5 cm **b** 2.5 cm and 3.5 cm
c 0.5 cm and 1.5 cm **d** 9.5 cm and 10.5 cm
8a 155.4 cm **b** 156 cm **c** 155.4 cm
9 Diameters 3.5 cm and 4.5 cm

Page 109　Exercise 3A

1a 4.1 m **b** 3.9 m, 4 m **c** Alexander **2** 147 mm
3 15 cm **4a** 2158 mm **b** 215.8 cm **5** 4.8 m
6a (i) 28.9 km (ii) 29.7 km **b** 58.4 km
7a 40 miles **b** 26 miles **c** 8 miles **8** 0.1 mm

Page 110　Exercise 3B

1a 360 cm **b** 60 cm **c** 60 **2** 5 cm **3a** Tall **b** Low
4 12 cm, Short; 4.8 cm, Low; 36 cm, Medium;
29.2 cm, Short
5a 135 mm, 70 mm, 80 mm, 80 mm **b** 200 mm, 167 mm,
130 mm

Page 111　Exercise 3C

1a 7, 8, 5, 6, 6, 12, 0 mm **b** 6 mm
c Sunday, Monday, Friday **d** Dry
2a £52.70 **b** £136 **3a** 20 **b** 51

Page 112　Check-up on Measuring Length

1 *Examples*: **a** 2 mm **b** 19 cm, 10 cm, 2½ cm
c 2 metres, 10 metres **d** 600 km **2** 50 mm, 7.4 cm
4a (i) 26 mm (ii) 2.6 cm **b** (i) 140 mm (ii) 14 cm
c (i) 103 mm (ii) 10.3 mm **5** 7 cm **6** 3.4 cm
7a 1 mm **b** 10 **8** £500

10　TILING AND SYMMETRY

Page 113　Looking Back

1a Rectangle, triangle, hexagon
2a House, moon, insect

Page 115　Exercise 1B/C

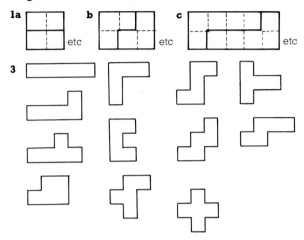

Page 116　Exercise 2A

1 b, c, d, g, h, i, j 2a 1 **b** 2 **c** 2 **d** 4 **e** 1 **f** 1
3a 1 **b** 1 **c** 2 **d** 0 **e** 3 **f** 1 **g** 2 **4 a, b, d, e**
5a A(3, 2), B(−3, 2), C(−3, 0), D(3, 0)
b A(−3, −2), B(3, −2)
c A(7, 2), B(−7, 2); C(−2, 6), D(2, 6)
6a A(2, 3), B(2, −3); C(0, −3), D(0, 3)
b A(4, 2), B(4, −2); C(0, 2), D(0, −2)
c A(6, 4), B(6, −4); C(−8, −5), D(−8, 5)
9a B(8, −5), C(−8, −5), D(−8, 5)
b F(2, 4), G(2, −4), H(−2, −4)
c J(4, 5), K(−4, 5), M(−4, −5), P(5, 0)
d S(3, −3), U(−3, −3), W(−3, 3), Z(0, 10), V(−10, 0)

Page 119　Exercise 2B

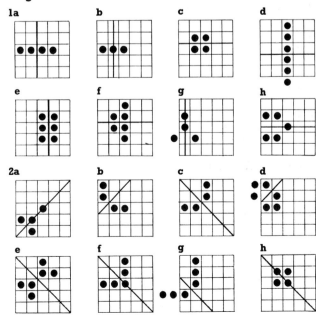

3 $(2,5)$, $(5,4)$, $(3,6)$, $(0,6)$, $(4,4)$, $(6,5)$, $(3,3)$, $(0,4)$;
x-coordinate
4 $(4,1)$, $(2,2)$, $(1,4)$, $(6,3)$, $(3,3)$, $(0,5)$, $(5,3)$;
y-coordinate

Page 120   Exercise 2C

1
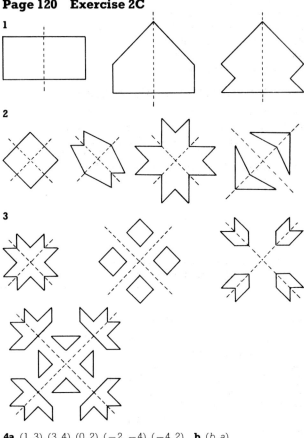

2

3

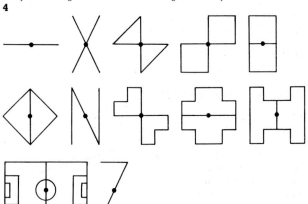

4a $(1,3)$, $(3,4)$, $(0,2)$, $(-2,-4)$, $(-4,2)$ **b** (b,a)
5a $(4,3)$, $(2,1)$, $(5,5)$, $(3,2)$, $(7,3)$, $(0,6)$
b Their sum is 5   **6** Image is the same for both

Page 122   Exercise 3A

1 Half-turn: **a**, **b**, **c**, **d**, **e**; Quarter-turn: **a**, **d**, **e**
2a $\frac{1}{2}$-turn   **b** $\frac{1}{4}$-turn   **c** neither   **d** $\frac{1}{2}$-turn **e** neither
3a $\frac{1}{4}$-turn   **b** $\frac{1}{2}$-turn   **c** neither   **d** $\frac{1}{2}$-turn **e** $\frac{1}{4}$-turn
4

5a (i) $(1,3)$ (ii) $(-1,-3)$ **b** (i) $(2,6)$ (ii) $(-2,-6)$
6a $(4,3)$, $(-4,-3)$ **b** $(-2,1)$, $(2,-1)$; $(1,2)$, $(-1,-2)$;
$(3,1)$, $(-3,-1)$
7 B$(0,6)$, C$(-6,2)$, D$(-6,0)$, E$(-2,-6)$, F$(0,-6)$,
G$(6,-2)$, H$(6,0)$

Page 124   Exercise 3B/C

1a 3   **b** 4   **c** 2   **d** 2   **e** 7   **f** 4   **g** 6   **h** 7   **i** 11
j 8
2a   **b**   **c**   **d**
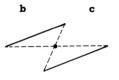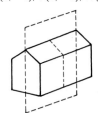

3a $(-2,-3)$ **b** $(-6,-1)$ **c** $(-4,-2)$
4 S$(3,-3)$, T$(0,-4)$, U$(-3,-3)$, V$(-4,0)$, W$(-3,3)$
5a $(-3,-3)$, $(-4,-5)$, $(-6,-2)$, $(-6,-4)$, $(-7,-1)$,
$(-9,0)$, $(-11,-1)$ **b** $(-3,3)$, $(-5,4)$, $(-2,6)$, $(-4,6)$,
$(-1,7)$, $(0,9)$, $(-1,11)$

Page 126   Check-up on Tiling and Symmetry

2a 2   **b** 4   **c** 5   **d** 4   **e** 7
3a A$(3,1)$, B$(1,3)$, C$(-1,3)$, D$(-3,1)$, E$(-3,-1)$,
F$(-1,-3)$, G$(1,-3)$, H$(3,-1)$
b P$(6,8)$, Q$(0,5)$, R$(-6,8)$, S$(-9,0)$, T$(-6,-8)$,
U$(0,-5)$, V$(6,-8)$, W$(9,0)$
4
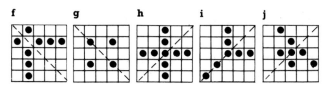

5a   **b**   **c**   **d**   **e**
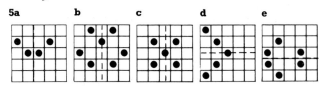

f   **g**   **h**   **i**   **j**

6b (i) $(3,-1)$, $(-1,-4)$, $(-2,2)$, $(5,3)$
(ii) $(-3,1)$, $(1,4)$, $(2,-2)$, $(-5,-3)$
7 $(1,3)$, $(4,-1)$, $(-2,-2)$, $(-3,5)$
8 $\frac{1}{4}$-turn: **a**, **c**, **d**, **f**, **h**. $\frac{1}{2}$-turn only: **b**, **e**, **g**
9 $(0,1)$, $(-2,3)$, $(-2,5)$, $(0,6)$, $(1,5)$, $(1,3)$; $(-1,0)$,
$(-3,-2)$, $(-5,-2)$, $(-6,0)$, $(-5,1)$, $(-3,1)$; $(0,-1)$,
$(2,-3)$, $(2,-5)$, $(0,-6)$, $(-1,-5)$, $(-1,-3)$
10 (i) **a** 3   **b** 4   **c** 0   **d** 2   **e** 7   **f** 4   **g** 6   **h** 7
i 11   **j** 8   (ii) **a** Neither   **b** $\frac{1}{4}$-turn   **c** $\frac{1}{2}$-turn
d $\frac{1}{2}$-turn   **e** neither   **f** $\frac{1}{4}$-turn   **g** $\frac{1}{2}$-turn   **h** neither
i neither   **j** $\frac{1}{4}$-turn

MEASURING AREA

Page 128   Looking Back

1a Length and breadth   **b** The size or area
2a 7   **b** 10   **c** 8   **d** 7   **e** 15   **f** 12   **g** 12   **h** 10
3a 16   **b** 34   **c** about 30   **4a** (i) 18 cm²   (ii) 27 cm²
(iii) 36 cm²   **b** 36 cm²

Page 129   Exercise 1A

1a 25 squares   **b** 18 squares   **c** 24 squares
d 20 squares   **e** 20 squares
Order **a, c, d** and **e, b**
2a 20   **b** 24   **c** 25   **d** 22   **e** 26; **e**
3,4a 2   **b** 9   **c** 24   **d** 8   **e** 6–7   **f** about 15   **g** 10–11
5a 8   **b** 12½   **c** 10   **d** 6
6a 24 sq units   **b** 8 sq units   **c** 28 sq units   **d** 32 sq units
e 28 sq units

Page 131   Exercise 1B

1a 54 cm²   **b** 800 mm²   **c** 225 cm²   **d** 162 cm²
e 207 cm²   **f** 1320 cm²   **g** 575 mm²   **h** 2400 cm²
i 360 000 mm²   **j** 9600 m²
2a 3 m   **b** (i) 16 m², 6 m²   (ii) 22 m²
5a 4 m   **b** (i) 36 m², 12 m²   (ii) 48 m²

Page 132   Exercise 1C

1 12 m by 1 m, 6 m by 2 m, 4 m by 3 m
2a 5 m   **b** 20 mm   **c** 80 cm
3a 81 m²   **b** 16 m²   **c** 65 m²
4a 75 m²   **b** 275 m²   **c** 230 mm²
5 7, 5, 14, 8, 50, 5; 9, 3, 12, 10, 40, 10; 32, 16, 52, 36,
180, 30; 63, 15, 168, 80, 2000, 50
6a 60 000 m²   **b** 6 hectares
7a 100 km²   **b** 10 000 m, 10 000 m   **c** (i) 100 000 000 m²
(ii) 10 000 hectares

Page 134   Exercise 2A

1a (i) 13 m²   (ii) £104   **b** (i) 9 m²   (ii) £72   **c** (i) 8 m²
(ii) £64
2a (i) 15 m²   (ii) £180   **b** (i) 8 m²   (ii) £96   **c** (i) 9 m²
(ii) £108   **d** (i) 6 m²   (ii) £72   **3a** 25   **b** 50 cm by 25 cm
4a 48   **b** 200   **5a** £199.80   **b** £335
6a £349.65   **b** £586.25   **7a** 12 m   **b** £216
8a 2 strips lengthwise is better   **b** £126

Page 135   Exercise 2B/C

1a 54 m²   **b** 8 m²   **c** 46 m²   **d** 2
e No. Two tins cover 70 m², but the area of walls and
ceiling is only 66 m²   **2** £435, £304.50, £210, £134.91
3a 4   **b** 168 m²   **c** 672   **d** £336
4a 17   **b** £80.75   **c** Seed, by £255.25
d It gives an instant lawn

Page 137   Exercise 3A

1a (i) 4   (ii) 2   **b** (i) 3   (ii) 1½   **c** (i) 6   (ii) 3
d (i) 2   (ii) 1   **e** (i) 9   (ii) 4½   **f** (i) 1   (ii) ½
g (i) 4   (ii) 2, all in square units
2a 4   **b** 1½   **c** 3   **d** 7½
3a 3 cm²   **b** 32 cm²   **c** 42 cm²   **d** 68 cm²
4a 6 mm²   **b** 60 cm²   **c** 60 m²   **d** 81 cm²
5 9 m², 24 m²   **6** 10 m²   **7a** 6 m², 10½ m²   **b** 16½ m²

8 96 m²   **9b** 15 sq units
10c 8, 4 units   **d** (i) 16 sq units   (ii) 32 sq units

Page 139   Exercise 3B/C

1a 4   **b** 2   **c** 6   **d** 4½   **e** 1½   **f** 6, all sq units
2a 14 cm²   **b** 36 mm²   **c** 33 m²
3a 84 mm²   **b** 60 m²   **c** 300 mm²   **4 c, a, b**
5a 10 m   **b** 21 m   **c** 15 m
6c (i) 9   (ii) 3, 1, 1½   (iii) 3½ sq units
7 5½ sq units   **8** 2 sq units

Page 141   Check-up on Measuring Area

1a 6 cm²   **b** 4 cm²   **c** 4½ cm²   **d** about 10 cm²
2a 45 cm²   **b** 56 cm²   **c** 2 m²   **d** 90 cm²   **e** 18 000 cm²
f 17.5 m²   **g** 64 mm²   **h** 13.2 m²   **i** 2000 mm²
j 8.55 cm²   **3a** 60 mm²   **b** 30 cm²   **c** 84 m²   **d** 24 cm²
4a 10 sq units   **b** 6 sq units   **5a** 12 m   **b** £5.50
6a 270 cm²   **b** 90 cm²   **c** 8 cm

LETTERS, NUMBERS AND SEQUENCES

Page 142   Looking Back

1a 7   **b** 4   **c** 5   **d** 3   **2a** 16   **b** 32   **c** 99   **d** 3
3a 2 × 4   **b** 6 + 1   **c** 4 × 4 + 5
4a 16, 20   **b** 28, 35   **c** 12, 15   **d** 13, 16
5a 3, 4, 5, 6; 6, 8, 10, 12; 9, 12, 15, 18; 12, 16, 20, 24;
15, 20, 25, 30   **b** 3, 5, 7, 9; 6, 10, 14, 18; 9, 15, 21, 27;
12, 20, 28, 36; 15, 25, 35, 45
6a Add 1   **b** Multiply by 2   **c** Add 5
d Multiply by 7
7a 6   **b** 16   **c** 32   **d** 60   **e** 60   **f** 150

Page 143   Exercise 1A

1a 9   **b** 4   **c** 14   **d** 0   **e** 16
2a 5   **b** 1   **c** 8   **d** 11   **e** 0
3a 20   **b** 30   **c** 40   **d** 50   **e** 100
4a 10   **b** 11   **c** 14   **d** 13   **e** 18
5a 12   **b** 7   **c** 0   **d** 15   **e** 4
6a 5   **b** 3   **c** 8   **d** 2   **e** 10
7a 9   **b** 3   **c** 18   **d** 9   **e** 39   **8** 3, 4, 6, 11
9 0, 3, 5, 8   **10** 10, 2, 18, 14   **11** 0, 3, 15, 30
12 4, 7, 10, 13   **13** 3, 1, 11, 15
14 5, 6, 11, 25; 1, 4, 1, 5   **15** 2, 8, 6, 10; 3, 10, 9, 19

Page 144   Exercise 1B

1a $P = 2x + y$ **b** 13 cm   **2a** $P = 4s$ **b** 24 cm
3a $P = 5t$ **b** 20 cm   **4a** $P = 2c + 2d$ **b** 26 cm
5a $P = a + b + c + d$ **b** 22 cm
6a $P = 2m + 2n$ **b** 70 cm   **7a** $P = 6h$ **b** 90 cm
8a $P = 2p + 2q$ **b** 38 cm
9a $P = 2u + v + w$ **b** 64 cm
10a $P = 2k + 2m + n$ **b** 30 cm
11a $P = 2s + 2u$ **b** 400 cm
12a $P = 2a + 2b + c$ **b** 57 cm

Page 145   Exercise 1C

1 3, 5, 7, 9   **2** 3, 7, 11, 15   **3** 2, 3, 5, 10; 6, 9, 15, 30
4 2, 8, 17, 29   **5** 2, 5, 8, 26   **6** 0, 1, 4, 7; 0, 12, 48, 84
7 0, 2, 4, 6; 6, 4, 2, 0   **8** 12, 14; 29, 36   **9** 8, 6, 2, 0
10 0, 3, 5, 9; 1, 7, 11, 19   **11** 4, 2, 10, 3; 11, 5, 29, 8
12 2, 5, 4, 8, 8; 1, 2, 2, 3, 4; 3, 7, 6, 11, 12; 1, 3, 2, 5, 4
13 5, 4, 6, 10, 18; 2, 3, 4, 5, 13; 3, 1, 2, 5, 5; 7, 7, 10, 15, 31
14 2*a*, 12, 14, 40, 28, 38, 18, 12, 34; *a* + *b*, 8, 10, 21, 16, 25, 12, 11, 22; *a*, 6, 7, 20, 14, 19, 9, 6, 17; *b*, 2, 3, 1, 2, 6, 3, 5, 5; *a* − *b*, 4, 4, 19, 12, 13, 6, 1, 12; 3*b*, 6, 9, 3, 6, 18, 9, 15, 15

Page 146   Exercise 2A

1a (i) Multiply by 2   (ii) 16, 18, 2*n*   **b** (i) Multiply by 5
(ii) 50, 55, 5*n*   **c** (i) Multiply by 4   (ii) 92, 96, 4*n*
2a (i) Multiply by 10   (ii) 130, 140, 10*n*
b (i) Multiply by 7   (ii) 119, 126, 7*n*
c (i) Multiply by 9   (ii) 270, 279, 9*n*
3a 2   **b** 4   **c** 6   **d** 8   **e** 20   **f** 200   **g** 2*x*   **h** 2*y*
4a 3   **b** 6   **c** 9   **d** 12   **e** 30   **f** 300   **g** 3*m*   **h** 3*n*
5a 24   **b** 40   **c** 4*k*   **d** 4*t*   **6a** 15   **b** 40   **c** 5*h*   **d** 5*d*
7a 20   **b** 2000   **c** 4*x*   **d** 4*y*
8a 6, 12, 18, ..., 6*m*   **b** 8, 16, 24, ..., 8*n*
c 12, 24, 36, ..., 12*t*   **d** 24, 48, 72, ..., 24*k*

Page 147   Exercise 2B/C

1a (i) Add 2   (ii) 12, 13, *x* + 2   **b** (i) Add 6
(ii) 26, 27, *n* + 6   **c** (i) Add 1   (ii) 5, 6, 18, 19, *k* + 1
d (i) Add 4   (ii) 8, 9, 95, 96, *m* + 4   **e** (i) Add 9
(ii) 13, 14, 133, 134, *t* + 9
2a (i) Add 3   (ii) *c* + 3, *m* + 3   **b** (i) Add 5
(ii) *x* + 5, *y* + 5   **c** (i) Add 11   (ii) *p* + 11, *q* + 11
d (i) Add 7   (ii) *u* + 7, *v* + 7   **e** (i) Subtract 1
(ii) *x* − 1, *r* − 1   **3** 2, 3, 4, 5, 6, 7, 11, *n* + 1
4 3, 4, 5, 6, 7, 8, 12, *n* + 2   **5** 2, 4, 6, 8, 10, 12, 20, 2*n*
6 3, 6, 9, 12, 15, 18, 30, 3*n*   **7** 4, 8, 12, 16, 20, 24, 40, 4*n*
8 8, 12, 16, 20, 24, 28, 44, 4*n* + 4

Page 149   Exercise 3A

1a (i) 8, 10, 20, 2*n*   (ii) *n* = 15   **b** (i) 12, 15, 30, 3*n*
(ii) *n* = 10   **c** (i) 20, 25, 50, 5*n*   (ii) *n* = 6
2a (i) 16, 20, 40, 4*n*   (ii) *n* = 200
b (i) 80, 100, 200, 20*n*   (ii) *n* = 40
c (i) 100, 125, 250, 25*n*   (ii) *n* = 32
3 5, 10, 15, ..., 5*x*   **4** 3, 6, 9, ..., 3*y*
5 4, 8, 12, ..., 4*b*   **6** 5*s*   **7** 19*b*   **8** 100*w*   **9** 7*n*
10 8*d*   **11** 6*m*   **12a** 7*r*   **b** 2*r*   **13a** 8*c*   **b** 50*c* pence
14a 12*n*   **b** 17*n*

Page 151   Exercise 3B/C

1a (i) 7, 9, 19, 2*n* − 1   (ii) 8   **b** (i) 9, 11, 21, 2*n* + 1
(ii) 14   **c** (i) 10, 12, 22, 2*n* + 2   (ii) 9
d (i) 13, 16, 31, 3*n* + 1   (ii) 12
e (i) 14, 17, 32, 3*n* + 2   (ii) 8
2a (i) 15, 19, 39, 4*n* − 1   (ii) 7   **b** (i) 17, 21, 41, 4*n* + 1
(ii) 12   **c** (i) 21, 26, 51, 5*n* + 1   (ii) 15
d (i) 22, 28, 58, 6*n* − 2   (ii) 20   **e** (i) 16, 19, 34, 3*n* + 4
(ii) 12   **3a** 10, 13, 16, 19, 37, 3*n* + 7   **b** 82
4a 6, 11, 16, 21, 51, 5*n* + 1   **b** 126
5a 7, 12, 17, 22, 52, 5*n* + 2   **b** 127
6a 5, 12, 19, 26, 68, 7*n* − 2   **b** 173
7a 12, 19, 26, 33, 75, 7*n* + 5   **b** 180
8a 8, 13, 18, 23, 53, 5*n* + 3   **b** 128

9a 6, 10, 14, 18, 42, 4*n* + 2   **b** 102
10a 7, 13, 19, 25, 61, 6*n* + 1   **b** 151   **11** 2*x* + 2
12 2*y* + 4   **13** 4*z* + 2

Page 154   Check-up on Letters, Numbers and Sequences

1a 85, 90, 5*n*   **b** 129, 132, 3*x*   **c** 31, *t* + 1
d *w* + 10, *k* + 10   **2** 2*c*   **3** 6*s*   **4** 5*h*   **5** 4*n*, 2*n*
6 4*t*, 2*t* + 2   **7a** 12   **b** 10   **c** 16   **d** 12   **e** 0   **f** 20
8a 10, 25, 40, 50   **b** 1, 4, 16, 36   **c** 1, 7, 13, 19
9 3, 4, 5, 6, 7, 8, *n* + 2; 3, 5, 7, 9, 11, 13, 2*n* + 1
10a (i) £16   (ii) £80   (iii) £16*n*   **b** (i) £20   (ii) £35
(iii) £50   (iv) £(15*n* + 5)
11a 348, 353, 5*w* + 3   **b** 499, 508, 9*r* − 5
c 231, 239, 8*k* + 7   **d** 2098, 2115, 17*t* + 7
e 2027, 2046, 19*c* − 6

13 TWO DIMENSIONS: RECTANGLE AND SQUARE

Page 156   Looking Back

1 (i) Circle   (ii) Rectangle   (iii) Square
(iv) Triangle   (v) Hexagon
(vi) Half-circle or semi-circle
2a (ii), (iii)   **b** (i), (vi)   **c** (ii), (iii), (iv)   **d** (v)
e (i), (ii), (iii), (iv), (v), (vi)   **f** (i), (ii), (iii), (v)
3 *Examples.* Rectangle: RT 90, FORWARD 110, LT 90,
FORWARD 220, LT 90, FORWARD 110, LT 90,
FORWARD 220. Square: RT 90, FORWARD 165, LT 90,
FORWARD 165, LT 90, FORWARD 165, LT 90,
FORWARD 165. Triangle: RT 90, FORWARD 250,
LT 90, FORWARD 250, LT 135, FORWARD 350
5 First picture: rectangles, triangles, pentagons,
parts of circle, possibly squares. Second picture:
triangles. Third picture: rectangles, triangles,
pentagons. Fourth picture: rectangles, circles

Page 157   Exercise 1A

1 12 cm, 15 cm
2a AB = 12 cm, BC = 8 cm   **b** EH = 7 m, HG = 14 m
c KN = 10 mm, NM = 30 mm
3a BC   **b** EF   **c** (i) NM   (ii) LM
4a 72 cm   **b** 54 cm   **c** 64 mm   **5c** B(8, 1), C(8, 3)
6b The edges remain the same distance apart
8a The train's wheels are a fixed distance apart
b Yes   **c** Yes
9a BC = 3 units, AB = 4 units, DC = 4 units
b AB ∥ DC, AD ∥ BC
10a S(2, 7)   **b** PQ = SR, PS = QR   **c** 3 units, 6 units
11a S(0, 5)   **b** OQ = SR, OS = QR   **c** 6 units, 5 units
12a Easy to make, and pass through   **b** 500 mm, 825 mm
13a 12.5 m   **b** 0.2 m
14a 100 cm   **b** 95 cm   **c** 115 cm
15a 6   **b** Base 30, 40, 30, 40 cm; top 30, 40, 30, 40 cm;
sides all 70 cm   **c** 560 cm

Page 159   Exercise 1B/C

1a 74 m   **b** 5 m
2a F(8, 3), H(3, 5)   **b** EF = HG = 5 units,
EH = FG = 2 units   **c** EF, HG; EH, FG

3a F(2, −1), H(−2, 3)   **b** EF = HG = 4 units,
EH = FG = 4 units   **c** EF, HG; EH, FG
4 14 units, 16 units
5 M(7, 2), N(7, −1) and M(−3, 2), N(−3, −1)
6 14, 1; 13, 2; 12, 3; 11, 4; 10, 5; 9, 6; 8, 7 metres
7 D(5, 7), E(3½, 3½)
8a 2, 4, 8, . . .   **b** (i) 128   (ii) 1024
(iii) 2 × 2 × 2 × 2 × . . . n times

Page 160   Exercise 2

1a   **b**   **c**

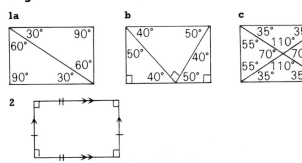

2

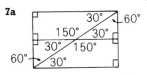

3 360°
4 ∠LKM = 25°, ∠NMK = 25°, ∠KNM = 90°,
∠KLM = 90°   **5** 90°. A rectangle   **6a** 28   **b** 15

7a

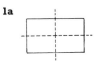

b Triangles
8 70°, 20°, 110°

Page 161   Exercise 3A

1a CD = 12 cm, AD = 5 cm, EC = 6.5 cm, AC = 13 cm
b QM = 30 mm, QP = 40 mm, OQ = 25 mm,
PM = 50 mm   **c** GH = 24 m, EH = 7 m, HF = 25 m,
HK = 12.5 m   **2c** OP = OQ = OR = OS = 5 cm
3a 110 m, 86 m   **b** (i) 70 m   (ii) 55 m   **c** 86 m, 140 m
5 (i) **c**, **b**, **a**, **d**   (ii) **d**, **a**, **b**, **c**   (iii) **c**, **b**, **a**, **d**
6b B(5, 1), D(1, 3), E(3, 2)   **7** B(2, −4), D(−2, 4), E(0, 0)
8 105 m   **9** The diagonal length of the screen is 51 cm

Page 162   Exercise 3B/C

1b E(2, −3), G(−4, 1), H(−1, −1)   **2** S(4, 8), T(3, 5)
3 55 m   **4** 3000 or 3200 m (AB shorter or longer side)
5a x = 30, y = 60   **b** x = 58, y = 29
c x = 60, y = 60   **d** x = 40, y = 50
6a 288 mm   **b** ½   **7** L(−1, 4), M(3, 0)

Page 163   Exercise 4

1 Rectangle
2 MOVE (2, 2)   **3** MOVE (0, 0)   **4** MOVE (3, 3)
   DRAW (2, 8)   DRAW (5, 0)   DRAW (7, 7)
   DRAW (6, 8)   DRAW (5, 2)   DRAW (5, 9)
   DRAW (6, 2)   DRAW (0, 2)   DRAW (1, 5)
   DRAW (2, 2)   DRAW (0, 0)   DRAW (3, 3)
5b DRAW (7, 1)   **6a** MOVE (1, 5) or (7, 1)
   DRAW (1, 1)   DRAW (7, 1)   (1, 5)
b MOVE (4, 3)
7b MOVE (7, 1)
   DRAW (7, 5)
   DRAW (13, 5)
   DRAW (13, 1)
   DRAW (7, 1)

d Rectangle congruent to original rectangle
8a A(3, 6), C(9, 2), P(6, 4)
b MOVE (6, 6) or MOVE (6, 6)
   DRAW (12, 6)   DRAW (6, 10)
   DRAW (12, 10) DRAW (12, 10)
   DRAW (6, 10)   DRAW (12, 6)
   DRAW (6, 6)   DRAW (6, 6)

Page 165   Exercise 5A

1 (i) 3   (ii) 7   (iii) 10
2a All equal; opposite sides parallel   **b** All 90°
c Equal   **3b** (i) 2 cm   (ii) 90°
4 *Examples* Chess or draughts board, wall or floor
tilings   **5** 900 m
6b A(3, 1), B(3, 4), C(6, 4), D(6, 1)
c P(−5, 3), Q(−5, −1), R(−1, −1), S(−1, 3)
7 (6, 0), (0, 6); (3, 3)
8b Four axes, two from the rectangle
9a 45°   **b** 90°   **c** 45°   **d** (i) OC   (ii) OB
10a PQ = QR = RS = 14 cm; OP = OQ = OR = 10 cm
b All 90° at O, 45° at corners of square (∠OPQ, etc)
11 AC = BD = 6 units; (3, 3)

Page 166   Exercise 5B/C

1 H(0, 3); (2, 3)   **2** M(7, 7), N(4, 7) or M(7, 1), N(4, 1)
3 (2, 0), (−2, −2); (0, −1)
4b 16x cm   **c** 8y cm   **d** 24x + 12y cm
5a S(2, 1), U(−4, −5)
b A(−1, −2), B(−7, −2), C(−7, 4), D(−1, 4)
c (−2½, −½)

Page 167   Exercise 6

1b DRAW (8, 1)   **2b** MOVE (1, 1)   MOVE (8, 1)
   DRAW (1, 1)   DRAW (8, 8)   DRAW (1, 8)
3b MOVE (2, 2)   **4b** Square   **5b** Square
   DRAW (2, 7)   **c** MOVE (5, 6)   **c** MOVE (8, 5)
   DRAW (7, 7)   DRAW (11, 6)   DRAW (12, 9)
   DRAW (7, 2)   DRAW (11, 12)   DRAW (8, 13)
   DRAW (2, 2)   DRAW (5, 12)   DRAW (4, 9)
                       DRAW (5, 6)   DRAW (8, 5)

Page 169   Check-up on Two Dimensions:
Rectangle and Square

1a   **b**

2a (i) DC   (ii) AD   (iii) BD   **b** OB, OC, OD
3a PQ, SR; PS, QR   **b** ∠s PQR, QRS, RSP, SPQ
4

5 C(3, 3) or (9, 3), D(3, 0) or (9, 0)
6a All sides 6 cm, all angles 90°
b Four half-diagonals 4 cm, angles at centre 90°,
other angles 45°   **7a** K(0, 8)   **b** 8 units, 5 units
8a 24   **b** 11

9a (i) T (ii) T **b** (i) F (ii) T **c** (i) T (ii) T
d (i) T (ii) T **e** (i) F (ii) T **f** (i) T (ii) T
g (i) F (ii) T **h** (i) T (ii) F **i** (i) F (ii) T
j (i) T (ii) T **10** F(6, 4), G(6, 6), H(2, 6)
11 (6, 7), (0, 7)

14 MEASURING VOLUME

Page 170 Looking Back

1 Arrows: **a** 2 marks up from 0 **b** 1 mark up **c** 3 marks up
2 $\frac{3}{4}$ litre **3** pint, litre **4a** (i) petrol (ii) milk **b** 3
5a (i) $1\frac{1}{2}$ litres (ii) 2 litres (iii) $2\frac{1}{2}$ litres (iv) $\frac{3}{4}$ litre
b It fills the jar **6a** (i) **b** (i) **7a** (v) **b** (i)
c (ii) and (iv)

Page 172 Exercise 1A

1a 4 **b** 6 **c** 8 **d** 12 **2a** 4 **b** 3 **c** 12 **d** 12
3a 4 **b** 4 **c** 16 **d** 16 **4a** 25 **b** 3 **c** 75 **d** 75
5 $8 \times 2 \times 2$; 32 **6** $7 \times 3 \times 4$; 84
7a $18\,\text{cm}^3$ **b** $24\,\text{cm}^3$ **c** $27\,\text{cm}^3$ **d** $20\,\text{cm}^3$
8a 8 cubes, or cm^3 **b** $6\,\text{cm}^3$ **c** $36\,\text{cm}^3$

Page 173 Exercise 1B

1a $96\,\text{cm}^3$ **b** $240\,\text{cm}^3$ **c** $40\,\text{cm}^3$ **d** $500\,\text{cm}^3$ **e** $8\,\text{cm}^3$
f $96\,\text{cm}^3$ **g** $720\,\text{cm}^3$ **h** $1000\,\text{cm}^3$ **i** $3600\,\text{cm}^3$
2 They pack easily and efficiently
3a $3\,\text{m}^3$ **b** $288\,000\,\text{mm}^3$ **c** $288\,\text{cm}^3$ **d** $560\,\text{cm}^3$
e $150\,\text{cm}^3$ **f** $63\,\text{m}^3$ **g** $4560\,\text{cm}^3$ **h** $240\,000\,\text{mm}^3$
i $112\,\text{m}^3$

Page 174 Exercise 1C

1a $53\,240\,\text{mm}^3$ **b** $405\,\text{cm}^3$ **c** $0.728\,\text{m}^3$ **d** $0.03\,\text{m}^3$
e $1125\,\text{cm}^3$ **2a** (i) $30\,000\,\text{cm}^3$ (ii) 30 litres **b** $6\frac{2}{3}\,\text{cm}$
3a 2 cm **b** 5 cm **c** $2\frac{1}{2}\,\text{cm}$
4a $192\,000\,\text{cm}^3$ **b** $459\,000\,\text{cm}^3$ **c** $216\,000\,\text{cm}^3$
5a 750 **b** 48 **c** 6 **6** 25 000

Page 175 Exercise 2A

1a 500 **b** 250 **c** 200 **d** 800 **2** 5 **3a** 10 **b** 20
4a $1000\,\text{cm}^3$, or 1 litre **b** 20 cm by 10 cm by 20 cm;
$4000\,\text{cm}^3$ **c** 75p **5a** 2000 **b** 3000 **c** 1500
6a $25 \times 12 \times 10\,\text{cm}^3 = 3000\,\text{cm}^3$ **b** 3000; 3
7a 5000 **b** 5 **c** £6 **8a** (i) 24 000 (ii) 24 **b** £12
9a (i) 12 mg (ii) 6 mg (iii) 2.4 mg **b** (i) $\frac{1}{2}$ litre
(ii) $\frac{1}{10}$ litre, or 100 ml
10a 1 000 000 **b** 1 000 000 **c** 1000

Page 176 Exercise 2B

1a $325\,000\,\text{cm}^3$ **b** 325 litres
2b Freezers: A–67 500 cm^3 or 67.5 litres; B–76 800 cm^3
or 76.8 litres. Fridges: A–180 000 cm^3 or 180 litres;
B–160 000 cm^3 or 160 litres **c** B has the larger freezer,
by 9.3 litres. A has the larger fridge, by 20 litres

Page 176 Exercise 2C

1 Volumes 75, 60, 48, 64, 120, 70 m^3. Radiator sizes 2, 1,
1, 1, 3, 2 **2a** 6.5 m **b** 5.5 m **c** 4.95 m; 3.25 m

Page 178 Check-up on Measuring Volume

1a 250 ml **b** 750 ml **c** 3 **2a** 2500 **b** 25
3a $6\,\text{cm}^3$ **b** $12\,\text{cm}^3$ **c** $18\,\text{cm}^3$ **d** $24\,\text{cm}^3$ **e** $30\,\text{cm}^3$
4a 16 **b** 7.5 cm
5a $3200\,\text{mm}^3$ **b** $466.2\,\text{cm}^3$ **c** $221\,\text{m}^3$ **6** 20 cm
7a 144 **b** 36 cm
8a (i) 100 cm, 1 cm, 0.1 cm (ii) $10\,\text{cm}^3$
b (i) 1000 mm, 10 mm, 1 mm (ii) $10\,000\,\text{mm}^3$

15 FRACTIONS AND PERCENTAGES

Page 179 Looking Back

1 $\frac{1}{4}, \frac{1}{5}; \frac{3}{5}, \frac{4}{5}; 33\frac{1}{3}; \frac{1}{4}, \frac{1}{2}; \frac{3}{4}, \frac{1}{4}; \frac{1}{2}, \frac{1}{4}; \frac{3}{4}, \frac{9}{10}; \frac{2}{3}, \frac{1}{3}; \frac{3}{4}, \frac{1}{2}; \frac{3}{8}, \frac{1}{4}; 1\frac{1}{2}, \frac{1}{4}; \frac{5}{9}$
2a (i) $\frac{1}{2}$ (ii) $\frac{1}{3}$ (iii) $\frac{4}{5}$ **b** (i) $\frac{1}{2}$ (ii) $\frac{2}{3}$ (iii) $\frac{1}{5}$
3a $\frac{1}{2}$ **b** $\frac{3}{4}$ **c** $\frac{1}{3}$ **4a** £5 **b** £2 **c** £6 **d** £3 **e** £10
5a $\frac{1}{3}$ **b** 4 cm **6a** (i) $\frac{1}{4}$ (ii) $\frac{1}{2}$ (iii) $\frac{1}{4}$ **b** 1
7 $\frac{1}{2}, \frac{1}{4}; \frac{1}{3}, \frac{1}{6}; \frac{4}{5}, \frac{1}{10}$
8 $\frac{1}{3}$ of 6 cm, $\frac{1}{10}$ of 30 cm, $\frac{1}{5}$ of 20 cm, $\frac{1}{2}$ of 10 cm
9a Shade: (i) 6 (ii) 9 (iii) 2 (iv) 8 squares
b $\frac{1}{6}, \frac{1}{2}; \frac{2}{3}, \frac{3}{4}$

Page 180 Exercise 1A

1a $\frac{1}{4}$ **b** $\frac{1}{2}$ **c** $\frac{3}{4}$ **d** $\frac{1}{8}$
2

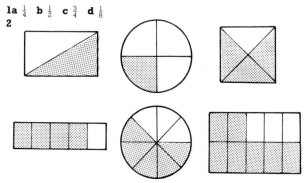

3a 7 **b** 2 **c** $\frac{2}{7}$ **4a** 12 **b** $\frac{3}{12}$ **5a** 10 **b** (i) $\frac{8}{10}$ (ii) $\frac{2}{10}$
6a $\frac{5}{11}$ **b** $\frac{2}{11}$ **c** $\frac{4}{11}$ **7a** $\frac{1}{4}$ **b** $\frac{5}{12}$ **c** $\frac{7}{10}$ **d** $\frac{1}{12}$ **e** $\frac{4}{5}$
8 $\frac{3}{4}, \frac{2}{5}; \frac{5}{7}, \frac{7}{12}; \frac{2}{3}, \frac{1}{4}; \frac{1}{2}, \frac{3}{8}; \frac{6}{8}, \frac{8}{9}$ **9a** 4 **b** 8 **c** 2 **d** 5 **e** 10
10 $\frac{2}{3}$ **11a** $\frac{13}{32}$ **b** $\frac{19}{32}$ **12** $\frac{1}{4}$

Page 181 Exercise 1B

1a $\frac{2}{5}$ **b** $\frac{3}{4}$ **c** $\frac{3}{7}$ **d** $\frac{2}{4}$ **2** $\frac{12}{25}$ **3a** $\frac{1}{6}$ **b** $\frac{3}{6}$ **c** $\frac{5}{12}$ **d** $\frac{9}{12}$
4a 1 **b** 2 **c** 4 **d** 6 **e** 7 **f** 8 **5a** $\frac{21}{50}$ **b** $\frac{9}{50}$ **c** $\frac{41}{50}$
6a $\frac{1}{8}$ **b** $\frac{3}{8}$ **c** $\frac{2}{8}$ **d** $\frac{200}{8}$
7a 1 mm **b** 1 cm **c** 1 g **d** 1 day **e** 1 minute
f 1 penny **8a** $\frac{1}{52}$ **b** $\frac{1}{365}$ **c** $\frac{1}{8760}$ **d** $\frac{1}{525600}$ **e** $\frac{1}{31536000}$
9a $\frac{1}{2}$ **b** $\frac{1}{2}$ **c** $\frac{1}{4}$ **d** $\frac{4}{52}$
10a 0 **b** 12 **c** 68 **d** (i) $\frac{20}{68}$ (ii) $\frac{17}{68}$

Page 182 Exercise 1C

1 $\frac{5}{12}$ **2** $\frac{1}{2}$ **3** $\frac{1}{6}$ and $\frac{1}{3}$
4 Divide it into **a** six **b** eight **c** fifteen equal parts
5a   **b**   **c**

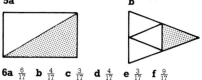

6a $\frac{6}{17}$ **b** $\frac{4}{17}$ **c** $\frac{3}{17}$ **d** $\frac{4}{17}$ **e** $\frac{3}{17}$ **f** $\frac{9}{17}$

Page 183 Exercise 2A

1a $\frac{1}{2}, \frac{2}{4}$ **b** $\frac{1}{2}, \frac{3}{6}$ **c** $\frac{3}{4}, \frac{6}{8}$

2a $\frac{1 \times 2}{2 \times 2}$ **b** $\frac{1 \times 3}{2 \times 3}$ **c** $\frac{3 \times 2}{4 \times 2}$

3a $\frac{1}{2}$ **b** $\frac{1}{3}$ **c** $\frac{1}{4}$ **d** $\frac{1}{2}$ **e** $\frac{1}{5}$ **f** $\frac{1}{4}$ **g** $\frac{1}{5}$ **h** $\frac{1}{3}$
4a $\frac{3}{4}$ **b** $\frac{2}{3}$ **c** $\frac{3}{4}$ **d** $\frac{4}{5}$ **e** $\frac{2}{3}$ **f** $\frac{3}{4}$ **g** $\frac{2}{3}$ **h** $\frac{9}{10}$
5a (i) $\frac{2}{4}$ (ii) $\frac{3}{6}$ (iii) $\frac{4}{8}$ (iv) $\frac{5}{10}$ (v) $\frac{6}{12}$
6a $\frac{1}{4}$ **b** $\frac{1}{2}$ **c** $\frac{3}{4}$ **d** $\frac{1}{3}$ **e** $\frac{2}{3}$ **7a** $\frac{1}{6}$ **b** $\frac{1}{4}$
8 $\frac{1}{2}, \frac{1}{5}, \frac{1}{4}, \frac{3}{5}, \frac{3}{4}, \frac{1}{10}$ **9a** $\frac{1}{2}$ **b** $\frac{1}{4}$ **c** $\frac{1}{3}$ **d** $\frac{3}{4}$
10 $\frac{1}{4}$ **11a** $\frac{1}{9}$ **b** $\frac{1}{3}$ **c** $\frac{1}{2}$ **d** $\frac{2}{3}$ **12** $\frac{3}{4}, \frac{1}{4}$

Page 184 Exercise 2B/C

1a $\frac{4}{8}$ **b** $\frac{3}{9}$ **c** $\frac{2}{10}$ **d** $\frac{3}{24}$ **e** $\frac{5}{10}$ **f** $\frac{10}{100}$
2a $\frac{2}{3}$ **b** $\frac{1}{2}$ **c** $\frac{2}{5}$ **d** $\frac{9}{10}$ **e** $\frac{1}{10}$ **f** $\frac{1}{5}$ **g** $\frac{4}{5}$ **h** $\frac{1}{4}$
3a $\frac{1}{4}$ **b** $\frac{4}{5}$ **c** $\frac{2}{3}$ **d** $\frac{3}{5}$ **e** $\frac{5}{4}$ **4a** $\frac{7}{10}$ **b** $\frac{3}{10}$ **5a** $\frac{4}{5}$ **b** $\frac{3}{5}$
6a $\frac{1}{6}$ **b** $\frac{1}{30}$ **7a** $\frac{1}{8}$ **b** $\frac{1}{2}$ **c** $\frac{4}{15}$ **8** $\frac{5}{12}$ **9a** $\frac{3}{5}$ **b** $\frac{5}{8}$
10a $\frac{3}{5}$ **b** $\frac{5}{6}$ **c** $\frac{1}{4}$ **d** $\frac{3}{4}$ **e** $\frac{22}{25}$ **11** $\frac{1}{4}, \frac{1}{8}, \frac{1}{8}$
12a $\frac{3}{4}$ **b** $\frac{2}{5}$ **c** $\frac{3}{10}$ **d** $\frac{1}{4}$ **e** $\frac{3}{5}$ **f** $\frac{3}{5}$ **g** $\frac{1}{2}$ **h** $\frac{13}{20}$
13 $\frac{8}{12}, \frac{9}{12}, \frac{3}{12}$ **14a** $\frac{9}{12}, \frac{10}{12}, \frac{6}{12}$ **b** $\frac{5}{6}, \frac{3}{4}, \frac{2}{3}$
15a $\frac{11}{15}, \frac{2}{3}, \frac{3}{5}$ **b** $\frac{3}{4}, \frac{5}{8}, \frac{9}{16}$

Page 186 Exercise 3A

1a 4 **b** 3 **c** 4 **d** 3 **e** 5 **f** 3 **g** 9
2a 5 **b** 6 **c** 5 **d** 3 **e** 10 **f** 12 **g** 6
3a 45 minutes **b** 20 minutes **4** 9p, 36p **5** 9, 21
6 14 **7** 9 m² **8** 2 m²
9a 10p **b** 60p **c** 75p **d** 250p **e** 40p **f** 100p
10 A-8, B-20, C-10, D-2 **11** 1200
12a 8 cm **b** 15 pupils **c** 12 grams **d** 21 days
13a 30 **b** 15 **c** 45 **d** 20 **e** 90
14a £285, £117, £99, £38 **b** £1.40, £33, £3.60, £0.90

Page 187 Exercise 3B/C

1a £75 **b** £12 **c** £15 **d** £14 **e** £18 **2a** 60 **b** 135
3 42 kg **4** 12 kg **5** $1\frac{1}{2}$ hours
6a 72 m **b** 140 kg **c** 360 pupils **d** 75 cm **e** £900
7a 90 m² **b** 4 m² **c** $1\frac{1}{2}$ m²
8a 71p **b** £4.58 **c** 28p **d** 33p **e** £6.93
9 225 km per hour
10a £116.99, 41p, £3.59, £40.95 **b** $\frac{9}{10} = 1 - \frac{1}{10}$
(i) $\frac{4}{5}$ (ii) $\frac{2}{3}$ (iii) $\frac{3}{4}$ (iv) $\frac{1}{2}$

Page 188 Exercise 4A

1a $\frac{1}{100}$ **b** $\frac{10}{100}$ **c** $\frac{9}{100}$ **d** $\frac{19}{100}$ **e** $\frac{60}{100}$ **f** $\frac{100}{100}$
2a $\frac{12}{100}$ **b** $\frac{35}{100}$ **c** $\frac{80}{100}$ **d** $\frac{5}{100}$ **e** $\frac{7}{100}$ **f** $\frac{50}{100}$
3a (i) **b** (iii) **c** (ii) **d** (v) **e** (iv)
4 10, 20, 30, 45, 50, 65, 80, 95, 100; $\frac{10}{100}, \frac{20}{100}, \frac{30}{100}, \frac{45}{100}, \frac{50}{100}$,
$\frac{65}{100}, \frac{80}{100}, \frac{95}{100}, \frac{100}{100}$ **5** 5%
6a 20%, 22%, 10%, 13%, 14%, 21%
b Salad, baked potato, filled roll, fish fingers, curry,
beans on toast **7** 11%, 9%, 8.5%, $7\frac{1}{2}$%, 5.8%, $3\frac{1}{2}$%, 1%
8a $\frac{1}{10}$ **b** $\frac{1}{4}$ **c** $\frac{1}{2}$ **d** $\frac{3}{4}$ **e** 1 **f** $\frac{7}{10}$ **g** $\frac{9}{10}$ **h** $\frac{3}{20}$ **i** $\frac{1}{20}$
j $\frac{1}{25}$ **k** $\frac{2}{25}$ **l** $\frac{22}{25}$
9a 100% **b** Petrol, servicing and repairs, licence,
insurance, parking, oil, extras
10a $\frac{3}{10}$ **b** $\frac{7}{10}$ **c** $\frac{3}{5}$ **d** $\frac{1}{5}$ **e** $\frac{2}{5}$ **f** $\frac{11}{20}$ **g** $\frac{4}{5}$ **h** $\frac{1}{100}$ **i** 2
j $1\frac{1}{2}$ **k** $\frac{1}{50}$ **l** 5

Page 189 Exercise 4B/C

1a $\frac{20}{100} = 20\%$ **b** $\frac{16}{100} = 16\%$ **c** $\frac{75}{100} = 75\%$
d $\frac{22}{100} = 22\%$ **e** $\frac{50}{100} = 50\%$ **f** $\frac{100}{100} = 100\%$
2a 38% **b** 95% **c** 121% **d** 273% **e** 7% **f** 1%
3a $\frac{33}{100}$ **b** $\frac{9}{25}$ **c** $\frac{77}{100}$ **d** $\frac{3}{50}$ **e** $\frac{14}{25}$ **f** 1
4 0.008, 0.8, 5, 8.375, 9.05, 9.25, 9.5, 9.52, 10.25, 12,
14.64, 40, 167
5a 55% **b** 64% **c** 70% **d** 98% **e** 60% **f** 25%
g 50% **h** 40% **6** 42.5% **7a** $\frac{1}{10}$ **b** 10%
8a $\frac{1}{4}$ **b** 25%
9a 75%, 70%, 60%, 80%, $66\frac{2}{3}$%
b History, English, Maths, Science, French
10a $\frac{4}{5}$ **b** $\frac{3}{10}$ **c** $\frac{7}{10}$ **d** $\frac{13}{50}$ **e** both the same
11a 20 **b** (i) 25% (ii) 20% (iii) 15% (iv) 30%
(v) 10% **c** 100%

Page 191 Exercise 5A

1a £20 **b** 50 g **c** 15 cm **d** 350 litres
2a £5 **b** £8 **c** £35 **d** £5 **e** £15 **f** £20 **g** £30
h 15p **i** 4p **j** 4p
3a 16 marbles **b** 160 people **c** 12 LPs **d** 2 books
4a 50p **b** 15p **c** £2.50. £1.50, 45p, £7.50
5a 4 pieces **b** 80 ml **c** 50 g **d** 3 cm
6a £6 **b** £6 **c** £10 **d** £21 **e** 25 m **f** 120 kg
g 500 people **h** £12
7a £2, £18 **b** £5, £20 **c** £1, £19 **d** £12, £68
e £4, £12 **f** £16, £16 **8a** 25% **b** 16 pages
9a 0.12 **b** 0.25 **c** 0.8 **d** 0.2 **e** 0.05 **f** 0.09
g 0.66 **h** 0.01

Page 192 Exercise 5B/C

1a £20 **b** £13 **c** £75 **d** £1 **e** £9.10 **f** £22.40
g £43.20 **h** 20p **i** £1.50 **j** 1p **2a** 1 hour **b** 20%
3a (i) 880 (ii) 140 **b** 1120 **c** 5%
4a (i) 4p, 32p, 14p, 11p (ii) 24p, £2.12, 94p, 71p
b Cereal, by 3p; loaf by 6p **5a** £60 **b** £55 **c** £50
6a 80% **b** (i) £29.75 (ii) £74.38 (iii) £27.08
7a £765 **b** £765
c Three times the increase on $\frac{1}{3}$rd the salary
8a £3.85 **b** £25.85 **9** Not really. £9880 to £19 760
10 £3837

Page 194 Check-up on Fractions and Percentages

1a $\frac{1}{2}$ **b** $\frac{3}{4}$ **c** $\frac{2}{5}$ **d** $\frac{1}{3}$ **e** $\frac{1}{2}$
2a month **b** second **c** hour **d** cent
3a $\frac{3}{4}$ **b** $\frac{1}{2}$ **c** $\frac{2}{3}$ **d** $\frac{3}{4}$ **e** $\frac{3}{10}$ **f** $\frac{2}{5}$ **g** $\frac{8}{9}$
4a $\frac{2}{15}$ **b** $\frac{1}{6}$ **c** $\frac{4}{15}$ **d** $\frac{11}{15}$
5a 10p **b** 60p **c** 80p **d** £2.50 **e** £56
6a 45 **b** (i) $\frac{2}{3}$ (ii) $\frac{1}{3}$
7a $\frac{1}{1}$ or 1, 100% **b** $\frac{2}{5}$, 40% **c** $\frac{3}{4}$, 75% **d** $\frac{1}{2}$, 50%
e $\frac{1}{4}$, 25% **8a** £10 **b** £12 **c** £15 **d** £15 **e** £10
9 540 **10a** £24 **b** £136
11 Blank, 1; 100%, $\frac{1}{4}$, 25%, $\frac{1}{5}$, 20%, $\frac{3}{4}$, 75%,
$\frac{1}{10}$, 10%, $\frac{1}{2}$, 50%, blank **12a** 25% **b** 50%

16 SOLVING MORE EQUATIONS

Page 195 Looking Back

1a 9 **b** 7 **c** 8 **d** 2
2a $x+2$ **b** $3y$ kg **c** £$2c$ **d** $3x+5$ cm
3a $3x$ **b** x **c** 0 **d** $8p$ **e** q **f** $6x$
4a $x=3$ **b** $y=6$ **c** $t=10$ **d** $p=7$ **e** $n=7$
f $k=4$ **g** $x=2$ **h** $y=2$ **5a** 7 **b** 14 **c** 10 **d** 6
6a $3x$ **b** 0 **c** $4y$ **d** 0
7a 10, 34, 36, $2x$ **b** 7, 29, 30, $n+2$
c 16, 100, 103, $3k+1$

Page 196 Exercise 1A

1 $x=3$ **2** $x=3$ **3** $y=10$ **4** $y=7$ **5** $a=7$
6 $b=4$ **7** $c=9$ **8** $d=15$ **9** $x=6$ **10** $x=10$
11 $y=7$ **12** $t=11$ **13** $x=4$ **14** $y=3$ **15** $t=9$
16 $u=7$ **17** $x=5$ **18** $k=4$ **19** $p=1$ **20** $t=2$
21 $a=9$ **22** $b=3$ **23** $c=3$ **24** $d=23$ **25** $x=3$
26 $y=1$ **27** $k=5$ **28** $t=1$ **29** $t=3$ **30** $u=0$
31 $v=5$ **32** $w=3$

Page 196 Exercise 1B

1 $x=2$ **2** $y=3$ **3** $y=4$ **4** $x=5$ **5** $x=1$
6 $x=6$ **7** $x=5$ **8** $x=8$ **9** $t=4$ **10** $x=1$
11 $x=2$ **12** $c=2$

Page 196 Exercise 1C

1 $x=2$ **2** $y=5$ **3** $a=2$ **4** $b=2$ **5** $x=8$
6 $y=0$ **7** $p=8$ **8** $k=9$ **9** $y=2$ **10** $x=4$
11 $n=2$ **12** $m=3$ **13** $p=3$ **14** $q=1$ **15** $t=2$
16 $u=3$ **17** $q=14$ **18** $h=13$ **19** $t=4$ **20** $x=5$

Page 197 Exercise 2A

1a 12 **b** 0 **c** 5 **d** 13 **e** 5
2a $5x$ **b** x **c** $4y$ **d** 0 **e** $7y$
3a $6a$ **b** $2a$ **c** $4b$ **d** $2b$ **e** $10c$
4a $2x$ **b** 0 **c** $2y$ **d** 0 **e** y
5a $3d$ **b** $8d$ **c** 0 **d** $2f$ **e** g
6a $4x+1$ **b** $5y-1$ **c** $2x+1$ **d** $2y-1$
7a 4 **b** 3 **c** $2n-4$ **d** $2m+1$
8a (i) $x+2$ (ii) 2 **b** (i) x (ii) $2x$ **c** (i) $2x$ (ii) x
d (i) $2x+1$ (ii) $3x+1$
9a (i) $2t+2$ (ii) $t+2$ **b** (i) $y+2$ (ii) $2y+2$
c (i) $w+3$ (ii) 3 **d** (i) $3k$ (ii) $2k$
10a (i) $x+3$ (ii) $2x+3$ **b** (i) $2m+1$ (ii) $4m+1$
c (i) $2c+2$ (ii) 2 **d** (i) $3n+2$ (ii) $n+2$
11a (i) $s+2$ (ii) 2 **b** (i) $h+3$ (ii) $3h+3$
c (i) $3p+3$ (ii) 3 **d** (i) $3x+4$ (ii) $6x+4$

Page 198 Exercise 2B/C

1a $2m-3$ **b** $n+2$ **c** $3t-1$ **d** $10x-5$ **e** 4
2a $4w+3$ **b** $7n+13$ **c** $4x+9$ **d** $4m+1$ **e** 3
3a $7+2a$ **b** 5 **c** 1 **d** $4+x$ **e** 6
4a (i) $x-2$ (ii) $2x-2$ **b** (i) $y-1$ (ii) $3y-1$
c (i) $t-4$ (ii) $4t-4$ **d** (i) $c-3$ (ii) $2c-3$
5a (i) $2d-2$ (ii) $4d-2$ **b** (i) $2y-1$ (ii) $3y-1$
c (i) $2c-2$ (ii) $6c-2$ **d** (i) $3x-4$ (ii) $6x-4$
6a (i) $-x$ (ii) 5 **b** (i) $-2x$ (ii) 3 **c** (i) $-5x$ (ii) 1
d (i) $-4x$ (ii) 1 **e** (i) $-7x$ (ii) 2 **f** (i) $-4x$ (ii) 0
g (i) $-2x$ (ii) 0 **h** (i) $-x$ (ii) 0 **i** (i) $+x$ (ii) 1
j (i) $+2x$ (ii) 3

7a (i) $+x$ (ii) 2 **b** (i) $+2x$ (ii) 4 **c** (i) $+3x$ (ii) 1
d (i) $-8x$ (ii) 2 **e** (i) $+2x$ (ii) 8 **f** (i) $-3x$ (ii) 4
g (i) $+3x$ (ii) 4 **h** (i) $-x$ (ii) 5 **i** (i) $+x$ (ii) 5
j (i) $-10x$ (ii) 10

Page 199 Exercise 3A

1a $x=6$ **b** $y=3$ **c** $a=4$ **d** $b=3$ **e** $x=2$
f $y=2$ **g** $m=1$ **h** $t=5$
2a $x=2$ **b** $m=3$ **c** $t=3$ **d** $w=1$
3a $m=1$ **b** $n=3$ **c** $k=4$ **d** $p=1$
4a $x=2$ **b** $y=3$ **c** $t=2$ **d** $u=3$
5a $x=4$ **b** $y=2$ **c** $a=3$ **d** $b=2$ **e** $s=3$
f $t=3$ **g** $u=1$ **h** $v=6$
6a $x=6$ **b** $x=7$ **c** $x=4$ **d** $x=15$ **e** $y=2$
f $y=6$ **g** $y=6$ **h** $y=2$ **i** $t=7$ **j** $t=5$ **k** $u=6$
l $v=10$

Page 200 Exercise 3B

1a $x=10$ **b** $x=3$ **c** $y=1$ **d** $n=3$ **e** $k=4$
f $t=10$ **g** $u=5$ **h** $v=4$ **i** $x=1$ **j** $y=15$
k $p=7$ **l** $s=10$
2a $x=4, 8$ cm **b** $x=5, 15$ cm **c** $x=5, 30$ cm
d $x=2, 10$ cm **e** $x=3, 3$ cm **f** $x=5, 10$ cm
g $x=6, 18$ cm **h** $x=3, 9$ cm
3a $3x=x+8$ **b** $4m$ **c** $12m$
4a $4x=2x+30$ **b** 15 cm **c** 60 cm
5a $5x=2x+90$ **b** 30 cm **c** 150 cm

Page 201 Exercise 3C

1a $x=3$ **b** $x=9$ **c** $x=2$ **d** $x=2$
2a 8th **b** 9th **c** 7th
3a $x=3$ **b** $x=8$ **c** $x=9$ **d** $x=1$ **e** $y=6$
f $y=2$ **g** $y=7$ **h** $y=6$ **4** 12p **5** 26p **6** 9p; 29p

Page 202 Exercise 4A

1a $x=2$ **b** $x=3$ **c** $y=6$ **d** $y=2$
2a $x=4$ **b** $x=1$ **c** $y=3$ **d** $y=2$ **e** $k=8$
f $t=4$ **g** $m=2$ **h** $n=2$
3a $2x+3=x+6, x=3$ **b** $3t+1=2t+5, t=4$
c $3w+2=w+4, w=1$ **d** $4k+2=2k+8, k=3$
e $2y+1=y+6, y=5$ **f** $4x+3=x+6, x=1$
4 Across: 12; 14; 32; 51 **Down:** 21; 43; 25; 10
5a $x=6$ **b** $x=0$ **c** $x=2$ **d** $x=3$ **e** $a=4$
f $b=4$ **g** $c=3$ **h** $d=4$ **i** $x=5$ **j** $y=5$
k $x=6$ **l** $y=5$
6a $a=4$ **b** $b=12$ **c** $c=3$ **d** $d=0$ **e** $x=6$
f $y=4$ **g** $k=4$ **h** $p=1$

Page 203 Exercise 4B

1a $k=6, 24$ cm **b** $x=4, 14$ cm **c** $m=6, 24$ cm
d $z=5, 18$ cm **e** $e=4, 16$ cm **f** $x=4, 16$ cm
g $v=8, 44$ cm
2 Across: 13; 27; 34; 21 **Down:** 17; 24; 31; 26
3a $x=7; 5$ **b** $y=4; 3$ **c** $x=4; 1, 4$ **d** $p=4; 1, 4, 4$
e $x=2; 1, 2, 2, 2$ **f** $t=6; 3, 6, 6$ **g** $x=7; 2, 7, 7$
h $x=1; 0, 1, 1, 1, 1, 1$ **i** $x=6; 2, 6, 5$
4a $x=3$ **b** $x=6$ **c** $x=1$ **d** $x=2$ **e** $x=2$
f $x=5$ **g** $x=4$ **h** $x=1$ **i** $x=4$ **j** $x=1$
k $x=4$ **l** $x=0$

Page 204 Exercise 4C

1a $2n, n+20$; 20th **b** $3n+1, n+51$; 25th
c $3n-1, n+79$; 40th

2a $x = 40$ **b** $x = 3$ **c** $x = 40$ **d** $x = 5$ **e** $x = 18$
f $x = 4$ **3** $m = 5$, 50 litres
4a (i) 32 (ii) $8x$ (iii) $8x + 32$ **b** (i) 35 (ii) $5x$
(iii) $5x + 35$ **c** $x = 1$; 40 **5** $x = 2$; 300 km

Page 206 Check-up on Solving More Equations

1a $x = 8$ **b** $x = 4$ **c** $y = 6$ **d** $y = 4$
2a (i) $x + 1$ (ii) 1 **b** (i) $2a$ (ii) a **c** (i) $3n + 2$
(ii) $4n + 2$ **d** (i) $2t + 5$ (ii) 5
3a 2 **b** 2 **c** $2m + 1$ **d** 1
4a $n = 4$ **b** $p = 4$ **c** $m = 7$ **d** $x = 5$ **e** $y = 2$
f $b = 5$ **g** $c = 10$ **h** $t = 2$
5a $y = 7$, 21 cm **b** $x = 15$, 60 cm **c** $n = 15$, 30 cm
6a $x = 2$ **b** $t = 4$ **c** $k = 6$ **d** $m = 2$
7a $x = 7$ **b** $n = 4$ **c** $k = 8$ **d** $x = 4$ **e** $n = 25$
f $x = 10$

17 THREE DIMENSIONS

Page 207 Looking Back

1a Cuboid **b** Cube **c** Pyramid **d** Cone
e Cylinder **f** Triangular prism **g** Sphere
2 Cube—beef cubes; cuboid—crackers, crunches,
soap powder, biscuits, tea; cone—choc ice;
cylinder—tomatoes, soup, peas, beans;
pyramid—milk; triangular prism—cheese, chews
3 d
4a A cube **b** All six faces are equally likely to show
on top, also it will stop when rolled
5a Squares **b** Squares or rectangles
c A square and triangles
d Triangles and rectangles or squares

Page 208 Exercise 1A

1 Cube has squares, cuboid rectangles or squares
2 Prism has 6, cuboid has 8
3 Pyramid has 8, cuboid has 12
4 Cone has 2, cuboid has 6
5 Sphere has 0, cuboid has 8
6 Cylinder has 2, cuboid has 12
7 Faces: 6, 5, 5, 2, 1, 3; Edges: 12, 9, 8, 1, 0, 2;
Vertices: 8, 6, 5, 1, 0, 0
8a Cuboids fit together without leaving spaces, and
make a smooth surface
b They may not build easily on each other, or make a
smooth surface, and may leave spaces

Page 209 Exercise 1B/C

1 Cube, square **2** Cylinder, circle **3** Sphere
4 Triangular prism (i) rectangle (ii) triangle
5 Pyramid, triangle **6** Cuboid, rectangle
7 Pentagonal prism (i) pentagon (ii) rectangle
8 Triangular prism (i) triangle (ii) rectangle
9 Hexagonal prism, hexagon
10a Cylinder **b** Triangular prisms, cuboids
c Cylinders, cuboids **d** Square pyramid, cuboids
11a Cube or cuboid **b** Sphere **c** Cone
d Triangular pyramid **e** Triangular prism
f Square pyramid **g** Cylinder
12 2-dimensional: **a**, **c**, **f**, **h**. 3-dimensional: **b**, **d**, **e**, **g**

Page 210 Exercise 2A

6a 3 by 1 by 2 units **b** 3 by 2 by 2 units
c 3 by 2 by 1 units

Page 211 Exercise 2B/C

1a 4 **b** 3 **c** 4 **d** 3 **e** 2 **f** 8 **g** 9 **h** 5
2 (i) **b** 3 **c** 5 **d** 4 **e** 3 **f** 5 **g** 5 **h** 9
(ii) **b** 7 **c** 11 **d** 10 **e** 7 **f** 13 **g** 11 **h** 16
(iii) **b** 9 **c** 15 **d** 13 **e** 9 **f** 17 **g** 15 **h** 21

Page 212 Exercise 3A

1 Yes; 6 **2** Yes **3a** 16 cm² **b** 96 cm²
4a 54 cm² **b** 150 cm² **5** 7
6 No. of dots (left to right, or top to bottom):
a 2, 4, 1 **b** 5, 6, 3 **c** 6, 2, 4 **d** 5, 4, 6 **e** 6, 4, 5
7 **a** and **c** will make cubes

Page 213 Exercise 3B

1a To fit together when the net is folded up
b (i) 1 of 600 cm², 2 of 60 cm², 2 of 40 cm² (ii) 800 cm²
c 30 cm by 20 cm. On any of the 20 cm or 30 cm
outside edges **2b** (i) 88 cm² (ii) 48 cm³
3b 38 cm² **c** 12 cm³ **4a** Yes **b** Yes
5 6 by 5 by 2 cm, 5 by 4 by 3 cm, 10 by 3 by 2 cm,
15 by 2 by 2 cm

Page 214 Exercise 3C

1a Two rectangles 100 cm by 50 cm, two 100 cm by
60 cm, two 60 cm by 50 cm **2a** 12 cm **b** 256 cm²
3b 54 cm²; 27 cm³
c Fit two rows of the nets onto the card, with five nets
side by side in each row.

Page 214 Exercise 4

1b 5, 9, 6 **2b** Yes; 108 cm² **4a** 5, 8, 5 **b** 4, 6, 4

Page 215 Exercise 5A

1a 4 of 12 cm, 4 of 9 cm, 4 of 6 cm **b** 8 of 12 cm
2a 48 cm **b** 120 mm **c** 64 cm
3a $4(5 + 4 + 3) = 4 \times 5 + 4 \times 4 + 4 \times 3$ **b** $16 \times 4 = 64$
c $30 \times 4 = 120$
4a 26 m **b** 52 cm **c** 42 cm **d** 38 m **e** 46 cm
f 45 mm **g** $49\frac{1}{2}$ cm **h** 68 cm **5** 18 cm

Page 216 Exercise 5B/C

1a 4 of 28 cm, 8 of 20 cm, 4 of 60 cm **b** 512 cm
c 80 cm, 60 cm, 4800 cm²
2a 1382 cm **b** 6; four 4-way joints
c roof 11 660 cm²; walls 29 600 cm²; total 41 260 cm²
d Four wires 80 cm long, four 75 cm long,
four 53 cm long, five 110 cm long; six 3-way joints,
four 4-way joints; plastic sheet for roof and walls
(total area 41 260 cm²)

Page 217 Exercise 6A

1a A, B, C, D **b** EFGH **c** AE, BF, CG, DH
d $\angle$ADC **e** DC, EF or HG **f** BAEF
2a DC, EF, HG **b** EH, FG, BC **c** BF, CG, DH
3a TUVW **b** TW, UV, QR **c** WS, TP, UQ
d $\angle$ s PSR, PSW, RSW
4a No **b** NM, RQ, OP **c** NMQR, OPQR, KLPO
d OK, KN, NR, LM, MQ, PQ, PL

5a EA, FB, GC, HD **b** Yes
c They are parallel and equal
d AB, EF, HG, DC; AD, BC, FG, EH **e** 3

Page 218   Exercise 6B

1a (i) ABED   (ii) ABC, DEF   (iii) DF   (iv) ∠BAC
(v) ∠s ABE, CBE **b** West
2a (i) PQ, PR, PS   (ii) ∠s QRS, RST, STQ, TQR
(iii) PSR, PST
b The line from P perpendicular to the base
3a (i) O, X, Y, Z   (ii) OX, OY, OZ, XY, YZ, ZX
(iii) OXY, OYZ, OXZ, XYZ   **b** (i) XZ   (ii) OXZ, XYZ
c ∠s XOY, YOZ, XOZ; 60°
d It is very streamlined, and pointed at the top; the corners are small and the roof low

Page 219   Exercise 6C

1a (i) SX, TW   (ii) VX, WY   **b** (i) SU, WY, VX
(ii) SV, UX, TY   **c** (i) VX   (ii) UX
2a Right   **b** Acute   **c** Right   **d** Right   **e** Right
f Acute   **3a** CE, DF   **b** OB, OC, OD, OE, OF, OG, OH
4a A right angle   **b** A rectangle   **c** OPMN
d OLMR, PQNK; LNRP, OKMQ
5a OPQRKL and KLMNRQ   **b** Triangular prism
6a Plane through midpoints of BC, FG, EH, AD   **b** 1
7 Two planes through midpoints of sides, two through diagonally opposite vertices
8 Three in **a**, four in **b**

Page 221   Check-up on Three Dimensions

1a Cuboid, cube
b Square pyramid, triangular prism
c Triangular prism   **d** Square pyramid
2a True   **b** False   **c** True   **3a** 3   **b** 9   **c** 7
4a 56 cm   **b** 48 cm
6a 126 cm²; 90 cm³   **b** 96 cm²; 64 cm³
7a EF, HG, DC   **b** AE, BF, CG, DH   **c** AF, AC, AH
d AG   **e** ∠s BAD, DAE, BAE   **8b** 85 cm²
9a A square pyramid   **b** A cuboid
10 14 cm; 1176 cm²

18   PROBABILITY

Page 222   Looking Back

1a Fair. Heads and tails are equally likely
b Fair. Even and odd numbers are equally likely
c Unfair. Only 1 and 2 are less than 3, leaving 3, 4, 5, 6
2a Certain   **b** Likely   **c** Impossible   **d** Unlikely
e Even chance in a mixed school   **f** Certain
3a 16   **b** (i) $\frac{1}{8}$ (ii) $\frac{1}{4}$ (iii) $\frac{3}{8}$
4a (i); 1 out of 2 better chance than 1 out of 4
b Even chance; each is the same as 1 out of 3
c (i) 2 out of 3 better chance than 2 out of 6

Page 223   Exercise 1

2a Even chance   **b** Certain
3a Impossible   **b** Certain   **5** Unlikely
6a Unlikely   **b** Impossible   **c** Even chance
d Certain   **8a** Unlikely   **b** Likely?   **c** Likely
9a Even chance   **b** Unlikely   **c** Unlikely

10a Unlikely   **b** Even chance   **c** Unlikely   **d** Likely
11a Unlikely   **b** Even chance   **12** Unlikely

Page 225   Exercise 2A

1a Unlikely   **b** 6   **c** 1   **d** $\frac{1}{6}$
2a Even chance   **b** 6   **c** 3   **d** $\frac{1}{2}$
3a Likely   **b** 6   **c** 5   **d** $\frac{5}{6}$ **4a** Head, Tail   **b** $\frac{1}{2}$
5a 4   **b** $\frac{1}{4}$ **6a** 5   **b** $\frac{1}{5}$ **7a** 6   **b** (i) $\frac{1}{6}$ (ii) $\frac{1}{2}$ (iii) $\frac{1}{3}$
8a 3   **b** (i) $\frac{1}{3}$ (ii) $\frac{2}{3}$ **9a** 26   **b** (i) $\frac{1}{26}$ (ii) $\frac{1}{13}$ (iii) $\frac{5}{26}$
10a $\frac{3}{5}$ **b** (i) $\frac{1}{4}$ (ii) $\frac{1}{2}$ **c** (i) $\frac{1}{5}$ (ii) $\frac{3}{5}$ (iii) 1
11a $\frac{1}{2}$ **b** $\frac{1}{6}$ **c** $\frac{1}{3}$ **d** 0   **12a** $\frac{1}{6}$ **b** 0   **c** $\frac{1}{6}$ **d** $\frac{1}{2}$

Page 226   Exercise 2B

1a $\frac{1}{8}$ **b** $\frac{1}{2}$ **c** $\frac{1}{4}$ **2a** $\frac{1}{10}$ **b** $\frac{1}{5}$ **c** $\frac{3}{10}$ **d** $\frac{2}{5}$ **e** $\frac{3}{5}$
3a She is correct; all the seats are available   **b** $\frac{2}{5}$
4a $\frac{1}{4}$ **b** $\frac{3}{4}$ **5** $\frac{6}{25}$ **6a** $\frac{1}{2}$ **b** $\frac{1}{3}$ **7a** (i) $\frac{3}{20}$ (ii) $\frac{1}{5}$
8a $\frac{1}{52}$ **b** $\frac{1}{26}$ **c** $\frac{1}{13}$ **d** $\frac{1}{4}$ **e** $\frac{4}{13}$
9a (i) $\frac{1}{8}$ (ii) $\frac{5}{8}$ (iii) $\frac{1}{4}$
b No-one else calls the lift; and he can reach all the buttons

Page 227   Exercise 2C

1a $\frac{1}{3}$ **b** $\frac{1}{6}$ **c** $\frac{1}{24}$ **d** $\frac{1}{3}$ **2a** $\frac{1}{4}$ **b** $\frac{1}{3}$ **c** $\frac{1}{6}$ **d** $\frac{5}{24}$ **e** $\frac{1}{24}$. 1
3a $\frac{1}{100}$ **b** $\frac{1}{25}$ **c** $\frac{9}{10}$ **4a** 0.143   **b** 0.083   **c** 0.017
5a (i)   **b** Even   **c** (ii)   **6a** $\frac{1}{7}$ **b** $\frac{4}{7}$ **c** $\frac{3}{7}$ **d** 0   **e** $\frac{2}{7}$
7a $\frac{3}{8}$ **b** $\frac{3}{8}$ **c** $\frac{3}{4}$ **d** $\frac{3}{8}$

Page 229   Check-up on Probability

1a Unlikely   **b** Likely   **c** Certain   **d** Even chance
e Impossible   **2a** $\frac{25}{60}$ or $\frac{5}{12}$ **b** $\frac{1}{6}$ or $\frac{10}{60}$ **c** Yes
3a $\frac{1}{4}$ **b** $\frac{1}{2}$ **c** 0   **4a** $\frac{4}{11}$ **b** $\frac{4}{11}$ **c** $\frac{7}{11}$ **5a** $\frac{13}{25}$ **b** $\frac{12}{25}$
6 $\frac{2}{3}$ **7a** $\frac{1}{100}$ **b** $\frac{1}{2}$ **c** $\frac{1}{10}$ **8a** $\frac{1}{5}$ **b** $\frac{1}{10}$ **c** $\frac{3}{10}$ **d** 0
9a $\frac{1}{28}$ **b** $\frac{1}{4}$ **c** $\frac{1}{7}$
10a (i) $\frac{1}{3}$ (ii) $\frac{2}{3}$ **b** The man in the picture!

REVISION EXERCISES

Page 230   Revision Exercise on Chapter 1: Whole Numbers in Action

1a K2, Mont Blanc, Ben Nevis, Scafell
b Twenty-eight thousand two hundred and fifty feet; three thousand two hundred and six feet
2a 306 km   **b** Reading to Swansea, by 15 km
3a 80 cartons, 8 boxes   **b** 750 cartons, 75 boxes
4a 1401   **b** 23   **5a** 288   **b** 30
6a 40   **b** 106   **c** 3000   **d** 5   **e** 26   **f** 6000
7a 31, 37; Add 6   **b** 162, 486; Multiply by 3
c 92, 90; Subtract 2
d 15, 21; Add 1 more than the previous difference
8a £100; £50   **b** 200, 100
9 6, 5, 1; 6, 4, 2; 6, 3, 3; 5, 5, 2; 5, 4, 3; 4, 4, 4
10a 13, 28; 41   **b** 57, 63; 120   **c** 348, 296; 644
d 32, 18; 14   **e** 102, 64; 38
11a 4000, 28 000, 16 000, 3000 feet
b 4400, 28 300, 15 800, 3200 feet
c 4410, 28 250, 15 770, 3210 feet   **12** Mrs Dawes; £900

Page 231   Revision Exercise on Chapter 2: Angles Around Us

1a Obtuse **b** Straight **c** Right **d** Acute
3a $\angle$ BAE; 110° **b** $\angle$ DAE; 20° **c** $\angle$ s BAD, CAE
4a 90° **b** 0° **c** 120° **d** 150°
5a (i) 180° (ii) 90° (iii) 45° (iv) 135° **b** NE, SE
6a 80° **b** 85° **7a** 45° **b** $22\frac{1}{2}$°
8a 4 m **b** 1 m **c** $1\frac{1}{2}$ m
9a (i) 20° (ii) 24° **b** Between 20° and 30°
10a $\angle$ PQS = 122° **b** $\angle$ XUW = 74° **c** $\angle$ CDB = 125°
d $\angle$ FKG = 50°, $\angle$ DKH = 150°
11a (i) AB, EF, DC (ii) EH, FG **b** $\angle$ BAD = $\angle$ ABC, $\angle$ ADC = $\angle$ BCD **12** 252°

Page 232   Revision Exercise on Chapter 3: Letters and Numbers

1a 14 **b** 10 **c** 7 **d** 2 **2a** 8 **b** 18 **c** 5 **d** 1 **e** 0
3a 5 **b** 13 **c** 7 **d** 12 **e** 7 **f** 56
4a $3x$ **b** $3y$ **c** $2t$ **d** $2p$ **e** $2x$ **f** $2y$ **g** $4x+6$
h 0
5 $a = 5, b = 8, c = 18, d = 12, e = 35$
6a $2x+2$ **b** $3t+5$ **c** $4y+4$ **d** $10n$
7 $x = 9; t = 5; y = 4; n = 2$
8a $x+4, x+5; x, x+1$ **b** $y+4; y; y-4$
c $t-1, t; t-5, t-4; t-9, t-8$
9a $4t$ **b** $10n$ **c** $5k+5$ **d** $2m+2$ **e** $p+1$ **f** $3x+3y$
g $2c$ **h** $u+v$

Page 233   Revision on Chapter 4: Decimals in Action

1a (i) 10.5 (ii) 250.21 **b** (i) Twenty point six
(ii) Four hundred and seven point nine
(iii) Nought point nought one
2a 7 **b** The final 1 **c** 9 **3** 1.01, 1.09, 1.1, 1.3, 8.9
4a £3.80 **b** £20.09 **5a** 0.7 **b** 2 **c** 4.1 **d** 5.5 **e** 7.2
6 9.95 **7a** £12 **b** £120 **c** 12p **8** 40.4 cm
9a (i) 48p (ii) £1.20 (iii) £4.80 **b** (i) 46p (ii) £1.32
(iii) £4.44 **c** 868 **10a** 76.93 **b** 6.8 **c** £1.75
11a 3.3 **b** 2.25 **c** 25.01 **12a** 204 mm **b** 28 mm
13 4 at £1.35 and 3 at £1.40 **14a** $434.38 **b** £14.30

Page 234   Revision Exercise on Chapter 5: Facts, Figures and Graphs

1a 20 **b** Roses **c** 86 **2b** $\frac{6}{36}$ or $\frac{1}{6}$
3a 13 pounds **b** 118 pounds **c** 5
5a Onion, cheese, bacon, plain **b** (i) $\frac{1}{2}$ (ii) $\frac{1}{4}$ (iii) $\frac{1}{4}$
6 Angles are 120°, 90°, 50°, 60°, 40°
7a June; £46 000 **b** May, £30 000 **c** £164 000
8 1–5, 1; 6–10, 6; 11–15, 11; 16–20, 9

Page 235   Revision Exercise on Chapter 6: Measuring Time and Temperature

1a February **b** April **c** November
2a 14 **b** 31 **c** 366 **3a** Thursday **b** 10
4a 3 h 15 min **b** 3.20 pm
5a 2 am or pm **b** 3.30 am or pm **c** 12.45 am or pm
d 2.25 am or pm **6** (i) 1 h 30 min (ii) 1 h 40 min
7a 02 00 or 14 00 **b** 03 30 or 15 30 **c** 00 45 or 12 45
d 02 25 or 14 25 **8** Fastest 17 48; slowest 14 55
9a London. 7°C **b** 13°C
10 −9°C, −4°C, 0°C, 1°C, 3°C, 8°C
11a 2.4°C; 0.6°C **b** 1.8°C
12a (i) Athens (ii) Helsinki **b** 24°C
13a 22 30 **b** 14 minutes

Page 236   Revision Exercise on Chapter 7: Coordinates, X marks the spot

1 A1 → D3, A2 → C3, A3 → C4, A4 → B3;
B1 → C2, B2 → B2, B3 → D4, B4 → A2;
C1 → D2, C2 → C1, C3 → A1 or A4, C4 → A3;
D1 → A4 or A1, D2 → D1, D3 → B1, D4 → B4
3a 45 **b** 55 **c** James **4** H(3, 2) **5c** $y = 6, y = -2$
6 b (2, −1)

Page 237   Revision Exercise on Chapter 8: Solving Equations

1a 2 **b** 7 **c** 0 **d** 12 **e** 16 **f** 4 **g** 6 **h** 0
2a $x = 7$ **b** $n = 10$ **c** $y = 15$ **d** $t = 22$
3 $y = 3, t = 4, x = 11, y = 2$
4a 4 **b** 2 **c** 5 **d** 2 **e** 4 **f** 7 **g** 1 **h** 0
5a $x = 4$ **b** $y = 6$ **c** $x = 8$ **d** $m = 6$
6a $28x$ cm **b** $28x = 56, x = 2$ **c** 2 cm, 4 cm, 8 cm
7a $t = 9$ **b** $t = 5$ **c** $t = 9$ **d** $t = 4$
8a 5 **b** 3 **c** 7 **d** 1 **e** 1 **f** 13 **g** 4 **h** 7 **i** 5
j 10 **k** 15

Page 238   Revision Exercise on Chapter 9: Measuring Length

1a Metres **b** Kilometres **c** Millimetres
d Centimetres
2a OA 35; OB 72; AB 37 mm **b** OA 3.5; OB 7.2;
AB 3.7 cm **3a** About 6.5 cm **b** 18 cm
4a 10; 22; 32 mm **b** 1; 2.2; 3.2 cm **5** 240 km
6 3.45 m **7a** 42 cm **b** 5 **9a** 325 km **b** 64
10a Just over 1 m; 6 m **b** 1.18 m, 6.52 m **11** £200
12a 8.125 km **b** 1.875 km

Page 239   Revision Exercise on Chapter 10: Tiling and Symmetry

2b (i) 1 (ii) 2 (iii) 2 (iv) 4 **c** (i) 360°
(ii) 180°, 360° (iii) 180°, 360° (iv) 90°, 180°, 270°, 360°
3a (i), (ii) **b** (i) **c** (ii) **d** (iii) **e** (i) **f** (i) **g** (i)
h (iii)
4a (−1, 1), (−2, 1), (−2, 3), (−3, 3), (−3, 4), (−2, 4),
(−2, 5), (−4, 5), (−4, 6), (−1, 6), (−1, 1)
b (1, −1), (2, −1), (2, −3), (3, −3), (3, −4), (2, −4),
(2, −5), (4, −5), (4, −6), (1, −6), (1, −1)
c (−1, −1), (−2, −1), (−2, −3), (−3, −3), (−3, −4),
(−2, −4), (−2, −5), (−4, −5), (−4, −6), (−1, −6),
(−1, −1)
5a 3 **b** 4 **c** 6 **d** 5 **e** 8 **f** 16 **g** 3 **h** 2

Page 240   Revision Exercise on Chapter 11: Measuring Area

1a 12 **b** 16 **c** 10 **d** 21 or 22 squares
2a 40 cm² **b** 72 m² **c** 120 mm² **d** 400 cm²
3a (i) 56 m² (ii) 12 m² (iii) 44 m² **b** £220
4a 30 cm² **b** 22 mm² **c** 9 m² **d** 3 m²
5a 12 cm **b** 7.5 mm **6a** 72 m² **b** 216 cm² **c** 55 m²
7a 24 m by 1 m, 12 m by 2 m, 8 m by 3 m, 6 m by 4 m
b (i) 24 m by 1 m (ii) 6 m by 4 m

Page 241   Revision Exercise on Chapter 12: Letters, Numbers and Sequences

1a 84, 91, $7x$ **b** 24, 25, $n+5$ **c** 92, 96, $4t$
2a $6x$ **b** $20y$ **c** $4m$ **d** (i) $4n$ (ii) $2n$ (iii) n
3a 6 **b** 23 **c** 11 **d** 36 **e** 6 **f** 12
4a 0, 1, 2, 3 **b** 16, 20, 24, 28 **c** 16, 25, 34, 43

5a $50+10t$ **b** $3t+4s$
6 4, 6, 8, 10, 12, 42, $2n+2$; 40, 70, 100, 130, 160, 610, $30n+10$ **7a** $p=2a+2b$ **b** 54

Page 242 Revision Exercise on Chapter 13: Two Dimensions, Rectangle and Square

1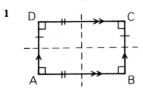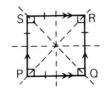

2a Diagonals **b** (i) 180 cm (ii) 90 cm (iii) 90 cm
c (i) 50° (ii) 40°
3 All sides 10 cm, all half-diagonals 7 cm, angles at Z 90°, angles at corners 45° (and 90°)
4a U(3, 6) **b** (5, 4)
5 15 m, 15 m, 7.5 m, 7.5 m; 16.5 m, 16.5 m, 6 m, 6 m
6a 2 **b** 4 **c** 2 **7** 8.7 cm, 5 cm
8b M(10, 1) or (0, 1), N(10, 6) or (0, 6); $(7\frac{1}{2}, 3\frac{1}{2})$ or $(2\frac{1}{2}, 3\frac{1}{2})$
9a (ii) **b** (i)
10a Rows: 24; 30, 18; 18, 30, 24; 15, 15, 15, 15 **b** 96 km

Page 243 Revision Exercise on Chapter 14: Measuring Volume

1a cm³ **b** m³ **c** mm³ **2a** litres **b** ml
3a 2000 **b** 40 **4a** 8 **b** 20 **c** 45 **d** 180
5a 480 mm³ **b** 512 000 cm³ **c** 1.28 m³
d 720 000 cm³ **6a** 720 000 **b** 720 **7a** 4 **b** 16 **c** 64
8a 25 cm **b** 7 cm **9a** The Arctic, by 10 litres
b The Icicle

Page 244 Revision Exercise on Chapter 15: Fractions and Percentages

1a $\frac{1}{4}$ **b** $\frac{2}{5}$ **c** $\frac{1}{2}$ **d** $\frac{5}{6}$
2 Shade **a** 3 parts **b** 1 part **c** 5 parts **d** 2 parts
3a $\frac{4}{9}$ **b** $\frac{5}{9}$ **c** $\frac{1}{3}$ **4a** $\frac{1}{2}$ **b** $\frac{2}{3}$ **c** $\frac{3}{4}$ **d** $\frac{3}{7}$ **e** $\frac{3}{5}$ **f** $\frac{8}{9}$
5a $\frac{1}{10}$ **b** $\frac{3}{20}$ **c** $\frac{12}{25}$ **d** $\frac{3}{4}$ **6a** £1.50 **b** £3 **c** £8 **d** £12
7a £16 **b** £36.66 **8a** $\frac{1}{2}$ **b** $\frac{1}{3}$ **c** $\frac{1}{10}$ **9** 20 m² **10** 30p
11a $\frac{7}{100}$ **b** $\frac{10}{100}$ or $\frac{1}{10}$ **c** $\frac{100}{100}$ or 1
12a 9% **b** 30% **c** 75% **d** 35% **e** 84%
13a £8 **b** £5 **c** £1.80 **d** £63

14a £30, £77, £9 **b** £120, £308, £36
15a E 70%, F 70%, M 74%, H 72%
b Maths, History, English and French equal
16 £21.85 **17a** 20 cm **b** $\frac{20}{20}$ or 1 **c** 100%
18a 10% **b** Golf £8100, tennis £2700, bowls £5400, putting £1800

Page 245 Revision Exercise on Chapter 16: Solving More Equations

1a 12 **b** 8 **c** 4 **d** 7 **e** 4 **f** 6 **g** 5 **h** 10
2a 2 **b** $3y-1$ **c** 4 **d** $-2t$ **e** $+2m$ **f** $2n+2$
3a $x+2$ **b** 5 **c** $4x+7$ **d** 3
4a 2 **b** 3 **c** 3 **d** 6 **e** 7 **f** 6 **g** 5 **h** 2
5a $r=2$ **b** $x=3$ **c** $m=4$
6a $3x=x+40$; $x=20$; 60 cm
b $5a=2a+75$; $a=25$; 125 cm
c $2t+28=4t$; $t=14$; 56 cm
7a 7 **b** 6 **c** 1 **d** 2 **e** 5 **f** 7 **g** 1 **h** 2
8a $3x+3=x+17$; $x=7$ **b** $x+12=4x+3$; $x=3$

Page 246 Revision Exercise on Chapter 17: Three Dimensions

1a (i), (iii), (iv), (vi) **b** (ii) Cone, spheres (v) Sphere
2a LM, KN, OR **b** PL, PO, QM, QR
c PL, QM, RN, OK **d** QMNR **3b** 24 cm², 8 cm³
4 10 cm by 10 cm
5a PQ, SR, WV, TU
b QR, RV, VU, UQ, PS, SW, WT, TP **c** TUVW
d ∠s SWT, SWV, VWT **e** PSWT, QRVU
f PV, QW, TR, US **6** 260 cm
7b (i) 37 500 cm³ (ii) 7000 cm²
8a A cube **b** A square pyramid
c A triangular prism
9a (i) Face diagonal (ii) Space diagonal
b (i) BG, DE, CF (ii) AG, CE, DF **c** 4

Page 247 Revision Exercise on Chapter 18: Probability

1a Certain **b** Impossible **c** Even chance
d (depends on year) **e** Likely
2a $\frac{1}{4}$ **b** $\frac{3}{4}$ **3a** $\frac{1}{5}$ **b** $\frac{3}{5}$ **c** $\frac{3}{10}$ **4** $\frac{1}{3}$ **5a** $\frac{1}{8}$ **b** $\frac{3}{8}$ **c** $\frac{1}{2}$
6a $\frac{3}{14}$ **b** $\frac{1}{7}$ **c** $\frac{3}{7}$ **d** $\frac{4}{7}$
7 Jonathan. He has 1 chance in 2, Kerry has only 1 in 6
8 60% **9b** $\frac{3}{5}=60\%$, but $\frac{5}{8}=62.5\%$